P9-EKS-154

02726198

DATE DUE

JAN 2 3 2001	
SEP 2 8 2001	
NOV 0 6 2001	
NOV 2 8 2001	
MAR 2 7 2002	
OCT 3 2002	
NOV 1 2 2002	
MAY 2 0 2003	
NOV 1 0 2003	

BRODART

Cat. No. 23-221

INTERVENTIONS FOR ADHD

BRITISH COLUMBIA

Interventions for ADHD

Treatment in
Developmental Context

Phyllis Anne Teeter

Foreword by Sam Goldstein

THE GUILFORD PRESS
New York London

© 1998 The Guilford Press
A Division of Guilford Publications, Inc.
72 Spring Street, New York, NY 10012
http://www.guilford.com

All rights reserved

No part of this book may be reproduced, translated, stored in a
retrieval system, or transmitted, in any form or by any means,
electronic, mechanical, photocopying, microfilming, recording,
or otherwise, without written permission from the Publisher.

Printed in the United States of America

This book is printed on acid-free paper.

Last digit is print number: 9 8 7 6 5 4 3 2 1

Library of Congress Cataloging-in-Publication Data

Teeter, Phyllis Anne.
    Interventions for ADHD : treatment in developmental context /
Phyllis Anne Teeter.
        p.   cm.
    Includes bibliographical references and index.
    ISBN 1-57230-384-0
    1. Attention-deficit hyperactivity disorder. 2. Attention-deficit
disorder in adults. I. Title.
RJ506.H9T44 1998
618.92′8589—dc21   98-39158
                                                            CIP

*To all my "friends" with ADHD—especially
to Andy, Griff, Nathan, Philip, Ted, and Mary,
and to your families. Thank you for your courage
and for teaching me so much.*

About the Author

Phyllis Anne Teeter, EdD, is Professor of Educational Psychology at the University of Wisconsin—Milwaukee. She is the author of *Child Neuropsychology: Assessment and Intervention for Neurodevelopmental Disorders,* and has written numerous book chapters and articles on ADHD. As the cochair of the Committee on Women in School Psychology, Division 16 of the American Psychological Association, Dr. Teeter is presently examining psychosocial issues that promote the well-being of girls and women.

Acknowledgments

This book compiles information gathered from research, as well as clinical insights developed over my years of working with children, adolescents, and adults with ADHD and their families. I have learned so much from all of you about how ADHD affects individuals on a personal basis. Although the challenges are many, I have always been impressed with the dignity, courage, and perseverance that you possess. You have been generous in teaching me so much, and I am grateful for the opportunity to have known you and worked with you over the years.

My colleagues in the Wisconsin ADD Consortium have also been a source of knowledge, support, and friendship. My thanks are extended to Paula Stewart, Kathy Hubbard, Barbara Downs, Joan Helbing, Lori Smith, Nancy Meyers, Donita O'Donnell, and JoEllen Waddell. You are a hard-working, talented group of women who have changed educational and psychological services for children and their families. Thank you for your time, energy, and commitment to children with ADHD and for sharing your expertise with me and with others. There are many who have shared the same goals. It has been a pleasure to learn from Stephanie Netzel, Pat Healy, Barb Senzig, Ellen Pizer-Kuppersmith, and Kathy Meredith. You have all been so generous. Ann Anderson was also one of the most talented of the teachers who taught me so much about life. You gave so much to all your students with ADHD and to the rest of us. We will miss you always.

I owe much to my family and friends—Steve, Stan, Mom, Donna, Tim, and Todd. You have been so understanding of the time lost and the engagements missed, and so tolerant of the enormous burden my writing this book placed on you. Thank you for your love and support.

Last but not least, thanks to all those teachers who have been compassionate and who helped calm down those anxious, rambunctious, and/or hyperactive children. We all have a part to play in the management of ADHD if individuals with the disorder are to be effective, happy, and productive. Thank you all for doing your part and for remaining optimistic even during the descending parts of the roller coaster ride.

Finally, my thanks are extended to Sharon Panulla at The Guilford Press. You have been a patient and supportive editor. Thank you for your help in getting this project completed. Jeannie Tang and the editorial staff at Guilford were meticulous and timely in the final stages of production. My genuine thanks to you all.

Foreword

In 1845, when Hans Hoffman wrote the story of Fidgety Phil (Papazian, 1995), few could have predicted that this poetic description of a hyperactive child defined the clinical features of what has become, 150 years later, a common yet complex disorder of childhood. Just over 50 years later, Englishman George F. Still described Still's Disease (1902) as a problem that resulted in a child's inability to internalize rules and limits characterized by a pattern of restless, inattentive, and over-aroused behavior. Following the prevailing thought developed in the 1890s that this pattern of behavior was the result of brain injury, Still hypothesized that at some point in their development these children had experienced neurological trauma. Still might be considered the Nostradamus of ADHD. Although in the following 100 years ADHD was alternately described in terms of its hypothesized cause (e.g., postencephalitic disorder, minimal brain dysfunction) as well as its core symptoms (e.g., hyperkinesis, hyperactivity, attention deficit), the start of a new millennium finds researchers and clinicians alike reaching a consensus that Still's description of cause, symptom, and consequence in ADHD appeared to be accurate.

ADHD is increasingly conceptualized and understood as a neurologically based condition, with genetics found to play a significant role in increasing the risk that an individual will experience the disorder. Differences in brain size, structure, and biochemistry as well as genetic variations in neurotransmitters have been identified in those afflicted with ADHD (for review see Goldstein & Goldstein, 1998).

From a symptom perspective, children with ADHD are not always inattentive or distractible (Douglas, 1983). It is increasingly recognized that problems with inhibition lead to faulty self-regulation and deficient executive function (for review, see Barkley, 1997). It is under circumstances in which inhibition is required that children with ADHD struggle most. When tasks are interesting, children with ADHD pay attention reasonably well. When sufficiently motivated by immediate consequences, they function better. However, when tasks are repetitive, effortful, uninteresting, and not of their choosing, they struggle. When consequences are delayed, infrequent, or unpredictable they quickly find something else to do. The current conceptualization of ADHD as resulting from a core deficit of faulty inhibition or impulsivity leading to poor self-regulation and executive function is now generally accepted and appears consistent with a large body of research. Thus, it is not surprising that Barkley has suggested that "ADHD represents a profound disturbance in self-regulation and organization of behavior across time" (Barkley, 1997, p. vii).

ADHD then may well be a disorder that affects children's ability to organize behavior over time and meet demands for present and future performance. Thus, to understand the disorder, one has to go where it lives. Over a longer period of time, laboratory tests may measure some aspects of ADHD but because this is a disorder of inconsistency as opposed to inability; a disorder that results not from lack of information but rather from not doing what one knows; it is not always captured or accurately reflected in brief laboratory observations or for that matter reports of parents and teachers.

Research in ADHD has increased exponentially over the past 10 years. As further studies are completed, ADHD is increasingly viewed not from a categorical perspective but on a dimensional basis. This shift to a dimensional view is supported by a robust literature suggesting that dimensional systems are not only better for defining severity but also much better predictors of outcome in later childhood and young adulthood (Fergusson & Horwood, 1995). ADHD appears to represent a set of qualities that do not define a distinct category of person but rather place an individual at an extreme position on a normal distribution with regard to inhibition and self-regulation (Levy, Hay, McStephen, Ward, & Waldman, 1997). This is how one would expect many polygenetic traits to be distributed. Rather than representing an advantage that others lack, qualities of ADHD represent a disadvantage that most people do not suffer from.

In the arena of consequence, we have increasingly come to recognize that symptom relief is not synonymous with changing long-term outcome. Symptoms of ADHD appear to act catalytically. Unfortunately, those afflicted with the disorder appear significantly more vulnerable than others to problems in coping with life's challenges, stresses, and demands. Stresses such as those involving family and environmental factors have been found to significantly contribute to adult outcome. Children with ADHD, in the absence of developing severe comorbid problems, may fare reasonably well into adulthood, though they may struggle somewhat academically and educationally. However, this group appears to be in the minority. An increasing body of research is demonstrating that nearly two-thirds of adults with histories of ADHD develop major depression, two-thirds have a history of substance abuse or dependence, while nearly one-fifth has a history of anxiety (Millstein, Wilens, Biederman, & Spencer, 1997). Nearly half the adult population with ADHD appear to develop a rather pessimistic, helpless, disorganized personality style (Robin, Bedwai, & Tzelepis, 1998). Thus, the consequences of ADHD appear worse than the symptoms. The combination of ADHD with other psychiatric disorders places afflicted individuals at significant risk to experience a lifetime of problems.

Over the past 50 years, the field of ADHD has withstood angry, inflammatory, and aggressive attacks from those who would seek to view afflicted individuals as bad, poorly parented products of a dysfunctional society, inappropriately fed, exposed to toxic chemicals, or deficient in minerals and vitamins (for review see Ingersoll & Goldstein, 1993). Through it all a cadre of dedicated researchers continued their important work by developing hypotheses, testing them rigorously, comparing findings to available data, and then slowly and patiently integrating proven findings into clinical care and practice. This is science. It is often difficult, frustrating, time consuming, and at times slow moving. It is, however, essential if we are to help rather than hinder those afflicted with ADHD. Even in the face of this work controversial treatments continue to be promoted. Those afflicted with ADHD and their families are often frustrated and confused.

So it was with great interest and pleasure that I read Phyllis Ann Teeter's *Interventions for ADHD*. Dr. Teeter's careful, scholarly review of the ADHD literature is deftly integrated with the science of normal human development. This text approaches ADHD from a developmental, dimensional perspective, setting the stage for what likely will be numerous texts to follow. In an intellectually honest fashion, Dr. Teeter describes research-proven treatments and what she refers to as "best practices." The latter represent those treatments that are not necessarily proven through double-blind, placebo control, but which, from a commonsense perspective, are consistent with what is known about ADHD and hold the promise of improving the lives of those afflicted. In my work with children, adolescents, and adults with ADHD, this is a text I will turn to time and time again. First, to reacquaint myself with normal developmental issues. Second, to develop, integrate, and implement reasoned and reasonable treatment plans for those with ADHD.

As we come to better understand what ADHD is and is not, we are increasingly aware that multiple developmental pathways ultimately contribute to an individual's life course. Although symptoms of ADHD are clearly impairing, they do not necessarily predict dire life outcome. The early identification and treatment of childhood ADHD is important not just because it relieves symptoms, but because symptom relief is likely to increase resilience and the capacity to deal with other adverse life stresses. Having this disorder demands a greater effort by affected individuals and those who live with and love them. Fortunately, ADHD can be treated and managed effectively, leading to more successful and happier lives for those who struggle with it. We must continue the work of serious scholarship in ADHD. Along the way we must also rededicate ourselves to the families and afflicted individuals with whom we work. Dr. Teeter's text will play an important role in this process.

SAM GOLDSTEIN, PHD
Neurology, Learning, and Behavior Center
Salt Lake City, Utah

REFERENCES

Barkley, R. A. (1997). *ADHD and the nature of self-control.* New York: Guilford Press.

Douglas, V. I. (1983). Attentional and cognitive problems. In M. Rutter (Ed.), *Developmental neuropsychiatry.* New York: Guilford Press.

Fergusson, D. M., & Horwood, L. J. (1995). Predictive validity of categorically and dimensionally scored measures of disruptive childhood behaviors. *Journal of the American Academy of Child and Adolescent Psychiatry, 34,* 477–496.

Goldstein, S., & Goldstein, M. (1998). *Managing attention-deficit hyperactivity disorder in children: A guide for practitioners* (2nd edition). New York: Wiley.

Ingersoll, B., & Goldstein, S. (1993). *Attention deficit disorder and learning disabilities: Realities, myths and controversial treatments.* New York: Wiley.

Levy, F., Hay, D. A., McStephen, M., Wood, C., & Waldman, I. (1997). Attention–deficit hyperactivity disorder: A category of a continuum? Genetic analysis of a large scale twin study. *Journal of the American Academy of Child and Adolescent Psychiatry, 36,* 737–744.

Millstein, R. B., Wilens, T. E., Biederman, J., & Spencer, T. J. (1997). Presenting

ADHD symptoms and subtypes in clinically referred adults with ADHD. *Journal of Attention Disorders, 2,* 159–166.

Papazian, O. (1995). The story of fidgety Philip. *International Pediatrics, 10,* 188–190.

Robin, A. L., Bedwai, A., & Tzelepis, A. (1998). Understanding the personality traits of adults with ADHD: A pilot study. *Attention, 4,* 49–55.

Still, G. F. (1902). The Coulstonian lectures on some abnormal physical conditions in children. *Lancet, 1,* 1008–10012.

Preface

This book presents the most current research on ADHD throughout the life span, and reviews empirically and clinically based interventions for addressing this disorder. Although there are numerous books on ADHD, this work provides a unique perspective on the disorder.

First, the book uses a developmental framework to show how ADHD develops over time. A developmental perspective is important because it shows how ADHD is manifested at various stages of life, helping to dispel the notion that ADHD is only a disorder of childhood.

Second, this book places ADHD within the context of normal developmental challenges. Specifically, normal challenges of the toddler/preschool, middle childhood, adolescent, and adult stages are explored. The impact of ADHD is considered for each age group. In order to appreciate how a particular disorder interferes with adjustment, it is critical to understand the major developmental milestones, issues, and conflicts prominent at each stage. Within this context, it is easier to see how disturbances of self-control, impulsivity, inattention, and hyperactivity add another complicating dimension to the developmental picture of individuals with ADHD.

Third, this book addresses ADHD within a biogenetic, neurodevelopmental framework. By understanding the genetic and neurodevelopmental basis of ADHD, clinicians are better able to develop appropriate interventions. Research shows that ADHD is highly heritable where a parent with ADHD is at risk for having an ADHD offspring (57%). The heritability of ADHD is a stronger factor in the development of the disorder than are environmental explanations such as poor parenting, poverty, or a chaotic family environment, and is useful in determining how ADHD in families might affect parent–child interactions and intervention efficacy.

Finally, research on the neurodevelopmental basis of ADHD shows that individuals are predisposed to deficits in executive control functions (i.e., self-regulation and self-control, planning, and organization) as a result of anomalies in neurochemical or neurotransmitter systems that primarily involve frontal lobe and frontal–basal ganglia neural networks. These neurodevelopmental anomalies interact with environmental factors to affect the overall cognitive, psychosocial, academic, and behavioral functioning of individuals with ADHD. However, these biogenetic vulnerabilities respond to a variety of interventions, including psychopharmacology, behavior management, parent/teacher training, and self-management techniques, to name just a few.

This book was written for medical, mental health, psychological, and educational professionals who work with individuals with ADHD. Parents will also find the techniques useful and will develop a better understanding of ADHD from the book. It provides detailed information about which interventions are most effective for which aspects of the disorder, including the cognitive, behavioral, psychosocial, and academic domains. The techniques that are described generally represent empirically based interventions. When research is not available, promising practice techniques are provided.

Contents

1

Introduction to Attention-Deficit/ Hyperactivity Disorder

Knowledge of the developmental course of attention-deficit/ hyperactivity disorder (ADHD) provides information about how symptoms vary at different ages and how personal characteristics affect adjustment, depending on the cognitive, academic, and psychosocial demands placed on the individual at specific developmental stages. A developmental perspective provides a framework for understanding the nature and course of ADHD, an understanding which is essential for planning long-term treatment. The typical age of onset is approximately 3 years (Barkley, 1989, 1996a), although research suggests that infant temperament is a predisposing factor in ADHD (Barkley, 1989; Kaplan & Sadock, 1985; Wender, 1987) and longitudinal studies show that a majority of children with ADHD do not outgrow the symptoms (Barkley, Fischer, Edelbrock, & Smallish, 1990; Weiss & Hechtman, 1993). The fact that ADHD is a lifelong disorder increases the need for a developmental perspective when designing interventions at various stages in the life of the child, adolescent, or adult with ADHD.

The core characteristics of ADHD (i.e., inattention, impulsivity, and hyperactivity) have adverse affects on a child's academic performance, school productivity, peer and family relationships, and overall psychosocial adjustment (Barkley, 1990a, 1990b; DuPaul & Stoner, 1994). Children who have difficulty meeting the expectations of parents and teachers often have grave concerns about their own self-worth and often frustrate

1

adults who do not understand the reasons behind the child's inability to accomplish age-appropriate tasks (Levine, 1994). Levine puts it poignantly when he states, "So much is at stake. Children who experience too much failure too early in life are exquisitely vulnerable to a wide variety of complications" (1994, p. 1). Others suggest that emotional, conduct, and learning problems may emerge as a result of poor self-esteem, a lack of success in school, and impaired relationships with peers and family members (Weiss & Hechtman, 1986, 1993; Weiss, Hechtman, Milroy, & Perlman, 1985; Wender, 1987). These patterns create chronic problems in individuals with ADHD that often persist into adulthood.

The purpose of this book is threefold: (1) to explain the challenges of ADHD throughout the life span; (2) to describe effective interventions in an effort to break the cycle of failure, self-doubt, and social maladjustment; and (3) to discuss how parents and medical, psychological, and educational professionals can assist in the intervention process. This book reviews the developmental course of ADHD, describes its pervasive effects, and addresses the behavioral, cognitive, academic, and psychosocial needs of individuals who have the disorder.

This chapter introduces the characteristics and symptoms of ADHD and presents a theoretical framework for understanding the dynamic effects of ADHD on an individual's life. A number of topics are discussed, including the characteristics and core features of ADHD, theoretical models for understanding ADHD, neuroanatomical substrates of ADHD, some considerations for designing multifaceted interventions, and an overview of the developmental course of ADHD.

CHARACTERISTICS AND CORE FEATURES OF ADHD

Research and clinical studies have shown that a complex set of behaviors has been observed in children and adolescents with ADHD. There is a general consensus that ADHD children and adolescents exhibit core symptoms of inattention, hyperactivity, and impulsivity in varying degrees and at different levels of severity (Barkley, 1990a, 1996a; DuPaul & Stoner, 1994; Weiss & Hechtman, 1993). To a lesser degree, studies suggest that children with ADHD also have primary difficulties in following rules or demonstrate deficits in rule-governed behavior and display tremendous variability in task performance (Barkley, 1981, 1982, 1990b).

Although inattention, impulsivity, and hyperactivity have been called the "holy trinity" of ADHD, behavioral disinhibition or poor regulation of behavior has been referred to as its hallmark (Barkley, 1990b, 1996a, 1997a). Disinhibition in its various manifestations (e.g., poor regulation of motor activity and impulsivity) seems to be the most powerful discriminating factor for differentiating individuals with ADHD from those without ADHD. The inability to plan, to control, and to regulate one's own behavior necessarily has broader ramifications and potentially more pervasive and severe effects than might be implied if ADHD is simply conceptualized as a disorder of inattention or hyperactivity. Further, Barkley (1990b, 1996a) suggests that inattention may be secondary to a child's inability to inhibit behaviors and that executive control dysfunctions or disinhibition underlie problems with inattention, hyperactivity, and impulsivity.

It is important to note that ADHD is a heterogeneous disorder and that individuals may differ in the type, level, and degree of characteristics they show. These individual variations, in conjunction with environmental factors, affect the overall impact of the disorder.

INCIDENCE RATES FOR ADHD

ADHD is one of the most common reasons for referring children to psychiatric and mental health agencies (Barkley, 1990b) and is the most common neurobehavioral disorder of childhood (Shaywitz & Shaywitz, 1992). Prevalence rates vary depending upon how the disorder is defined (Frick & Lahey, 1991); some suggest that approximately 3–5% of the school-age population has ADHD (American Psychiatric Association, 1994; Barkley, 1990b; McBurnett, Lahey, & Pfiffner, 1993), whereas others estimate that 10–20% of this age group has ADHD (Shaywitz & Shaywitz, 1992). The estimates by Shaywitz and Shaywitz (1992) represent the high end of the continuum and may be a result of the combined dimensional and categorical paradigm that the Yale team employs in diagnosis (Shaywitz, Holahan, Marchione, Sadler, & Shaywitz, 1992). Dimensional paradigms describe behaviors on a dimension depending on the severity of symptoms (e.g., a T score above 70 on the impulsive–hyperactive scale), whereas categorical approaches use criteria to determine the presence or absence of a disorder based on specific symptoms (e.g., DSM-IV criteria for ADHD).

Estimates are harder to determine for adolescents and adults (APA, 1994). Studies report that approximately 71% of children do not outgrow ADHD symptoms in adolescence (Barkley, Fischer, et al., 1990) and that about 66% of adults still demonstrate at least one of the major "disabling" symptoms of childhood ADHD (Weiss & Hechtman, 1993). Although most ADHD adults show fairly good outcomes, Spitzer, Williams, Gibbon, and First (1990) found that 41% had a comorbid disorder, including mood disorders, substance abuse, and antisocial behaviors. In addition to the core symptoms, adults also show stubbornness, poor frustration tolerance, and chronic conflicts with spouses, friends, and authorities (Biederman et al., 1993). These findings for adolescents and adults are discussed in later chapters.

Some gender differences appear in incidence rates of ADHD. Males are more likely to be diagnosed with ADHD (Barkley, 1996a), and Szatmari (1992) reported a 3:1 ratio of males to females with the disorder. However, recent attention has been given to the notion that ADHD may be underreported and underdiagnosed in women (Ratey, Miller, & Nadeau, 1995). Clinic-referred samples suggest a higher incidence of oppositional defiant disorder and/or conduct disorder in males (Barkley, 1996a), while school-based referrals show higher rates of aggression and behavioral symptoms in boys (Carlson, Tamm, & Gaub, 1997). Szatmari (1992) also found that gender ratios are not significantly different when comorbid diagnoses are controlled. The increased incidence of the aggressive, antisocial dimensions of the disorder in boys may lead researchers to overlook girls who have ADHD (Ratey et al., 1995). However, Carlson et al. (1997) found that girls with disruptive behavior disorders have more social problems than boys. Furthermore, Ratey et al. (1995) suggest that women frequently exhibit depression and anxiety symptoms that often mask those of ADHD and that even the best clinicians overlook ADHD in women. As a result, women tend to be diagnosed later in life than most men. Other factors, including intellectual, academic, and neuropsychological functioning, may contribute to our understanding of gender differences in ADHD. In a pilot study, Seidman et al. (1997) found higher rates of intellectual (Freedom from Distractibility on the Wescher Scales) and academic deficits in ADHD girls compared to non-ADHD girls, while performance on measures of executive functions were less impaired than on those previously reported for boys. Future research should clarify these important differences.

Ratey et al. (1995) suggest that there are a number of issues that detract from our ability to diagnose ADHD in women:

> These issues are neurobiological, as gender-related neurobiological tendencies may make diagnosis more difficult; they are psychological, as a woman's trend toward internalization rather than externalization and acting out makes diagnosis more complicated; and they are social and cultural, as our gender-related norms and expectations not only color our own ability to recognize ADD but also influence and complicate the lives of women in ways that are damaging and painful, leading to low self-esteem and a global sense of failure. (p. 261)

Ratey, Greenberg, Bemporad, and Lindem (1992) found that low doses of tricyclic antidepressants (imipramine and desipramine) or stimulants in combination with antidepressants were helpful for many women with ADHD.

THEORETICAL MODELS OF ADHD

Researchers have formulated a number of integrated theories to explain ADHD and the dynamic relationship among various symptoms and clinical features of the disorder. These theories include a cognitive interactional model (Douglas, 1983), a behavioral inhibition model (Barkley, 1996a, 1996b), and a transactional, neurodevelopmental model (Teeter & Semrud-Clikeman, 1995, 1997).

The Cognitive Interactional Model

The cognitive interactional paradigm describes the multiple processes involved in ADHD and incorporates diverse research findings in an effort to further explain the disorder within an integrated perspective. In a comprehensive review of research investigating cognitive processes associated with ADHD, Douglas (1983) advanced a paradigm for understanding and ultimately treating individuals with ADHD. The model suggests that primary-process deficits (i.e., attention, inhibition, arousal-modulation, and reinforcement deficits) result in secondary-process deficits (i.e., deficits in reasoning, and social interaction and academic difficulties).

The interactional model introduced by Douglas (1983) is useful because, rather than providing a list of symptoms or seemingly unrelated characteristics, this paradigm theorizes that attentional, inhibitory, and arousal problems affect, interact, produce, and sustain high-order cognitive and behavioral deficits in individuals with ADHD. The extent to which primary process deficits interfere with cognitive, academic, and social adjustment partly determines the severity of ADHD in individual children and adolescents.

Primary-Process Deficits Associated with ADHD

Primary-process deficits interfere with the way an individual attends to stimuli and controls and organizes responses. Douglas (1983, p. 323) indicates that primary deficits of ADHD include the following: (1) impaired attention and effort; (2) inhibitory deficits; (3) arousal-modulation deficits; and, (4) a tendency to seek immediate reinforcement. According to Douglas, these primary deficits contribute to secondary deficits, including (1) an impaired development of higher-order reasoning; (2) difficulty developing schemata, including concepts, strategies, and academic operations; (3) impaired metacognitions; and (4) poor effectance motivation.

Impaired Attention. Inattention is considered one of the cardinal symptoms of ADHD (Barkley, 1990b; Frick & Lahey, 1991). Inattention typically refers to a complex set of processes, including (1) an inability to complete two tasks simultaneously (divided attention), such that the child is unable both to listen and to take notes while the teacher is talking; (2) an inability to attend to the task at hand (focused attention), such that the child appears to daydream or be preoccupied with other thoughts or activities; (3) an inability to ignore competing or irrelevant stimuli (selective attention), such that the child is easily distracted by noises or other stimuli; and (4) an inability to maintain attention when completing a task (sustained attention), such that the child rarely finishes assignments (Goldstein & Goldstein, 1990). Vigilance or readiness to respond is often included in discussions of attentional processes, and children with ADHD often have trouble listening, attending, and getting ready to respond.

Research suggests that deficits in attention are particularly evident under repetitive or boring conditions (Zentall, 1985), which might occur during classroom seatwork or when tackling tedious homework (Barkley, 1990b). Furthermore, inattention may affect the child's ability to engage in free play for long periods of time (Barkley & Ullman, 1975) and to participate in organized sports such as baseball (Pelham et al., 1990). Thus inattention can affect both academic and social functioning in children with ADHD.

During complex tasks, Douglas (1983) contends that attention comprises three processes related to self-regulation, including (1) maintaining attention over time; (2) organizing and self-directing attention; and (3) investing effort to attend to tasks. These self-regulatory features of attention suggest an interplay between the child's abilities to expend energy to focus attention and to inhibit impulsive responding. Furthermore, a developmental progression has been demonstrated wherein the attention of young children

> is frequently controlled by salient, curiosity-producing features of stimuli and by reinforcement-correlated features in the environment. In older children, these diffuse, exploratory behaviors tend to be replaced by self-governed, organized search strategies that enable the children to extract the particular information from their environment. (Douglas, 1983, p. 285)

The presence of difficulties in self-regulation and self-direction is a central feature of ADHD and permeates other aspects of the disorder, including motor regulation and inhibition of motor responses. Children with ADHD can have difficulties in strategic, systematic, and organized attention that ultimately affect their ability to meet the challenges of school, play, and social interchange.

Children with ADHD are not consistent in the amount of effort they expend to accomplish tasks (Douglas, 1972). Variability in work completion is particularly problematic with tasks that have multiple parts or that require sustained effort. Performance is highly variable and changes from "moment to moment, trial to trial and day to day in the same setting" (Barkley, 1990b, p. 46). It is this variability in performance that often leads to so much misunderstanding and misdiagnosis of attentional deficits. Teachers and parents are baffled by the observation that a child can do something one moment but not the next. In these instances, it is not so much a failure to perform that is problematic but the fact that the child has been successful that leads to so much misunderstanding. Once a child shows that she can accomplish a task, adults expect that performance to be maintained; when it is not, they interpret the variability as laziness, manipulation, noncompliance, or simple misbehavior. Barkley (1990b) views this variability in performance as one of the signs that can be useful in diagnosing ADHD, particularly when other core symptoms are present. Performance variability may also be associated with deficient reinforcement mechanisms, which are described later.

Disinhibition–Impulsivity. Disinhibition affects a range of behaviors, including the ability to attend, to complete projects, and to control emotions and verbal responses. Disinhibition or impulsivity appear as cardinal symptoms of ADHD in children and adults (Barkley, 1990b, 1996a; Douglas, 1983). Weiss and Hechtman (1993) indicate that "impulsivity problems (or series of problems) are the most serious and most sustained of the childhood clusters of symptoms" (p. 40). Hyperactivity and poor concentration appear less problematic for adults with ADHD, although impulsivity continues to be a major impeding factor. Difficulties with impulsivity or the inability to inhibit one's behavior might be manifested as blurting out answers in school, having difficulty waiting one's turn, and/or interrupting or intruding on others (American Psychiatric Association, 1994). These clinical symptoms appear in numerous situations, particularly when there are few external controls or when children are absorbed by something that is especially interesting or reinforcing (Douglas, 1983).

Impulsivity or disinhibition appears in many situations that can be frustrating for parents, teachers, and peers who interact with children with ADHD. For example, children with ADHD are often unable to wait. They are demanding and inflexible, and, at times, they appear to others to be selfish. They may insist on being first in every game; they may butt into line to get ahead of someone else; or they may want to take another turn because they cannot wait until their turn comes again. These problems are particularly acute in situations where children must delay gratification. Children with ADHD are unable to work for long periods of time without a reward; they cannot wait for the teacher to pay attention to them; and they cannot wait to get through the grocery line before ripping open a candy bar and devouring it. Children with ADHD often begin tasks before directions are given; they may work quickly and impulsively without thinking; and they may make many careless errors in an effort to finish quickly.

Impulsive behaviors often lead to social rejection by peers, criticism from teachers, and exasperation and exhaustion in parents. As Barkley (1990b) describes them, children with ADHD leave the impression of "irresponsibility, immaturity or childishness, laziness, and outright rudeness. Little wonder they may experience more punishment, criticism, censure, and ostracism by adults and their peers" (p. 42).

Impulsivity and hyperactivity interfere with work and interpersonal relations and affect the self-esteem and psychiatric well-being of both children and adults (Weiss & Hechtman, 1993). Individuals with ADHD may say whatever is on their minds without realizing the social consequences of their remarks; they may be so blunt as to appear rude and overbearing. Children and adults may be emotionally labile and prone to emotional outbursts that do not seem appropriate to the circumstance or situation.

Arousal-Modulation Deficits. Despite several theoretical and methodological shortcomings of the concept, Douglas (1983) includes arousal-modulation deficits among the primary-process difficulties exhibited by children with ADHD. Arousal-modulation deficits refer to an inability to react or be alerted to stimuli. Arousal-modulation deficits appear related to "expectancies," that is, to the readiness to respond to a situation or a stimulus. Expectancies are most likely affected by one's prior learning experiences. Thus ADHD appears to be a disorder that affects both arousal and alertness; these deficits then negatively affect learning. Children with ADHD often do not function at optimal arousal states (Douglas & Peters, 1979); they are not alert to important features of a task (especially when tasks are dull or repetitive); or they may become so overly excited about specific aspects of the task that they are unable to respond effectively to the task demands (Douglas, 1983). Thus arousal states and the ability to control or modulate them appear to be affected by ADHD.

Tendency to Seek Immediate Reinforcement. In conjunction with attentional, arousal, and inhibitory deficits, Douglas (1983) found that children with ADHD responded abnormally to rewards; such responses are presumed to be a manifestation of a defect in self-regulation. Douglas and Parry (1994) suggest that children with ADHD "(1) have an abnormally strong tendency to seek immediate reward, (2) are unusually vulnerable to possible arousing and distracting effects of reward, and (3) become abnormally frustrated when anticipated rewards fail to appear" (p. 281). Douglas and Parry (1994) hypothesize that hypersensitivity to the presence of reinforcers and/or the possibility of losing anticipated rewards produces a state of emotional arousal in children that ultimately results in frustration and task interference. This hypersensitivity to reinforcement further reduces the child's ability to delay gratification. Parry and Douglas (1983) suggest that because children with ADHD may pay so much attention to the rewards they fail to realize that a particular behavior is being reinforced. Douglas and Peters (1979) also found that, when given rewards, children with ADHD actually become highly aroused and more impulsive.

Variable schedules of reinforcement dramatically alter the performance of children with ADHD. When reinforcement is continuous (100% of the time), children with ADHD sustain attention longer and respond more accurately than when reinforcement occurs only 50% of the time (Freibergs & Douglas, 1969; Parry, 1973), although Douglas and Parry (1994) did not find these differences until reinforcers were dropped to below the 30% level. Frustration appears to be greatest following a decrease in reinforcement from 100% during initial learning trials to zero during extinction (Douglas & Parry, 1994). Douglas (1983) hypothesizes that children with ADHD have a production deficit rather than a mediation deficit. That is, if children can produce a response (use a mediator) that was not used spontaneously after reinforcement, then the mediational process is probably intact, and reinforcement mechanisms are implicated.

According to Sagvolden, Wultz, Moser, Moser, and Morkrid (1989), stimulant medication (e.g., Ritalin) seems to increase the reinforcing effects of stimuli by "lengthening the delay gradient" of reinforcers. Beninger (1989) suggests that an altered response to reinforcement may be related to low levels of dopamine in children with ADHD. Dopamine is important in the control of motor behavior and also in "reward learning." Reward learning increases attention to the stimulus that has been reinforced or signals that rewards are forthcoming, and because this mechanism may be impaired, children with ADHD may "move more frequently from stimulus to stimulus leading to an apparent hyperactivity" (Beninger, 1989, p. 335). Because Ritalin enhances dopamine, it may "lead to better incentive learning, more attention to stimuli signalling reward and a resultant reduction in activity" (p. 335). Information concerning the reinforcing properties of specific tasks may provide better clues to how children with ADHD learn best.

Barkley (1990b) argues that the magnitude of the reinforcer is an important influence on the performance of children with ADHD. When watching television, playing video games, or engaging in highly reinforcing activities, children with ADHD may perform at normal or near-normal levels. This performance enhancement is thought to be a function of the schedule (high rates of immediate reinforcers) and magnitude (highly rewarding activities) of the reinforcers that are inherent in the activity itself. A differential response to rewards obviously has a dramatic impact in the classroom; reinforcements there may be quite sparse because it may be difficult for teachers both to maintain high rates of reinforcement and to routinely alter rewards when they lose their potency or effectiveness. However, research shows that efforts to modify reinforcers, to increase schedules of reinforcement, and to change reinforcers frequently produces positive behavioral changes in children with ADHD. Medication also has a positive effect on the response to rewards and, in combination with high rates of reinforcement, may produce the best overall performance outcome for children with ADHD.

Summary of Primary Process Deficits. As a group, children with ADHD are less able than other children to control their own arousal levels to meet the demands of tasks. They may seek stimulation because of their sensitivity to rewards; they may fail to inhibit strong response tendencies inherent in some stimuli; and they may have difficulty modulating their own arousal states, especially when tasks are boring (Douglas, 1983). Because of these dysfunctional processes, children with ADHD may not adequately "learn" from previous experiences. Douglas "emphasizes the role of experience in developing 'expectancies' or readiness to respond to particular aspects of a situation" (1983, p. 289). Children with ADHD may experience long-term developmental deficits in cognitive and academic areas because they have not developed elaborate expectancies about given situations.

Secondary-Process Deficits Associated with ADHD

Douglas (1983) suggests that the primary-process deficits found in children with ADHD are interrelated; that attentional, arousal, and inhibitory deficits vary across individuals; and that these primary problems give rise to secondary difficulties in planning and reasoning and in social processes.

Planning and Reasoning Deficits. Reasoning and planning deficits have been associated with ADHD (Hynd & Willis, 1988; Teeter & Semrud-Clikeman, 1995, 1997). Children with attention deficits exhibit weaknesses on neuropsychological tests and show signs of perseveration, poor reasoning, and impaired judgment (Chelune, Ferguson, Koon, & Dickey, 1986). Children diagnosed with ADD differed significantly from a control group on measures requiring sustained attention, flexible problem solving and thinking, fluid monitoring and regulatory abilities. As a group, children with ADD demonstrated a tendency to ignore feedback concerning the correctness of responses, and their perseveration errors (persisting in giving the same incorrect response regardless of feedback) were twice as high as normals on the Wisconsin Card Sorting Test. Douglas (1983) suggests that the perseverative response pattern observed in children with ADD may be a function of "overfocusing" on one element of a task and that the "unique" response pattern may reflect an impulsive, unconventional strategy or approach to tasks rather than dysfunctional thought processes.

Further evidence of reasoning and problem-solving deficits in children with ADD was found in a study conducted by Tant and Douglas (1982). Children with ADD failed to identify all the possible alternative solutions to tasks presented, to effectively use the solutions they did find, and to develop good questions for finding solutions. Tant and Douglas (1982) concluded that children with ADD fail to develop metacognitive strategies when solving problems and that they do not know how to develop an overall strategy for problem solving. The extent to which academic tasks demand flexibility, problem-solving, and reasoning skills may determine the extent to which children with ADD will show generalized cognitive deficits and academic delays. Also, the extent to which later learning is dependent upon early learning may predict that children with ADHD will develop serious "learning problems" as they get into middle and high school. The cognitive complexity of tasks and the need to develop mental schemata and to access prior knowledge to perform them may explain why a large portion of children with ADD fail to progress academically.

Social Processes. The degree to which impaired attention, poor inhibitory control, arousal-modulation difficulties, and altered reinforcement mechanisms (primary processes) affect the social adjustment of children with ADHD has been of interest. Numerous research articles report that children with ADHD often have significant social-emotional problems (Barkley, 1990b, 1990a; Weiss & Hechtman, 1993). Pelham (1993a) indicates that the "typical child with ADHD has an impulsive, interrupting, overbearing, and immature style of relating to peers" (p. 203). Children with ADHD often have trouble making and keeping friends (Guevremont, 1990), which over time may lead to social isolation, sadness, and depression; they also show a failure to reciprocate (e.g., respond to questions) in social interactions with peers (Cunningham & Siegel, 1987; Milich & Landau, 1989).

Others have found that hyperactivity and aggression frequently cooccur (Loney & Milich, 1982) and that approximately 50% of children with ADHD are aggressive with peers (Pelham, 1993a). Aggressive characteristics often result in social rejection by peers (Landau & Moore, 1991), which is predictive of poor long-term outcome (Parker & Asher, 1987). Walker, Lahey, Hynd, and Frame (1987) found that conduct disorders were also exacerbated by hyperactivity and that when conduct disorder occurs in children with ADHD, a pattern of antisocial behaviors ensues that is more persistent than are problems found in children with conduct disorder alone. Further, hyperactive delinquents are more antisocial than are their nonhyperactive peers (Offord, Sullivan, Allen, & Abrams, 1979).

Summary and Critique of the Interactional Model

Although Douglas (1983) includes reasoning and planning as secondary-process deficits, current research is exploring the possibility that these deficits are primary and part of a larger pathology involving executive-control or frontal-lobe dysfunction (Barkley, 1996a; Pennington & Ozonoff, 1996). Even though further research is necessary to resolve measurement and specificity issues (i.e., global, diffuse vs. discrete, focal deficits), a review of current research by Pennington and Ozonoff (1996) suggests that executive control deficits are primary rather than secondary deficits in ADHD.

Executive control functions include inhibiting or deferring responses to a later time; strategically planning a series of actions; and creating a mental representation of the task, which includes encoding relevant aspects of stimuli in memory and goal-directedness (Pennington & Ozonoff, 1996). The issue of whether executive control dysfunctions are primary to ADHD is important in conceptualizing this disorder. Furthermore, the relation of disinhibition and executive control deficits to frontal lobe dysfunction is becoming recognized as a viable primary explanation for this disorder. Research investigating the paradigm of ADHD as an executive control disorder will no doubt lead to a better understanding of how an inability to inhibit affects the planning and execution of motor responses, reasoning and problem solving, goal-directedness, and memory functions. The executive dysfunction paradigm may also provide important insight into the pathophysiology of ADHD and may help in differentiating common disorders of childhood (e.g., ADHD, conduct disorder, autism, and Tourette's disorder) that often coexist.

Although the interactional model of ADHD developed by Douglas (1983) does not highlight hyperactivity as a primary characteristic of ADHD, Barkley (1990a) considers hyperactivity to be the third primary characteristic of ADHD, along with inattention and behavioral disinhibition or impulsivity. Hyperactivity may manifest itself as over-activity, restlessness, fidgeting, unnecessary body movements, constant movement that appears purposeless, and/or excessive speech. DSM-IV criteria list a number of hyperactive/impulsive symptoms for children, including behaviors such as leaving a seat frequently, running about or climbing excessively, having difficulty playing quietly, and appearing to be constantly "on the go" or "driven by a motor" (APA, 1994). Hyperactivity is still considered one of the cardinal features of the disorder in the latest DSM revision. It permits a diagnosis of subtypes that depend on the presence of primary or predominant characteristics: attention-deficit/ hyperactivity disorder, combined type; attention-defi-cit/hyperactivity disorder, predominantly inattentive type; and atten-tion-deficit/hyperactivity disorder, predominantly hyperactive-impulsive type. Although Douglas's (1983) original research emphasized atten-tional and impulse control rather than hyperactivity as defining charac-teristics and influenced earlier diagnostic criteria (DSM-III; American Psychiatric Association, 1987), subsequent research reinstated the im-portance of hyperactivity and was thus included in the latest revision of diagnostic criteria.

There is some question as to the overlap of impulsivity and hyper-activity. In some factor analytic studies, impulsivity and hyperactivity appear strongly related (Achenbach & Edelbrock, 1983; Milich & Kraemer, 1985), and many items on rating scales commonly used for diagnosing ADHD often show an overlap of these symptoms (Barkley, 1990b). Impulsive and disinhibited behavior is the most powerful char-acteristic differentiating ADHD from other disorders and from normal development. Based on these findings, Barkley (1990b) argues that "greater weight should be given to the behavioral class of impulsive and hyperactive characteristics than to inattention in conceptualizing the disorder and its clinical presentation" (p. 45). In spite of this impressive differentiating power, it is unclear whether hyperactivity and impulsivity are both part of the more global characteristic of disinhibition, resulting from executive control deficits and abnormal frontal lobe activity.

Two other integrated theories of ADHD rest on executive control and neuropsychological underpinnings and suggest a greater role for these deficits in explaining the secondary and/or associated problems found in individuals with ADHD.

The Behavioral Inhibition Model

Barkley (1996a, 1996b) proposes an integrated model of ADHD that posits behavioral disinhibition as the central deficit that negatively influences four executive functions, including prolongation or working memory; self-regulation of affect, motivation, and arousal; internalization of speech; and, reconstitution, or analysis and synthesis. This theory is predicated on the "race" model of inhibition that suggests that an event or stimulus triggers both activating and inhibiting response processes in the brain that compete (or race) to be executed first (Barkley, 1996a). Schachar, Tannock, and Logan (1993) hypothesize that children who are disinhibited (e.g., individuals with ADHD) are slower to produce inhibitory responses. Barkley's (1996a) theory seeks to explain how basic disinhibition affects and accounts for other secondary or associated deficits found in many individuals with ADHD. This model incorporates earlier explanations of the disorder and provides a basis for further research.

Aspects of executive control dysfunction may hold the key to our understanding of how seemingly unrelated deficits result from some core or executive control deficit. Behavioral inhibition serves as the starting point for the other executive functions (e.g., prolongation, self-regulation of affect, internalization of speech, and reconstitution); when inhibition is dysfunctional, these related functions are affected adversely (Barkley, 1996a). Taken together, all these functions underlie self-regulation, help to bring behavior under control over time, and allow the priority of long-term or future consequences over immediate ones. Barkley (1996a) argues that the interaction of these executive control functions allows individuals to predict and control what happens in their environment. Furthermore, control over these events maximizes the beneficial consequences of future actions by enhancing one's ability to affect positive outcomes or to profit from one's experiences.

The following six assumptions underlie this theoretical model of ADHD: (1) Behavioral inhibition begins earlier in development than the other four executive controls. (2) These executive controls emerge at different developmental stages. (3) The impairments in the four executive functions associated with ADHD arise from the primary behavioral-inhibition deficit; if and when this primary deficit is altered, the other functions improve. (4) Behavioral-inhibition deficits result from genetic and neurodevelopmental factors. (5) Secondary deficits in self-regulation create further primary deficits in behavioral disinhibition because self-regulation enhances restraint or inhibition. (6) The model does not explain the occurrence of ADD without hyperactivity (Barkley, 1996a).

Barkley (1996a) indicates that behavioral inhibition is

> comprised of two related processes: (1) the capacity to inhibit prepotent response, either prior to or once initiated, creating a delay in the response to an event (response inhibition); and (2) the protection of this delay,

the self-directed actions occurring within it, and the goal-directed behaviors they create from interference by competing events and their
prepotent responses (interference control). (p. 71)

Prepotent responses are those that are subject to immediate reinforcement or for which there is a strong historical context for reinforcement.
The ability to postpone a response under these conditions and the period
of delay allow the other executive functions to exert influence over or
to modify a response to an event.

> The chain of goal-directed, future-oriented behaviors set in motion by
> these acts of self-regulation is then also protected from interference
> during its performance by this same process of inhibition (interference
> control). And even if disrupted, the individual retains the capacity or
> intention (via working memory) to return to the goal-directed actions
> until the outcome is successfully achieved or judged to be no longer
> necessary. (Barkley, 1996a, p. 71)

Prolongation or Working Memory

Prolongation or working memory is dependent on the ability to inhibit,
which allows the development of mental representations (Barkley,
1996a). By delaying a response, an individual exercises the ability to
hold a mental image while acting on some data. This "provisional
memory" allows a person the opportunity to prepare and to execute a
response that, once executed, is no longer a part of working memory.
Prolonged mental representations can be stored in long-term memory,
can be called back into working memory, and can be used in considering
a response to some new event. The ability to sequence these memories
and to analyze the temporal sequence for recurring patterns or themes
affects the ability to anticipate what happens next—to conjecture or
hypothesize. This process allows the individual to create an "anticipatory
set" and to develop forethought, or a sense of "future-thinking," which
in turn permits him or her to assign greater value to future rather than
to immediate consequences (Barkley, 1996a). Barkley hypothesizes that
these mechanisms are linked to inattention and disinhibition and that
they help to explain the forgetfulness that is so commonplace in
individuals with ADHD.

Self-Regulation of Affect

Behavioral inhibition includes the process of inhibiting the initial emotional valence that is elicited by prepotent responses. This inhibition does

not mean that the child does not experience the emotion; it means that he or she can control the emotional reaction or the behavioral response that is associated with the event. This delay of or control over emotions allows the child to engage in self-directed behaviors that modify not only the behavior itself but the emotional reaction it elicits. One can then gain objectivity in a situation and can determine the response one will make to an event. This process "permits the child to actually learn to induce drive or motivational states that may be required for the initiation and maintenance of goal-directed behavior" (Barkley, 1996a, p. 73).

When extended to the child with ADHD, Barkley (1996a) suggests that executive control deficits will predict greater emotional reactivity, less objectivity, diminished social perspective-taking, and decreased ability to generate drive and motivation to facilitate goal-directed behaviors.

Internalization of Speech

Speech development plays a role in the process of executive-control functions. As children progress through developmental stages, speech serves not only a communication function but also a control or behavioral inhibitory function. Increased behavioral inhibition permits language to be "turned on the self" (Barkley, 1996a, p. 73). Language is used to influence the behavior of others ("Give me milk!") and to control one's own behavior ("Better not take the cookie. Mom will get upset with me"). Progressive language development from public to subvocal to private is associated with an increase in control over one's behavior. Both language and knowledge of rules of acceptable behavior grow in influence over behaviors and are related to the capacity for self-control and the ability to plan and to direct behavior toward a goal (Barkley, 1996a).

Barkley (1996a) hypothesizes that the process of internalization of speech may be related to the prolongation or working-memory mechanisms, although the exact relationship is not known at this time. Given this theory of ADHD, internalization of speech would be expected to be less mature and more public (resulting in excessive talking), less reflective, less organized, less influential in controlling one's behaviors, and less rule oriented. As such, self-control and rule-governed behaviors would be compromised because the internalization of speech is not functional.

Reconstitution

The last executive function considered in the behavioral inhibition model is reconstitution, or the ability to analyze and synthesize that develops from the processes of internal speech, mental prolongation, and behavioral inhibition (Barkley, 1996a). New ideas can be generated from this process, and creativity or new combinations of ideas and problem solving also appear. Verbal fluency affects this process, and as tasks become more goal-directed, speech becomes rapid, efficient, and even creative in forming the internal verbal message that precedes the action. Thus the model predicts that individuals with ADHD will have trouble analyzing and synthesizing a response to a specific event. Problem solving will be affected because of difficulty in generating multiple plans of action or alternatives. Although verbal fluency deficits are not documented for ADHD, the ability to analyze a situation and to quickly, accurately, and efficiently put together a verbal plan of action to accomplish a goal has been shown to be deficient in individuals with ADHD.

Motor Control and Fluency

Behavioral inhibition and the various other executive functions influence one's ability to inhibit task-irrelevant behaviors, to execute and persist in goal-directed motor responses, to complete novel or complex motor responses, to reengage once interrupted, and to control one's behaviors through mentally represented stimuli (Barkley, 1996a). The primary cortex of the frontal lobes controls motor output and planning and executing of motor responses, and behavioral inhibition is controlled in adjacent regions of the cortex. Fine and gross motor skills thus depend on inhibition to

> preclude the initiation of movements located in neural zones adjacent to those being activated. Inhibition provides an increasing "functional pruning" of the motor systems such that those actions required to accomplish the task are initiated by the individual. Although the pruning action is believed to be distinct from actual synaptic pruning that may occur in neural development, the two processes may not be entirely unrelated. Over development, such powers of inhibition also permit the construction and execution of lengthy, complex, and novel chains of goal-directed behavior, protecting them from disruption by interference until they have been completed. (Barkley, 1996a, p. 74)

The prefrontal cortices are involved with more complex motor planning and execution. Given the model, individuals with ADHD would be expected to show difficulty with motor coordination and with planning and executing motor responses, particularly when lengthy, complex, goal-directed behaviors are required. Research shows problems in motor development and motor execution, but more research is needed to determine whether problems are most pronounced under novel, lengthy, or complex conditions (Barkley, 1996b).

Summary and Critique of the Behavioral Inhibition Model

The model of behavioral inhibition and its relationship to other executive control functions provides a paradigm that can be tested through systematic research. Barkley's (1996a, 1996b, 1997a) model suggests that there is a linkage between executive function, self-regulation, and goal-directed persistence that results from self-control and that this link explains the relationship between disinhibition and hyperactivity–impulsivity. Disinhibition is the primary deficit according to this model. Further research will be needed to determine the casual links between disinhibition, working memory, self-control, goal-directed persistence, and interference control, particularly in the presence of "prepotent" responses.

The Transactional, Neurodevelopmental Model

Teeter and Semrud-Clikeman (1995, 1997) proposed a transactional, neurodevelopmental model for ADHD, where biogenetic and environmental factors affect brain development and brain function, creating biogenetically based vulnerabilities, particularly executive control dysfunctions. Subtle brain anomalies in turn have consequences on the cognitive–intellectual (i.e., memory, language, processing, and attentional) functioning of children. These vulnerabilities also interact with and affect school (i.e., learning and academic performance) and psychosocial (i.e., interpersonal and family interactions) adjustment. In turn, the environment (i.e., home, school, and social) also has an impact on this process whereby biogenetic vulnerabilities can be modulated by modifying and controlling environmental factors (e.g., the presence or absence of reinforcers). This transactional model serves as a paradigm for explaining the bidirectional nature of the relationship between brain functioning and associated cognitive–intellectual, academic, behavioral, and psychosocial problems found in individuals with ADHD and provides a model for intervention planning.

Emerging research in the neurosciences suggests that children with ADHD have a biogenetically based disorder that results in complex problems of inattention, disinhibition, and impulsivity, problems that are not simply the result of willful disobedience, thoughtlessness, or lack of motivation. Although the growing evidence that ADHD is a neurobiological disorder may cause some parents and professionals to think that nothing can be done about the disorder, research suggests otherwise. This book examines intervention strategies that have proven effective for treating children, adolescents, and adults with ADHD.

CONSIDERATIONS FOR DESIGNING INTERVENTION PROGRAMS

Several factors are important to consider when designing intervention programs for individuals with ADHD. First, intervention plans should be developmentally based and sensitive to the various cognitive, social, and emotional demands that characterize each major developmental stage. Second, because of the pervasive and chronic nature of this disorder, interventions must be multifaceted in order to address the behavioral, academic, and psychosocial features of ADHD (Atkins, Pelham, & White, 1989; Barkley, 1990a; Pelham & Murphy, 1986). Interventions must also span a longer period of time than short-term approaches or programs might otherwise indicate (Atkins et al., 1989; Guevremont, 1990; Pelham, 1993a). Unfortunately research investigating the efficacy of long-term developmental interventions is long overdue. However, there is sufficient evidence to suggest that once interventions (i.e., behavioral management or pharmacotherapy) are discontinued, problems reemerge for children with ADHD (Pelham, 1993a).

The third factor is that disorders such as conduct, oppositional, and depressive-anxious disorders, and learning problems coexist in a majority of children with ADHD (Biederman, Newcome, & Sprich, 1991; Biederman & Steingard, 1987; Semrud-Clikeman, Biederman, et al., 1992). Comorbid disorders may need to be addressed separately when designing intervention plans because these problems do not necessarily improve with interventions that target ADHD symptoms alone. For example, interventions for a child with ADHD and a learning disability in reading should address the attentional, behavioral, and impulsive features of ADHD, as well as academic weaknesses, including the core phonological awareness and/or language deficits that are so common in children with learning disabilities. Therapies, such as medication and behavior management, that are designed to improve work completion, attention, and impulsivity will not be sufficient for increasing reading skills when a reading disability is also present. Furthermore, there is evidence that the coexistence of conduct and/or aggressive disorders with ADHD is predictive of poor adolescent and adult outcomes (Weiss & Hechtman, 1986, 1993) and occurs in families with high rates of parental psychopathology (Lahey, Piacentini, et al., 1988). When significant conduct or aggressive disorders accompany ADHD, then intervention must also focus on family systems and psychosocial components. Comorbid disorders typically increase the severity of the problems that are present in ADHD and must be addressed in treatment.

Interaction between ADHD Characteristics and Environmental Expectations

One of the major theses of this book is that interventions for ADHD must be viewed within an interactional framework. Whereas specific problems that are prominent in early childhood can be effectively addressed with intervention, the core features of ADHD are often manifested differently in older children, adolescents, and adults because of the unique challenges or environmental expectations of later stages of development. Furthermore, activity levels, disinhibition, and impulsivity change with age and are manifested differently at different ages.

The extent and the manner in which characteristics express themselves at different stages depends highly on an interaction between child (e.g., temperament, neuropsychological, and cognitive resources) and environmental factors (e.g., responsive and supportive caretaking in the home and in the school). Although ADHD has a strong biogenetic basis (Barkley, 1990a; Teeter & Semrud-Clikeman, 1995, 1997), environmental factors can affect the adaptation and expression of these characteristics. Although factors such as family dysfunction, parental psychopathology, and ineffective behavioral management affect children with ADHD, this does not imply that these environmental factors form the etiological foundation of the disorder. So whereas biology influences and, to some degree, formulates the nature of the actor, the environment sets the stage for a myriad of expressions and actions. The extent to which we can alter the environment may reduce the impact of symptoms of ADHD and the overall adjustment of individuals.

Thomas and Chess (1977) and Thomas, Chess, and Birch (1968) explored the relationship between temperament and environment and found that neither factor alone sufficiently explains atypical development. It is rather a "goodness of fit" between a child's characteristics and the expectation and support of the environment that appears to be critical. Barkley (1990a) further suggests that "the goal of treatment is to improve the 'goodness of fit' between the child and primary caretakers including parents and teachers. Thus, specific interventions may be targeted at (1) enhancing the child's capabilities and/or (2) adjusting the environmental demands" (p. 228).

The Need for Multifaceted Interventions for ADHD

Perhaps more than any other disorder, intervention programs for children with ADHD are typically multifaceted, drawing from various theoretical paradigms that include medical, behavioral, psychosocial, and family systems approaches (Teeter & Semrud-Clikeman, 1995).

Multifaceted intervention programs usually incorporate pharma-cotherapy, behavioral management, academic interventions, social skills training, problem-solving or anger-control training, and parent/family interventions (Abramowitz & O'Leary, 1991; Barkley, 1990b; DuPaul & Stoner, 1994).

There has been an increased interest in investigating how a combination of intervention strategies affects the overall adjustment of individuals with ADHD (e.g., psychopharmacological with behavioral and/or psychosocial interventions; Teeter & Semrud-Clikeman, 1995). A comparative analysis of different treatment modalities is often difficult because children with ADHD are an extremely heterogeneous group, such that the nature and severity of characteristics varies across children (Whalen & Henker, 1991). There may also be differences in outcome studies depending on the referral source (i.e., school versus clinic; Barkley, 1996a). Children seen in clinics tend to be more disruptive, whereas school-based referrals often focus on children who have greater problems concentrating. There is a growing need to determine how interventions affect specific problems and the additive effects of multi-modal treatments.

AN OVERVIEW OF THE DEVELOPMENTAL COURSE OF ADHD

Teeter (1991, 1993) argued for developmentally based treatment programs that address the specific behavioral challenges of each age and reflect the changing nature of the symptoms of ADHD across the life span. The developmental course of ADHD usually begins in the toddler stage, when parents note excessive levels of activity when the child first begins to walk (American Psychiatric Association, 1994). Although overactivity is fairly common in toddlers and although many active toddlers do not have ADHD, it appears that the behavior of children at the extremes of the continuum maintains a similar rank order over time (Campbell, 1990a). The diagnosis of ADHD often occurs when the child reaches school age because of emerging behavioral and academic difficulties.

Despite a growing number of longitudinal studies investigating the developmental course of clinic-referred children, the prediction of adolescent and adult outcome depends on multiple interacting variables, including the severity of symptoms, the presence of comorbid disorders, a family history of ADHD or parental psychopathology, childhood aggression, and treatment responsivity. Although symptom expression remains highly individualized and characteristics may change in adolescence (e.g., a decrease hyperactivity), almost 75% of adults with ADHD continue to show associated problems (see Table 1.1). In adults who do not demonstrate all of the symptoms of ADHD but continue to experience some functional impairment, partial remission may be indicated (American Psychiatric Association, 1994).

Table 1.1 shows that although the signs and symptoms of ADHD persist over time, the core features of the disorder affect children and adults differently because the developmental challenges of each age vary so dramatically. The core symptoms of ADHD make it extremely difficult for children and adults to adjust to the structure, demands, and challenges of school, work, and interpersonal relationships.

ADHD is a disorder that appears early and persists throughout the life span for most individuals who are diagnosed in childhood. The primary features of the disorder interfere with academic and work productivity, behavioral adjustment, and psychosocial interactions. There is growing evidence that interventions reduce the negative impact of the disorder especially when strategically administered and when combined with medication.

AN OVERVIEW OF SUBSEQUENT CHAPTERS

In Chapter 2, etiology is explored within a transactional model that shows the interaction of biogenetic, neuropsychological, cognitive, academic, and psychosocial correlates of ADHD. Chapter 3 reviews the challenges of the infancy/toddler/preschool stage of development. Interventions for addressing positive parent–child relationships, cognitive and speech delays, psychosocial deficits, and behavioral difficulties are presented in Chapter 4. Chapter 5 reviews the challenges of middle childhood and includes a discussion of how the symptoms of ADHD affect school performance, behavioral adjustment, and psychosocial interactions. Effective interventions for this age group are reviewed in Chapter 6, including combined strategies (e.g., psychopharmacology with behavior management). Chapter 7 addresses the unique challenges of adolescence and discusses outcome variables, and Chapter 8 explores intervention techniques for this age group. The characteristics of ADHD in adults and intervention strategies for this group are discussed in Chapter 9. Finally, Chapter 10 explores future research trends.

TABLE 1.1. Signs and Symptoms to Look for in Children and Adults with ADHD (Based on Wender's [1995] Clinical Research Studies

Signs and symptoms	Correlates at developmental stages	
	Childhood	Adulthood
Attentional difficulties	Child has short attention span and rushes from one thing to another in play; is unmotivated; cannot follow instructions in school; cannot sustain listening and has trouble remembering; leaves things half finished in home and school. Does best with one-to-one supervision. Attention is most impaired in boring tasks, but good in novel and interesting tasks; attention is not under social control; attention increases with age but child still has trouble focusing attention when necessary	Particularly problematic for college students; other adults may not complain about attention problems—but may self-select jobs with low demand for constant, careful attention. May have difficulty keeping mind on reading; can concentrate when necessary for 5–10 minutes; rarely sits through a TV show; has trouble listening to conversations or interrupts in social interactions; may learn to minimize distractions; misplaces little things (e.g., keys, wallets, etc.)
Motor problems	Shows gross and fine motor hyperactivity, drumming fingers, kicking feet, moving in seat; rushes around; acts "driven." Excessive activity is observable in classroom; hyperactivity is present even in utero. Is restless and active; inadvertently breaks things; constantly fidgets; is overtalkative. May show impaired coordination, poor handwriting, poor eye–hand coordination in sports, soft neurological signs (e.g., clumsiness)	Many adults remain hyperactive, fidgety, and restless; may be uncomfortable sitting still; may dislike being inactive, and cannot relax; would rather stand than sit. Forced immobility may produce anxiety; fidgets; exhibits foot movements, "cross-knee" foot jiggle, or foot tapping. Sports ability and handwriting may be poor.
Impulsivity	Cannot delay gratification, is easily frustrated; is impatient; gets upset when expectations are not met; blurts out in class or interrupts; is reckless and has no concern for safety (e.g., jump off roof with sheet as parachute, chases ball into street without looking); acts before thinking; has frequent accidents	Has ability to inflict serious self-damage; acts on spur of moment; makes decisions without thinking; shows little reflective ability (e.g., quits job, marries or divorces hastily)
Disorganization	Assignments are not written down or are lost; work is not finished on time or at all; assignments are poorly organized on paper; locker, room or backpack may be messy beyond ordinary sloppiness	Shows untidiness and failure to plan; keeps messy work space or desk; is often late on work assignments; trouble keeping paperwork or records complete; has cluttered or unkempt home; may do two or three things at once and not finish in a timely manner.

(continued)

TABLE 1.1. cont.

Signs and symptoms	Correlates at developmental stages	
	Childhood	Adulthood
Altered response to social reinforcement	Fails to comply, usually because of forgetfulness or distraction; feels remorse; shows temperament of the "terrible twos." Deprivation, rewards, and physical punishment are unsuccessful. May be seen by parents as stubborn, negative, obstinate, forgetful. Responds to immediate reinforcement but effects are temporary. Cycle of negativity, criticism, and noncompliance develops between parents and children.	Remembers getting in trouble for not complying; has history of disobedience and needed firm rules in school or home. No data available on adult noncompliance
Interpersonal relations	May be described as bossy, stubborn, or bullying. Shows social immaturity and athletic clumsiness; has few friends; is socially avoidant. Shows insatiable demand for attention, and may act as class clown or try to win friends by stealing; is easy "to get a rise out of"; lacks awareness of others' feelings, behaviors, or motivations.	No systematic data available. May show subtle or complex changes on medication (e.g., seeing self more realistically or as others do)
Emotionality: temper and mood	Has labile moods, from dysphoric to overexcited. Pleasurable stimuli results in excessive excitement; unpleasurable stimuli produces temper tantrums or outbursts. May get overexcited and lose control; may have short fuse and history of fighting (more typical of conduct disorder). Has difficulty experiencing pleasure and does not seem happy; may have coexisting depression or may be demoralized because of failure, negative feedback from adults, constantly disappointing adults, or peer problems (e.g., being teased or left out); may have biological factors linked to self-esteem and mood.	Similar lability to that seen in children; mood shifts common throughout day; spontaneous "ups" are reduced in adults but "downs" persist, described as boredom or discontentment, but not like major depressive disorder. May engage in sensation-seeking behaviors as teens (e.g., drinking and driving, drug use); constantly gets into demoralizing situations because of academic, work, or interpersonal problems; has explosive temper but may calm down quickly; seems always irritable; destructive to relationships; seems easily provoked to anger by stimulus
Stress intolerance	No systematic studies available. May have difficulty staying with things under pressure.	May report overreacting to normal stress or pressure; may respond inappropriately to ordinary demands; is unable to handle things out of the ordinary; may describe self as "stressed out," "discombobulated," or "hassled." Becomes anxious when stressed and becomes more impulsive, disorganized, and less competent

Note. See Wender (1995) for an in-depth discussion of these signs and symptoms.

2

Etiology and Associated Features of ADHD: A Transactional, Neurodevelopmental Model

In order to accurately diagnose and effectively treat attention deficit disorders, we must have a thorough understanding of the etiology of ADHD. The problems that children and adolescents with ADHD often display have been erroneously attributed to a number of factors, including laziness, lack of motivation, low intelligence, willful misbehavior, and poor parenting, to name just a few. Although children with ADHD may in fact have some of these difficulties, these factors do not cause attentional, impulsive, hyperactive, and inhibitory problems. The fact that the behaviors of so many individuals with ADHD are misunderstood by teachers and parents increases the need for those adults working with children to be knowledgeable about the etiology and to be aware of the biogenetic basis of the disorder.

Acknowledging the biological etiology of a disorder does not mean that remedial or intervention efforts should be abandoned. Furthermore, Whalen and Henker (1991) caution that responsivity to treatment does not necessarily tell us anything about the etiology of the disorder. For example, the fact that performance improves with methylphenidate (Ritalin) does not prove that ADHD is a neurodevelopmental disorder, because most of us will perform better on some tasks with stimulant medication. At present, there are no medical tests that tell us who does and who does not have ADHD, and a positive response to treatment is not diagnostically conclusive. However, by understanding that ADHD is a neurobiological disorder, we may avoid the misunderstandings that lead to misdiagnosis and mistreatment of individuals with ADHD. Furthermore, there is sufficient evidence from diverse research laboratories using different methodologies and technologies that ADHD is related to anomalies in brain development and brain function (Filipek, 1996; Heilman, Voeller, & Nadeau, 1991; Hynd, Semrud-Clikeman, Lorys, Novey, & Eliopolus, 1990; Semrud-Clikeman et al., 1994; Zametkin et al., 1990) and that stimulant medication produces positive short-term effects in most individuals with ADHD, particularly when combined with psychosocial or behavioral treatments (Pelham, 1993a).

Although critics argue that environmental factors cause behavioral, attentional-hyperactive, and impulsive problems in children, Barkley (1990b) indicates that "little if any evidence supports the notion that ADHD can arise purely out of social or environmental factors, such as poverty, family chaos, diet, or poor parent management of children" (p. 104). Although family dysfunction, parental psychopathology, and poor parental management skills may exacerbate the problems a child experiences and certainly may complicate treatment, these factors do not form the etiological basis of ADHD. However, the impact of environmental factors (e.g., family stress and conflict) need to be addressed so that treatment may have the most benefit.

There is mounting evidence demonstrating that ADHD is a biogenetically based disorder most likely involving frontal lobes, basal ganglia, and other attentional networks that control and regulate motor activity, attention, and inhibition (Teeter & Semrud-Clikeman, 1995). Complex neurological networks interact with the child's temperament and environment in such a way as to produce multiple cognitive, attentional, memory, reasoning, and perceptual difficulties. These difficulties interfere with achievement and learning, often have negative impact on social interactions, and frequently result in behavioral problems in the classroom and at home. Thus a complex set of behaviors appears to emerge from subtle neurodevelopmental dysfunctions that probably involve morphological, metabolic, and neurochemical anomalies interacting with and producing associated academic, psychosocial, and behavioral difficulties.

The premises of a transactional, neurodevelopmental model are that ADHD is a genetically based disorder that appears early in life and that is related to subtle neurodevelopmental anomalies that interfere with performance (e.g., work and school), psychosocial adjustment (e.g., family and peer relations), and other challenges (e.g., planning and achieving goals) throughout the individual's life span (Teeter & Semrud-Clikeman, 1995, 1997). In this chapter, particular emphasis is placed on how neurodevelopmental factors interact with environmental and contextual variables to produce the array of associated features that characterize ADHD.

THE BIOGENETIC BASIS OF ADHD

Studies investigating causative factors of ADHD show strong support for the heritability of ADHD (Faraone, Biederman, Chen, Milberger, & Tsuang, 1995; Gillis, Gilger, Pennington, & DeFries, 1992). In their investigation of twins, Goodman and Stevenson (1989) found that genetic transmission of ADHD was highest for monozygotic twins (59%), with rates somewhat lower for dizygotic twins (33%). Biederman et al. (1995) also found that if a parent has ADHD, the risk of ADHD in his or her offspring is 57%. Environmental factors were not as powerful for predicting ADHD symptoms when adverse family factors, perinatal risk factors, and rater biases were controlled. Genetic effects accounted for approximately 50% of the explained variance in the symptoms of ADHD, including hyperactivity and inattention (Stevenson, 1992). Furthermore, when children were grouped on severity of ADHD, heritability indices were even higher in twins with clinically significant rates of symptoms (64% for symptoms of hyperactivity and inattention). Levy et al. (1997) reported heritability estimates of .75 to .91, which were robust for twins and siblings when ADHD was defined in both dimensional (high end of the continuum) and categorized (DSM-III-R) approaches.

Others have documented genetic links between differences in infant temperament, including activity levels and distractibility (Torgensen & Kringlen, 1978); psychomotor activity (Rutter, Korn, & Birch, 1963); and attentional problems, school competence, and behavioral problems (Edelbrock, Rende, Plomin, & Thompson, 1995). Despite a wide phenotypic expression of this disorder, Faraone, Biederman, Chen, Krifcher, et al. (1992) suggest that familial ADHD may be transmitted through a single major gene. Furthermore, multifactorial polygenetic, cultural, and environmental transmission of ADHD seems unlikely. Research conducted by Stevenson (1992), showing that only up to 30% of the variance of ADHD symptoms can be accounted for by environmental factors, is consistent with these findings. Goodman and Stevenson (1989) also found that nongenetic factors (e.g., child rearing) accounted for less than 10–15% of the variance in symptoms. Barkley (1996a, p. 95) indicates that these influences "may also contribute to an apparent link between poor child management by a parent and ADHD"—that is, child-rearing practices may be adversely affected by ADHD symptoms in parents.

Although the primary gene or genes involved in ADHD have not been isolated, apparently an abnormal dopamine receptor gene may alter the expression of the major gene that is casually related to ADHD (Comings et al., 1991; Cook et al., 1995). Barkley (1990b) indicates that a genetic predisposition may underlie ADHD, and he further hypothesizes that "it may be that what is transmitted genetically is a tendency toward dopamine depletion in, or at least underactivity of, the prefrontal–striatal–limbic regions" (p. 104).

PROPOSED NEURODEVELOPMENTAL SUBSTRATES OF ADHD

The neurodevelopmental, morphological, and neurochemical substrates of ADHD have been investigated, and various neuroanatomical hypotheses for ADHD have been advanced (Teeter & Semrud-Clikeman, 1995). Zametkin and Rapoport (1987) indicate that there are at least 11 different prevailing theories that identify subcortical and/or cortical regions of the brain in the pathogenesis of ADHD. Hypotheses implicating the thalamus, the hypothalamus, or the reticular activating system (Laufer, Denhoff, & Solomons, 1957) are referred to as subcortical or "bottom-up" theories (Wender, 1971), whereas more recent evidence suggests a "top-down" model of ADHD in which cortical dysfunction of the frontal lobes (Zametkin et al., 1990) and prefrontal/sagittal regions are implicated (Borchgrevink, 1989). The frontal–basal ganglia loop may also be implicated in ADHD in that frontal regions feed back into lower brain structures for the inhibition, planning, and control of responses. These cortical areas, with lower brain stem regions, also make up the dopamine pathways of the brain. The various neurological systems that are involved with ADHD may account for the heterogeneity of the disorder.

Studies suggest that neural systems are likely involved in the pathogenesis of ADHD (see Table 2.1), and the behavioral manifestations appear related to structural or functional variations in these systems (Teeter & Semrud-Clikeman, 1997). Although neurological examinations do not reveal gross abnormalities, and neuroimaging techniques, including computerized tomography (CT) and magnetic resonance imaging (MRI), do not reveal brain lesions, some morphological variations have been found in the brains of children with ADHD (Riccio, Hynd, Cohen, & Gonzalez, 1993). Measures of cerebral blood flow and glucose metabolism show decreased activation in specific neural regions intimately involved with the control of attention and executive functions.

Table 2.1 summarizes research investigating the neuroanatomical substrates of ADHD which suggests involvement of the major brain structures associated with attention, motor planning, and executive

TABLE 2.1. Proposed Neuroanatomical and Biochemical Substrates of ADHD

Study	Proposed neuroanatomical or biochemical substrates	Proposed behavioral manifestations
Butter, Raposak, Watson, & Heilman (1988)	Right dorsolateral frontal	Inattention, motor impersistence, response disinhibition and initiation
Casey et al. (1997)	Caudate > symmetry (right > left), right prefrontal, left globus pallidus	More variable and longer reaction times for simple control tasks and complex inhibitory tasks
	Prefrontal regions	Reduced performance on inhibitory tasks; suppresses attentional and behavioral responses
	Caudate and globus pallidus regions	Reduced performances on inhibitory and control tasks; execution of behavioral responses
Castellano et al. (1996)	Smaller cerebellar regions	Motor planning
Filipek et al. (1997)	Smaller anterior right frontal regions, smaller caudate regions, smaller globus pallidus regions	Attentional networks orienting/shifting attention network, executive network, and alerting/arousal network
Heilman & VanDenAbell (1980)	Right hemisphere	Attentional controls
Heilman, Voeller, & Nadeau (1991)	Methylphenidate	Redress asymmetric imbalances of neurotransmitters
	Right hemisphere deficits	Disinhibition of left hemisphere control
Hunt, Mandl, Lau, & Hughes (1991)	DA—nucleus accumbens DA—hippocampus and frontal lobes NE—locus ceruleus SE—serotonin	Inhibits distraction Ongoing attention Hypervigilance Behavioral inhibition

(continued)

TABLE 2.1. cont.

Study	Proposed neuroanatomical or biochemical substrates	Proposed behavioral manifestations
Hynd et al. (1993)	Reversed asymmetry of caudate nucleus (left < right) Smaller left caudate nucleus	Possible DA deficiencies
Hynd, Semrud-Clikeman, Lorys, Novey, & Eliopolus (1990)	Bilaterally smaller anterior cortex Reversed asymmetry of anterior cortex (right < left hemisphere)	
Hynd et al. (1992)	Smaller genu (corpus callosum)	Interhemispheric regulation
Kertesy, Nicholson, & Cancelliere (1985)	Right frontal lobe	Sustained motor activity motor impersistence
Koella (1982)	NE and SE DA and Ach	Perceptual responsivity Motor readiness
Lou, Henriksen, & Bruhn (1984)	Hypoperfused mesial frontal cortex	
McGuinness & Pribram (1980)	Integration of NE/SE and DA/ACh transmitters	Attentional system
Tucker & Williamson (1984)	Left hemisphere (premotor cortex) Dopaminergic activity—left lateralized Right hemisphere Norepinephrine—right lateralized Anterior cortex Posterior cortex	Motor control Process of activation Perception Substrate of arousal Motor—activity level Sensory—attentional

Note. Adapted from Teeter & Semrud-Clikeman (1995). Copyright 1995 by Elsevier Science, Inc.. Adapted by permission. DA, dopamine; NE, norepinephrine; SE, serotonin; Ach, acetylcholine.

control functions. Specifically, research shows that in individuals with ADHD, the anterior right frontal regions appear to be somewhat smaller, the caudate nucleus is asymmetrical, suggesting anomalies in the frontal–striatal systems; there is anomalous morphology of the corpus callosum (smaller splenium); and there are anomalies in bilateral posterior–occipital regions (Filipek et al., 1997). These regions play a critical role in attentional and executive controls, and motor planning functions, all of which are core features of ADHD. Neurochemical deficiencies in dopamine, norepinephrine, and serotonin are also implicated.

Structural and Metabolic Anomalies in ADHD

Structural Anomalies

Posner and Petersen (1990) and Posner and Raichle (1994) hypothesize that there are three major networks involved in attentional control: (1) the *orienting/shifting* (*selective*) attention network that appears localized in parietal, midbrain, and thalamic regions; (2) the *executive* network that involves the anterior cingulate gyrus (deep frontal structure) and basal ganglia (subcortical regions); and, (3) the *alerting/arousal* (*vigilance*) network found in the right frontal region. Filipek (1996) states that these structural sites have been the focus of investigation, and studies provide some support for this model.

Heilman et al. (1991) hypothesize that the innerconnections between dorsolateral and medial frontal regions to the basal ganglia are implicated in the pathogenesis of ADHD and propose that "in ADHD there is a disorder in this gating system such that volition is not correctly transcoded into action. This defect leads both to a form of inattention where stimuli that should lead to action do not and to defective response inhibition where stimuli that should not lead to action do elicit a response" (p. S78). Furthermore, stimulants improve behavior because they act on this frontal–striatal loop.

Rapoport (1996) provided evidence for frontal–basal ganglia dysfunction in children with ADHD. Data from 200 MRI scans with 100 repeat scans showed that children with ADHD (1) have smaller anterior frontal regions; (2) show less or no asymmetry in the globus pallidus and caudate in the basal ganglia, whereas in normal children the right side is larger than the left; and, (3) have smaller total brain volume. In females with ADHD, the differences were found to the same degree and may be even more striking than in males. Rapoport (1996) suggests that these morphological differences occur early in brain development and that these gray matter abnormalities are related to the inhibitory problems found in children with ADHD. The basal ganglia–frontal loop is involved in the ability to appreciate the context and appropriateness of responses and in the planning and control of responses.

The variability of symptom expression between individuals with ADHD may be explained by anomalies in different parts of this circuitry. Stimulants act on dopamine and norepinephrine, neurotransmitters that are active in the basal–frontal circuitry. Further research may help to clarify subtypes of ADHD based on involvement of different areas of the basal ganglia–frontal loop and to determine the genetic linkage and behavioral expressions of these variations. Research is needed to determine the relationship of morphological anomalies, metabolic activation, and specific patterns of neuropsychological and behavioral deficits found in children with ADHD. Although preliminary research provides that this link is present (Casey et al., 1997), there is probably more than one neural system involved in attentional processes that may correspond to different deficits displayed by individuals with ADHD (Colby, 1991; Posner & Raichle, 1994).

Metabolic Anomalies

Cerebral blood flow research comparing children with ADHD and aphasia to a control group found functional differences in central frontal and caudate regions. Specifically, children with ADHD displayed a pattern of hypoperfusion (low arousal) in the mesial frontal areas, primarily in the white matter, with increased arousal in sensory and sensorimotor regions (Lou, Henriksen, & Bruhn, 1984). Lou, Henriksen, Brunn, Borner, and Nielsen (1989) found that cerebral blood flow was more reduced in the right compared to the left hemisphere. Children with ADHD showed decreased metabolic activity in cortical areas thought to be responsible for the regulation of attention and inhibition. When Ritalin was administered, structures intimately involved in moderating distractibility and motor activity became more aroused, thereby exerting regulatory influences over once underactivated structures. Heilman, Voeller, and Nadeau (1991) indicate that these studies support a frontal–striatal system dysfunction for ADHD, primarily in the right hemisphere. Preliminary evidence suggests a link between neuroanatomical arousal, neurochemical activity, and behavioral symptoms in children with ADHD.

Zametkin et al. (1993) applied positron emission tomography (PET) scans to adolescents with ADHD. Although overall brain glucose metabolism measures were not significantly different for those with ADHD than for controls, participants with ADHD did have reduced metabolism in 6 of 60 brain regions. Of specific interest was the finding that reduced metabolism in left anterior frontal regions was related to the severity of symptoms of ADHD. PET results are not consistent with MRI findings that implicate right frontal regions. Future studies need to clarify these inconsistencies. It may be that the two hemispheres assume different functions in the control of attention and inhibition. Schaughency and Hynd (1989) hypothesize that the two hemispheres may be differentially implicated, depending upon the presence or absence of hyperactivity, with (1) possible right-posterior region deficits in children with attention deficit disorder/without hyperactivity (ADD/WO) and (2) left anterior region deficits in children with attention deficit disorder/with hyperactivity (ADD/H). There is a need for further research investigating morphological and metabolic differences between ADD/WO and ADD/H to confirm these hypotheses.

Single photon emission computed tomography (SPECT) studies corroborated reduced activation in the prefrontal cortex of adolescents with ADHD. When adolescents were challenged on intellectual tasks, the prefrontal cortex was significantly deactivated in 65% of participants with ADHD compared to only 5% of the control group (Amen, Paldi, & Thisted, 1993). Using SPECT imaging, Sieg, Gaffney, Preston, and Hellings (1995) also found decreased activation in the left frontal and left parietal regions.

Future research investigating neuroanatomical and metabolic substrates of ADHD will help resolve some of the present inconsistencies and may provide stronger support for Posner's model in which attention is spread over various brain regions depending on the cognitive features involved (i.e., orienting/shifting, executive, or arousal/alerting).

Neurochemical Substrates of ADHD

Although a single-neurotransmitter theory for ADHD seems remote, the catecholamines, dopamine and norepinephrine, figure prominently in research studies to date (Comings, 1990; Weiss & Hechtman, 1993). Dopamine and norepinephrine levels influence a variety of behaviors, including attention, inhibition, motor activity, and motivation (Riccio et al., 1993). Deficiencies in serotonin may also play a role in attention difficulties, and studying these may prove helpful for understanding ADHD symptoms in some individuals (Comings, 1990; Hunt, Lau, Ryu, 1991; Hunt, Mandl, Lau, & Hughes, 1991; see Table 2.2).

Table 2.2 illustrates how neurochemical and anatomical substrates might play a role in different disorders of behavior, including inattention, hyperactivity, impulsivity, and emotional dysregulation (e.g., alcoholism, aggression, depression, etc.). Although neurotransmitters are distributed throughout the brain, dopamine, norepinephrine, and serotonin do have higher concentrations in specific brain circuits, and biochemical abnor-

TABLE 2.2. Proposed Neurotransmitter Circuits, Brain Regions, and Functional Activity

Neuro-transmitter	Brain circuits	Functional activity

DA	• Nigrostriatal pathway
	  Substantia nigra → caudate
	  → striatum
	• Mesocortical–limbic pathway
	  Brainstem → prefrontal
	  Brainstem → limbic system
		Stimulates movement
		  ↓ DA ↑ muscle rigidity and
		  tremors (e.g., Parkinson's)
		  ↓ DA ↑ jerky movements, tics
		  (e.g., Tourette's)

	• Tuberoinfundibular pathway
	  Hypothalamus → pituitary
		Modulates emotions
		  ↑ DA ↑ hallucinations and
		  paranoia (e.g., schizophrenia)
		  ↓ DA ↑ disinhibition of
		  subcortex
		  ↓ DA ↑ hyperactivity
		  ↑ inattention
		  ↑ temper
		  ↑ aggression

NE	• LC → spinal cord
	• LC → cerebellum
	• LC → thalamus
	• LC → frontal → limbic
		Regulates DA and NE in
		  prefrontal region
		Alternative hypothesis for
		  Tourette's disorder and ADHD

SE	• Caudal raphe nuclei → cerebellum
	• Rostral raphe nuclei → thalamus
	• Rostral raphe nuclei → prefrontal
	  → limbic
		Inhibits large brain regions
		• Frontal (ADHD)
		• Striatum (tics)
		• Hippocampus (memory and
		  learning)
		• Septum and limbic (emotional
		  lability)

	• Feedback loop
	  Raphe nuclei inhibit habenula →
	  feedback → inhibits raphe nuclei
		May increase/decrease symptoms
		Decreased SE
		• Alcoholism
		• ADHD
		• Aggression
		• Borderline personality
		• Bulimia
		• Depression
		• Impulsivity and inattention
		• Self-mutilation (Lesch–Nyhan
		  syndrome)
		• Premenstrual syndrome
		• Tourette's disorder
		• Violent behavior
		• Violent suicide

Note. From Teeter & Semrud-Clikeman (1997). Copyright 1997 by Allyn & Bacon. Reprinted by permission. DA, dopamine; NE, norepinephrine; LC, locus ceruleus; SE, serotonin.

malities in these various regions may help explain the diverse functional difficulties across various disorders including ADHD.

The relationship between altered dopamine and norepinephrine systems in individuals with ADHD have been postulated for some time (Shaywitz & Shaywitz, 1989) based on research from diverse paradigms, including cerebral blood flow (Lou et al., 1984; Lou et al., 1989) and neurotransmitter studies (Shaywitz, Shaywitz, Cohen, & Young, 1983; Shekim, Javid, Dans, & Bylund, 1983). Deficiencies in one or both of these neurotransmitters appears related to the underactivity of brain regions intimately involved with dopamine and norepinephrine activity (Barkley, 1990b; Seiden, Miller, & Heffner, 1989). Comings et al. (1991) suggest that the dopamine receptor D_2 is associated with a variety of psychiatric disorders, including schizophrenia, Tourette's disorder, and ADHD, and abnormalities in these receptors are thought to be genetically linked.

In their review, Riccio et al. (1993) suggest that attentional controls may be moderated by two neurochemical systems: dopamine appears involved with motor control centered in the left hemisphere, whereas, norepinephrine appears related to arousal and perceptual orienting centered primarily in the right hemisphere. Dopamine and norepinephrine neural systems work in concert with each other to control attention, inhibition, and motor planning. Impairment of mesocortical dopaminergic systems may explain dysfunction of the frontal lobes (Heilman et al., 1991) and/or of basal ganglia dopaminergic circuits from the prefrontal lobe to the striatum (Levy, 1991). Serotonin may also be involved with ADHD but to a lesser degree than are dopamine and norepinephrine systems (Weiss & Hechtman, 1993; see Table 2.3). Table 2.3 summarizes proposed neurochemical abnormalities in major psychiatric disorders. Increases and decreases in dopamine, serotonin, and norepinephrine in different brain regions appear to produce behavioral effects that accompany different disorders. Table 2.3 also show that different behavioral features of psychiatric disorders may result in subtle imbalances in the neurotransmitters.

Dopamine appears to play a strong role in the inhibitory functions of the frontal lobes (Comings, 1990). Dopamine receptors can be either inhibitory (D_1 receptors) or excitatory (D_2 receptors), and, although it is distributed in the caudate, the putamen, and the limbic system, there is a higher synthesis of dopamine in prefrontal regions. Imbalances in dopamine will likely affect prefrontal functions more than in other brain regions. Serotonin and norepinephrine also are known to affect dopamine levels in the prefrontal lobe either directly or indirectly. Given these interactions, disturbances of one of the neurotransmitter systems may have an adverse affect on other neurotransmitters. Stress signifi-

TABLE 2.3. Proposed Neurotransmitter Levels, Psychiatric Disorders, and
Behavioral Effects

Psychiatric disorder	Neurotransmitters	Behavioral effects
Tourette's disorder	↓ DA frontal regions	Frontal lobe syndrome
	↑ DA nucleus accumbens and striatum	Motor and vocal tics, hyperactivity
	↓ DA substantia nigra	ADHD symptoms
		Learning and conduct problems
		Mimics frontal lobe syndrome
	↓ SE	Aggression and self-injury
		Hypersexuality
ADHD	↓ DA frontal regions	Disinhibition of subcortex
		Hyperactivity and irritability
	↓ SE	Aggression
Schizophrenia	↑ NE	Hyperarousal
	↑ SE	Particularly in brain atrophy
	↓ SE	Two types of schizophrenia
Depression	↓ NE	Depression
	↑ NE	Mania
	↓ SE	Severe depression
Anxiety	↑ NE	Anxiety and fear
Obsessive–compulsive disorder	Hypersensitive SE receptors	Obsessive–compulsive symptoms
		Linkage of depression, anxiety, and aggression in obsessive–compulsive disorder

Note. From Teeter & Semrud-Clikeman (1997). Copyright 1997 by Allyn & Bacon. Reprinted
by permission. DA, dopamine; SE, serotonin; NE, norepinephrine.

cantly reduces the amount of dopamine in the prefrontal regions, which
has deleterious effects and further exacerbates problems associated with
ADHD.

Norepinephrine modulates other neurotransmitter systems, particularly dopamine, which is similar in chemical structure (Comings, 1990).
Norepinephrine is more widespread than the other two transmitters
(dopamine and serotonin), originates from its major source in the
adrenal glands in the locus ceruleus (brainstem region), and spreads to
the cerebellum, the limbic system, and the cerebral cortex. Norepinephrine appears to play a role in the individual's alertness and
sensitivity to the environment, and locus ceruleus arousal increases when
novel or challenging stimuli are present. Serotonin has an inhibitory

effect on norepinephrine neurons, whereas norepinephrine activates serotonin nerves. Too little norepinephrine results in depression, and too much norepinephrine produces mania and symptoms of ADHD (Comings, 1990; Kalat, 1975).

Medications used for various psychiatric disorders enhance or reduce neurotransmitters at the synapses. Subsequent behavioral changes result. Table 2.4 summarizes common medications, their effects on neurotransmitters, and their effects on behavior.

Because of the complex nature and interaction of neurotransmitters, it is not surprising that different medications can alter these activities. Although stimulants remain the first-line medications for the treatment of ADHD symptoms, antidepressants or antianxiety medications may be used as second-line alternatives or in conjunction with stimulants in individuals with comorbid disorders (e.g., ADHD with depression).

TABLE 2.4. Proposed Medication Effects on Neurotransmitters

Medications	Neurotransmitter effects	Behavioral effects
Stimulants	↑ DA in frontal regions	Frontal lobe inhibits subcortex Decreases ADHD symptoms Increases Tourette's symptoms
Haloperidol	Stimulates synthesis and turnover of DA ↑ SE	Decreases aggression Decreases Tourette's symptoms Decreases self-injury
Pemoline	↑ SE	Decreases ADHD symptoms
Clonidine	↓ NE ↑ SE ↑ DA frontal regions Inhibits production of NE	Decreases anxiety and panic attacks Decreases ADHD Decreases Tourette's symptoms
Tricyclics	↓ Locus ceruleus activity ↑ NE	Decreases depression
Imipramine	Inhibits reuptake of NE	Decreases depression
Clomipramine	↑ SE	Decreases obsessive–compulsive behavior Decreases panic attacks
Fluoxetine	ì SE Increases synthesis or decreases reuptake of SE	Decreases depression

Note. From Teeter & Semrud-Clikeman (1997). Copyright 1997 by Allyn & Bacon. Reprinted by permission. DA, dopamine; SE, serotonin; and, NE, norepinephrine.

Neuropsychological Correlates of ADHD

A search for frontal lobe impairment on neuropsychological measures in populations with ADHD has produced mixed results (McBurnett, Lahey, & Pfiffner, 1993). Some researchers have documented perseveration, poor reasoning, and impaired judgment in children with ADHD based on scores of the Wisconsin Card Sorting Test (Chelune et al., 1986). Developmental deficits in functional brain systems related to inhibitory and attentional processes were found in about 85% of children with attention deficit disorders (Chelune et al., 1986). Children who rated high on inattention/overactivity also had more errors on all subscores of the Wisconsin Card Sorting Test when compared to children who were rated high on aggressive/defiance scales (McBurnett et al., 1993). However, when compared to learning-disabled and control groups, children with ADHD did not demonstrate significant differences on the WCST, according to another study (Barkley, Grodzinsky, & DuPaul, 1992).

Boucugnani and Jones (1989) suggest a link between test performance and possible frontal lobe dysfunction in individuals with attentional disorders. Deficits were found in planning, maintaining a strategy, shifting strategies, verbally mediating responses, and executing a visual motor task. Kozoil and Strout (1992) found that children with ADHD also had verbal fluency difficulties associated with frontal lobe weaknesses.

Research investigating the relationship between neuropsychological, behavioral, and cognitive functions in ADHD provides further insight into how neurobiological mechanisms affect performance across a variety of domains. Output mechanisms of the frontal lobe allow for the inhibition of motor activity, the activation of attention, and the planning and execution of complex motor responses (Teeter & Semrud-Clikeman, 1995). These output mechanisms may be deficient in children with ADHD (Borchgrevink, 1989). Dysfunction of frontal regions, specifically orbital-limbic connections through the striatum, may account for the disinhibition, self-regulatory deficits, and defective reinforcement systems that have been observed in children with ADHD (Lou et al., 1984; Sagvolden et al., 1989).

TRANSACTIONAL MODEL FOR THE STUDY OF ADHD

The manner in which neurodevelopmental anomalies interact with and affect the cognitive, psychological, behavioral, social, and family adjustment of individuals with ADHD suggest that a transactional, neurodevelopmental model is required for understanding the complex nature of this disorder (Teeter & Semrud-Clikeman, 1995). See Figure 2.1 for a depiction of this transactional model.

This model was first introduced by Teeter and Semrud-Clikeman (1995, 1997). A transactional model hypothesizes that brain development and maturation are influenced by various factors, including genetic, temperament, and prenatal and postnatal environmental factors. A bidirectional relationship between cortical and subcortical regions of the brain (neural networks that control attention, inhibition, and motor activity) influence the cognitive–intellectual, perceptual, motor, attentional, and memory capacity of the individual. The expression of characteristics and the overall adjustment of individuals with ADHD is further affected by their environment, including the home, social, and school/work setting. A transactional, neurodevelopmental model is proposed as a paradigm for describing the complex interaction between brain development and function and the subsequent cognitive, behavioral, and psychosocial manifestations of the disorder that are also influenced by contextual variables (e.g., school or work environment and family stress and dysfunction).

Table 2.5 summarizes select research showing the various manifestations of ADHD within each of these domains. These various factors interact differently in individuals but research suggests that deficits in functional skills (e.g., intelligence, attention, memory, reasoning, and planning, etc.) are related to anomalous brain functions which ultimately affect overall academic (e.g., work completion, off-task behaviors), psychosocial (e.g., peer rejection, increased psychiatric disorders), and family adjustment (e.g., disrupted parent–child relationships).

COGNITIVE–INTELLECTUAL
AND ACADEMIC PROBLEMS

Cognitive, academic, and behavioral problems associated with ADHD are well documented and tend to persist across the life span. Although the primary features of ADHD are often described from a behavioral perspective, associated problems suggest a need to explore cognitive and social interactional systems as well. Although single paradigms (e.g., behavioral or psychosocial) might sufficiently describe specific features of ADHD, an integrated approach provides for more accurate diagnosis and treatment (Teeter & Semrud-Clikeman, 1995), particularly given that the behavioral symptoms of ADHD are often present in other childhood disorders (Barkley, 1990b; Biederman et al., 1991; Platzman

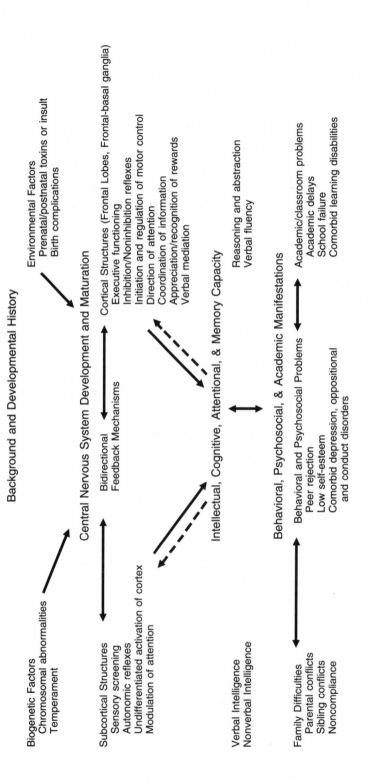

FIGURE 2.1. Transactional, neurodevelopmental model of ADHD. Adapted from Teeter & Semrud-Clikeman (1995). Copyright 1995 by Elsevier Science, Inc. Adapted by permission.

TABLE 2.3. A Summary of Specific Defects Associated with ADHD

Biogenetic factors
- 59–84% MZ
- 33–29% DZ
- Independent genetic code differs from reading
- Familial ADD transmitted by single gene
- Single gene has not been isolated—probably dopamine receptor gene

Temperament
- Genetic linkage
- Activity level
- Distractibility
- Psychomotor activity
- Attentional problems, school competence, and behavioral problems

Environmental factors/Prenatal/postnatal
- Multifactorial, polygenetic, cultural and environmental transmission seems unlikely
- Poverty, overcrowding, chaotic family style, pollution, food additives account for very little variance
- Common environmental factors: 0–30% variance

Birth complications
- No known correlates

Structural and functional anomalies
- Underactivated frontal lobe
- Decreased activation of left frontal and left parietal
- Left hemisphere underactivation

- Smaller total brain volume
- Smaller anterior cortex in right hemisphere
- Reversed asymmetry of anterior cortex (right < left)
- Reduced metabolic activity in right caudate region
- Reversed asymmetry of caudate nucleus (left < right)
- Smaller left caudate nucleus
- Right hemisphere deficits (disinhibition of left hemisphere)
- Smaller cerebellar regions
- Genu (corpus callosum) smaller
- Rostrum and rostral bodies are smaller
- Imbalances of dopamine in basal ganglia, from prefrontal to striatum

Intellectual
- Range of IQ
- Low coding
- IQ may be 7–15 points lower
- Language delays

Memory
- Low verbal
- Working memory
- Low verbal fluency

Attentional
- Poor sustained
- Poor selective
- Poor alternating/divided

Reasoning and neuropsychological
- Decreased response inhibition
- Poor sustained effort
- Poor complex problem solving
- Poor executive functions
- Poor organizational skills

Academic/behavioral
- Motivational problems
- Underachievement
- Comorbid learning disability
- Out-of-seat behavior
- Noncompliant behavior
- Decreased work completion
- Increased off-task

Psychosocial
- Rejection by peers
- Low social status
- Comorbid depression
- Comorbid aggression, oppositional and conduct disorders
- Low self-esteem
- Increased psychiatric disorders
- Increased negative attention

Family
- Increased stress
- Increased tension in parent–child relationship
- Disrupted parent–child attachment
- Increased negative parent–child interactions

Note. Adapted from Teeter & Semrud-Clikeman (1997). Copyright 1996 by Allyn & Bacon. Adapted by permission. MZ, monozyotic twins; DZ, dizygotic twins.

et al., 1992; Rutter, 1989). The chronic and pervasive nature of and the influence of situational and task variables on ADHD and the fact that other childhood disorders share common characteristics increase the need for careful assessment and treatment of ADHD within an integrated perspective (Teeter & Semrud-Clikeman, 1995).

Cognitive–Intellectual Correlates of ADHD

The degree to which general cognitive–intellectual deficits are associated with ADHD is somewhat controversial (DuPaul & Stoner, 1994). Although children with ADHD are represented in all ranges of intelligence, some studies report IQ scores below those of normal peers (Fischer, Barkley, Edelbrock, & Smallish, 1993; McGee, Williams, Moffitt, & Anderson, 1989). It is true that standardized IQ scores for these children may range between 7 and 15 points lower than those of control groups (Barkley, 1990a), but it is difficult to determine whether attentional difficulties interfere with performance on specific tests or whether "true" cognitive–intellectual (e.g., verbal or nonverbal) deficits account for these differences. Early research included samples of participants with comorbid learning disabilities, so it is difficult to compare studies investigating the affects of ADHD on intellectual performance (Barkley, 1990b). August and Garfinkel (1989) found that individuals with ADHD and controls did not differ on IQ measures when learning disability was controlled; thus comorbid learning disability may affect IQ scores more than ADHD does (DuPaul & Stoner, 1994).

Weiss and Hechtman (1993) indicate that whereas it is sometimes difficult to determine the influence of neurological dysfunction on adjustment of individuals with ADHD, the relationship between IQ and adolescent and adult outcome is much stronger. For individuals with ADHD, intelligence levels in childhood appear highly correlated with the ability to be self-supporting in adulthood (Menkes, Rowe, & Menkes, 1967). Initial IQ levels at 5 years of age were also highly predictive of school success for adolescents (Fischer et al., 1993), whereas initial levels of hyperactivity–distractibility were somewhat less predictive (Weiss, Minde, Werry, Douglas, & Nemeth, 1971).

Predicted outcomes for children with ADHD are most guarded when low or compromised intellectual abilities occur with other risk factors, including a history of neurological involvement, poor parental and family adjustment, family economic status, attitudes of aggression and noncompliance in the child, and impaired mother–child relationships (Minde, Weiss, & Mendelson, 1972; Barkley, 1996a). Longitudinal studies provide support for the contention that there is an interaction between neurological, cognitive–intellectual, and psychosocial factors that affects the overall adjustment of children with ADHD. For example, Fischer et al. (1993) found that family instability was related to grade retention for adolescents. Thus cognitive abilities appear as important outcome variables, particularly when other risk factors are present.

Children with ADHD who have high IQs (at or above 115) show the potential to be talented and creative (Shaw & Brown, 1991). In this study, the high-IQ/ADHD group made better use of nonverbal, diverse, and poorly focused information. High-IQ students with ADHD also demonstrated high levels of figural creativity compared to individuals without ADHD. This study is important because ADHD is so often discussed within a deficit framework that emphasizes the negative attributes and characteristics of individuals while ignoring or overlooking the positive characteristics (e.g., humor, creativity, and energy level). Furthermore, these data show that individuals with ADHD can be very talented (Shaw & Brown, 1991).

Academic Correlates of ADHD

Many of the behaviors associated with ADHD interfere with normal classroom adjustment, including distractibility and difficulties in following instructions, sustaining attention, listening, and completing tasks. High incidences of out-of-seat, noncompliant, and disruptive behavior also have a negative impact on academics. Barkley (1996a) suggests that executive control deficits in working memory, speech–language skills, and verbal fluency also interfere with measured achievement and classroom performance on academic tasks.

Children with ADHD have high rates of developmental disorders, learning disorders, language delays, and communication problems. Lambert and Sandoval (1980) reported that more than one-third of hyperactive children have learning problems; this number is three times higher than that reported for a control group. Barkley (1981) reported that other studies suggest that between 60% and 80% of hyperactive children have learning problems, and Cantwell and Satterfield (1978) found that 76% of hyperactive children were achieving below expected levels in at least two areas. Barkley (1981, p. 23) further states that "the risk for school failure has been estimated to be two to three times higher in hyperactive than normal children, with many being retained at least one grade before entry into the middle or junior high school years."

Children with ADHD have been shown to have high rates of comorbid learning disability (Cantwell & Baker, 1992; Cantwell & Satterfield, 1978; Dykeman & Ackerman, 1992; Semrud-Clikeman et al., 1992), delayed speech (Szatmari, Offord, & Boyle, 1989); problem-solving deficits (Tant & Douglas, 1982); disorganized, inefficient problem-solving strategies (Zentall, 1988); and motivational weaknesses (Douglas, 1983; Weiss & Hechtman, 1986). These diverse problems obviously have great impact on the child's performance in the classroom and on the ability to 'profit from instruction; subsequently, overall academic attainment is affected.

In a review of studies, Platzman et al. (1992) found that excessive activity levels, negative verbalizations, and off-task behaviors reliably differentiated children with ADHD from children in a control group. It is important to note that Platzman et al. (1992) found that direct classroom observations were more effective for differentiating individuals with from those without ADHD than were observations conducted in laboratory or clinic settings. Furthermore, there is evidence that classroom environments affect the manner in which characteristics are manifested, where informal versus formal classrooms (Jacob, O'Leary, & Rosenblad, 1978), unstimulating or boring conditions (Milich, Loney, & Landau, 1982), and self-paced versus other-paced activities (Whalen, Henker, Collins, Finck, & Dotemoto, 1979) appear to be important distinguishing factors. Other classroom factors also affect how the disorder can be managed: Fewer attentional deficits have been found in children with ADHD when tasks and/or situations are varied (Frick & Lahey, 1991), when tasks are novel and stimulating (Zentall & Dywer, 1988), and when rates of reinforcement are optimal (Douglas, 1983), frequent, and immediate (Pfiffner & Barkley, 1990). These findings have important implications for intervention plans because environmental factors can be altered to reduce the negative impact of ADHD in the classroom.

Academic Outcome: Longitudinal Studies

Even when more serious learning disabilities are not present, children with ADHD have a great deal of trouble in academic settings and experience high rates of failure in school. Approximately 40% are placed in exceptional-education programs for learning or emotional disorders, and 20–25% are likely to experience difficulties learning to read (Barkley, 1990a). Weiss and Hechtman (1993) suggest that "poor school achievement in hyperactive children is a close-to-universal problem in both elementary and secondary schools" (p. 42). Longitudinal studies show that adolescents continue to demonstrate academic difficulties: (1) 58% were retained in at least one grade (Brown & Borden, 1986); (2) 25% were placed in special education and 2% in training schools (Mendelson, Johnson, & Stewart, 1971); (3) 10% were school dropouts (Barkley, Fischer, et al., 1990); and (4) achievement scores on reading, spelling, and math were within the low average range (Barkley, Fischer, et al., 1990).

The academic problems noted in adolescents continue into adulthood. Approximately 30% drop out of high school and only 5% finish college (Barkley, 1990b). Despite intellectual abilities ranging from low average to gifted, adults with ADHD may not be academically successful, a development that ultimately affects employment and career opportunities.

Effects of Comorbid Disorders on Academic Adjustment

Faraone, Biederman, Lehman, Spencer, et al. (1993) investigated the relationship among intelligence, school failure, and comorbid psychological problems (e.g., conduct, depression, and anxiety disorders) in children with ADHD and their siblings. Children with ADHD had higher rates of learning disabilities, grade retention, special class placement, and special tutoring than a control group. However, comorbid disorders were more predictive of special education placement than were academic failure or intelligence scores. Even without comorbid psychological disorders, children with ADHD had more school-related failures and lower IQs than the control group. Furthermore, the siblings of children with ADHD also were more likely to have intellectual deficits, supporting a genetic component to ADHD.

Using strict criteria with a carefully diagnosed group of ADHD subjects and a comparison group consisting of children with oppositional defiant disorder, conduct disorder, and normals, Barkley, Du Paul, et al. (1990) found that the presence of conduct disorder did substantially increase the risk for expulsion from and dropping out of school, although suspensions and dropout rates were greater in children with ADHD compared to normals. Furthermore, hyperactivity alone accounted for significantly higher rates of grade retention without the added complications of conduct disorder (Barkley, 1990b).

PSYCHOLOGICAL, SOCIAL, AND FAMILY CORRELATES OF ADHD

Psychological Correlates

The psychological correlates of ADHD include low self-esteem (Campbell, Endman, & Bernfield, 1977; Weiss & Hechtman, 1986; Wender, 1987); depression (Barkley, 1989; Biederman, Newcome, & Sprich, 1991; Weiss & Hechtman, 1986); high rates of aggressive, oppositional, and antisocial behaviors (Blouin, Bornstein, & Trites, 1978; Ross & Ross, 1982); and drug and alcohol abuse, usually associated with antisocial behaviors (Blouin et al., 1978). However, children differ in how they display these symptoms depending on the presence or absence of hyperactivity (see Table 2.6). High rates of psychiatric disorders in adolescence are more frequent in individuals with pervasive versus situational hyperactivity (Schachar, Rutter, & Smith, 1981).

A review of Table 2.6 shows that associated psychological, behavioral, cognitive, and social problems depend on the presence or absence of hyperactivity. Barkley, DuPaul, and McMurray (1990) also report significant differences between the two groups on attentional, memory, psychosocial, and familial correlates. Furthermore, Trommer, Hoeppner, Lorber, and Armstrong (1988) found that the two groups differ on measures of impulse control. Although both groups show difficulties with impulse control during the initial stages of tasks, children without hyperactivity (ADD/WO) improve with training while children with hyperactivity (ADD/H) do not show improvement.

Comorbid psychiatric disorders also differ between groups of children depending upon the presence or absence of hyperactivity (Lahey, Schaughency, Hynd, Carlson, & Nieves, 1987; Lahey, Schaughency, Strauss, & Frame, 1984). Children with attention deficits without hyperactivity are more likely to have a diagnosis of tension–anxiety or anxiety/depression than are children with hyperactivity. On the other hand, children with attentional deficits with hyperactivity are more likely to have symptoms of aggression, antisocial activity, and impulsivity even when a codiagnosis of conduct disorder (CD) is not given. The ADD/WO group shows signs of coexisting internalized disorders, while the ADD/H group displays signs of accompanying externalized disorders. In addition, children with pervasive, severe hyperactivity appear to be a more disordered group, show symptoms at an earlier age, and have lower IQs, more neurodevelopmental problems, and more language delays compared to children with moderate levels of ADHD (Taylor, 1989).

In a series of carefully designed studies, Lahey et al. (1987) reported that children with attentional difficulties without hyperactivity could be reliably differentiated from those with hyperactivity in a clinic setting, although both groups had a high frequency of codiagnoses with other childhood disorders (ADD/WO at 68% and ADD/H at 61%). The behavioral differences between the two groups were also important. The ADD/H group was found to have a higher incidence of and a more severe type of conduct disorder, and its members were more impulsive. In contrast, "children with ADD/WO are more sluggish in their cognitive tempo and are more likely to display coexisting internalizing disorders" (Lahey et al., 1987, p. 721). These data were consistent with those

TABLE 2.6. Psychological Correlates of Attention-Deficit Disorder with Hyperactivity (ADD/H) versus Attention-Deficit Disorder without Hyperactivity (ADD/WO)

Study	ADD/H	ADD/WO
Barkley (1990a)	Sustained attention	Focused attention Sluggish information processing
Barkley, DuPaul, & McMurray (1990)	Family members—high rates of ADHD and substance abuse Child—signs of: ↑ Disinhibition ↑ Aggression ↑ Placement in emotionally disturbed classes ↑ School suspensions ↑ Referrals for psychological services ↓ Persistence ↓ Working memory May need higher mediation dosages	Family members—high rates of anxiety and learning disorders
Biederman, Faraone, Keenan, Benjamin, & Krifcher (1992)		↓ Comorbid psychiatric conditions
Carlson, Lahey, & Neeper (1986)	Lower Full Scale IQ Lower Verbal IQ	

(continued)

TABLE 2.6. (cont.)

Study	ADD/H	ADD/WO
Hynd, et al. (1991)	No significant achievement problems ↑ Motoric activity ↑ Impulsivity ↑ Comorbid diagnosis of conduct disorders (40%) ↑ Social skills problems "Right hemisphere" weaknesses (social skills and visual-spatial deficits)	↑ Reading and math disorders 60% Comorbid diagnosis of reading and math disorder Low on rapid naming tasks ↓ Comorbid diagnosis of conduct disorders
Lahey, Schaughency, Strauss, & Frame (1984)	↑ Externalizing disorders	↑ Internalizing disorders ↑ Social withdrawal
Lahey, Schaughency, Hynd, Carlson, & Nieves (1987)	61% Comorbid diagnosis ↑ Severe conduct symptoms ↑ Impulsivity	68% Comorbid diagnosis ↑ Sluggish, apathetic ↑ Hypoactive ↑ Anxiety ↑ Depression
Lahey, Pelham, & Piacentini (1988)	Higher parental psychopathology in ADD/H with conduct disorders than in ADD/WO groups ADD/H with conduct disorder have fathers with high rates of illegal activities, aggression, and imprisonment	
Szatmari (1992)	More common, 85% of ADD in childhood	More common in adolescence

Note. Evidence suggests that ADD/H is similar to ADHD/combined type, whereas ADD/WO is similar to ADHD/predominantly inattentive type (Barkley, 1996a).

48

reported earlier by Lahey, Strauss, and Frame (1984), where ADD/H children showed signs of externalizing disorders and ADD/WO children showed signs of internalizing disorders. Even when Lahey et al. (1987) eliminated all children with a codiagnosis of conduct disorder, the ADD/H and ADD/WO groups showed a different cognitive tempo and varying levels of anxiety.

Finally, Carlson, Lahey, Frame, Walker, and Hynd (1987) demonstrated that children from both groups are not popular with peers. Although these findings seem to contradict a distinction between these two groups, the authors found that hyperactive children with comorbid disorders (i.e., ADD/H plus conduct disorders), started more fights with their peers than did the ADD/WO children with a codiagnosis (i.e., ADD/WO plus conduct disorders or with major depression).

A disturbing psychological pattern tends to emerge over time, especially when ADHD co-occurs with conduct and oppositional defiant disorders (Teeter & Semrud-Clikeman, 1995). Children with associated conduct disorder and/or oppositional defiant disorder features tend to develop more serious antisocial and criminal activity over time (Blouin et al., 1978; Mendelson et al., 1971; Weiss & Hechtman, 1986). Furthermore, Forehand, Wierson, Frame, and Kempton (1991) found that ADHD does have an additive effect on adolescents with coexisting conduct disorder that influences the development and chronicity of juvenile delinquency in this comorbid population.

Social Correlates

The primary features of ADHD often interfere negatively with an individual's ability to interact effectively with peers, family members, friends, and colleagues. Temperamental and behavioral deficits observed in young children with ADHD interfere with normal social interactions, according to Campbell (1990a). In middle childhood, children with ADHD are often rejected by their peers (Milich & Landau, 1989), have lower social status than their peers (Whalen & Henker, 1985), and are more unpopular than even children described as aggressive (Milich, Landau, Kilby, & Whitten, 1982). Social rejection occurs even after very brief encounters with children who have ADHD (Pelham & Bender, 1982). This disturbing picture is further complicated by the fact that children with ADHD often receive more negative attention from teachers (Milich & Landau, 1989) and from parents (Barkley, 1990b).

Normal social interaction patterns appear to be affected by the numerous problems associated with ADHD, including off-task, rule-breaking, aggressive, bossy, and intrusive behaviors (Milich & Landau, 1989; Pelham & Bender, 1982). Differences in attributional style may also be a factor impeding social interactions. Specifically, children with ADHD often misinterpret social situations and are more likely to ascribe negative intentions to others in neutral situations (Milich & Dodge, 1984). In adolescence, difficulties with social interactions can persist and may develop into more serious forms of psychopathology or antisocial problems. In an effort to be accepted, teens with ADHD may engage in various risk-taking behaviors (e.g., drug and alcohol use) to be accepted (Barkley, 1990b). However, the degree to which risk-taking behaviors result in higher rates of alcohol or drug use is in question. Some studies suggest that adolescents with ADHD do show increased rates of drug and alcohol abuse, whereas others report higher rates only for drug use (Barkley, 1990b). Caution seems warranted when interpreting research in this area because a number of these studies did not utilize standardized rating scales; moreover, the studies were conducted prior to the publication of DSM-III and DSM-III-R, so the diagnostic criteria may vary dramatically from guidelines presently in use (Barkley, 1990b). Furthermore, the extent to which these studies included children with mild or borderline characteristics of ADHD or with comorbid conduct and/or oppositional disorders that increase the likelihood of substance abuse problems is not clear.

Weiss et al. (1971) also found that antisocial behaviors in young ADHD children predict the same problems for adolescents and adults. Aggression seems to be a critical factor in this pattern, although it is important to note that most children with antisocial tendencies do not display problems with aggression in adulthood (Robins, 1978). Antisocial behaviors that often begin in early adolescence can be problematic for between 20% and 45% of adults; 25% display antisocial personality disorder (Barkley, 1990b). In general, there appears to be a strong relationship between early and later social adjustment difficulties and early aggression and later antisocial behaviors. Finally, longitudinal studies suggest a rather guarded social outcome for adults with ADHD, as evidenced by high divorce and separation rates (Weiss & Hechtman, 1993).

Family Correlates

Children with ADHD are challenging even for the most patient and knowledgeable parent. Parents frequently complain of problems with noncompliance and express concerns about their child's academic failure and social rejection (Barkley, 1990b). Barkley (1990b) suggests that these are the most frequent reasons why parents seek professional help in clinics. So beyond the issue of coping with the symptoms of ADHD, parents' primary concern is the impact these symptoms have on the child's social, school, and home adjustment (Barkley, 1990b). Parents are often pressured by other adults to "fix" their noncompliant child and feel guilty when their child/teen continues to be such a problem for everyone around them. The stress that parents experience and the difficulty they have trying to "normalize" their children indicates the need for investigating the impact of ADHD on the family and for including parents and family members in the intervention plan.

It has long been recognized that parenting a child with ADHD places an undue amount of stress on the family system. Campbell and her colleagues (Campbell, 1985, 1990a; Campbell, Ewing, Breaux, & Szumowski, 1986; Campbell, Breaux, Ewing, Szumowski, & Pierce, 1986) describe tensions in the parent–child interactions of young hyperactive children with behavioral problems. Excessive crying, feeding problems, and sleep disturbances are frequently displayed by infants who are later diagnosed with ADHD (Campbell, Szumowski, Ewing, Gluck, & Breaux, 1982; Weiss & Hechtman, 1986, 1993; Werry, Weiss, & Douglas, 1964). A complex interaction between the child's characteristics and parents' behavior has also been observed. It is likely that the difficulties inherent in parenting an infant who is not cuddly, who does not engage in reciprocal smiling, and who is difficult to soothe contribute to parent–child attachment problems (Weiss & Hechtman, 1986, 1993). In addition, toilet training difficulties (Campbell, Schleifer, & Weiss, 1978), insecure parent–toddler attachment patterns between 12–18 months of age (Sroufe & Waters, 1982), and fewer positive and more negative mother–child interactions (Battle & Lacey, 1972) may contribute to the social and developmental problems that have been well documented in preschool children with ADHD.

Barkley's work has also been extremely helpful in describing the family dynamics associated with raising children with ADHD. Barkley (1981) was one of the first researchers who called attention to the effects of coercive child behaviors and the negative cycles of parenting that often ensue as a result of this interaction. Furthermore, Barkley (1981, 1990b) cautioned professionals not to blame mothers for the behavioral problems of their children with ADHD, and he described differences in parenting styles that may account for differences in children's compliance with mothers and with fathers.

From a developmental perspective, family conflicts often continue throughout childhood and may intensify during the adolescent stage because teenagers with ADHD often have difficulty following rules and assuming responsibilities (Barkley, 1989). Robin and Foster (1989) describe the family systems problems found in homes with troubled adolescents. Antisocial behaviors, such as fire setting and stealing both inside and outside the home (Barkley, Fischer, et al., 1990; Mannuzza, Gittleman, Konig, & Giampino, 1992), also place stress on families who try to control the behavior of adolescents with conduct-related disorders.

Parental psychopathology also influences this interaction and increases the likelihood of comorbid disorders in children with ADHD. However, parental psychopathology is higher in families with children diagnosed with conduct disorder and with conduct disorder and ADD/H (Biederman & Steingard, 1987; Lahey, Piacentini, et al., 1988). Both parents are more likely to display antisocial behavioral problems, fathers have high rates of substance abuse, and mothers have high levels of depression along with antisocial, substance abuse, and somatic complaints. Although parental psychopathology was not related to ADD/H, children diagnosed with ADD/H and conduct disorder were more likely to have fathers with a higher incidence of illegal activities, aggression, and imprisonment. These are important findings, as they suggest the need for family systems and parent-focused strategies, along with child-focused interventions, for the treatment of children with ADHD.

PREDICTORS OF ADOLESCENT AND ADULT OUTCOME: FURTHER EVIDENCE FOR A TRANSACTIONAL MODEL OF ADHD

Studies addressing the long-term outcome of ADHD have investigated whether child and/or family characteristics are predictive of poor adolescent adjustment (Barkley, 1990b; Weiss & Hechtman, 1993). A number of factors appear as significant predictors of positive or negative outcomes.

First, parental psychopathology or poor mental health, poor parent–child relationships, and harsh parenting styles are predictive of antisocial behavior in adolescents (Weiss, Minde, Werry, Douglas, & Nemeth, 1971). Unsocialized, aggressive children with hyperactivity tend to have antisocial fathers (Stewart, deBlois, & Singer, 1979). Although parental psychopathology appears to be an important predictor variable, Weiss and Hechtman (1993) caution that it is not clear what form of psychopathology other than the aggression–antisocial link is most predictive.

Second, Weiss and Hechtman (1993) report that well-adjusted adolescents come from families who improve over time, whereas poorly adjusted teens come from families who deteriorate over time. The deterioration occurs in the "emotional climate of the home, child-rearing practices, and total family score, though *not* in the marital relationship or parental mental health scores" (Weiss & Hechtman, 1993, p. 231). Patterns of parent–child relationships and parenting styles affect outcome. Punitive discipline practices (Weiss et al., 1971), fewer mother–child interactions (Barkley & Cunningham, 1980), and high levels of parental control (Loney, Kramer, & Milich, 1981) are related to negative child outcomes. On the other hand, consistent, respectful, and firm parenting (Werner & Smith, 1977) is related to positive outcomes. Critical, disapproving, harsh, and unaffectionate parent–child interactional styles appear related to child misbehavior, and studies have shown that these parental behaviors change when the child's behavior improves following stimulant medication (Barkley & Cunningham, 1980).

Third, family socioeconomic status (SES) and the intellectual abilities of the child are related to educational outcomes, including academic attainment and employment level (Barkley, 1990b). Although SES factors are related to certain parenting styles (e.g., easygoing, inconsistent, or lax) (Paternite, Loney, & Langhorne, 1976), SES may be more predictive of global versus specific outcomes (Weiss & Hechtman, 1993). Other variables appear to interact with SES, including place of residence (e.g., urban environments) and family size. Furthermore, child drug use and academic performance levels also enter into the equation, such that more antisocial behaviors occur when all these factors are combined (Weiss & Hechtman, 1993).

SUMMARY

In summary, research provides evidence that ADHD is a biogenetically based neurodevelopmental disorder. This review illustrates how neurobiological factors predispose children to certain behavioral, academic, and psychosocial problems. A transactional model for understanding ADHD suggests an interaction among factors, where biogenetic vulnerabilities (e.g., morphological and metabolic anomalies) interact with environmental (e.g., classrooms) and family systems factors to affect the overall academic, psychological, and social adjustment of children, adolescents, and adults with ADHD.

Studies investigating the various correlates of ADHD are important for several reasons. First, many studies indicate that children with ADHD display difficulties early in life that persist into adolescence and adulthood. Second, adolescent and adult outcome data suggest that more serious problems may emerge, especially when coexisting psychological disorders, such as oppositional defiant or conduct disorders, are also present. Some researchers argue that psychological, conduct, and school problems emerge as a result of a cycle of low self-esteem, poor academic progress, and impaired relations with peers and family (Weiss & Hechtman, 1986, 1993). It is also likely that ADHD does not cause the associated problems cited; rather, it may be that these difficulties emerge concurrently and have a bidirectional influence on each other. Because it is likely that there is not a straight predictive line from ADHD to these associated features, investigating one factor without the other gives only part of the clinical picture (Teeter & Semrud-Clikeman, 1995). Finally, longitudinal research provides further evidence of the need for an integrated, neurodevelopmental approach to the study of ADHD. Other theoretical models also support an interactive framework and describe complex interactions among neurodevelopmental anomalies and the subsequent cognitive, psychological, academic, and social problems associated with ADHD (Barkley, 1990b, 1996b; Douglas, 1993).

3

Developmental Challenges of the Toddler/Preschool Stage: The Impact of ADHD on Normal Development

M*ost young children* do not obtain a diagnosis of ADHD until the preschool years; thus research conducted at the toddler stage has focused on children who have high levels of activity, temperamental difficulties, and compliance problems (Campbell, 1990b). However, it has been noted that children diagnosed with ADHD at later stages generally have a history of difficulties beginning in infancy and/or the toddler stage; and by the time the child is between 3 and 4 years of age, there is an increase in referrals for hyperactivity (Weiss & Hechtman, 1986).

This chapter reviews developmental challenges of the toddler/preschool stage and describes how characteristics of ADHD affect development in this stage. In order to provide a foundation for understanding the challenges observed in the preschool stage, information regarding the infancy stage is briefly reviewed.

DEVELOPMENTAL CHALLENGES OF INFANCY AND THE TODDLER/PRESCHOOL STAGE

Infancy and the toddler/preschool stage are marked by rapid development across numerous domains, including motor, cognitive–language, emotional, and social areas. In order to determine the impact of extreme levels of inattention, hyperactivity, impulsivity, and disinhibition on these domains, a number of variables that are critical to the overall well-being and normal development of the child must be considered. These variables includes (1) attachment and bonding; (2) initiative/self-exploration; (3) self-regulation/self-control; (4) cognitive–language development; (5) emotional development and socialization; and, (6) early preschool adjustment. Developmental variations or deviant patterns of growth in these specific areas have been found to be associated with childhood and adolescent psychopathology in general and with ADHD in particular (Wenar, 1994).

Attachment and Bonding

Attachment is the powerful emotional bond established between the child and his/her primary caretakers, who are generally the child's parents and most frequently the mother. This reciprocal relationship is manifested by the infant's tendency to send emotional signals (e.g., smiling, cooing, cuddling, etc.) and to seek closeness to the mother. The mother in turn pays attention to the child's biological and emotional needs by feeding, holding, rocking, and smiling at the infant. Development of the mother–child bond has been shown to have profound effects on infants in a number of important ways.

Ainsworth (1979) studied various forms of attachment and found that infants could be described as either securely attached, avoidant, or ambivalent/resistant. A securely attached infant or toddler cries when his/her mother leaves the room and is happy when she returns. When the mother is present, the toddler actively explores the environment and periodically returns to the mother for support and reassurance. These infants and toddlers attend to their environment openly and rarely show anger. Avoidant infants do not cry when left, nor do they approach their mothers when they return. These children do not like to be held, they do not seek out maternal attention when they are stressed, and they often appear angry (Papalia & Olds, 1992). Furthermore, avoidant infants fail to cling when they are picked up and are also indifferent to others including their mothers. Ambivalent/resistant patterns of attachment describe infants who become very upset when their mothers leave the room, and may stay angry (pushes mom away) upon their mothers' return.

Children have a set of built-in behaviors (e.g., sucking, clinging, crying, smiling, and moving toward the mother) that elicit emotional–physical bonding from their parents (Bowlby, 1969). Attachment develops in stages, from birth to about age 2, and the enduring ties that emerge from this process affect relationships the child has with other people in later developmental stages. Bowlby (1969) indicates that the infant's ability to evoke positive reactions from his/her parents, as well as the parent's responsivity to the infant, affect this bond. Variations in infant temperament affect the child's ability to elicit positive, responsive reactions from parents.

Temperament

The notion that infants are born with biologically determined qualities or characteristics that affect their approach and response to the environment has long been postulated (Davidson, 1994). Although the term "personality" is used to describe differences in the manner in which adults customarily react and behave, psychologists refer to "temperament or characteristic emotional responses" when discussing infants (LeFrancois, 1995, p. 256). Personality that develops later in the toddler stage is thought to evolve from an interaction between inborn temperament and the child's environment (Carey, 1989). Temperament traits are presumed to be inherited (Buss & Plomin, 1985) and have a biological basis (Thomas & Chess, 1977). Although a child's temperament appears to be largely biologically based, environmental events interact in meaningful ways to influence the infant's development (Campbell, 1990b). Thus characteristic emotional reactions in infancy are influenced by both biological and environmental factors.

Thomas, Chess, and Birch (1968, 1970), and Thomas and Chess (1977) pioneered investigations into infant temperament in an effort to identify differences in infants and to determine the relationship between temperament and adjustment in later developmental stages (LeFrancois, 1995). Classifications of infant temperament have proven useful in the discussion of individual differences. LeFrancois (1995) summarizes temperament characteristics of infants on the basis of (1) level of motor activity; (2) regularity of eating, sleeping, and eliminating; (3) withdrawal or approach in novel situations; (4) adaptability to a changing environment; (5) sensitivity to environmental stimuli; (6) intensity of responses and energy level; (7) mood or disposition (e.g., cheerful, cranky, friendly); (8) distractibility; and (9) attention span and persistence when engaged in activities.

Classifications of Infant Temperament. Characteristic styles of approaching and reacting to people and/or to objects form the basis of determining differences in infant temperament. In the New York Longitudinal Study, Thomas, Chess, and associates followed 133 individuals from infancy through adulthood and found nine basic components of temperament (cited in Papalia & Olds, 1992). Depending on their emotional and behavioral responses, infants can be classified into three basic types: easy, difficult, and slow-to-warm (LeFrancois, 1995). *Easy infants* are described in terms of regularity (i.e., eating and sleeping), adaptability to novelty and change, and low intensity of responses (i.e., good mood). *Difficult infants* are more irregular, intense, moody, and withdrawn and in general are less adaptable. *Slow-to-warm infants* fall somewhere in between easy and difficult infants on temperament patterns and are described as somewhat negative in mood, with moderate to low intensity of reaction to stimulation (LeFrancois, 1995).

Although these categories are helpful for describing differences in infant temperament, Thomas and Chess (1981) indicate that about 35% of all infants do not fit these types and that there may be other types of temperament. It is also important to note that infants will not always react in the same manner to all situations. Environmental factors, including parental responses to the child, affect the manner in which infants respond (LeFrancois, 1995).

Brain Activity and Temperamental Characteristics. Although temperament has long been presumed to be biologically based (Thomas & Chess, 1977), it has only been recently that research employing electrophysiological measures have provided evidence of such a linkage. Temperamental characteristics (i.e., approach or withdrawal to novel stimulation) are more likely to have "direct links with underlying biological processes than more complex traits, such as obedience to authority" (Davidson, 1994, p. 518). In a series of studies, Davidson and his colleagues have found that infants and toddlers have patterns of cerebral activation in response to emotional arousal similar to patterns recorded in adults. Specifically, Davidson and Fox (1982) found that 10-month-old infants showed differential electroencephalographic (EEG) activity depending on the emotions portrayed in a videotape. Infants showed more left hemisphere activation in frontal brain regions during positive emotional depictions (laughter vs. distress)—a pattern similar to those found in adults. Neonates also showed more right-sided frontal lobe activation to tastes that produced negative facial reactions (Fox & Davidson, 1986).

In other efforts to measure "behavioral inhibition," Davidson and Fox (1989) found that infants who show a greater right hemisphere activation when at rest are more likely to express intense emotional reactions under stress conditions (i.e., maternal separation) than infants with greater left-sided activation. Different patterns of brain activation have also been found in infants who have a tendency to withdraw from novel or unfamiliar situations (behaviorally inhibited) compared to those children who are likely to approach novel toys (behaviorally uninhibited). Davidson (1994) found that behaviorally inhibited children (mean age of 31 months) showed decreased activation in approach-related brain regions (left frontal hemisphere) rather than hyperactivation of withdrawal systems (right frontal regions). Furthermore, the pattern of underactivated left frontal regions found in behaviorally inhibited children was similar to patterns found in adult depressives (see Davidson, 1994, for a more detailed discussion). Davidson and colleagues are currently investigating whether children who are behaviorally uninhibited are likely to show impulsivity and sensitivity to reward situations— characteristics that are associated with ADHD.

In other research, Kagan and Snidman (1991) found that infants who had a tendency to avoid novel stimuli also cried more easily and were less active than children who approached unfamiliar stimuli. Kagan and Snidman indicate that "this implies but does not prove that variation in the excitability of brain areas that mediate motor activity and crying participates in the actualization of the temperamental categories" (1991, p. 856). Furthermore, temperamental differences appear quite consistent for the first 2 years of life.

Although this selected research shows variation in brain activity in children with different temperaments, environmental factors are known to affect the manner in which the child's personality develops.

Environmental Influences on Temperament. Development is probably best viewed as an interaction between the child's biological makeup and his/her environmental setting. So even though genetic influences on temperament are well documented, the environment has a significant influence over the development of the child's personality (LeFrancois, 1995). Furthermore, by understanding the child's temperament, caretakers can begin to alter the environmental context in an effort to reduce its adverse effects on difficult infants.

Sameroff (1975) described a transactional process whereby organismic–child factors and environmental determinants interact in constantly evolving ways. In his model, Sameroff assumes that the child actively participates in his/her development and that interactions between the parent and child are bidirectional, each influencing the other (Campbell, 1990b). This relationship is constantly evolving and changing. Furthermore, the child has strong biological "self-righting" tendencies that strive for "normal development" (Campbell, 1990b). The effect of these "self-righting" tendencies cannot be underestimated as the child moves into more complex social and cognitive functioning.

The dynamic interaction between child and parent is critical for the development of normal personality and social-emotional functioning in children. When parents attend to and meet the child's needs (e.g., hunger, fatigue, and cuddling) in a warm and responsive manner, the child typically shows normal adjustment. Papalia and Olds (1992) suggest that "unusual events or parents' handling of a child can change temperamental style" (p. 153). The Thomas and Chess (1984) reported several case studies that found that children with "difficult" temperaments were well-adjusted, whereas "easy" children got into trouble, depending on the circumstances and influences of their environment. These findings provide information that can be helpful for designing and implementing effective intervention strategies for this stage, where parent–child relationships are the focus.

Implications of Differences in Temperament. Among the most important findings of this research are the fact that temperament appears to be relatively stable over time (Kagan & Snidman, 1991) and that infants with "difficult" temperaments are likely to develop psychiatric problems (Thomas & Chess, 1981). About one-third of the infants in the New York Longitudinal Study study developed mild disturbances at 3 to 5 years; some of these were resolved by adolescence, while other problems persisted into adulthood (Papalia & Olds, 1992). Although none of the temperament types were resistant to problems, there were some factors that seemed to increase the likelihood of adjustment problems later in life. Healthy adjustment seems highly related to a "goodness of fit" between the child's temperament and his/her environment.

"Goodness of fit" occurs when the child's style of behaving (i.e., temperament) matches the child-rearing practices of the parents (Thomas & Chess, 1977; Chess & Thomas, 1984). When there is dissonance between the two—a "poor fit"—maladaptive functioning and developmental abnormalities are more likely (Berk, 1989). The optimal situation occurs when parents accept their child's temperamental style and modify their expectations or parenting style to meet the needs of the child.

The interactional nature of child-rearing practices and behavioral styles can place stress on the parents as well as the child. For example, "difficult" infants require more careful, consistent, and adaptable parenting, whereas "easy" infants may respond well to a variety of parenting styles (LeFrancois, 1995). The concept of the "good-enough mother" (Winnicott, 1953) has been proffered to describe the instance where a parent may be "good enough" for the "easy" child but may not be effective with the more demanding, reactive, negative, and intensely "difficult" child. Parents also react differently depending on the behavioral style of their child: "easy," highly responsive infants elicit pleasure and a sense of well-being, whereas "difficult," unresponsive children elicit feelings of inadequacy and unhappiness in parents (Thomas & Chess, 1981).

Numerous studies suggest that mothers of "difficult" infants are less responsive and interact less frequently with their children (Bates, 1987; Crockenberg, 1986). Infants' difficult behaviors (e.g., being fussy, demanding, or slow to soothe) tend to leave mothers feeling incompetent, anxious, and angry, particularly if they also have their own problems, such as depression or impatience (Campbell, 1990b). Mothers who are stressed and overwhelmed withdraw from their infants; in turn, infants become more demanding in these situations because their needs are not being met (Bates, 1987). Early mother–child conflicts or mismatches predict later serious social problems for the child. Furthermore, parental psychopathology, distress, hostility, and marital problems can also interact with "difficult" child characteristics to either moderate or exacerbate behavioral problems, placing the difficult child at risk for ADHD (Barkley, 1990b).

Temperament and Later Behavioral Adjustment. The extent to which researchers can use infant temperament to predict later adjustment problems largely depends on their theoretical orientation—research can be used to support either continuity or discontinuity in child development (Campbell, 1990b). Principles of continuity suggest that later problems would be predicted by a "difficult" temperament in infancy, whereas, discontinuity theories suggest that "difficulty" in infancy is a developmental phase without necessary implications for later development (Campbell, 1990b).

Although disagreement exists about the ultimate outcomes for "difficult" children, there is relative consensus on the need to reestablish warm and accepting parent–child relations early in the child's life (Berk, 1989; Campbell, 1990b). Berk cautions that it is important to change impaired relations early "before unfavorable temperament-environment relationships heighten difficult behavior and are hard to change" (1989, p. 439). It is particularly important to address the parent–child relationship in the 1st year of life, creating consistent, firm, and reasonable parental expectations so that the child is able to master new developmental challenges (Berk, 1989). A lack of "goodness of fit" that affects the mother–child attachment has implications for the child's socialization with individuals outside the family later in life.

Disturbances in Attachment

Disturbances in attachment can occur for a variety of reasons related to the child, the parent, or the interaction between the two. (1) Infants may exhibit behaviors or have temperaments that do not elicit warmth, caring, and proximity from their mothers. (2) Infants may have mothers

who abandon, neglect, and abuse them. (3) Parents may not be responsive to their child's biological and emotional needs. (4) Infants may have
lost their parents and been institutionalized. (5) Infants and children may
have been hospitalized for illness (Berk, 1989; Papalia & Olds, 1992).
These attachment disturbances can have serious consequences.

Although the quality of parenting, typically characterized as warm,
responsive, affectionate, and sensitive, is critical to the attachment
process, recent theorists indicate that it is an interaction between the
temperamental style of the infant and the quality of caregiving that
affects attachment (Berk, 1989). Sameroff and Chandler (1975) found
that children who were abused often had difficult births or had illnesses
as infants that made them particularly difficult to take care of, thus
placing added stress on the parents. Although the relationship between
temperament and attachment is a complex one, Sroufe (1985) suggests
again that maternal sensitivity to the child's temperamental characteristics is important. The "goodness-of-fit" paradigm also applies,
whereby a mother can adjust to her child even though the child may be
irritable and difficult. Other individuals close to the child, including the
father, grandparents, and other caretakers, can also play a role in the
attachment process and can serve to reduce the stress that mothers with
"difficult" infants experience.

The long-term negative effects of poor attachment have been documented in numerous studies. Avoidantly attached infants had few
positive interactions with peers at 4 years of age, and ambivalently
attached infants were involved in more instances of aggression and
resistance in preschool (Jacobson & Wille, 1986). Children who were
ambivalently attached were also viewed as disruptive, difficult, and
prone to temper tantrums in preschool (Sroufe, 1983). Children who
experience high levels of support from their mothers are better adjusted
in kindergarten (Pianta & Ball, 1993), and, in general, securely attached
individuals are more competent, more independent, better at problem
solving, and more curious (LeFrancois, 1995).

In Erikson's (1959) model of psychosocial development, he describes the infant's developmental challenge as one of "trust versus
mistrust." During the 1st year of life, the infant develops a sense of trust
or mistrust based on his/her interactions with the primary caretaker—
most frequently the mother (LeFrancois, 1995). If this basic conflict is
resolved, the infant develops a sense that the world is "predictable, safe,
and loving" (LeFrancois, 1995, p. 56). If the infant is rejected or not
well cared for, the infant may see the world as an unfriendly and hostile
place. Thus attachment can affect the resolution of this very basic and
critical psychosocial stage.

In summary, attachment and early mother–child relationships affect adjustment during the toddler/preschool stage and on into middle childhood and adolescence.

> Both psychoanalytic and ethnological theories predict that the inner feelings of security and affection that emanate from a healthy attachment relationship provide the foundation for virtually all aspects of later psychological functioning, including exploration and mastery of inanimate environment and cooperative, sociable interactions with others. (Berk, 1989, p. 455)

Initiative/Self-Exploration

Autonomy and self-exploration are cardinal developmental challenges for toddlers between 18 months and 2 or 3 years of life, whereas initiative is a developmental feature that appears between the ages of 2 and 6 years of age, according to Erikson (as cited in LeFrancois, 1995). Toddlers begin to realize that they have control over their actions, and they begin to exercise this control. Erikson (1961) indicates that if their actions and their movement toward autonomy are thwarted, toddlers develop a sense of shame and doubt. If infants are to develop a sense of autonomy, it is important that their attempts to explore the environment are encouraged by parents. A balance between firmness or parental limit setting and flexibility allows the toddler to develop autonomy, whereas overprotectiveness may lead to doubt and shame (LeFrancois, 1995).

Wenar (1994) describes the development of initiative as an outgrowth of the child's natural inquisitiveness and curiosity. As the toddler begins walking, he/she begins to venture out and explore; and with the development of language, the child begins to ask questions, to understand answers, and to imagine a variety of things (LeFrancois, 1995). These developmental milestones (walking and talking) facilitate exploration, which in turn is naturally reinforcing—that is, the environment is interesting and encourages further exploration. Through this process, the child develops a sense of "self-as-agent" (e.g., "I can do it!"), which is in conflict with parental directives (e.g., "Stop!" "Get down!" "Be careful!") and prohibitions (Wenar, 1994). If the child's initiatives and pleasurable explorations are thwarted, the toddler often reacts with tantrums or resistance. Although battles between parents and toddlers are common, if the child's efforts toward mastery are met with criticism, ridicule, or punishment, then young children develop a sense of guilt (Sroufe & Cooper, 1988).

During this stage, several things are important. First, the child begins to develop a sense of self-worth with every growing competency (e.g., walking, talking). Second, the child begins to deal with parental rules, regulations, and roadblocks to physical exploration (e.g., "Don't touch!" "Stay out of the street!"). This delicate process, allowing and encouraging initiative within limits, sets the stage for future feelings of competence, and it gives the child his first experiences with compliance. The critical aspect of the development of initiative and self-exploration is that the child needs to be encouraged and supported within boundaries and reasonable expectations. This process of parental regulation sets the stage for the child to learn self-regulation and self-control.

Self-Regulation/Self-Control

Developmental challenges during infancy typically involve developing self-soothing abilities, establishing regular daily eating and sleeping routines, developing and regulating motor activity, and attending to environmental stimuli (Sroufe, 1979). Infants who are difficult to soothe, have irregular schedules, and have excessive activity levels often develop hyperactivity (Bates, Maslin, & Frankel, 1985). These infants are generally difficult to care for, and these behaviors often interfere with normal parent–child attachment (Campbell, 1990b). When the fussiness and lack of routine persist, the parent–child relationship may be at risk for disruption.

Neonates have some capacity to self-soothe and to regulate their own physiological tension (Wenar, 1994). Sensitive, nurturing parents help children to develop both tolerance for frustration and important self-soothing abilities in infancy. Furthermore, infants begin to develop methods of regulating external stimulation by turning away. Sander (1975) describes the early development of self-regulation as a process whereby "two person regulation" (parent–child) evolves into self-regulation. Initially, the parent meets the infant's biological needs; later the infant becomes more active in making his/her needs known to the parent, which is followed by the child's move to control events (Sroufe & Cooper, 1988). Kopp (1982) suggests that infants learn to modulate their own responses as a result of predictable and responsive parenting that also reduces overwhelming frustration in the infant.

Infants begin to comply to parental requests by the end of the 1st year (Kopp, 1982). Self-regulation at this age is dependent on the child's cognitive development (i.e., object permanence, language skills, and memory capacity), and true self-control emerges at about the age of 2 years, when children are able to comply and to inhibit without external constraints (Campbell, 1990b).

As a toddler, the child's intentional attempts to control the environment may be in contrast or opposition to the parent's wishes. When conflicts between autonomy and acceptance of limit setting are appropriately resolved, the child becomes more aware of his/her own motivational states and desires. The basis of self-regulation is the child's growing awareness of the desire to act and the feelings that are engendered by this desire; the child becomes guided by these feelings. "Finally, if the parents reinstate a harmonious relationship after the child expresses anger or aggression, the child can experience a continuity in self, which is the key to flexible self-management" (Sroufe & Cooper, 1988, p. 389). If this conflict is met with harshness, unresponsiveness, or extreme negativity from the parent, or if the parent–child relationship is not reestablished in response to "the child's feelings of anger or destructiveness," then healthy development can be compromised (Sroufe & Cooper, 1988, p. 390). Wenar (1994) notes that a failure to develop self-control can result in acting out, in aggressiveness, or in delinquent behavior disorders (externalizing) in adolescence; whereas overcontrol can result in internalizing disorders, including anxiety, depression, and/or eating disorders.

During the toddler/preschool stage, the child develops more sophisticated self-regulation and self-control in response to rewards and punishments delivered by parents (Wenar, 1994). The child learns to control his/her own behavior in an effort to gain rewards (e.g., toys, activities, treats, etc.) or to avoid punishments. Rewards and punishments also come in the form of love and acceptance or withdrawal and criticism from parents. Thus the child learns to behave, to control, and to regulate himself or herself in an effort to please the parent and to avoid disapproval. The desire to please and to obtain approval from parents forms the basis for compliance and cooperation and for later socialization with others including the development of empathy.

The process of developing self-regulation and self-control is affected by numerous temperamental characteristics (Bates et al., 1985), as well as by the child's ability to delay gratification (Maccoby, 1980), to tolerate frustration, and to inhibit his/her actions (Sroufe & Cooper, 1988). These child factors interact with parental discipline styles (Wenar, 1994) and other environmental factors, such as extreme stress and chaos in the family, that either facilitate or impede the child's ability to develop self-regulation. In the toddler/preschool stage, self-regulation can be enhanced through proper supervision and guidance by adults outside the home (e.g., in the preschool setting). Furthermore, self-regulation and self-control are facilitated by the child's increasing language ability and cognitive development, which occur rapidly through this stage. For the biologically vulnerable child, self-regulation is not so predictable and may be impaired in spite of parental efforts.

Cognitive–Language Development

The scope of cognitive development is too broad to cover adequately in this review. See Berk (1989), LeFrancois (1995), Papalia and Olds (1992), and Sroufe and Cooper (1988) for in-depth treatment of language and cognitive development in the toddler and preschool stages. For purposes of this chapter, the development and maturation of language, reasoning, attentional, and memory abilities are briefly reviewed because developmental variations have been found in these domains in young children with ADHD.

Language Development

Language development undergoes rapid quantitative and qualitative changes in the infancy, toddler, and preschool stages. Productive or expressive language development is quite remarkable from toddlerhood to preschool, where estimates suggest that children learn five to eight new words a day and acquire anywhere from 8,000 to 14,000 words by the time they reach 6 years of age (Sroufe & Cooper, 1988). The development of receptive vocabulary is even more dramatic; estimates indicate that children may be learning up to 22 words a day during the same time period (Sroufe & Cooper, 1988). Qualitative changes are just as impressive, as children learn the sound patterns of words, word meanings and usages, morphological rules (nouns, verbs, prefixes, suffixes, etc.), and the syntactic rules (ordering of words) of language (Sroufe & Cooper, 1988).

   Although the development of language is thought to be biologically predetermined and genetically based, the environment plays a critical role in the normal acquisition of language. Language and cognitive development go hand and hand; that is, language is another type of representational thought (Sroufe & Cooper, 1988).

Symbolic Thinking and Reasoning

The development of symbolic thinking and reasoning is slow and continues into adulthood, according to most developmental psychologists. Although reasoning is not fully developed in toddlers and preschool children, there are some features of symbolic thinking that are undergoing change in this stage. The symbolic capacities that emerge during the toddler stage "pave the way for more complex social interactions, for make-believe play, and for new kinds of problem solving" (Sroufe & Cooper, 1988, p. 291).

   With the development of language, the child expands his/her repertoire from perceptual and physical action to mental action or representational thought (Sroufe & Cooper, 1988). Although the notion that thinking and language are related is generally accepted, it is not known which precedes the other (LeFrancois, 1995). Vygotsky (1962) suggests that thought and language develop independently at first, with thought preceding language, but that eventually these processes become highly interrelated. Vygotsky suggests that language has three major functions: (1) social speech (up to age 3), which is directed at others and is intended to control the activity of others or to communicate (e.g., "Give me milk!"); (2) egocentric speech (between 3 and 7 years) acts to control the child's own actions and behaviors (e.g., "The car goes vroom, vroom!"); and (3) inner speech or self-talk (after age 7) serves to direct the child's own thoughts and behaviors (LeFrancois, 1995). Vygotsky believes that inner speech is the foundation for all higher level mental activity, and A. R. Luria views language as the mechanism for "internalizing rules" to control one's own behavior (cited in Sroufe & Cooper, 1988).

Attention and Memory

The development of attentional and memory controls is important in the consideration of ADHD. Information-processing theories define attention as the process by which information moves from the sensory (e.g., visual, auditory, etc.) register phase to short-term memory, whereas memory refers to processes whereby information is transferred from short-term memory to long-term or permanent memory (Sroufe & Cooper, 1988).

> Between birth and the end of the early childhood period (around age 6), children learn and remember an overwhelming assortment of things; the identities of people and animals; the locations of things; numbers, letters, and songs; and thousands of words and all sorts of complex rules for putting them together. (LeFrancois, 1995, p. 302)

We also know that infants, even neonates, have the ability to learn and remember things and that they are more competent than originally believed (Bower, 1989). However, the memory capacity of infants and toddlers differs dramatically from that of older children and adults in that young children do not systematically use strategies to remember things (LeFrancois, 1995). By the age of 2 years, toddlers do seem to have a rudimentary understanding of memory and will consciously pay attention and try to remember when prompted to do so (Wellman, 1988). Although they do recognize that some information needs to be remembered, young children (even by the age of 6 years) are not able to develop good strategies for remembering (Sroufe & Cooper, 1988).

Wellman (1988) indicates that preschool children remember information using *incidental mnemonics*. Incidental mnemonics are not intentional strategies but arise from the act of attending to a repeated stimulus over time (LeFrancois, 1995). Although remembering at this stage is involuntary, memory strategies are nonetheless developing. Wellman (1988) found that preschool children can employ simple memory strategies when instructed to do so. Furthermore, preschool children as young as 3½ years make use of past knowledge of information to help them remember (Wellman, Sommerville, & Haake, 1979).

Between the ages of 3 and 5 years, memory strategies begin to develop and become more effective (Heisel & Retter, 1981). Although 3-year-olds are able to apply simple strategies systematically, their approaches are often ineffective. Memory strategies become more deliberate, more efficient and effective, less distracted by irrelevant information, and, with practice, habitual and automatic as the child moves through preschool to elementary age (Ornstein, Baker-Ward, & Naus, 1988).

Young children from the ages of 2 to 4 years differ in their ability to divide their attention between two interesting things (e.g., television and toys). Young children tend to play with toys more frequently, whereas older children become progressively more able to watch television and play at the same time (Anderson & Levin, 1976). Attentional processes are further complicated by the fact that even in kindergarten, children are still developing the ability to select information, focus attention, and ignore other information (Sroufe & Cooper, 1988). Preschool children develop the ability to rehearse, to use active memory strategies, and to improve their memory capacity under the supervision of teachers. Levy (1980) provides normative data on the development of sustained attention and inhibition in preschool children. Obviously, the capacity of young children to develop and have control over their attentional and memory processes will be critical for future learning and academic competencies.

Emotional Development and Socialization

Social development is an important milestone at this stage. The patterns laid down here set the stage for interaction patterns in middle childhood and later adolescence. As indicated in the discussion on attachment, early socialization is affected by healthy mother–child bonding and attachment patterns. Socialization is the "process by which children learn behaviors that are appropriate for people their age and sex" (LeFrancois, 1995, p.

348). During the toddler and preschool stage, children undergo rapid changes in their acquisition of the "rules of society"—when and how to express their feelings, how to play, and how to interact with others.

Interpreting, Expressing, and Controlling Emotions

In infancy, children gradually become aware that they are separate from others—that they are individuals—and that they have feelings (Kopp & Brownell, 1991). Infants eventually become aware of others and realize that their feelings exist apart from others (LeFrancois, 1995) and that emotions or subjective feelings (e.g., sadness, joy, and fear) are universally experienced by "normal human beings" and serve to motivate behaviors (Papalia & Olds, 1992). Although everyone experiences emotions, individuals do differ in how often they feel emotions, which events trigger emotions, and how they react to these emotions, and these differences essentially "form a fundamental element of personality" (Papalia & Olds, 1992, p. 148).

Papalia and Olds (1992) outline the major time frames in which specific emotions become present from infancy to toddlerhood. (1) Interest, the spontaneous neonatal smile, the startle response, the distress cry, and the disgust response to unpleasant tastes and odors are present at birth. (2) A social smile emerges between 3 and 6 weeks. (3) Anger, surprise, and sadness appear between 2 and 4 months. (4) Fear becomes evident between 5 and 7 months. (5) Self-awareness, empathy, shame, jealousy, shyness, pride, guilt, and contempt emerge between 12 and 18 months. Although the emergence and sequence of emotions have a biological basis, experiences can alter this process. For example, abused children show fear earlier than other infants (Gaensbauer & Hiatt, 1984).

The developmental process of communicating emotions is a function of the interaction between infants and the adults around them—a process of "mutual regulation" (Papalia & Olds, 1992). Quite early, infants can "read" the emotions of others, and they appear to change their behaviors in an effort to elicit reactions from others. That is, they can "read" anger, depression, and happiness in others, and they attempt (e.g., make faces, sounds, and gestures) to alter the way the other person is responding to them. Parents, on the other hand, interpret the emotional signals babies send out and alter their own behaviors to match those of the child. This mutual relationship insures the emotional well-being and development of the child and facilitates the attachment process. When this relationship breaks down, because, for example, the child has temperamental difficulties or because the parent may have inadequate parenting skills or maternal depression or may be overwhelmed by the stress of parenting, the child is likely to develop problems in later stages. For example, children of depressed mothers are at risk for a variety of problems. Infants have lower birth weights and tend to squirm and cry more; toddlers show less symbolic play activity; older children experience more cognitive problems and more accidents; and adolescents show more behavior problems (Zuckerman & Beardslee, 1987). Dawson (1994) found that babies of depressed mothers have reduced EEG activation in the left frontal lobe, which processes feelings of well-being; this finding mirrors the activation patterns of the depressed mother. When mothers can control their depressive symptomology in their interactions with their children, young children show normal activation patterns. This again reinforces the biology–environment interaction and shows that vulnerability does not necessarily lead to pathology.

The socialization process includes developing an awareness of and control over one's emotions. This is difficult for young children and coincides with the development of other abilities. As the young child develops language, he/she begins to express feelings in words rather than simply in actions. Before the child can understand the impact his/her behavior has on others, the child must have achieved sufficient cognitive development to take the perspective of others before acting. Finally, the child must have also begun developing self-control and inhibition of his/her actions when verbally instructed to "stop." This is a complex process and occurs with repeated experiences interacting with others.

According to Goodenough (1931), the "period between 1 and 4 years is the high-water mark for unvarnished expression of rage, the developmental trend being from explosive, undirected outbursts of temper to directed attacks, and from physical violence to symbolic expression of anger" (cited in Sroufe & Cooper, 1994, p. 57). Temper tantrums appear to peak at about 3½ years of age, and the accompanying behaviors (e.g., kicking, biting, hitting, and screaming) can be quite destructive in some children. Some parents know the embarrassment of being at the grocery store or at the mall when a child who doesn't get his/her own way screams, falls on the floor, and kicks or hits. Aggression directed toward others is rare during the 1st year, but retaliatory anger increases with age and can be fairly common (one-third of angry outbursts) in 4- and 5-year-olds (Sroufe & Cooper, 1988).

The emergence of directed anger coincides with the child's cognitive development. Until the child is aware of objects, he/she cannot really be angry at someone, and, although the toddler can be intentionally aggressive, he/she is not aware until about 3 years of age that aggressive behavior can hurt someone else (Sroufe & Cooper, 1988). Sroufe and Cooper suggest that this is when the child is first capable of being aggressive; they define aggression as "behavior that has injury or destruction as its goal, and anger or hatred as its accompanying effect" (1988, p. 57).

Physical aggression is usually replaced by verbal, "psychological" aggression, which some might see as an improvement in aggressive tendencies. However, Sroufe and Cooper (1988) suggest that verbal aggression can be just as harmful and may be more damaging than a "beating." Verbal aggression usually replaces physical aggression between 2½ to 5 years of age (Maccoby, 1980). Aggression during this stage is typically instrumental, that is, "aggression used as an instrument to reach a goal" (Papalia & Olds, 1992, p. 222). Children grab to get a toy or make threatening gestures to get what they want. Social aggression that occurs during play is generally viewed as "normal," and children who engage in this behavior may actually be "the most sociable and competent" of their group (Papalia & Olds, 1992, p. 222).

Toddlers and preschool children often express anger in situations in which their initiatives have been thwarted or their actions have been inhibited. Children develop self-control and self-management in later preschool years, but as toddlers they are generally unable to exercise this control (Sroufe & Cooper, 1988). As they develop language skills, young children become capable of asking instead of grabbing. As children develop a sense of empathy, they become aware of how others feel; they begin to understand how their behaviors affect others; and they engage in more positive behaviors in their interactions with others (Papalia & Olds, 1992). This progression generally occurs as children move out of the stage of egocentric thinking at about the age of 6 or 7 years.

Unfortunately, some children do not show a decrease in angry behavior and do not learn to control these powerful emotions. Patterson, DeBaryshe, and Ramsey (1989) found that aggression in young children can be a reaction to parenting practices in the home. When young children are not reinforced for good behavior or receive harsh or inconsistent punishment when they misbehave, they often do not adjust well to school, are rejected by others, and experience depression (Papalia & Olds, 1992). Children who have these experiences do not typically develop healthy friendships with others; they imitate aggressive models experienced in real life (parents or friends) or seen on television; and they are reinforced for aggressive behaviors (Papalia & Olds, 1992). This early pattern has strong influences into adolescence, and aggression that occurs as a result of this dynamic parent–child interaction is difficult to decrease.

Importance of Play

One of the major ways young children learn to control aggressive tendencies and to develop prosocial behaviors (e.g., altruism, empathy, cooperation) is through play. Play "is the 'laboratory' where the child learns new skills and practices old ones" (Sroufe & Cooper, 1988, p. 385). Through play, the child learns to deal with conflict and to master fearful or painful experiences. Preschool children "work out" their anxieties, bring their fears into their play, and learn to cope with these experiences during play.

In social play, preschool children learn to cooperate and to develop friendships (LeFrancois, 1995). Friendship patterns are quite stable (Park, Lay, & Ramsey, 1993), and children who are the most cooperative and least aggressive are the best liked (Denham & Holt, 1993). Although cooperative play is not typical until about the age of 4 to 5 years, younger children do display cooperation in some instances. Young children who comfort others, show compassion, and share with others at younger ages (i.e., 3 years) tend to be advanced in their ability to take another person's perspective; they show self-confidence and mature reasoning and appear to be securely attached (Papalia & Olds, 1992). Although prosocial behaviors and cooperative play are related to complex developmental changes in the young child (e.g., cognitive, language, self-control, etc.), altruism can be fostered in the home. Modeling, reinforcement, and selective use of punishment can be critical factors that encourage the development of prosocial behavior in young children (Papalia & Olds, 1992). As such, parents have a positive impact on this process, and early experiences with same-age peers also helps in the development of cooperative play (Rubin, 1980).

Early Preschool Adjustment

The importance of preschool experiences is intensified by the fact that young children between the ages of 4 and 5 years are undergoing rapid, complex developmental changes across major domains. However, the types and kinds of preschool educational experiences that are best for young children are hotly debated. Some argue that we are pushing young children too quickly and are in effect creating the "hurried child" who is missing out on childhood (Elkind, 1987), whereas others argue for structured, formal instruction in academic areas, including exposure to reading, foreign language, and musical instruments (LeFrancois, 1995).

Children are exposed to a variety of preschool settings, including day-care centers, kindergartens, intervention programs, and compensatory programs such as Head Start (LeFrancois, 1995). Obviously, the more structured, formal attempts at instruction will affect children in different ways depending on their individual development, temperament, and family–home experiences. In many kindergarten classrooms, children are being taught to read, to write, and to count—tasks once introduced in first grade (Papalia & Olds, 1992). The pressure to teach academics early often leaves less free time for play, whereas more time is devoted to worksheets and to learning to read (Egerton, 1987).

Kindergarten programs that have "one academic program to fit all developmental sizes" may be creating problems for young children, who show a wide range of "normal" variation in the acquisition of skills (i.e., language, motor, self-control, attention and memory, and socialization) that are needed to perform well and adjust to the school setting. For children prone to difficulties resulting from developmental delays or temperamental variations, kindergarten and/or day care may be the first but not the last time that they demonstrate trouble meeting the expectations of others. Papalia and Olds caution that "unless motivation comes from children themselves, and unless learning arises naturally from their experiences, their time might be better spent on the business of early childhood" rather than on academic preparation (1992, p. 206). Despite the controversies, many early childhood experts believe that preschool settings should provide children the opportunity to play, to explore and choose learning experiences, and to interact with same-age peers under guidance from knowledgeable and caring adults.

Summary

In summary, normal development during infancy, toddlerhood, and preschool periods is rapid and complex. Children are developing across broad domains, and this growth and maturation depends on a delicate balance between the child's biogenetic makeup and his/her environmental experiences and interactions with others. Early attachment and bonding with the parent, especially the mother, serves as a foundation for future relationships, for language and cognitive development, and for the emergence of self-control and self-regulation. These attachment processes are also a function of interactions among child, parent, and environmental/experiential forces that shape and influence the manner, rate, and overall development of the child. The probability that a child will develop later adjustment problems in academic and social settings is related to the extent to which the child has genetic and/or neurodevelopmental abnormalities in combination with poor attachment and bonding; harsh, insensitive, or abusive parenting; and inadequate environmental stimulation. Clinicians considering a diagnosis of ADHD in the preschool stage typically consider normal developmental patterns across these major areas and investigate the number, type, and severity of presenting problems.

The following sections review difficulties associated with children displaying symptoms of ADHD in the toddler/preschool stage. Most young children do not receive a diagnosis of ADHD until the preschool years; thus research conducted at the toddler stage has focused on children who have high levels of activity, temperamental difficulties, and compliance problems (Campbell, 1990b). It has been noted that children diagnosed with ADHD at later stages generally have a history of difficulties beginning in infancy and/or the toddler stage. The following describes how characteristics of ADHD affect development in the toddler/preschool stage.

ATTENTIONAL, HYPERACTIVITY, AND IMPULSIVITY DEFICITS IN THE TODDLER/PRESCHOOL STAGE

It is important to remember that most children identified as having ADHD show symptoms in the toddler/preschool stage (Barkley, 1990b) and that the number of referrals for hyperactivity increases for children 3 to 4 years of age (Weiss & Hechtman, 1986). The rise in referral rates at the preschool stage appears related to the increased expectations placed on the child, whereby parents and other adults (e.g., preschool teachers and/or childcare staff) expect children to conform, to comply to requests (i.e., inhibit on command), to develop symbolic language, and to play cooperatively (Weiss & Hechtman, 1993). Although not all children will be identified this early, diagnosis usually occurs when the problem behaviors exceed expected norms and when "society can no longer tolerate" the ADHD symptoms (Weiss & Hechtman, 1993, p. 22). Lakey et al. (1998) found that structured diagnostic interviews of parents and DSM-IV checklists completed by teachers were valid for identifying all three DSM-IV subtypes of ADHD in children 4 to 6 years of age. Children who met DSM-IV criteria showed a variety of social, behavioral, and academic difficulties consistently associated with ADHD.

Despite the fact that most ADHD symptoms appear early, there have been a limited number of well-designed prospective research studies on infants. Consequently, much of our understanding of this age group comes from retrospective accounts from mothers, who are asked to recall earlier developmental patterns. These retrospective accounts may not always be reliable (Weiss & Hechtman, 1993). Other research has focused on children who have not been formally diagnosed but who have shown serious problems with inattention, hyperactivity, impulsivity, and/or noncompliance at an early age and have later been diagnosed as having ADHD.

The developmental correlates of ADHD in the toddler/preschool stage are summarized in Table 3.1. An inspection of research findings shows that young children with ADHD symptoms or characteristics demonstrate a variety of developmental problems. It is important to note that individual children may differ in the number and severity of problems they possess at any given time; and, even at an early age, children diagnosed with ADHD are a very heterogeneous group of individuals.

THE IMPACT OF ATTENTIONAL, HYPERACTIVITY, AND IMPULSIVITY DEFICITS ON ADJUSTMENT IN THE TODDLER/PRESCHOOL STAGE

ADHD symptoms affect normal development and adjustment in many areas, including attachment and bonding, initiative/self-exploration, self-control/self-regulation, cognitive development, social and emotional development, and early preschool adjustment.

Attachment and Bonding

About one-third of mothers with hyperactive children report that problems are present in the first year of life (Werry, Weiss, & Douglas, 1964)—excessive crying, sleep difficulties, delays in vocalization, feeding problems, and physical anomalies—and that their babies exhibit less smiling and cuddling behavior (Weiss & Hechtman, 1993). Excessive crying in "hyperactive" infants is particularly problematic because these troubled infants do not readily respond to parental attempts at soothing (e.g., rocking, holding) or other parental attention (cuddling and comforting; Weiss & Hechtman, 1993). A lack of reaction to these maternal efforts reduces the number of positive mother–child interactions and reduces the amount of time the infant can spend exploring his/her environment and thus affects the cognitive development of the "hyperactive" infant (Weiss & Hechtman, 1993). Other sleeping and/or feeding difficulties in "hyperactive" infants also have a negative effect on mother–child relationships.

Although research in the infancy stage is "sketchy," evidence does suggest that "difficult" infants develop a variety of subsequent problems, including hyperactivity (Wenar, 1994). Temperamental difficulties alone, however, are not sufficient for predicting later ADHD; parental caretaking skills, family stress, and parental dysfunction appear related to the emergence of behavioral problems in young children (Campbell, 1990b). Intrusive parenting and insensitive or abusive caretaking tends to interact with child characteristics to produce later problems. In keeping with the interactional model, mothers of young children with hyperactivity also

TABLE 3.1. Characteristics of ADHD in the Infancy, Toddler, and Preschool Stages

Study	Child characteristics
	Infancy
Campbell, Szumowski, Ewing, Gluck, & Breaux (1982)	Excessive crying, drowsiness; colic, feeding problems; sleep disturbances
Kaplan & Sadock (1985)	Undue sensitivity; aversive response to stimuli; sleep disturbances; excessive crying; irritability
Knobel, Wolman, & Mason (1959)	EEG abnormalities (occipital lobe)
Waldrop, Bell, McLaughlin, & Halverson (1978)	Head and facial abnormalities
Weiss & Hechtman (1986)	Difficulties being soothed; excessive or little sleep; restless or easily disturbed sleep; unresponsivity; colic, poor sucking; crying while eating; irregular eating; lateness in babbling; resistant to cuddling; little smiling
Wender (1987)	Temperamental difficulties; deficient neurotransmitters; likelihood of siblings or fathers with ADD/ADHD
Werry, Weiss, & Douglas (1964)	Early mother–child difficulties due to excessive crying, colic, and feeding problems
	Toddler
Battle & Lacey (1972)	Negative feelings of mother toward child; less frequent interactions; less affection; less compliance of child

Reference	Description
Mash & Johnston (1983)	High stress and lower self-esteem in mothers (leading to perception of worse problems in child); stress in mother–child relationship
Sroufe & Waters (1982)	Relation in attachment ratings at age 12–18 months to attending, focusing, and social readiness in preschool

Preschool

Reference	Description
Barkley, Karlsson, & Pollard (1985)	Zenith of parental stress occurring when child is between 3 and 6 years
Campbell et al. (1978)	Excessive activity; noncompliance; difficulty in toilet training
Campbell et al. (1982)	Shifting of activities in free play; high activity levels during structured activities; impulsive responding
Pelham & Bender (1982)	Rejection by peers
Schleifer et al. (1975)	Similarity of hyperactive children to normal children in free play; true hyperactives (symptoms in home and school) doing less well than situational hyperactives (problems in one setting); more frustration and stress in parents of true hyperactives than in parents of normals or situational hyperactives; differences between true hyperactives on impulsivity and field independence
Weiss & Hechtman (1986)	Increase in number of referrals for hyperactivity in 3- to 4-year-olds; increasing environmental demands on child; negative encounters between child and others

show more depression, lower self-esteem, and higher stress than mothers of normal children (Mash & Johnston, 1983). Problems during the toddler stage typically center on issues related to exploration and regulation of behaviors.

Initiative/Self-Exploration

As exploratory and autonomous behaviors develop during the toddler/preschool stage, high activity levels, inattention, and defiance may be difficult to differentiate from the normal behaviors of the active toddler who explores and exerts him or herself (Campbell, 1990b; Wenar, 1994). Although ADHD behaviors are hard to distinguish from those of normal, active toddlers, some differences can be seen in children who have excessive levels of problem behaviors. When exploration is characterized as "frenzied" and unfocused; when it interferes with problem solving and mastery; when inattention results in "flitting from one object to another without becoming involved in any one"; and when oppositional behaviors are expressed as frequent tantrums, the child is more likely to have ADHD (Wenar, 1994, pp. 165–166).

Research suggests that extreme levels of early noncompliance and high levels of activity are predictive of adjustment problems in elementary school (Campbell, Ewing, et al., 1986). Children at the extremes of the continuum of these behaviors may be more susceptible to adverse environmental factors, particularly chronic, unstable, and negative situations that further affect problem behaviors (Lewis, Feiring, McGuffog, & Jaskir, 1984).

Self-Control/Self-Regulation

In preschool, children with characteristics of ADHD often are difficult to toilet train and are noncompliant, defiant, overactive, and mischievous (Barkley, 1989). Safer and Allen (1976) indicate that children with ADHD are characterized by their parents as "excessively restless, temperamental, meddlesome, and disruptive . . . frequently shift from one activity to another . . . destroy toys by tinkering repeatedly with them . . . and bedwetting at night is also fairly frequent" (p. 44). These behaviors present major challenges in the home, and parental stress is at its zenith when the child is between the ages of 3 and 6 years (Barkley, 1989).

Parental efforts to control or limit extreme behavior problems may in turn elicit high levels of noncompliance from children and often results in frustration for both the parent and the child. Children may develop tantrums and noncompliance (Campbell, 1990b), while at the same time mothers may become more directing, demanding, and disapproving of their children (Cunningham & Barkley, 1979). In parent–child relationships with high levels of conflict, mothers often show signs of depression and may disengage from their children because parenting is often an unrewarding and unsuccessful experience (Barkley, 1990b). The reciprocal interaction between child characteristics and parenting styles creates a complex and dynamic behavioral pattern that should be addressed in intervention programs for young children with ADHD symptoms.

The role of the father in disciplining difficult, noncompliant children should not be overlooked, particularly in cases where the mother–father relationship is troubled. Campbell (1990b) noted that mothers of difficult-to-control young children usually act as "crisis managers," coping with the daily conflicts and challenges of raising noncompliant youngsters. In these instances, fathers often withdraw from unpleasant discipline situations, subsequently creating an uneven parent-role differentiation.

Withdrawal behavior or lack of participation on the part of fathers creates a number of ramifications in the family dynamic. (1) Mothers feel isolated and unsupported. (2) Mothers may feel angry, resentful, and frustrated, and thus may be less effective as parents. (3) Children miss out on fathers' parenting and nurturing influences. (4) Mothers' attempts at disciplining are subtly undermined by lack of involvement of fathers (Campbell, 1990b). These dynamics frequently create marital friction and may be another source of stress in an already tense situation. Family systems problems should be explored when planning interventions for the toddler/preschool stage.

It is often hard for parents to find babysitters, which increases the burden many mothers have when caring for a young child with high levels of inattention, impulsivity, and hyperactivity (Barkley, 1990b). Mothers are often criticized by friends and relatives for not being able to control their hyperactive children, and often become isolated when their children are quite young. As such, mothers of children with ADHD often feel alone and inadequate as parents, which further increases stress, depression, and other self-esteem problems, including a lack of confidence in their parenting skills. This pattern suggests that clinicians need to pay attention to the parenting styles, family dynamics, and family support systems available when addressing the needs of difficult children and their parents.

Cognitive Development

There is emerging research identifying the cognitive correlates of ADHD symptoms in young children. Language and attention and memory difficulties may be present early.

Language

Speech and language delays often appear in a variety of childhood disorders, including learning disabilities, conduct disorders, and ADHD. Ornoy, Uriel, and Tennebaum (1993) found that 80% of children aged 2 to 4 years who showed "soft" neurological signs, including inattention, hyperactivity, and speech delays, were diagnosed with ADHD between the ages of 7 and 14 years. In a study of 399 children between 4 and 12 years of age in psychiatric care, children with subtle as well as previously diagnosed language disorders also had symptoms associated with ADHD (Cohen et al., 1993). Moreover, children with subtle or previously "unsuspected" language problems showed the most serious externalizing disorders. The largest study to date followed 600 children with speech–language impairment. Children showed increased rates of both learning disabilities and ADHD when early speech–language problems were present, and, learning disabilities and ADHD were strongly associated with speech–language impairment in the sample of 1- to 16-year-olds, both at initial and follow-up testing (Cantwell & Baker, 1992).

Other research shows that IQ may-be an important variable in the development of behavior problems in children with significant developmental language delays. Specifically, Benasich, Curtiss, and Tallal (1993) found that language-impaired children, originally identified at 4 years of age, demonstrated more behavior problems as a function of IQ than of ADHD at 8 years of age. Low IQ may-be more significant than language impairment alone for predicting behavior problems in young children. These issues need further investigation to clarify the contributions of low IQ and language delays to the development of future behavioral problems, especially ADHD and learning disabilities. Such research may help to establish better predictive pathways for these two disorders. These distinctions may also be helpful for differentiating among the disorders at an age when early intervention may reduce the emergence of secondary psychosocial and self esteem problems.

Attention and Memory

Although children with ADHD show signs of attentional and memory problems at school age, few studies have been conducted on preschool children. Generally, research suggests that memory improves with age and emerges with the development of cognitive and language skills (Campbell, 1990b). Although the research is sparse on this topic, Campbell et al. (1982) did find that children referred for problems with attention, tantrums, and defiance were less attentive on structured tasks and more impulsive on laboratory tasks (e.g., the Cookie Delay Task) than control children between the age of 2 and 3 years.

More research is needed on attention and memory capacities for this age group before definitive statements can be made about how ADHD interferes with skill development in preschool. It has been suggested that preschool children may miss out on academic readiness activities due to inattention and the constant discipline (e.g., exclusion from play) they receive for problem behaviors (DuPaul & Stoner, 1994). Attention and memory deficits will be explored in more detail in the discussion of middle childhood.

Social and Emotional Development

Although children with ADHD may appear highly "sociable," it has long been suggested that the symptoms of the disorder interfere with normal social interactions and that young children show problems early in their interactions with others (Campbell, 1990b). Alessandri (1992) observed 4–5-year-old children in a preschool setting. Young children with ADHD showed signs of impaired play and social interactions when compared to a control group, including fewer overall play activities, less functional motor play, less competence in social interactions, and less attention and cooperation during group activities. Furthermore, hyperactive pre-schoolers were found to be more negative and noncompliant (Mash & Johnston, 1982).

It is interesting to note that differences in play activities were most prominent under conditions of "free play" versus "structured play." Hyperactive children can be indistinguishable from normal preschool children during "free play" activities but are significantly different from a control group during structured activities, such as sitting at a table or completing quiet tasks (Schleifer et al., 1975; Weiss & Hechtman, 1993). Hyperactive children stood at the table and left their seats more frequently and were more aggressive (e.g., hitting, biting, kicking, throwing things) than normal children. Furthermore, children with "situational" hyperactivity (i.e., problems only in some situations) did not differ from "true" hyperactives or children with pervasive problems (present in all settings) during structured situations.

Campbell, Endman, and Bernfeld (1977) conducted a three-year follow-up of children in the Schliefer et al. (1975) study. These children were in the first and second grades and were between the ages of 6 and 8 years. Children identified as hyperactive (both "situational" and "true") continued to show behavior problems (i.e., disruptive, off-task, and out-of-seat behaviors), although "true" hyperactives were higher on these dimensions than "situational" hyperactives. Furthermore, signs of low self-esteem were present in the hyperactive children, and these children had a negative effect on other children in the classroom. Thus early problems with peers persist, and by the time a child reaches school age, hyperactive children have trouble making and keeping friendships.

Early Preschool Adjustment

During the preschool stage, children are beginning to learn to inhibit on command, to attend for longer periods, to persist at play, and to become less restless and hyperactive. However, many preschool children are reported to be highly active (Barkley, 1990b), and as many as 40% of 4-year-old children are considered inattentive (Palfrey, Levine, Walker, & Sullivan, 1985). Campbell (1990a) found that with maturation most of these children improved and most did not display ADHD symptoms 3 to 6 months later. Palfrey et al. (1985) found that only 10% of children with symptoms at 3 to 4 years of age developed serious patterns of inattention at 7 years of age. These are important findings because, although inattention and overactivity may be problematic for 3- and 4-year-olds, most children do not show persistent deficits into later childhood (Barkley, 1990b). However, Campbell (1990b) showed that when management problems emerge at age 3 and persist through age 4, children are more likely to be hyperactive and aggressive and frequently display problem behaviors at later ages.

IMPLICATIONS FOR ASSESSMENT OF ADHD IN THE TODDLER/PRESCHOOL STAGE

Although one of the more important elements of intervention is proper and early diagnosis, the identification of ADHD in the toddler/preschool stage is complicated. First, approximately 40% of 4-year-olds display problems of inattention, based on reports by teachers and parents (Palfrey et al., 1985); yet the majority of these problems do not persist after 3 to 6 months (Campbell, 1990b). Furthermore, Palfrey et al. (1985) found that only 10% of the problem group continued to show inattention resulting in academic difficulties or behavioral problems by the second grade. Thus not all children who display early problems are significantly impaired or show significant ADHD symptoms in later grades.

Second, there is a great deal of developmental variability among normal children on behaviors that usually constitute ADHD characteristics, including inattention, noncompliance, overactivity, low frustration tolerance, and poor social interactions during play activities (DuPaul

& Stoner, 1994). Third, more reliable methods of assessment are needed for this age group (Barkley, 1990b; DuPaul & Stoner, 1994); see Lahey et al. (1998) for guidelines. Fourth, parent and teacher behaviors (i.e., discipline practices, expectations, and environmental constraints) also influence child behaviors, including compliance and attention.

Although these cautions are important when considering a diagnosis of ADHD in the toddler/preschool stage, ignoring behavioral problems during this stage is troublesome in that children may develop sustained peer relationship difficulties and low self-esteem, particularly related to academic functioning (DuPaul & Stoner, 1994). Thus rather than ignoring these early signs, efforts to reduce problems should be initiated for children with troubling, disruptive, and problematic behaviors, even without a diagnosis of ADHD.

SUMMARY

Research exploring the effects of ADHD on normal challenges in the toddler/preschool stage is sparse. Studies have focused on children with high levels of inattention and hyperactivity. ADHD symptoms are associated with language delays, cognitive deficits, and impaired social relations. Parent–child relationships may also be strained due to the challenge of parenting a difficult to control preschooler. Mothers may experience depression and may feel inadequate as parents. Family stress may be high, and mother–father relations may also be strained.

4

Intervention Strategies and Therapeutic Techniques for the Toddler/Preschool Stage

*T*his chapter presents selected interventions that address the developmental challenges of children with ADHD and children who display problematic behaviors at higher than expected levels in the toddler/preschool stage. In this stage, interventions typically focus on psychosocial (e.g., parent–child bonding and attachment) and peer relations (e.g., play activities and social skills) and behavioral adjustment (e.g., parenting skills and classroom management techniques). A number of young children with ADHD also display language-related delays, thus interventions will be discussed for these difficulties. Finally, a discussion of medication options and cautions for this age group are explored.

Despite difficulties making a firm diagnosis of ADHD at the toddler/preschool stage, Blackman, Westervelt, Stevenson, and Welsch (1991) recommend the following interventions for preschool children to effectively address ADHD symptoms: (1) parent training and support; (2) structured, tolerant preschool experiences; (3) social skills training and self-control; and, in severe cases, (4) medication. Generally, most interventions for this stage are caregiver-focused (e.g., parent- or teacher-focused) rather than child-focused, although several interventions do address social interaction techniques for the child (e.g., waiting, sharing, etc.); medication regimens also focus on the child.

PARENT AND FAMILY INTERVENTIONS

Parent and family interventions are typically necessary because later behavioral disorders in children with difficult temperaments are significantly influenced by problems in the family, including excessive stress, parental psychopathology, and poor parenting practices (Barkley, 1990b). Negative, critical, and demanding parenting styles during the preschool years are associated with chronic and significant behavioral problems at 4, 6, and 9 years of age (Campbell, 1990b). Preschoolers with a history of attachment problems are frequently hostile, avoidant, and aggressive toward peers, or they may be socially isolated (Troy & Sroufe, 1987). Techniques for increasing parent–child attachment and for developing effective parenting techniques are described first.

Building Positive Parent–Child Relationships

During the infancy, toddler, and preschool stages, treatment may need to focus on building positive parent–child relationships, particularly if this bond is not securely and positively established. Timely parental interventions can improve mother–child attachment (Sroufe, 1985; Campbell, 1990b), whereas a lack of intervention during this stage may result in the child's developing a sense that the environment is unresponsive, rejecting, and distressing.

Important elements of parenting that affect parent–child relationships include the following: (1) attentiveness, (2) physical contact, (3) verbal stimulation, (4) material stimulation, and (5) responsive care (LeFrancois, 1995). Mothers can be instructed in specific ways to attend, interact, and stimulate the child positively. Bromwich (1981) developed a model for parent–infant interaction that focuses on the bonding and attachment process for temperamentally at-risk infants. This program has two major foci: assessing the nature of the mother–infant relationship and intervening to improve the relationship. The program works on changing the perceptions and behaviors of the parent in an effort to optimize the child's development (Seitz & Provence, 1990). Attempts are made to make the parent–child relationship mutually reinforcing, thereby enhancing the bond between the two. Parents are taught how to observe their child, to understand the importance of play, and to anticipate the needs of their child (Seitz & Provence, 1990). Further, as parents become more confident in their ability to affect their child's development, they develop a better sense of their adequacy as parents.

Nezworski, Tolan, and Belsky (1988) developed the Penn State Family Intervention Program for addressing parenting styles, marital problems, and maternal personality issues that affect the bonding/attachment between mother and child. In this model, several key components are featured: (1) improving the mother's negative views and perceptions of herself and her world (e.g., "I'm not worthy of nurturance or love"; "I can't trust people."); (2) exploring stressful parenting and family experiences (e.g., clingy babies, parental discord, etc.); and (3) examining the emotional reactions of mothers in the parenting role (e.g., feeling overwhelmed, disappointed, resentful, etc.).

Therapists seek to establish "emotionally supportive, nonjudgmental" relationships with mothers in order to help facilitate exploration of "negative core beliefs" and to change the way these beliefs are manifested during ongoing mother–child interactions (Nezworski et al., 1988). Infants are included in therapy sessions so that work can be done on the real parenting issues facing the mother, such as controlling temper tantrums. Twelve weekly sessions are provided, but the program is flexible and mothers are able to select the number of sessions they want or need. The goals of therapy sessions are to provide "corrective emotional experiences" to improve self-esteem, functional relationships, and parenting effectiveness; it is not parent training per se.

Initial pilot research suggests that the program is successful in increasing the mother's trust in the therapist, and mothers express a continued interest in getting more help. The extent to which the treatment produces long-term effects on the child have not been assessed. However, there are reasons to be optimistic about the short-term help that may be provided to mothers for the duration of the program.

There is need for more research investigating the usefulness of interventions aimed at changing mother–child attachment problems in infancy. Furthermore, if for some reason the mother–child relationship is severely disrupted and resistant to interventions because of maternal psychopathology or drug and/or alcohol abuse, then attempts should be made to encourage attachment and bonding between the child and other significant adults, including the father, grandparent, aunt or uncle, or other childcare provider (Papalia & Olds, 1992). Thus the clinician may encourage and foster attachment with other adults in these extreme conditions. Responsive parenting during the toddler/preschool stage may be an important protective factor for the child over time.

It is important to note that some resilient children with insecure attachment relationships who received good parenting during the preschool period did not display later behavioral problems (Erickson, Egeland, & Sroufe, 1985). Thus when parents are able to provide an environment with appropriate play materials, parental support and encouragement, respect for child autonomy, clear instructions, consistent limit setting, and low levels of hostility, there is reason to suggest that the negative outcome of early attachment problems can be minimized

(Nezworski et al., 1988). Therapy goals would thus focus on helping the parent become more supportive and effective and less reactive when dealing with challenging behaviors.

Parent Management Techniques

Parent management techniques have proven effective for increasing compliance in toddler and preschool children, for helping parents set clear and consistent limits, and for improving the parent–child relationship. The basis of most parent training programs include methods for dealing with "difficult, noncompliant" children by focusing on using consistent and firm limit setting, with reasonable and fair expectations (Barkley, 1987, 1997b; Forehand & McMahon, 1981). These programs generally attempt to improve the parent–child relationship as well. Activities focus on teaching parents to attend to positive behaviors and to use praise and reinforcement to increase their child's compliance (Newby, Fischer, & Roman, 1991). Pisterman et al. (1989) found that parent–child interactions and child compliance increased in families with young children who received a 10-week training program with these components.

Regardless of the particular approach taken, a number of factors, techniques, and methods for changing the way parents interact with their ADHD child appear relevant. Goldstein and Goldstein (1990) describe the following model for increasing parental competence.

First, helping parents understand the nature of ADHD and the primary reason why children behave the way they do is important. Goldstein and Goldstein suggest that "many published materials or clinical services available to parents stress the use of techniques at the expense of understanding" (1990, p. 349). Thus parent education is necessary because many techniques "may be intermittent and short-lived unless parents develop an understanding of the ADHD child's behavior, their interaction with the child and the effect problems with attention and arousal level are going to have upon the child on a long-term basis" (Goldstein & Goldstein, 1990, p. 349).

In an effort to accomplish this goal, "seeing the world through the eyes of the ADHD child is important" and helps parents move beyond simple behavioral techniques that will not produce long-lasting behavioral changes in and of themselves (Goldstein & Goldstein, 1990, p. 349). Clinicians are advised to consider differences in parenting styles and parental temperament prior to skill training. This information can be gathered during the interview process. Parents may need help to control their own frustrations, impulse control problems, or other issues that may interfere with effective parenting. This extends the concept of "goodness-of-fit" described by Chess (1986) whereby interventions optimize a "fit" between the parent's abilities and the demands placed on the parent by the child's ADHD problems.

Second, parents need to distinguish children's noncompliance from incompetence (Goldstein & Goldstein, 1990). This distinction is particularly important with very young children because parents often overestimate the developmental capabilities of their child. By learning that the symptoms of ADHD make it difficult for the young child to stop, to wait, to stay calm, to deal with frustration, and to be purposeful, parents are taught not to punish children for their ADHD symptoms. Also, by knowing that the next time the child is in a similar situation, "the impulsive need for gratification will outweigh any capacity to stop, to think and plan, resulting in reoccurrence of the problem," the parent can begin to relabel their child's behavior and to modify their own responses to the situation (Goldstein & Goldstein, 1990, p. 351).

Third, parents are taught how to give "positive directions." This step increases the parents' ability to distinguish between compliance and competence and also helps parents to determine when to punish and when to help the child build or develop skills. In this step, Goldstein and Goldstein suggest that clinicians should encourage parents to tell children "what they want instead of what they don't want" (1990, p. 352) and to practice saying this in sessions before trying it out in the home. Parents also begin to appreciate that some behaviors are due to incompetence resulting from ADHD and require the parents to act as the "control system for their child" and that positive directions need to be repeated so that the child can experience small successes (Goldstein & Goldstein, 1990). For example, the parent is taught to ask the child to remember to follow directions the next time, which begins a process of helping the child to develop inner or self-control mechanisms. During these first three steps, parents begin to appreciate how their parenting responses interact with their child's behavior.

Finally, Goldstein and Goldstein (1990) encourage parents to end their interactions with their child on a successful note. For example, if a child is sent out of the room for noncompliance, he/she should return to the situation and comply with parental requests. "Parents are directed to use short punishment periods designed to clearly give the message that the parent is dissatisfied and to quickly return the child to the problem situation, allowing an additional try at compliance" (1990, p. 353). This entire process helps the parent to understand that the child's ability to change may be limited but that with the proper use of negative consequences (e.g., a toy is taken away as a penalty for rough play) and positive reinforcement (e.g., the child receives a new toy or a big hug for appropriate play) the child's behavior does improve.

This paradigm sets the stage for helping parents to have realistic expectations for their child, to understand how ADHD affects their child's behavior, to distinguish between incompetence and noncompliance, and to use consequences to shape behavior. This structure provides an opportunity for the child to behave in more positive ways while strengthening the parent–child bond.

Structured Parenting Programs

There are a number of commercially available parenting programs for clinicians looking for methods to improve parents' discipline practices and parent–child interactions. These programs can be used for either group or individual parent training. For the most part, the strategies utilize behavior management and family systems techniques.

Select programs and procedures for parents, including Barkley's (1987, 1997b) program for defiant children and Forehand and McMahon's (1981) program for noncompliant children, are described next. Related research on parenting programs is also presented.

Parent Training for Defiant Children (Barkley, 1987, 1997b)

Barkley (1987, 1997b) developed a parent training program for families with defiant children between the ages of 2 and 11. The program is based on behavioral principles and is conducted in 8 to 10 sessions. Parents are trained either in groups or individually depending on their own family needs and the severity of presenting problems. The program includes an assessment, an intervention, and a follow-up phase. A Spanish-language supplement is also available (Barkley, 1997b).

During the assessment phase, the clinician obtains specific information about the child's behavioral functioning in the home utilizing rating scales and observational and interview techniques. The purpose of the assessment is to determine the nature and extent of the child's compliance difficulties and the parents' response to these problems. The revised manual includes scales to assess parents who may also have symptoms of ADHD or oppositional deviant disorder (Barkley, 1997b). Parents learn the reasons behind their child's misbehavior and are taught more effective techniques for increasing child compliance. The sessions are personalized, and specific family problems are addressed based on inventories and checklists that identify family stressors and conflict situations. Parent–child, sibling, and marital relationships are all facilitated through the training process (Weiss & Hechtman, 1993).

The training phase consists of systematically teaching parents the principles of behavior management, including reinforcement and punishment. The sessions are arranged to teach parents the reasons underlying noncompliance, how aspects of their child's behavioral problems interact with their own characteristics, and how situational and stress factors affect parenting skills. Techniques for dealing with problem behaviors are then introduced (Barkley, 1987, 1997b). The timing and sequencing of the management techniques are important. Reinforcement principles are introduced before punishment procedures (time-out and response cost). Parents who may have troubled and conflictual relationships with their child are taught to attend to, play with, and reinforce their child while avoiding critical or "corrective" directives. Parents are taught techniques such as "catching their child being good" and giving direct and effective commands. Parents are encouraged to create highly reinforcing, positive relationships with their child before reductive punishment techniques are introduced. Parents are taught to use a token economy in the home before response cost techniques (i.e., losing points for noncompliance) are introduced.

Although many parents of children with ADHD have used some form of time-out, they frequently misapply important aspects of this technique. Some of the common errors that Barkley point out include (1) inconsistent use of time-out; (2) time-out periods that are too long for the child's age; (3) arguing, yelling, and/or verbally interacting with the child during time-out; and (4) using time-out for every infraction. Parents are taught to avoid these pitfalls and are given detailed instructions and handouts for the appropriate use of time-out.

The training program eventually leads parents to plan for and practice managing their child's behavior in public places. Misbehavior and noncompliance in public are generally quite challenging for most families. Parents develop skills in setting up rules for behavior, in working with the child to identify rewards for compliance, and in responding when children comply or defy the rules in a public setting. Finally, the program offers booster sessions to address particularly resistant problems or to reinforce parents for continuing to utilize the various management techniques.

Barkley's parent training program incorporates several strategies for increasing parent effectiveness, including homework assignments and related readings in conjunction with weekly instructional sessions where common problems with or impediments to using the skills in the home are also discussed. Identifying impediments to changing behaviors in the home is a particularly useful component; it helps the clinician to identify common reactions to specific strategies and helps parents anticipate potential difficulties ahead of time (Newby et al., 1991). Thus the clinician anticipates the concerns and heads off issues that are raised before and after each technique is introduced. Parents' unwillingness or inability to comply in carrying out management strategies is a typical problem and accounts for difficulties in maintaining contingency management in the home (Weiss & Hechtman, 1993).

Helping Parents with Noncompliant Children (Forehand & McMahon, 1981)

Forehand and McMahon (1981) developed a program to help parents reduce noncompliance. Although not specifically designed for children with ADHD, this program can be useful with this group because it provides strategies for handling problems with rule-governed behaviors (Newby et al., 1991). The Barkley and Forehand–McMahon methods are heavily influenced by Constance Hanf and by Gerald Patterson and his colleagues, and both feature social learning and behavioral theories (Newby et al., 1991). The concepts of "coercive escalation" and "reinforcement traps" are central to the program, and parents are taught to understand and alter these particular cycles. Negative behaviors are inadvertently reinforced when parents give in to, pay attention to, or succumb to children's tantrums and angry outbursts. "Coercive escalation" occurs when the child threatens to misbehave and parents withdraw their requests in order to avoid a confrontation ("Okay, you can watch TV for 30 more minutes") or give in to the child's demands ("Okay, you can have the candy bar if you stop screaming!"). Parents learn about the coercive nature of these patterns of child noncompliance and are taught how to alter their responses to these situations.

This program includes an initial evaluation of the problem using interviews and rating scales, observation of parent–child interactions, videotaping in the home, and 10 instructional sessions (Newby et al., 1991). Forehand and McMahon (1981) incorporate direct instruction of parenting strategies in parent–child dyads, using techniques such as role play, cued practice, and coaching. Once skills are learned in the therapy sessions, parents are taught how to use the strategies in the home. The sessions also teach parents how to pay attention to the child, how to reinforce the child's positive behaviors and to ignore negative behaviors, how to give commands and consequences for noncompliance, and how to use time-out effectively (Forehand & McMahon, 1981).

The Forehand–McMahon program is very intensive, with repeated opportunities for parents to receive supervised and coached practice sessions, modeling and role-playing of effective techniques, and extensive explanations of how to use the techniques. During practice sessions, the clinician provides feedback and coaching to parents through a "bug-in-the-ear" microphone (Newby et al., 1991). The program focuses on improving day-to-day interactions related to compliance issues.

Pisterman et al. (1989) evaluated the effects of a parent-mediated training program for preschool children with ADHD. The program adapted elements of the Barkley and Forehand–McMahon approaches and found positive treatment effects for child compliance, parental interaction styles, and managment skills. Newby et al. (1991) suggest that although generalization from the clinic to the home is often observed in programs emphasizing parent training, school behavior remains problematic. They suggest that the school psychologist might play a role in designing and implementing a home–school program.

Other Research Findings

Several well-designed studies have shown parent training to be effective for improving behaviors of infants, toddlers, and preschool children. Some present techniques for helping infants develop regular sleeping patterns, as sleep-related difficulties are often reported by parents with temperamentally difficult children. Other research investigates management strategies for parents with toddlers and preschool children.

Establishing Sleep Patterns in Infants. Sleep difficulties in infants and young children are fairly common reasons why parents seek consultation from pediatricians and psychiatrists. In fact, Coates and Thoreson (1981) indicated that 26% of problems addressed by pediatricians and 61% of the problems addressed by psychiatrists were sleep related.

Wolfson, Lacks, and Futterman (1992) were able to help first-time parents establish "early, stable" sleeping patterns in infants using a short-term (two weekly and two booster sessions) behavioral program. Parents were taught to promote independence in their infants by using gradual shaping techniques, to use scheduled nightly feeding times, and to help their infants develop appropriate day/wake–night/sleep cycles. Parents were able to successfully alter their infants' sleep patterns, and they also showed less stress and more confidence in their parenting skills compared to "untreated parents." Although the infants were not considered temperamentally difficult, the techniques described by Wolfson et al. (1992) may have some utility for this group as well. Parental behaviors that promote independence in their child may also be beneficial to mother–infant bonding and attachment. Parents who are less stressed, less tired, and more confident may be more responsive to their infants during waking hours, when attachment and bonding during feeding and other times are enhanced. These factors should be considered when clinicians are consulted by parents with "temperamentally difficult" children or children with sleep-related difficulties. Further preventive measures may improve attachment and bonding in parent–child relationships.

Parent-Mediated Treatment for Preschool Children with ADHD. Pisterman et al. (1989) adapted techniques from Barkley and Forehand–

McMahon in their treatment research. A 12-week parent training program for families with 3- to 6-year-old children with ADHD was highly effective for increasing child compliance but did not decrease the child's inattention (Pisterman et al., 1989). Using didactic instruction, modeling, rehearsal, and role playing, parents were taught how to attend to appropriate behaviors and to ignore negative behaviors, how to give appropriate commands, and how to use time-out.

Parents improved their management skills, and the style of parent–child interaction also improved following treatment. Parents were more consistent in rewarding their children for compliance and were able to decrease the number of beta (i.e., vague and unclear) commands given to their children. Pisterman et al. (1989) caution that nontargeted behaviors do not improve, so issues related to generalization need further consideration. However, short-term maintenance was assessed, and the effectiveness of treatment was shown at a 3-month follow-up.

Access to Parent Training

Historically, interventions for parents and families have not been typically available through school systems that provide exceptional educational services to young children. However, early childhood legislation provides for such services and mandates that family intervention components must be included for handicapped infants and toddlers (Public Law 99-457). The extent to which a young child with ADHD has exceptional educational needs is probably related to the presence of other coexisting developmental delays (e.g., speech–language, cognitive, and/or psychomotor) that determine the eligibility for special education services, including family support and parent training through the schools. Provisions under Section 504 of the Rehabilitation Act may also apply to young children identified as ADHD; however, this avenue of accessing family intervention services for young children is relatively untested.

In instances where no other developmental delays can be documented, family intervention services can be obtained at local universities, medical colleges, hospital settings, or mental health facilities. Family interventions can be administered in parent groups, where stress reduction techniques are introduced, specific problems are discussed (e.g., toilet training and noncompliance), and management options are generated. However, Barkley (1989) suggests that families also need individual sessions to discuss their unique problems and issues. Family services are essential to reducing early and later adjustment problems; hence, they should be an integral part of intervention plans for this age group.

Family Therapy

Campbell (1990b) suggests that therapists incorporate other therapeutic approaches to strengthen parent–child relations and to address family interaction patterns that influence child behaviors. Although Campbell advocates the use of operant behavioral conditioning for aggressive, noncompliant, and disruptive problems, other dynamic techniques that increase positive interactions between parents and children are essential components. Efforts should be made to increase parental awareness of behavioral management techniques and to help them develop ways of interacting positively despite their child's temperamental difficulties, noncompliance, and impulsivity. Warm, responsive, flexible, and consistent parental interaction styles should be systematically taught and encouraged.

Parent Support Groups

It is important to help parents establish a network of social support because it has been noted that parents, particularly mothers of children with ADHD, often feel isolated and cut off from relationships with other people (Barkley, 1990b). The sense of isolation is highly related to a mother's perceptions of her child's behavior problems and to subsequent success in parent training programs (Barkley, 1990b). Dunst and Trivette (1990) state that "a maxim and fundamental of successful social support is an adequate determination of a family's needs as a basis for identifying resources and mobilizing support from personal social network systems" (p. 327).

The largest national–international organization for parents of children with ADHD is known as CH.A.D.D., Children and Adults with Attention-Deficit Disorders (Fowler, 1992). CH.A.D.D. was founded as a political action group (Barkley, 1990b) with the intent to provide "family support and advocacy, public and professional education, and encouragement of scientific and educational research" (Fowler, 1992, p. xi). CH.A.D.D. has more than 350 chapters around the United States, with international chapters established in a number of countries.

CH.A.D.D. generally holds local meetings for parents and professionals on a monthly basis. Meetings typically provide parents with current research about ADHD and effective interventions for various problems (e.g., home or school noncompliance, effects of medication on academic and behavioral outcomes, family and marital stress from coping with ADHD, etc.); information about resources and other services available in the community; and an opportunity for networking with parents who are experiencing similar problems. This support helps parents recognize and accept their child's problems and develop effective advocacy and management techniques for coping with ADHD.

Support groups may also be used to organize day-care "pools" or shared babysitting arrangements through which mothers can get some free time and can interact with other parents who face similar challenges. This is particularly helpful for single parents who may not have another adult to share the responsibility of raising a child with ADHD. The need for support systems outside the home should not be overlooked when designing intervention programs for parents of children with ADHD. Having a support system often makes a great difference in a parent's ability to cope with the many problems inherent in raising a child with ADHD (personal communication from a parent of a preschool child with ADHD).

PREVENTION OF AND INTERVENTION IN DISRUPTIVE, EXTERNALIZED DISORDERS OF CHILDHOOD

In an effort to prevent the development of serious antisocial behavioral problems in middle childhood and adolescence, Tremblay, Pagani-Kurtz, Masse, Vitara, and Pihl (1995) developed a prevention program for kindergarten boys identified as disruptive. Although their techniques were not specifically developed for children with ADHD, the interventions may be considered when coexisting disruptive problems are present.

The prevention program included two major intervention foci—the parent and the child. Parent training was provided to families based on the Oregon Social Learning Center model developed by Patterson and associates. Parents were taught to monitor their child's behavior, to reinforce prosocial behavior, to give appropriate commands, to manage crisis situations, and to transfer these techniques to new problem situations (Tremblay et al., 1995). The mean number of sessions was 17.4, with a maximum number of 46 sessions. Children were given social skills training over a 2-year period. During year 1, children received nine sessions of prosocial-skills training. Disruptive children were trained with other "prosocial" children in small groups of four to seven, with three to four prosocial peers to each at-risk child. During year 2, children were taught how to solve problems and to use self-control in conflict situations. Sessions were initiated when the boys were 7 years of age and continued until they were 9 years old.

The intervention program appeared to differentially affect the boys depending on a number of factors, including the child's developmental stage and age, the domain under study, and the data source (Tremblay et al., 1995). The program was effective in improving global school adjustment during elementary age, although not through adolescence; in increasing the probability of a child's staying in age-appropriate class placement; and in decreasing delinquent behaviors in boys from 10 to 15 years of age. Extensive efforts to improve parenting practices and to increase social skills in young children did appear to have a positive effect on later adjustment.

The extent to which prevention techniques can be useful for boys with both ADHD and disruptive behaviors warrants investigation. It is important to note that the Tremblay et al. study was a long-term, 2-year treatment program; such a time span may be needed to prevent serious disruptive disorders. It is possible that research results that show little or no gains using similar interventions may be a function of the length of the treatment. Too often we look for short-term fixes for chronic, lifelong disorders and are disappointed when we do not produce a significant impact on the child's problems following treatment. Also, the program included both a parent and a child component, a combination that appears necessary for preventing severe disruptive disorders in later childhood. It is imperative that we reassess our clinical and educational programs with these two things in mind—the length of treatment and the use of multimodal strategies.

BEHAVIORAL, ACADEMIC, AND SOCIAL INTERVENTIONS IN THE PRESCHOOL AND CHILDCARE SETTING

As the young child enters preschool, kindergarten, or day care, problems associated with ADHD are noticeable and begin to interfere with early school adjustment. It is not uncommon for children with severe symptoms of ADHD, particularly high activity, impulsivity, and aggression, to be "kicked out" of preschool (Barkley, 1990b). In one instance, a mother of a preschool child seen in our university clinic came for an evaluation of her young daughter. This angelic-looking little 4½-year-old had already been asked to leave three successive day-care centers and was having significant behavioral problems in her present kindergarten classroom. Although the mother was concerned about her hyperactive and noncompliant child, she was not able to accept the possibility that the child had a serious problem. The mother "blamed" unresponsive, overly strict teachers for her daughter's problems. During our clinic evaluation, it was apparent that the young girl had severe ADHD, and we were able to help the mother see the "problematic" and "intrusive" behavioral problems during assessment and structured "free time" in our clinic. It was only after she observed her daughter in a highly structured, responsive setting that the mother was able to accept that her child had ADHD and that she was truly a management problem. The parent was able to see some of the problem behaviors reported by the teacher.

This parent–teacher dynamic can be played out in numerous ways. For example, a teacher may see a significant problem, whereas the parent does not; or the parent may be highly concerned about the possibility of ADHD, whereas the teacher views the child's problem as a function of poor parenting, a lack of follow-through at home, or a result of "bad boy" or "bad girl" behavior. Either way, differences between parent–teacher perceptions and understandings about how and why children with ADHD behave the way they do is a serious problem that generally needs to be addressed early in and maybe even throughout the child's academic career.

Gordon (1991) says that

> for an educational treatment program to fly, all aboard must first be knowledgeable about the nature of ADHD and accept its legitimacy as a *bona fide* disorder. No amount of educational techniques, tips for teachers, or lists of educational options can overcome the attitude that ADHD children are just "irresponsible," "lazy," "immature," or "spoiled" (p. 105).

Thus helping teachers to become knowledgeable about ADHD and to understand how this disorder affects the child's behavior in the class-room and in social situations serves as the foundation of educational interventions. This principle holds true throughout the developmental stages of this disorder, from preschool through college. Teachers need to understand the nature of ADHD in order to effectively help the child learn and succeed in the academic setting.

Training Teachers in the Principles of ADHD

Just as Goldstein and Goldstein (1990) suggest that parents need to understand how ADHD affects the child's behavior in the home, teachers need to understand how this disorder interferes with the child's school adjustment and social interactions. The type of information teachers obtain about ADHD is important. First, it is critical that teachers have access to the latest research concerning the biogenetic basis of ADHD. This has proven to be a good way to dispel the misconceptions that may exist in some educational circles. As a result of recent legislative changes specifying that children with ADHD are eligible for special education services through a variety of avenues (e.g., Section 504 of the Rehabilitation Act or Other Health Impaired section of the Individuals with Disabilities Educational Act; Teeter, 1991), there has been an effort to educate teachers about the nature of this disorder. However, "school officials have only a dim conception of the disorder and usually are unfamiliar with the degree of complexity and effort involved in helping these children" (Gordon, 1991, p. 106). This lack of understanding and training must be remedied in educational settings.

Second, school staff must become knowledgeable about the need for educational modifications for many young children with ADHD. Of utmost importance is the understanding that although the child has a biogenetically based disorder, he/she may function better in some situations than in others. Furthermore, there are specific "classroom and specific teacher factors that may minimize or escalate the child's problems" (Goldstein & Goldstein, 1990, p. 73). Educational interventions often focus on modifying the environment, altering teacher expectations, and changing input and output demands rather than solely focusing on changing the child. Teachers are often disappointed when confronted with the notion that their behaviors, not the child's, are the focus of interventions. Thus attitudes must also be addressed when teaching teachers about ADHD and when developing educational interventions. One of the most powerful ways to facilitate attitudinal change is to educate teachers about the biogenetic, neurodevelopmental basis of ADHD. Explaining genetic and functional brain anomalies related to ADHD helps teachers understand that ADHD is real and that the child may be handicapped by these variations.

Third, educational professionals need to understand that the "typical classroom is a terrible place for an ADHD child . . . after all, we are asking children who have profound problems attending, organizing, and controlling their actions to spend hours per day attending, organizing, and controlling their actions" (Gordon, 1991, p. 107). This is not to say that the school setting cannot be modified, but the point is important because it shows the need to do just that. Modifying classroom environments and utilizing management strategies to produce positive and successful experiences for young children with ADHD are the key to early educational interventions.

Fourth, teachers need to learn how to use empirically based educational interventions to reduce behavioral, academic, and psychosocial problems in the classroom. In an extensive review of the literature and an analysis of field-based research, the following techniques have been found to be generally effective: positive reinforcement; behavior reduction (mildly aversive reduction or reprimands); response cost; task stimulation (increase novelty of the task itself); and parent or family training (Chesapeake Institute, 1993).

Finally, teachers must become knowledgeable about the developmental course of ADHD and about other intervention options, including medication, parent training, social skills interventions, and so forth. Understanding the course and developmental outcome of this disorder will help teachers appreciate the complexity and severity of ADHD and the need for multimodal intervention strategies.

There are a number of ways to provide teacher training, including preservice course work, in-service workshops, and/or structured curriculum, to name just a few. See Chapter 6 for an example of a structured teacher training curriculum: the Kenosha ADD Program Trainer's Manual. Clinicians might also address the problem of teacher training through case consultation, where published articles, books, and other written materials can be shared with individual teachers. Problem solving for specific classroom-related behavioral problems can then be conducted in consultation with the clinician, the child's teacher, and the parent. The success of educational interventions is predicated on the need for knowledgeable classroom teachers who are well versed in the symptoms, etiology, developmental course, and treatment options for ADHD.

School-based intervention strategies and techniques may also prove helpful for ADHD children in preschool and kindergarten classrooms. Such interventions address behavioral difficulties in the classroom and present techniques for promoting social interaction and strategies for handling cognitive and language-related difficulties.

Classroom Management Techniques

Many preschool children with ADHD are placed in day-care or kindergarten programs with teachers who find it difficult to control extreme levels of disruption, aggression, and noncompliance (Barkley, 1990b). When children begin to show significant problems, therapeutic preschool programs are recommended, although very little is known about the potential effectiveness of such environments (Campbell, 1990b). So in many ways, the need for effective strategies and appropriate preschool environments for ADHD children outweighs the availability of published research demonstration projects (projects designed to reflect the best therapeutic practices available) telling us exactly what to do for this age group.

Although few studies have been conducted on classroom management for ADHD children in this age group, several model projects for preschool children with behavior disorders suggest that interventions with this group are not entirely effective. Anderson, Long, Leathers, Denny, and Hilliard (1981) reported some limited success with a program for children between the ages of 3 and 6 years. Children were placed in a half-day therapeutic setting and a half-day nursery school setting, and services included academic and social skill development for the child, combined with training and family support for parents. Improvement was more frequently reported in those children described as anxious and withdrawn, whereas children having problems with aggression did not significantly improve (Campbell, 1990b).

In a more extensive program, Cohen, Bradley, and Kolers (1987) focused on improving language and cognitive development, social adjustment, and parent–child interactions, and decreasing disruptive and aggressive behaviors. Children between the ages of 3 and 6 years with developmental delays showed the most significant gains compared to children with behavior disorders. These intensive interventions did not produce improvements on teacher ratings for social competence, aggressive, or disruptive behavior, but parents did report positive changes in their children with behavioral disorders. However, it was not evident that the program provided specific techniques to help parents reduce disruptive/noncompliant behaviors, nor was it clear how teachers addressed these problems (Campbell, 1990b). A paucity of research suggests the need for more powerful and effective interventions for children with significant behavioral and social interaction problems in the classroom.

University of Massachusetts Medical Center (UMMC) Prevention/Treatment Program for Kindergarten Students with ADHD

A preschool project at the University of Massachusetts Medical Center (UMMC) was developed to study the school environments of young children with ADHD or other oppositional and behavioral difficulties. This project is ongoing and evaluates state-of-the-art behavioral and educational techniques. Although there are no published data on effectiveness to date, there is reason to be optimistic given initial unpublished findings (Shelton, 1996, personal communication). Staff at the UMMC utilized some of the techniques developed at University of California–Irvine Child Development Center (UCI-CDC) under the direction of James Swanson. See Chapter 6 for a description of the UCI-CDC project.

The University of Massachusetts program was developed to meet the educational needs of kindergarten children at risk for ADHD or oppositional behaviors (Chesapeake Institute, 1993). The UMMC program employs techniques developed in the Paraprofessional Model of the UCI-CDC project, in which educational interventions are delivered in the regular classroom by a specially trained teacher's aide.

Three factors were considered in the development of the UMMC program: (1) empirically based educational needs of children with ADHD and effective interventions; (2) data from the UCI-CDC program; and (3) the specific needs and strengths of the young kindergarten child (Shelton, 1992). The program provides strategies for behavioral interventions, social skills training, and academic curriculum.

Behavioral Interventions. This component of the UMMC program includes techniques for providing frequent and immediate reinforcement using explicit and consistent feedback (Shelton, 1992). Positive behaviors, including attending and complying, are encouraged and maintained using a "rich system of feedback"; response cost mechanisms are employed to reduce undesired behaviors. A highly reinforcing environment is necessary, in which praise and verbal reinforcers are a keystone. The child receives at least 10 "big deal" stickers per day for attending, cooperating, or showing a good attitude. Reinforcers are given at a 2:1 ratio to negatives, and group contingencies are awarded for good behavior. Competition is minimized, and children are encouraged to work together to achieve positive results.

Verbal reinforcers or feedback are given every 10 minutes when a prerecorded tone sounds (Shelton, 1992). Teachers comment on good behavior (e.g., "I like the way Jennifer is paying attention") and go out of their way to "catch the child being good." Other techniques are incorporated into the management program, including (1) proximity control, in which the "problem child" sits close to the teacher; (2) private reminders—the teacher whispers to the child (e.g., "Nice job listening"); (3) preventing negative behaviors before they occur, such as giving a pat or rub on the back to calm the child down before he/she misbehaves (Shelton, 1992).

Response cost techniques are utilized because positive comments and rewards are not usually enough to reduce oppositional behaviors. Noncompliance, disruption, and aggression are specifically targeted in the following way. Teachers or aides immediately address the problem behavior, and behaviors are charted every 30 minutes. Three color codes are used to track the child's behavior, with feedback periods followed by administering consequences (e.g., activity rewards). Time-out procedures are employed but are reserved for repeated noncompliance or aggression. "Doing tasks" are another strategy to help reduce negative behaviors. When a child gets a yellow (initial noncompliance) or blue (repeated noncompliance) card for a rule infraction, the teacher or aide tells the child to do a specified number of prescribed tasks. Desks are set aside for these writing activities. The child returns to the group and can then start earning positive feedback again depending upon completion of the classroom assignment. This technique serves to stop the negative behavior, allows the child to cool down, and keeps behaviors from escalating. Parents also receive daily notes describing their child's progress in school.

Social Skills Training. The social-skills component of the UMMC program includes strategies developed by McGinnis and Goldstein (1990). Skills are taught and practiced in the natural classroom setting to increase the potential for maintenance and generalization (Shelton, 1992). Role play, modeling, and problem solving are used to help children stop and think before they act, to select an appropriate behavior, and to demonstrate the appropriate behavior in social situations.

Reinforcement of "trained" skills occurs in the classroom during normal play and work activities. Specific goals of the skill training are reinforced by all professionals in the classroom. Parents are also informed of the targeted social skills so that reinforcement can occur in the home as well.

Academic Curriculum. The development of preacademic and readiness skills (e.g., time, size, perspective taking, etc.) vary across children; therefore, the curriculum is highly individualized (Shelton, 1992). Children are taught to use problem-solving strategies, such as stopping, reading directions, and checking and evaluating work products. Small group and one-to-one instruction are available, although group activities are gradually increased to help the child prepare for the academic demands of first grade. Preliminary data suggest that the classroom segment of the program is effective (Fowler, 1992). The extent to which other strategies, including social skills training and academic curriculum, are effective is presently under study.

A few other educational and classroom techniques have been recommended for this age group. Home–school notes have been utilized with success, and classroom modifications may prove helpful in reducing problems in the school setting.

Home–School Notes

McCain and Kelly (1993) found that daily home–school notes effectively reduced problems with inattention, disruptiveness, and activity levels in a 5-year-old child with ADHD. Teachers evaluated the child's behaviors every day, and parents delivered consequences for positive or negative classroom behavior. This technique did improve attentiveness, behavior, and activity levels in the classroom.

Other general classroom modifications may prove successful for preschool/kindergarten children. The following suggestions are proposed as "promising practices."

"Promising Practices"

Although these recommendations have not been systematically re-searched, DuPaul and Stoner (1994) suggest the following classroom modifications for preschool settings. First, change the physical space of the classroom to reflect the activities that will be carried out in each area. Use bookshelves or other furniture barriers to separate play and work space. Tables for preacademic structured activities should be positioned away from highly distracting areas (e.g., bulletin boards, water/paint locations).

Second, introduce and complete activities in a step-by-step fashion. Take out and put away materials for activities one at a time (e.g., papers, crayons, scissors, then the glue) to reduce distractors and potential disruptions. Place children with ADHD in close proximity to the teacher, and do not place seats too close together.

Third, analyze daily activities and transition times. Scheduling changes are an easy way to reduce potential problem behaviors (e.g., two short circle sessions rather than one long session). Reducing the amount of time between activities may also be helpful. Use transition cues (e.g., lights, bells, songs, etc.) to signal that it is time to move to something else. Be flexible when considering whether everyone has to line up. Try to find the best time of day for sitting, and rearrange activities to best fit the child's internal controls.

Fourth, vary the curriculum, utilizing interesting, fun, and creative activities (e.g., puppets). Fifth, give directions clearly, individually, and simply. Group directions may not work, and indirect commands should be avoided (e.g., "Jeff, what are you supposed to be doing now?"). Use direct, single-step commands (e.g., "Jeff, please pick up the blocks"). Have the child repeat the directions. Finally, a low child-to-adult ratio is preferable. Volunteers (e.g., parents, grandparents, college students) can be useful for providing individualized help to children with ADHD during transition times, work activities, and circle sessions. This allows for more consistent follow-through for classroom-based interventions.

Social skills problems are common in children with ADHD or oppositional defiance. Finding effective intervention approaches for these problems is difficult because skills don't always transfer from training sessions to natural classroom and play settings. With this in mind, the following suggestions may be helpful as part of a comprehensive inter-vention plan for this age group.

Social Interaction and Play Group Techniques

Social skills training for children in kindergarten may be necessary because "learning to share, to take turns, to wait, to attend to the needs of others, not to grab toys or to hit—all important social behaviors that are learned in preschool peer groups—will be particularly difficult for the hyperactive child to master" (Campbell, 1990b, p. 86). Efforts should focus on helping the child develop skills for interacting with peers in nonaggressive ways and for increasing self-control in play situations.

Behavioral techniques provide numerous ways of accomplishing these treatment goals, and most available programs combine positive reinforcement, role playing, and response cost techniques to teach social skills to disruptive children (Walker & Hops, 1979; Hops, Walker, & Greenwood, 1987). Campbell (1990b) suggests that when behavioral approaches do produce gains in young children, these relatively unidirectional, mechanistic approaches do not produce changes that generalize to other settings or persist once treatment has ended. Thus reinforcement in natural settings such as the playground and the classroom is critical for maintaining changes over time.

There are several widely-used commercial programs available for building social skills in preschool and kindergarten children. McGinnis and Goldstein (1990) developed a systematic program to teach prosocial skills to children with withdrawal or aggressive tendencies; with normal development and "periodic deficits" in prosocial behavior; and with learning, communication, behavioral, and other handicaps (McGinnis & Goldstein, 1990). The program was designed for classroom teachers and other professionals and provides instructional methods for increasing prosocial skills in preschool and kindergarten children. Components of the program include modeling, role playing, performance feedback, and transfer training. The program provides a method for assessing social skills problems in young children and for selecting appropriate therapy and training goals.

McGinnis and Goldstein (1990) utilize a basic problem-solving model in which children are taught to answer the following questions: "(1) Why should I use the skill? (2) With whom should I use the skill? (3) What skill should I use? (4) Where should I use the skill? (5) When should I use the skill? (6) How should I use the skill? and (7) What should I do if the skill is unsuccessful?" (p. 110). Teachers and facilitators are provided with specific activities to enhance 40 different prosocial skills, including beginning social skills (e.g., listening, saying "thank you"); school-related skills (e.g., asking a question, following directions, not interrupting); friendship-making skills (e.g., joining in, waiting one's turn, sharing); skills in handling feelings (e.g., knowing one's feelings);

alternatives to aggression (e.g., dealing with teasing or anger); and handling stress (e.g., relaxing, being honest, accepting losing). The sessions are broken down into steps for each skill, and group activities and related activities are suggested for each session. Finally, management techniques for handling behavioral problems in the group sessions are also described.

To date, systematic research addressing the efficacy of this program has not been conducted. However, Campbell (1990b) indicates that efforts at developing preventive programs using problem solving and conflict resolution do produce positive effects on children with low SES, family disruption, social relations problems, and mild to moderate behavior problems. Improvements in social functioning and self-esteem were noted; however, long-term effects were questionable because of a lack of parental involvement. Further research is needed to determine how effective social skills programs are for young children with ADHD. Research with older children has shown that generalization and mainte-nance issues are a problem, so these factors should be specifically built into the program.

Speech–Language and Cognitive–Academic Interventions

Despite the fact that a number of young children with ADHD are delayed in cognitive and language development, there are few studies that investigate intervention in these areas. The limited research that has been done is ongoing and has not been published (see the preceding discussion on the UMMC program).

Almost one-third of children with significant speech–language de-lays develop problems with inattention and hyperactivity (Baker & Cantwell, 1987). In preschool children, subtle as well as more complex language problems may go unidentified because these delays may be manifested as behavioral or as self-control difficulties (Goldstein & Goldstein, 1990). Language development coincides with the child's increased ability to control him/herself, and speech becomes a substitute for actions. Thus early speech–language delays may be viewed as behavioral problems instead of communication problems. If parents and teachers misunderstand the connection between speech–language devel-opment and behavioral self-control and place unrealistic demands on the child, young children may respond with temper tantrums. "When parents and teachers inadvertently continue to place pressure upon the language-disordered child to conform behaviorally, a chronic pattern of behavioral, attention and arousal-level problems may develop" (Gold-stein & Goldstein, 1990, p. 165).

Deciding whether to focus on behavior or language delays can be tricky and may set a course of treatment that does not address the child's underlying problems (Goldstein & Goldstein, 1990). In situations where children with ADHD have coexisting language impairment, behavioral problems may improve with an appropriate language-based intervention program that has a parent training component. In instances where overarousal and attention problems are a result of speech–language delays, behaviors may improve when language-based interventions are initiated. The clinician must be careful to assess the presence of language delays, because these deficiencies often result in a variety of behavioral problems in young children.

There are no published studies that specifically address interventions for language–speech problems in preschool children with ADHD. The research that exists has been conducted on children with developmental delays and/or children from disadvantaged or at-risk populations. Generally, language-based intervention programs are rather global in nature and stress ecologically based approaches such as social communication skills (Bricker & Veltman, 1990). Generally speaking, narrowly focused interventions such as articulation therapy are not recommended "since cognitive, social, communicative, and motoric development are so interrelated in the behavioral repertoires of young children" (Bricker & Veltman, 1990). Other programs have been successful when parents have been taught to be "language teachers" to their young developmentally delayed children (Lombardino & Mangan, 1983) or have been taught how to increase imitation and attentional skills in their preschool children (Goodman, Cecil, & Barker, 1984).

Although there are no systematic studies for language-impaired preschool children with ADHD, it is important for the therapist or teacher to understand how the child's behavioral problems interfere with speech–language therapy. Behavior management strategies, high levels of reinforcement, and short therapy sessions are recommended. Ecologically based interventions for young children, wherein functional language skills are emphasized and social communication is the goal, may also prove useful. More specific, narrowly based interventions for language problems may be more appropriate for school-aged children or for those children with moderate to severe language deficits.

In a review of the effects of early intervention with disadvantaged and disabled preschool children, an interesting finding was reported (Farran, 1990). Young children display more aggressive behaviors in situations where academics are heavily emphasized than in other preschool settings (Farran, 1990). More research is needed to determine whether preschool classrooms should be heavily academically focused, particularly if these environments produce more behavioral and social problems in children with ADHD. Furthermore, clinicians should avoid making recommendations for individual children based on these results. Rate of cognitive and language development, social interaction skills, and self-control skills also need to be considered when deciding which type of academic setting is most appropriate for any given child. However, Gordon (1991) argues that the "typical classroom is a terrible place for an ADHD child" (p. 107), so flexibility and a willingness to modify the learning environment is imperative if the young child with ADHD is going to be successful academically.

PSYCHOPHARMACOLOGICAL INTERVENTIONS

Pharmacological interventions may be considered for young children with severe ADHD symptoms, particularly in cases where the child's social, academic, and family adjustment are significantly compromised. However, medication effects are more variable, and side effects can be more problematic in young children with ADHD.

Although medication may be part of an intervention regimen for older children, the decision to medicate younger children with ADHD is complex and controversial. There are a number of factors that contribute to this controversy. In general, younger children appear to have a less clear-cut positive response to methylphenidate (Ritalin) and often show more adverse side effects to medication (Goldstein & Goldstein, 1990). Younger children do not respond as consistently or dramatically to Ritalin as do older children (Conners, 1975), and irritability and solitary play tend to occur in preschool children on medication (Schleifer et al., 1975). The U.S. Food and Drug Administration has approved dextroamphetamine (Dexedrine) for children as young as 3 years of age, and it may be the treatment of choice for children up to age 6, although many physicians appear to prefer methylphenidate (Green, 1991). Dexedrine also has side effects that are of concern (Speltz, Varley, Peterson, & Beilke, 1988).

Another reason for the controversy surrounding medicating young children is the fact that the use of stimulants in preschool children is not well researched. In one of the few studies reported for this age group, Barkley (1988) investigated the effects of Ritalin on 27 children with ADHD between 2½ and 4 years of age. Effects of medication were positive for reducing the amount of off-task behaviors in these young children and for increasing their rate of compliance to maternal commands. Furthermore, maternal commands decreased even in children receiving low dosages of medication. Alessandri and Schramm (1991) also found that a

4-year-old diagnosed with ADHD was unable to sustain attention and control impulses in play activities prior to medication. Medication was effective for this child by significantly improving attention during play and group activities and by increasing sequential and symbolic play.

Although medication may be initiated for a small percentage of preschool children with ADHD, several cautionary factors appear relevant. Early studies with methylphenidate suggest that young children show fewer positive responses (Conners, 1975) and higher incidences of side effects such as irritability and solitary play (Schleifer et al., 1975). Others suggest that although some improvement was noted in that tantrums decreased, social isolation was a major concern for preschool children taking dextroamphetamine (Speltz et al., 1988) and methylphenidate (Schleifer et al., 1975). Campbell (1985) suggests that the hazards outweigh the benefits and that medication for preschool children with ADHD should be considered only in the rare cases in which parental support and systematic monitoring can be ensured. Campbell (1990b) further cautions that even with older children medication effects are most positive when combined with psychosocial and family intervention approaches.

In summary, the use of stimulant medication for young children has not been adequately researched. Although in some cases positive results have been reported, negative side effects appear likely. Clinicians considering medication as a treatment option for preschool children should consider multimodal interventions, including parent training (e.g., behavior management), family therapy (e.g., attachment and bonding), and school-based interventions (e.g., classroom management; social skills development; language and academic readiness), depending on the child's particular constellation and severity of symptoms.

In cases when medication is considered, the manner and degree to which ADHD symptoms are interfering with the child's overall psychosocial, academic, and behavioral adjustment must be weighed against the potential adverse side effects. Even in young children with severe and pervasive ADHD, medication may not always be as effective or predictable as with older children. Because careful medication monitoring is also necessary, the mental health and psychological resources of the child's parents also must be assessed. Family stress, marital discord, maternal depression, and alcohol or drug dependency may be factors that could interfere with proper medication monitoring; these factors may interfere with other psychosocial treatment options as well. Similar family issues should be considered when medicating older children; they often add to the complexity of treatment planning and implementation for children and adolescents with ADHD as well.

SUMMARY

Although not all children with ADHD will have difficulties across all of these areas, the following intervention goals and strategies have either been proven or promise to be effective with children in the toddler/preschool stage.

1. Improve parent–child relationships and family adjustment by teaching effective parenting skills and providing family therapy for parent–child attachment and bonding, family cohesion and problem solving, and stress management.
2. Improve adjustment in day-care and preschool settings using teacher training in the nature and characteristics of ADHD and in effective management techniques (e.g., use of reinforcement and response cost).
3. Improve social interaction skills by providing the child structured, supervised play and by teaching social interaction skills with reinforcement in natural settings (e.g., on the playground).
4. Decrease symptoms of ADHD in children with severe adjustment problems by utilizing medication after other psychosocial and behavioral therapies have been tried and by monitoring medication benefits and side effects.

By improving attachment and bonding, using behavioral management techniques in the home and at school, and providing academic and social readiness training, the negative effects of ADHD may be reduced. These interventions may also increase overall adjustment and decrease the development of later, more serious secondary problems (e.g., conduct disorders) and poor self esteem associated with school failure and social rejection.

5

Developmental Challenges of the Middle Childhood Stage: The Impact of ADHD on Normal Development

B$_y$ *the age of* 6 years, the child with ADHD differs noticeably from normal age peers on the primary symptoms of the disorder, including inattention, impulsivity, and restlessness (Barkley, 1989). Despite strong biological correlates, some of which are causal, Weiss and Hechtman (1993) indicate that behavioral patterns interact with and are influenced by the environment and other psychosocial factors. Moreover, if the primary problems of ADHD are not adequately addressed between the ages of 6 and 12 years, they may result in serious secondary problems (e.g., oppositional defiant or conduct disorders) that frequently persist into adolescence and adulthood. Aggression may develop during middle childhood, if it has not emerged earlier; and children with ADHD who develop antisocial conduct problems often display severe maladjustment later in life (Barkley, 1989). Thus coexisting aggressive and conduct-related problems must be addressed during this stage.

Investigating the impact of ADHD in middle childhood is important for several reasons. First, diagnosis of ADHD becomes more clear-cut because differences between normal and abnormal behaviors (e.g., activity level and self-regulation) are more easily discernible and less variable than in earlier stages. Second, the characteristics of the disorder can be detrimental to the major developmental challenges of this stage—schooling and peer relationships. Third, if the primary problems associated with ADHD are not resolved, a number of secondary problems can emerge—aggression, low self-esteem, academic failure, depression, and/or social isolation or rejection. Finally, there are a number of strategies that have proven effective for this age group and that, when used in combination, can reduce the negative impact of ADHD. This chapter presents a selective review of normal developmental challenges of middle childhood and describes how characteristics of ADHD interfere with development during this stage.

DEVELOPMENTAL CHALLENGES
OF MIDDLE CHILDHOOD

Development in the middle childhood stage is characterized by complexity and increased expectations for self-control, cooperation, compliance, and independence in the home, in the classroom, and in social situations. The following developmental domains are briefly reviewed: (1) parent–child relationships and attachment; (2) initiative and self-worth; (3) self-regulation and self-control; (4) cognitive development; (5) emotional development; (6) socialization and peer interactions; and (7) school adjustment. Although there is no doubt that other developmental changes occur during middle childhood, the factors that are reviewed here are adversely affected by the manner in which ADHD is manifested during this stage (Wenar, 1994).

It is important to note that, even though developmental domains will be discussed separately, adjustment across these domains is interdependent. For example, bonding/attachment patterns with parents and family members affect the child's social relationships with peers and other adults, achievement motivation and success in school, cognitive and language development, and overall psychosocial adjustment (i.e., self-esteem). In turn, the child's temperament, self-control, and cognitive and emotional development also affect attachment, social relationships, and school adjustment and achievement. The child's social relationships affect his/her self-esteem and psychological adjustment. Finally, the child's academic adjustment affects social relations with peers, teachers, and parents and his/her overall psychological well-being, including self-esteem. So these developmental domains should be viewed as interdependent, with child factors (e.g., temperament, attention, self-control, compliance) interacting with environmental factors (e.g., home environment, peer and teacher relationships, expectations, and demands) to affect the overall adjustment of the child.

Parent–Child Relationships and Attachment

Although the literature on how attachment affects relationships during the infancy/preschool stage is abundant, "the descriptive picture of attachment in middle childhood grows dim" (Wenar, 1994, p. 38). Discussions on this topic do suggest that the patterns established early in life serve as a foundation for the quality of parent–child interactions in later stages (Maccoby & Martin, 1983). If the child as a toddler views the parent as supportive and responsive even when more restrictions are placed on his/her actions, then he/she is more likely to seek harmonious relationships with parents during middle childhood (Ainsworth & Bell, 1974). The give and take of the parent–child relationship serves as the basis for the child's development of empathy, which underlies relationships with others (Sroufe & Cooper, 1988). This interaction reinforces the child's perceptions of the parent as the authority figure, which also influences the child's perceptions of other adults (e.g., teachers) as authority figures. These perceptions, as well as a desire to please and to be close to others, serve to increase the child's compliance to requests and his/her willingness to set aside desires when conflicts arise.

Although early attachment patterns are important in the overall social-emotional development of the child, Lamb, Thompson, Gardner, Charnov, and Connell (1985) report that the continuity and quality of care the child receives is also critical. It is interesting to note that parents seem to spend about one-third less time caring for their children between the ages of 5 and 12 years than they did during the preschool years (Hill & Stafford, 1980). At a time when the child is developing cognitive, social, and emotional competencies and when environmental demands are increasing (e.g., school and friendships), the job of parenting is far from complete (Papalia & Olds, 1992). Contemporary changes in family demographics, including divorce, marital discord, single parenthood, and the increasing number of working mothers may further reduce the amount of time parents and children spend together.

Parenting Styles

Parenting styles have a significant impact on the child's socialization patterns and on the emergence and further development of self-control and self-esteem. Differences in the ways in which parents approach child rearing can be classified according to degrees of warmth–hostility and restrictiveness–permissiveness (Sroufe & Cooper, 1988). In order to relate parenting styles to child adjustment, it is important to consider the complexity of the parent–child relationship and to avoid one-, two-, or even three-dimensional models to explain this interaction. With this in mind, Baumrind (1968, 1977) found that parents who were labeled "authoritative" were nurturing while being responsive to their child and were likely to be rational and democratic, rather than power-assertive, when parenting. High standards for maturity were communicated in conjunction with firm limits, the child's point of view was not ignored, and children were encouraged to express their opinions. "Authoritative" parents tended to have children who were high on initiative and who were able to meet the challenges they faced at 8 and 9 years of age (Sroufe & Cooper, 1988).

Other parenting styles have differing impact on the child's subsequent behavior. (1) Authoritarian parents, who are demanding and controlling, who place high value on conformity and obedience and limit child autonomy and self-control, and who are unresponsive or rejecting, tend to have children who are withdrawn and unhappy, anxious and insecure with peers, hostile when frustrated in preschool, and angry, defiant, and unmotivated in middle childhood. (2) Permissive parents, who are nurturant, communicative, and low on authority and control, tend to have children who are immature, who have trouble controlling impulses, who are less involved in classroom activities, and who are disobedient and explosive when confronted with rules. (3) Uninvolved parents, who are undemanding, indifferent, and rejecting, tend to have children who are noncompliant, demanding, and disruptive (Baumrind, 1968, 1971, 1977; Martin, 1981; Maccoby & Martin, 1983). Baumrind (1968, 1971, 1977) suggests that parenting styles have different effects on boys and girls. Furthermore, it is important to determine social, cultural, and ethnic variations in child-rearing practices and to consider how these factors affect parent behaviors.

Parent/Family Stress Factors

Despite consistency across time and siblings, parental and family stress factors do have an impact on the effectiveness of child-rearing practices (Papalia & Olds, 1992; Sroufe & Cooper, 1988). Parental and family stress have been associated with divorce, parental conflict, single parenthood, working mothers, and low socioeconomic status. Although these factors do not necessarily have a negative impact on parenting practices, they may place undue pressures on parents and may erode their confidence and ability to be responsive and effective when caring for their children.

Divorce affects children in different ways depending on their age. Children in middle childhood appear to react with various emotions, including masked anger, intense hostility toward one or the other parent, shame, sadness, resignation, depression, low self-esteem, poor school performance, and poor social relationships (LeFrancois, 1995). Research suggests that boys show more adverse effects of divorce, specifically in terms of noncompliance, hostility, and "demandingness" (Guidubaldi & Perry, 1985; Wallerstein & Kelly, 1980), whereas girls show more internalized problems, sadness, withdrawal, and self-criticism (Hetherington, Cox, & Cox, 1982). Although both sexes may show declines in school achievement, boys tend to be treated with less nurturance by mothers and teachers, and their externalized behaviors may be more difficult to empathize with and more difficult to manage. Although school performance may improve, long-lasting feelings of sadness and unhappiness over the divorce seem to persist over time (Wallerstein, 1985).

It may not be divorce per se that produces these negative effects in children; it may be the level of parental discord associated with the breakup and the inconsistent discipline and parenting that affect the child's adjustment to the change in the family's status. When divorcing parents maintain regular visitations and fathers maintain an active role in their children's lives, improved long-term outcomes have been reported, especially for sons (Hetherington, Cox, & Cox, 1982). With adequate support from extended family and friends, professional advise, and/or family therapy, the custodial parent may further reduce some of the negative effects of divorce, particularly as it relates to parenting and child-rearing practices.

Maternal Employment and Childcare Issues

For a variety of economic and personal reasons, there are more mothers working now than in the past 30 years (Berk, 1989). The effects of maternal employment on child development depend on numerous issues, including the child's age and gender and the economic status of the family. Working mothers tend to report higher levels of satisfaction, self-esteem, self-worth, and less ambivalence about their child's independence, and their children also seem to show positive benefits, including better social and emotional adjustment (Berk, 1989). Other factors appear related to these positive outcomes. (1) Working mothers may schedule more special time with their children. (2) Working mothers may be more consistent with rules and parenting. (3) Children may take on more responsibilities at an earlier age, which may be related to improved self-esteem. (4) Children may be exposed to fewer sex-typed roles (e.g., boys help with dishes) and activities (Berk, 1989).

Some cautionary notes are important when investigating the effects of maternal employment on child development. First, if work places undue demands on the mother's time and energy, she may not be able to adequately monitor her child. This seems particularly important for boys. Working mothers tend to view their sons as more demanding, noncompliant, and active than nonworking mothers (Alvarez, 1985). It may be that working mothers are not able to spend the amount of time needed to adequately socialize their sons in the formative years. The support of the father in these situations is a critical factor. However, even when fathers participate highly, mothers still carry the overwhelming burden of running the household and of parenting children (Baruch & Barnett, 1986).

Access to adequate childcare further complicates the issue of parenting for working mothers. The high number of latchkey children increases the likelihood that adult supervision after school is less than optimal. A lack of adult supervision has been related to antisocial behaviors, to higher susceptibility to peer pressure to engage in antisocial activities, to ineffective social skills, to lower self-esteem, and to poorer school performance in some children (Berk, 1989). However, when parents do provide supervision in absentia (e.g., through telephone calls or by leaving notes at home) and when the time the child spends alone is structured, these negative effects can be reduced (Steinberg, 1988).

The Resilient Child

Over the years, a number of researchers have observed that children react to stressful experiences (e.g., divorce, abuse, neglect, poverty) in different ways (Papalia & Olds, 1992). Resilient children appear to flourish in spite of their circumstances or experiences—they perform and develop into productive adults and lead interesting, full lives. Resilience generally refers to children who despite adversities and risk for significant psychopathology (1) avoid negative outcomes, achieve, and become successful adolescents and adults; (2) are competent even in high-stress situations; or (3) recover from various traumas (Mash & Dozois, 1996). Children at risk include those with temperamental difficulties or early conduct disorders, or those who live in extremely negative environmental conditions (e.g., severe poverty or abuse). These children are considered to be "vulnerable" and susceptible to negative developmental outcomes. Rutter (1985) explains that genetic and temperamental factors place the child in a vulnerable position and when these factors interact with high-risk environments, negative outcomes are likely.

"Rather than a direct causal pathway leading to a particular outcome, resilience involves ongoing interactions between a series of protective and/or vulnerability factors within the child and his or her surroundings and particular risk factors" (Mash & Dozois, 1996, p. 19). "Protective factors" may help to explain how some children are able to withstand experiences that typically produce problems or disorders in other children. Protective factors include the child's personality, family, and learning experiences, the number of risk factors the child has been exposed to, and compensatory experiences the child may have enjoyed (Rutter, 1984). Rutter (1987) thinks of protective factors as processes rather than absolutes, which serve either as protective or vulnerability factors depending on the context in which they occur (e.g., placement in a foster home because of an abusive home life).

Rutter (1979, 1984) describes how protective factors contribute to resiliency. First, resilient children tend to be positive, friendly, sensitive, and able to cope. High self-efficacy and self-esteem are generally present, and intelligence levels also play a role—academically capable children may be more resilient and successful in the long run. Second, family factors, including close, supportive, and loving relationships with parents, are related to resiliency. If these relationships do not exist with a parent, then resilient children tend to be close to another adult who provides care, trust, and interest in the child's activities. Third, resilient children have experiences solving problems, coping with frustration, and making the "best of it" in "spite of it all." In the face of challenges, resilient children figure out a way to cope and exert control over their stressful conditions and experiences.

Fourth, children are more able to overcome adversity when only one stressor is present; when two or more are present, psychopathology is more likely. So, in isolation, parental discord, economic adversity, a disturbed or antisocial parent, and/or divorce or adoption may be overcome, but when several of these factors are combined, the child is less likely to cope with the adversities. Finally, compensatory factors, such as academic excellence, athletic abilities, artistic or musical skills, or other successful experiences (e.g., supportive neighbors, family religious beliefs) also seem to "protect" the child from the effects of poor relationships and adverse experiences in early stages of life (Papalia & Olds, 1992; Wenar & Smith, 1992). Protective factors may prove helpful for the clinician when looking for ways to buffer children in adverse situations, dysfunctional families, and/or impoverished environments.

Initiative and Self-Worth

Wenar (1994) suggests that the developmental course of initiative involves the emergence of self-worth and self-love. Although children are not necessarily capable of expressing feelings of self-worth in middle childhood, they are aware of their own social acceptability and competence. So at this stage children tend to develop a sense of pride in themselves when they can do something or when others like them.

Furthermore, Wenar (1994) indicates that self-worth is also affected by the child's sense of his/her own physical abilities. When children perceive themselves as incompetent either socially, physically (in ability or attractiveness), and academically, they may not develop a sense that they are worthwhile.

Children tend to value themselves based in part in how others view them. During middle childhood, children are able to compare themselves to peers; they become more realistic in terms of their assessment of their own performance; and their self-assessments approximate teacher ratings, observations, and test scores (Berk, 1989). Self-evaluations are related to the child's everyday behavior and performance (Berk, 1989). Furthermore, high self-esteem in academic areas tends to influence the child's motivation, interest and persistence and curiosity in the face of challenging tasks (Harter, 1981), whereas children with high social self-esteem are viewed as "better liked" by peers (Harter, 1982).

Berk (1989) suggests that the following variables affect the child's development of high self-esteem: (1) child-rearing practices including high expectations, standards for behavior and performance, and warmth and support that set the stage for the child to make sensible choices, particularly when encouraged by parents, and (2) achievement motivation and attributional thinking that stresses effort and persistence. During the middle childhood stage, children can differentiate ability and effort, and, when successful in school, they develop "mastery-oriented attributions." Thus success is viewed as a function of the child's ability, which is a positive characteristic that can be counted on in other situations. Children come to expect to succeed, and when they do not, they are likely to believe that they did not work hard enough or that the task was too difficult. Subsequent tasks are approached with interest and increased effort, rather than with expectations of defeat and/or fear of failure. High self-esteem predicts success in school and is related to academic achievement, including reading (Markus & Nurius, 1984).

Finally, self-esteem in children is fairly stable over time. High self-esteem in middle childhood can be predicted from adjustment in preschool and from the quality and strength of attachment in infancy (Sroufe, Jacobvitz, Mangelsdorf, DeAngelo, & Ward, 1987). Children who develop positive regard for themselves during middle childhood typically are able to meet the challenges of adolescence and adulthood with more confidence; they have more faith in their own judgments; and, in general, they have positive approaches to life experiences. Thus efforts to establish high self-esteem in middle childhood are important for future self-appraisals and are related to success in school and the development of positive peer relationships.

Self-Regulation and Self-Control

During middle childhood the child begins to exert more self-control and self-regulation over his own behaviors, which reduces the necessity for constant parental supervision (Papalia & Olds, 1992). Wenar (1994) characterizes the period between 6 and 9 years of age as "the high point of self-control," when children are described as "conforming, practical, industrious, self-motivated, and self-controlled" (p. 46). There is a tendency for children to be more internal in their thinking and more adept at controlling momentary feelings and impulses during this stage.

Self-control reflects both the child's developing self-concept and the ability to match his/her behavior to fit the desires or demands of parents, teachers, and other adults. Maccoby (1984) describes the period of middle childhood as a transitional stage of *coregulation* in which the parent and the child share power. The child conforms to the wishes of others because of the developing awareness of what others will think if he/she misbehaves. In this stage, children begin to anticipate the consequences of their actions and to shape their actions accordingly. Children are less aggressive and selfish in their actions, and other negative tendencies (e.g., blaming, snatching, ridiculing) are also on the decline (Wenar, 1994).

During the middle childhood stage, parents influence children by setting standards that the child uses to monitor his/her own behaviors (Maccoby, 1984). Thus the process of self-regulation is established and influenced not only by the child's own central nervous system but also by his/her environment. The child becomes aware of society's expectations based on the standards set by his/her parents and controls his/her behavior to conform to these expectations in order to receive praise, affection, and positive regard from other people. If the child is ignored or does not receive positive feedback for appropriate self-control, or if parents do not set standards that are consistent with society's expectations, then trouble can ensue. The child may struggle with issues of compliance, may not incorporate a sense of what is "right," and may see no reason to control him/herself. In effect, the child sees no advantage in controlling his/her behaviors because there are no incentives to do so. The advantages of breaking the rules are viewed as more rewarding (e.g., "I get to do what I want," "Who cares what she [mom or teacher] thinks about it," "She can't make me do it").

Although the parent–child relationship affects this process, self-regulation also develops in conjunction with the child's increasing cognitive capabilities (e.g., anticipating consequences). Language development also facilitates this process, as children begin to use "inner talk" to control and guide their behavior (e.g., "I better not take that cookie,

Mom is really going to get mad at me"; or "If I hit Mark 'cause I'm mad at him, he might not play catch with me later"). Vygotsky (1986) theorized that language development undergoes stage-like changes that correspond to the child's development of self-control. In Stage 1 (up to age 3), social-external speech attempts to control the actions of others ("Give me that toy"); in Stage 2 (ages 3 to 7), egocentric speech bridges the gap between internal and external speech and serves to control the child's own behaviors; and in Stage 3 (age 7 and up), inner speech or self-talk begins to direct thinking and behaving and is the foundation for all mental functions (LeFrancois, 1995). Furthermore, language development is shaped by the child's culture and occurs through the child's interaction with important adults and competent peers. Vygotsky described the child's potential for development—*proximal zone of development*—as the "distance between the actual developmental level as determined by independent problem solving and the level of potential development as determined through problem solving under adult guidance or in collaboration with peers" (Vygotsky, 1978, p. 86).

Even though the child's biological capacities are influential, Vygotsky believed that interaction with the environment, context of the child's development, may be more important than the child's biological predispositions or vulnerabilities in terms of overall developmental capacity. In the instance of ADHD, this reciprocal approach to understanding child development means that we must consider the environmental opportunities and demands that are placed on the child, and that we cannot ignore the significance of the environment in determining how this disorder will ultimately affect the child. Furthermore, this theoretical orientation suggests the need both to consider environmental factors when designing intervention programs, and to modify the child's home and school environment rather than simply trying to "fix" or change the child.

Cognitive Development

Cognitive development during middle childhood is often described as a stage in which children try to make meaning out of their experiences, their world, and those around them. They are in the process of developing an understanding of symbols, and they use concrete principles of logic when dealing with these symbols. Major developmental changes occur in three areas: conservation, classification, and memory abilities. These cognitive changes are intricately linked together, occurring as language and communication skills increase.

Reasoning and mental operations during this stage are linked to conservation and reversibility. According to Sroufe and Cooper (1988), conservation refers to the notion that properties of objects do not change despite transformations in size or shape, whereas reversibility refers to the notion that substances maintain their quantity when changes in size or shape are reversed (i.e., the quantity of liquid remains the same when poured from a short, wide flask into a tall, slender flask and back again). Children develop an understanding that appearances may be misleading as they acquire a sense of conservation of liquids, length, volume, area, and mass. Cognitive maturation is marked by the child's development of a sense of permanence and stability of physical aspects of the world.

Classification is also central to cognitive development during middle childhood and refers to a child's ability to group objects, to develop a system of categories, and to discern similarities and differences between objects in order to classify or categorize. Classification allows children to "impose structure on the many things around them," and these skills "provide part of the basis for logical thinking" (Sroufe & Cooper, 1988, p. 423). Although children in middle childhood are able to learn hierarchical classification systems, they do not typically appear to understand abstract, logical structures of these schemes until adolescence. Thus classification is a means by which the child organizes information and solves problems. The last phase of this cognitive process occurs when the child understands the logic behind the classification hierarchies. The period from middle childhood into adolescence marks the change from concrete to abstract thinking for some but not all children.

Language

Vocabulary development is rapid during middle childhood. Children use words more precisely to organize and classify objects, to connect verbal labels to underlying concepts, to explain meanings of words, and to interpret words on more than one level (e.g., to understand figures of speech and humor; Berk, 1989). Linguistic subtleties are more readily understood at this age as grammatical (word usage) and semantic (word meanings) complexity increases.

Language becomes more pragmatic during this stage, as children expand their ability to receive and send messages in social situations. Listening skills and the ability to recognize whether a received message is clear are necessary for effective communication. Children begin to acquire the necessary language skills to become adept conversationalists. Language becomes a mechanism for social interchange, and social acceptability can be influenced by the child's use of appropriate language (e.g., "please," "thank you," "hello"; Berk, 1989). In this stage children understand social expectations and begin to express this understanding through speech.

Language development also facilitates increased self-control. As the child develops more elaborate language systems, control of behaviors, thoughts, and feelings become more likely. In effect, the child uses language to express intentions, thoughts, and feelings, whereas at younger ages he/she acted on these feelings because there were few options for expressing them. So, rather than snatch the toy away, the child can ask for the toy; and rather than hitting a playmate, the child can say, "Leave me alone." Thus language influences a number of developmental domains, including cognitive (e.g., thinking, abstraction), social (e.g., communication), and inhibitory (e.g., self-control) functions.

Memory

Middle childhood is marked by increased complexity in cognitive processes. LeFrancois (1995) describes children as "consumers and processors of information—as little organisms that shed their ignorance as they build up a store of memories" (p. 409). During this stage, children become aware of themselves as learners and begin to see themselves as "knowers" who are capable of using and evaluating strategies to develop knowledge. Metacognition, or "knowing about knowing," becomes important in this process. Children also become aware that by using strategies they can remember more information.

Memory capacity increases with age, and after the age of 6 years, children use relatively sophisticated strategies, including organization, elaboration, and external aids to remember events and information (Papalia & Olds, 1992). Organizing or arranging information in terms of relationships are techniques for remembering that do not naturally occur in young children. However, by the age of 10 or 11 years, children can be taught to organize; or they may imitate organizational strategies when instructed to remember more information (Chance & Fischman, 1987).

Elaboration strategies, such as attaching a picture or story to new information in an effort to form associations between new material and what is already known, helps children remember information. Older children utilize these techniques more readily than younger children, and when they create their own elaborations instead of using those made up by someone else, they are able to remember more information (Papalia & Olds, 1992). Children use more spontaneous elaborations by the age of 12 (Justice, 1985), and competency in strategy development continues to grow into adulthood (Berk, 1989).

Using rehearsal or repetition as a means to remember also does not occur in younger children (Berk, 1989). By about the age of 10 years, children begin to use rehearsal strategies to aid in remembering. With time, children become more sophisticated in the type of rehearsal they use. For example, when asked to use rehearsal strategies to remember a list of words, 8-year-olds simply repeat words in isolation, whereas 12-year-olds repeat words in a string, thereby linking together the words to be remembered (see Berk, 1989). Rehearsal is also facilitated by the way in which information is organized. For example, by grouping things that go together, children can remember more. Once children begin to use grouping strategies, they start to notice associations, they think about these connections, and they begin to consciously utilize mature ways of associating items or information (Bjorklund & Jacobs, 1985). Memory is facilitated when information is placed within a meaningful context. Other external aids also help memory functions, and children begin to use things such as lists, notes, or other reminders during middle childhood (Papalia & Olds, 1992).

Context for Memory. Educated children tend to remember more information than uneducated children do, particularly when strategies are required (Berk, 1989). Schooling provides numerous opportunities and activities to promote deliberate memorization of information. This practice tends to increase the development of memory strategies, and the environmental context, the classroom, is important in this process. Cultural and environmental conditions can either help or impede the development of memory strategies.

Knowledge Base. Another important developmental issue is the extent to which memory performance is related to the rapidly growing knowledge base of the school-age child. A number of theorists believe that "cognitive development is largely a matter of acquisition of domain-specific knowledge—knowledge of specific content areas that subsequently renders new, related information more familiar and meaningful and therefore easier to store and retrieve" (Berk, 1989, p. 296). As the child becomes more knowledgeable in a specific area, strategy use becomes more efficient. In a series of studies, Chi (1978, 1982) found that a child who is more knowledgeable about specific subject areas may have superior memory abilities in those areas than adults do.

Just as differences in the quantity of information or knowledge in a domain appear to be important, differences in structure of knowledge may also help explain age-related changes in memory development (Chi & Koeske, 1983). That is, expert and novice learners may actually differ in the ways they connect concepts and information together, and these differences may make the memory process more efficient. Furthermore, children use previously acquired information to access and clarify the meaning of new information, such that successful learners are more adept at utilizing available knowledge to learn and at making sense of new information than are less successful learners (Bransford, Stein, Shelton, & Owings, 1981). When children do not ask themselves how previously learned information contributes meaning and significance to new material, the learning process is seriously compromised.

Attention

Attentional controls undergo rapid development during middle childhood. By the age of 8 or 9 years, children become aware that they need to employ attentional strategies when studying information. Attentional processes determine the sources of information that the child considers when confronted with a specific task or a problem (Berk, 1989). In this stage, attention becomes more controlled and sustained, as well as planned. Children develop more control and adapt attentional processes, depending upon environmental demands or in response to their own learning.

Older children use more effort to attend to information when irrelevant or distracting stimuli are present (Higgins & Turnure, 1984). Older children become more attentive and are in effect more successful at focusing attention under these conditions. Focused attention affects the amount of incidental learning a child demonstrates. Incidental learning increases until about the age of 11, when there is a decline— apparently with age children become more adept at ignoring irrelevant information (Maccoby & Hagen, 1965; Hagen & Stanovich, 1977). This may help explain how some children with ADHD appear to learn in early grades, but when later learning requires sustained and directed attention, academic delays become more apparent.

The ability to shift attention depending upon task demands increases with age. Thus middle childhood is characterized by greater attentional adaptability, flexibility, and efficiency (Berk, 1989). These attentional processes are related to the complexity of the task in such a way that older children can make decisions about what they already know and what they need to spend more time studying. Proficient learners are better at this assessment than are less proficient learners (Masur, McIntyre, & Flavell, 1973). In summary, attentional processes become more deliberate, focused, planned, flexible, and adaptive during middle childhood.

Emotional Development

Developmental psychologists acknowledge that emotions influence various psychological processes, including learning, cognition, social adjustment, and physical well-being, in children (Berk, 1992; Mash & Barkley, 1989, 1996; Lewis & Miller, 1990). Fear, anxiety, depression, and anger are emotions that affect the child's overall adjustment and sense of well-being. These emotions are particularly relevant to the discussion of ADHD because when undercontrolled or extreme they may be considered as comorbid disorders requiring intervention.

Anxiety

Anxiety usually signifies anticipation of the pain of some upcoming event and often serves to forewarn the individual to avoid the situation (Wenar, 1994). Normal fears and anxieties in middle childhood include fear of harm and fear of failure. These fears are signals for the child to act in a certain manner to avoid the fearful event. For example, a child may avoid a bully on the playground to keep from getting beaten up, or a child might study to avoid failing a test in school. When fears become irrational or uncontrolled, the more serious problems can ensue.

Anxiety can have both a positive and a negative influence on development. Anxiety alerts the child to behave in socially acceptable ways, and serves to increase motivation to perform well. On the other hand, inappropriate or self-defeating fears distort the child's thoughts and actions and thus impede development. For example, school phobia—an unrealistic fear that often keeps children from attending school—may occur in children between the ages of 5 and 15 (Papalia & Olds, 1992). Although phobic children tend to be above average in intelligence and usually perform well in school, they may have unrealistic fears about their performance or they may be overly sensitive to social rejection (real or perceived) from teachers and peers.

Depression

For children in middle childhood, depression, like anxiety and anger, is a normal emotion and likely occurs in reaction to some stressful event, such as failure to accomplish a goal or the loss of a loved one through divorce or death (Wenar, 1994). Normal feelings of sadness are not the same thing as severe or chronic depression. However, the differences between depressive feelings and major depression in children appears to be one of degree: feelings of "dejection, discouragement, and loneliness are the central features of the depressive experience" (Wenar, 1994, p. 193).

Other emotions, such as shame and guilt, typically are related to injury to the child's sense of self (Berk, 1989). Shame is associated with self-criticism and low self-esteem, whereas guilt appears related to a sense of failure for not having "lived up" to some internalized standard (Wenar, 1994). Although shame first appears in the toddler stage, it becomes relatively stable and associated with depression in middle childhood. On the other hand, guilt is not considered a sufficiently stable emotion to play a role in depression until later stages of middle childhood.

Aggression

Aggression undergoes major changes from toddlerhood to middle childhood because older children are more able to control the "attack" reaction (Wenar, 1994). Aggression becomes more intentional, and the aspect of "getting even" can be characteristic of this stage. The manner in which aggression is expressed also expands with children's increased cognitive abilities, as they begin to tease, bully, swear, and quarrel and to use prejudice and cruelty to express angry feelings toward others (Wenar, 1994).

Children in this stage have the capacity to feel remorse for their angry reactions, and they begin to develop a conscience. The ability to take the perspective of others and the internalization of society's expectations help in this process. Children feel badly when they strike out, either physically or verbally, and they begin to exert appropriate control over their angry feelings. When children are not sensitive to the feelings of others, they may strike out and attack others with little remorse. Children without remorse can be dangerous; these children frequently have not bonded with or been adequately nurtured by significant adults early in life.

Situations that elicit anger are typically those things or events that are important to the child. Issues related to fairness (e.g., cheating); being "bossed around," lectured, ignored or neglected, or punished unfairly; and the child's own ineptness or inability to accomplish something are all common reasons for anger at this age (Wenar, 1994). Other situations in which the child's pride is at stake also tend to be potentially volatile. Children at this stage are generally more able to differentiate intentional from accidental injuries or provocations, but children with very low self-esteem may be more susceptible to acting on these "slights" than children with intact or healthy opinions of themselves. These dynamics play an important role in the development of more serious forms of aggression, such as conduct disorders.

There are a number of factors that affect the child's expression of angry feelings. Affectionate parents provide discipline, have high expectations and standards, and teach or model problem solving and reasoning, all of which help the child control angry feelings (Wenar, 1994). Adults can also help children channel aggression into socially acceptable avenues (e.g., sports, acting, or writing). Children who develop severe aggressive problems tend to have underlying feelings of "being unloved, the humiliating sense of insignificance, the self-loathing" (Wenar, 1994, p. 60).

Parents of aggressive children are often unskilled in effective techniques to control their child (Patterson, 1982). Unskilled parents often use punishment as a means of discipline for misbehavior and fail to reinforce and model prosocial behaviors for their child. Children develop coercive patterns in which aggression is employed as a means to control the behavior of others. Thus aggression alters the child's social environment; a short-term payoff occurs when the victim gives in to the child's demands. Furthermore, high rates (95th percentile) of coercion are stable over time, across settings and situations. Coercive and aggressive behavior patterns are associated with rejection, poor school performance, poor social skills, and a host of other problematic behaviors (e.g., truancy, school drop out, serious conduct disorders).

Although family interaction patterns no doubt form the basis of aggression in children, there are other factors that may contribute to a child's propensity for aggressive, violent behavior. Television viewing has been viewed as a possible causal link.

There is growing concern that violent themes or events portrayed in the media are associated with an increase in violent behaviors in youth. Early studies investigating the relationship between watching violence on TV and hostile, uncontrolled dispositions showed strong positive correlations (Berk, 1989). For example, 9-year-old children who watched a great deal of violence on TV were more likely to be rated as aggressive by 19 years of age (Lefkowitz, Eron, Walder, & Huesman, 1972). This relationship also predicted adult antisocial aggression (e.g., spousal abuse, criminal convictions, etc.) at age 30 (Huesmann, 1986). Furthermore, aggressive children prefer to watch violent TV shows, and these programs often teach children violent problem-solving techniques. Watching violence on TV also desensitizes the child to violence, and children begin to view the world as it is depicted on TV.

Although most researchers investigating the relationship between violence on TV and aggression in children conclude that there is a link between the two, the relationship is not a simple one. Singer (1982) suggests that it is not TV violence per se that stimulates aggression but that it may be that children who watch too much TV are deprived of social opportunities to develop skills that promote problem solving, conflict resolution, and other prosocial skills rather than aggression. That is, excessive TV watching may interfere with play activities where these social skills are developed and refined.

Similar concerns have been raised about violence in rock videos, video games, and films on videocassette (LeFrancois, 1995). Although there is little research on the effects of these media sources, critics suggest that these do have a negative influence on children because they are replete with violent themes. Although the debate over these influences will certainly be informed by controlled studies, parents are encouraged to monitor TV watching and to promote social and intellectual (e.g., reading, conversing, etc.) activities in their children, especially when aggressive tendencies are observed (Anderson, 1983).

Awareness, Expression, and Control of Feelings

Between the ages of 6 and 12 years, children become adept at regulating their emotional reactions to events and situations (Berk, 1989). Children 10 to 12 years of age are better able to control negative feelings and to separate their actions from their feelings than are 6- to 8-year-olds. Children of all ages do show some slippage (i.e., some emotions slip out or are not easily hidden), particularly when they are trying to control positive feelings. It may be that social rules are clear-cut for controlling negative emotions but more ambiguous for masking positive feelings (Shennum & Bugenthal, 1982).

Children become more aware of their feelings and of the rules for expressing them during middle childhood. Some psychologists believe this process is influenced by reinforcement and punishment, as well as by the child's desire to please others (Saarni, 1982). Awareness of and ability to control one's emotions develop in conjunction with cognitive and language development, perspective taking, and better muscle control over facial, vocal, and gestural expressions (Berk, 1989). Furthermore, the child's social experiences provide a context for learning the standards of emotional expression.

Socialization and Peer Interactions

In middle childhood, children adopt a sense of the *social self*; that is, the awareness they have of themselves is in part a function of their social group membership (Sroufe & Cooper, 1988). They describe themselves in terms of their affiliations with certain groups and their social context (e.g., "I'm in the fifth grade at Richards School, I play forward in the Bavarian Soccer Club, and I'm in the ski club"). Children also begin to make comparisons and to evaluate themselves depending on how they rank or compare to other kids in their peer group. For example, the 11-year-old described above might further comment on his performance on the soccer field when talking about himself (e.g., "I scored more goals than anyone in the club," or "I have the fastest downhill time for skiers in the U-12 group.").

The social self is not only tied to one's social affiliations but is also highly related to how the child judges his success or failure in these groups. In a competitive social context in which the child compares unfavorably to his peers, it is likely that self-evaluations will be harsh and self-esteem will be negatively affected. When children find a niche, when they compare favorably or are in less competitive settings, then self-esteem flourishes.

Perspective Taking

During middle childhood, children develop a sense of what others are thinking and feeling, and they begin to modify their actions in ways that take into consideration how other people feel. Perspective taking influences social relations, academic and cognitive achievement, and communication skills (Berk, 1989). The ability to consider the feelings and reactions of others and to share these feelings also forms the basis for empathy (LeFrancois, 1995). Empathy becomes a strong emotional bond between self and others whereby children curb their aggressive, mean tendencies so as not to hurt or harm others. When empathy is lacking, significant social maladjustment can occur.

Selman (1980) described four stages of social cognition that children pass through as they develop and express their understanding of how others feel. In stage 0 (the egocentric stage, 0 to 6 years), children are generally unaware of perspectives other than their own. They identify the feelings of others in terms of how they would feel in that particular situation. In stage 1 (the social-informational stage, 6 to 8 years), children become aware that others have perspectives that differ from their own, but they still refer to their own feelings when judging other peoples reactions. In stage 2 (self-reflective stage, 8 to 10 years), children know that two perspectives—their own and the other person's—exist, but they generally respond in terms of either one or the other, not both, perspectives. At stage 3 (the mutual stage, 10 to 12 years), children begin to make sense of both perspectives and can evaluate a situation by moving from one perspective to the other in a more objective manner. Finally, in stage 4 (the social and conventional stage, 12 to 15 years and older), adolescents begin to apply principles and ideologies when assessing their own perspective as well as those of others.

The ability to understand how others think and feel is an important cognitive variable in the development of effective interpersonal relationships (Berk, 1989). Although social problem solving, social acceptability, altruism, and effective interpersonal behaviors tend to be associated with good perspective taking, children may not always be able to "see" from or understand the perspectives of others who are different from themselves in obvious ways, such as in race or gender. So the social context becomes an important variable in the way in which children demonstrate their perspective taking awareness. Furthermore, there is not a simple relationship between perspective-taking and social behavior. For example, the 10-year-old who constantly and effectively annoys his sister may be quite adept at understanding exactly what bothers her, but he uses this knowledge to irritate rather than to get along with her. Temperament and personality factors also affect whether a child will act on his/her accurate perspective-taking skills; and in cases of extreme antisocial behavior, children generally do not feel remorse or guilt when harming or mistreating others (Berk, 1989).

Friendship Patterns

Friendship patterns change dramatically during the middle childhood stage and are directly related to the development of perspective taking (Papalia & Olds, 1992). In earlier stages, children make friends on the basis of proximity (e.g., "She's my friend 'cause she lives near me") or physical or material attractiveness (e.g., "She's my friend because she lets me play with all her Legos"), whereas children in middle childhood begin to develop friendships based on intimacy and affection, as well as their mutual interests (Hartup, 1989). Males and females differ on these dimensions, as females tend to develop fewer but more intimate friendships than males do (Selman & Selman, 1979). During middle childhood, friendships become an important means for sharing feelings and secrets and enables children to do things together, although jealousies and possessiveness may also occur.

Friendships provide a mechanism for the child to learn and practice problem-solving skills, inhibition of impulses, and working through conflicts in mutually agreeable ways. Children who are unpopular or who do not establish friendships during this stage may miss these important learning opportunities, in addition to missing the emotional support that comes along with friendships. Popular children tend to exhibit positive qualities such as physical attractiveness, cooperation, self-assurance, maturity, adaptability, dependability, humor, affection, and creativity, whereas unpopular children are often aggressive, silly, immature, anxious, withdrawn, unsure of themselves, unattractive, or cognitively delayed (Berk, 1989).

Unpopular children may come to believe that others are not going to like them and thus act in ways that do not promote friendships. Once a child attains low status among peers, he/she behaves in unpopular ways (e.g., with aggression or withdrawal) and elicits reactions from others that perpetuate that status (Dodge, Pettit, McClaskey, & Brown, 1986). Negative friendship experiences can be extremely painful for the child and the parent and often produce lasting emotional scars that affect on the child's sense of self-worth and self-esteem into adulthood.

Children in middle childhood begin to form relatively stable peer groups, and these groups begin to define who the child is and to exert influence on standards of acceptable behavior (Sroufe & Cooper, 1988). Group norms or rules of conduct are important during this stage and serve to ensure group harmony and cohesiveness (Streater & Chertkoo, 1976). Rigid adherence to rules is common at this age, and rewards (praise, food, toys) are often distributed on the basis of the child's performance abilities (who is the fastest, funniest, smartest, toughest) on whatever standard of behavior the group defines as important (sports, playground activities, schoolwork, "street smarts," etc.).

Group norms provide strong influences on how the child behaves, particularly in terms of gender-related behaviors. Group memberships in middle childhood are uniformly divided on the basis of gender, and males and females interact only in heavily prescribed ways. For example, males will tease a peer in order to discourage him from interacting with girls, and this teasing in effect defines the group boundaries of what is acceptable and what is not (Thorne, 1986). During middle childhood, children are able to make assessments that differ from the group norm, even though they feel pressure to conform and will consider the group norm in their decision making. Children at this age are able to express these differences in direct ways, and friendships become a context in which they learn how to develop arguments, to accept criticism, and to disagree (Berk, 1989).

Despite the concerns expressed in the media and by parents and teachers, children do tend to have moral standards that reflect those of their parents, and they behave in ways that are generally consistent with parental values (Hartup, 1983). So again the role of the parent/family comes into play as a factor in setting the stage for developing values and standards of conduct, although the peer group is also a major socialization factor in the child's life (Sroufe & Cooper, 1988).

School Adjustment

Erikson (1950) identified middle childhood as a time for resolving the conflict of "industry versus inferiority." Children resolve this conflict when they are productive and when they develop skills that are deemed important by parents and teachers. Children develop academic self-esteem when they are successful in the resolution of this conflict—when they are competent. By completing tasks, producing work, and comparing favorably to peers on these dimensions, children come to view themselves as competent (Papalia & Olds, 1992).

Self-efficacy, or the child's assessment of him/herself as a competent, capable learner, is related to success in school (LeFrancois, 1995). Children who view themselves as competent set high goals for themselves, and they persist during challenging tasks; those who do not view themselves positively on this dimension set lower goals and give up quickly when they begin to fail (Bandura, 1989). These self-perceptions appear to affect the use of strategies and techniques that facilitate learning. For example, children who have positive beliefs about their own memories will use strategies, particularly when they think these strategies will help them memorize (Rebok & Balcerak, 1989). So children become better learners when experiences increase their confidence in themselves as learners and when they view themselves as competent and capable of knowing and remembering information.

During middle childhood, children are developing academic competencies in reading, mathematics, writing, and speaking. These skills are dependent on numerous factors, including cognitive, language, attentional, and memory abilities, as well as motivation and self-efficacy. Children spend a great deal of time in school, where there are high expectations that they learn and that they become compliant, cooperative, and socialized. The educational setting and teacher variables thus are important elements in this equation.

Educational Setting and Teacher Variables

The effects of the educational setting and teacher variables on the learning process have been of great interest to educational psychologists. The way in which classrooms are set up, the expectations teachers have about their students, the activities that are provided, and the management techniques that are utilized all affect the child's learning and development of self-control.

Classroom Environments. Different classroom arrangements produce different learning outcomes for children. For example, circular seating arrangements facilitate student participation and attentiveness during classroom discussions, whereas cluster seating (in small groups) is superior to row–column seating for increasing student engagement and on-task behaviors (Rosenfield, Lambert, & Black, 1985).

Teacher Expectations. Teacher expectations and beliefs about a child's learning capacity have been shown to have an affect on academic outcomes of children. The concept of the *self-filling prophecy* suggests that children live up to the expectations that teachers or other adults have of them. Children in effect become as good or as competent as we think they can be. Although this is not a simple or perfect relationship, teacher's expectations do affect the quality of their interactions with students and of student learning (Brophy, 1983; Brophy & Good, 1974). Teachers who believe that their children can learn do things that promote this learning— they give extra time to children who need help, they are affectionate, and they are generous (Pederson, Faucher, & Eaton, 1978).

Tone of voice, facial expressions, touch, and posture may also convey teacher expectations and attitudes to children (Rosenthal & Jacobson, 1968). Teachers may also react differently to children based on their ethnic, racial, or economic backgrounds in ways that promote stereotypic, negative, and/or self-fulfilling prophecies (Irvine, 1986). Teachers, even in preschool, teach differently (e.g., giving less verbal stimulation) when they have low-income children versus middle-income children in class.

Parental Influences. Parents play a critical role in how well their children do in school. Generally, it has been shown that high-achieving children have parents who do the following: (1) talk to, read to, and listen to their children; (2) provide a place for the child to study; (3) have structured schedules for eating, sleeping, homework, and making school deadlines; (4) monitor TV viewing and after-school activities; and (5) show an interest in their child's lives, including school events, problems, and successes (U.S. Department of Education, 1986).

Teacher Influences. Teachers' management practices have the greatest impact on student achievement in the classroom (Berk, 1989). Effective classroom management reduces disruptive behaviors and provides for smooth transitions between learning activities. Teacher factors will be explored in more detail in Chapter 6, in the discussion on classroom and educational interventions.

Other Developmental Changes

Self-regulation is another developmental change that affects academic performance in middle childhood. Children become adept at *comprehension monitoring* when reading; that is, they become aware of inconsistencies, ambiguities, or contradictions when reading, and they slow down or reread passages in order to comprehend what they are reading (Markman, 1979). Thus, self-regulation, conscious awareness, planning, and self-correcting skills are important variables that facilitate learning.

In addition, metacognitive awareness improves with age and develops in conjunction with language.

Summary

Middle childhood is marked by considerable progress in self-regulation; cognitive functioning, including increased memory and attentional abilities; control and expression of emotions; and social interaction abilities. Supportive parent–child relations help to ease this growth process and set the foundation for positive behavioral, academic, and psychosocial adjustment.

THE IMPACT OF ADHD ON ADJUSTMENT IN MIDDLE CHILDHOOD

The ways in which ADHD affects the normal developmental challenges of middle childhood can be profound and widespread. In children with pervasive ADHD, every developmental domain may be affected, including cognitive, academic, social-emotional, and behavioral. In children with situational ADHD, these symptoms may influence these areas differentially (see Table 5.1).

The inability to regulate and to inhibit one's behavioral responses, referred to as "executive control deficits," can have a negative impact on all of a child's social interactions and thus can affect both behavioral adjustment in the classroom and general psychological well-being. Furthermore, it may not be hyperactivity and inattention per se but rather the whole constellation of disinhibitory problems, including off-task, out-of-seat, and disruptive behaviors, that are of most concern to teachers and parents (Weiss & Hechtman, 1993).

The inability to stop and to maintain behavioral responses such as paying attention, as well as deficits in self-control (i.e., weak executive control mechanisms), often result in impulsivity, carelessness, poor planning and problem solving, and disorganization. Furthermore, the child's insensitivity to the consequences of behavior also interferes with future learning because children with ADHD may not sufficiently profit from their experiences in a normal or predictable pattern. Barkley (1990b) refers to this as a deficit in "rule-governed behaviors," or the inability to learn the relationship between behavior and its antecedents and consequences. Again, the implications of these difficulties can be more far-reaching than what might typically be implied when conceptualizing ADHD as simply a problem of inattention or overactivity (Barkley, 1997b).

TABLE 5.1. Characteristics/Correlates of ADHD in the Middle Childhood Stage

Source	Child characteristics
Barkley (1989)	Poor school adjustment; failure to finish tasks; disruptive behavior in classroom; poor peer relations; learning disability may be apparent
Barkley (1990b)	Greater response to parental commands from father
Biederman, Newcome, & Sprich (1991)	25% comorbid anxiety disorders; 20–30% comorbid mood disorders
Boucugnani & Jones (1989)	Perseverative response patterns; deficits on measures of self-regulation, inhibition, attention, and planning
Campbell (1990)	Difficulties in socialization, particularly with chaotic, punitive home life; sometimes helped by consistent, supportive, structured home; change in symptoms over time
Chelune et al. (1986)	Executive control deficits; failure to sustain goal-directed behaviors
Douglas (1983)	Primary deficits: attentional, inhibitory, arousal, and reinforcement; secondary deficits: low motivation, impaired metacognition, limited higher order schemata (concepts and strategies)
Douglas & Peters (1979)	Extreme sensitivity to presence and absence of reinforcers
Friebergs & Douglas (1969)	Normal learning rates with 100% reinforcement
Hoza et al. (1993)	No differences between ADHD and controls on self-esteem
Milich (1994)	Learned helplessness; less persistence on complex tasks; quick to give up; high frustration rates
Satterfield et al. (1994)	Defiance ratings predict antisocial behaviors
Taylor (1994)	Self-blame by mothers; mothers' energy spent protecting ADHD child from rejection; maternal stress and depression high
Weiss & Hechtman (1993)	Concern by parents with social adjustment of ADHD child; improved activity levels based on parent report
Weiss & Hechtman (1986)	Grades 1–3 most referred; behavioral and cognitive disorders that resemble syndrome; constellation of behaviors; negative impact on achievement; increased demands (structure); low attention in boring, repetitive, nonreinforcing, unmotivating environment; cycle of poor self-esteem and depression related to poor school performance
Wenar (1994)	Difficulty accepting responsibility; need for constant supervision; immaturity; temper tantrums; vulnerability exacerbated by family factors

(continued)

TABLE 5.1. *cont.*

Source	Child characteristics
Wender (1987)	Low frustration tolerance; cycle of social difficulties, temperament, and experience resulting in low self-esteem; risk-taking and dangerous acts to gain attention and enhance self-image; family stress and sibling rivalry
Zentall et al. (1993)	Deficits in organizing events and objects

Attachment and Family Relationships

Parent–child relationships come under a great deal of stress due to behavioral excesses and difficulties associated with ADHD, including poor inhibitory control, inability to regulate behaviors, and impulsivity. These characteristics are often manifested as noncompliance to parental requests or commands. Parents may also experience stress related to the problems their children experience in school. Battles over homework often are prolonged and traumatic for everyone involved. Furthermore, parents, particularly mothers, experience social isolation, depression, and stressful parent–child interactions; self-blame and marital discord are common effects.

Parent–Child Relationships

The parent–child relationship is often strained when children with ADHD fail to complete household chores, argue and fight with siblings, and throw tantrums when asked to do things for themselves, such as eating and getting dressed (Barkley, 1990b). During this developmental stage, parents complain that their children have problems accepting responsibility, need constant monitoring for such activities as dressing and bathing, have temper tantrums, and are immature (Wenar, 1994).

It may be difficult for clinicians to appreciate the extent of the difficulties parents experience in their attempt to get their children with ADHD to comply. In some households, daily routines, such as catching the school bus, are marked by stress and tension because of the yelling, threatening, cajoling, and bribing that may occur every morning. I am reminded of the story told by one mother of two children with ADHD and oppositional problems. By the time her third-grade son finally finished combing his hair while screaming at his father, he had missed the bus, so Dad had to drive him to school. (It turned out that the boy had been harassed on the bus during the first week of school and that a pattern of behaviors was starting to emerge—ways to avoid the bus ride.) Once the older boy was out of the house, his brother threw all of his clothes out of the dresser trying to find a pair of pants that didn't scratch. He was hypersensitive to how different materials felt on his skin. He also missed the bus after spending his morning complaining that shoes should have socks sewn into them so the seams would not get scrunched into the toes of his tennis shoes. Scenes of this nature are all too common; many parents struggle with getting their kids to comply with simple everyday routines—eating breakfast, getting dressed, and catching the bus on time for school.

Disturbed parent–child relationships have been widely reported in families who have children with ADHD. For example, McLeer, Callaghan, Henry, and Wallen (1994) found that ADHD was the most frequent diagnosis in both sexually abused and nonabused children between the ages of 6 and 16 years who had been referred for psychiatric evaluation. The difficulties children have in obeying rules, following directions, listening, and sitting still require increased supervision by parents. The stress this places on parents may make children with ADHD susceptible to other forms of physical and/or emotional child abuse (Barkley, 1990b). The nature of the parent–child relationship should be assessed when clinicians are gathering developmental and medical histories.

Parenting Styles: Interactional Patterns. Just as temperamental characteristics of the toddler/preschool child interact with parenting styles, reciprocal interactions occur between parental behavior and child characteristics in middle childhood. Battle and Lacey (1972) described this interactional pattern, in which mothers were described as critical, unaffectionate, and punitive in their interactions with their hyperactive sons. Mothers did not display these behaviors when interacting with high-activity daughters. Although it has been hypothesized that parenting factors are etiological factors in hyperactivity, others suggest that these negative patterns of maternal behaviors are reactive to the child's difficulties (Bell & Harper, 1977).

Research evidence supports observations made by Bell and Harper. Barkley and Cunningham (1979) found that although the controlling and intrusive parent behaviors occurred in response to the child's overactivity, impulsivity, and inattention, the commanding and less reinforcing maternal behaviors also contributed to the child's difficulties. When medicated, hyperactive males were more compliant, and mothers were less commanding and more responsive (Barkley & Cunningham, 1980). Although medication improved mother–child interactions, the level of responsiveness was still not equal to that found in mother–child relationships in a control group. Studies of father–child interactions revealed similar results, although hyperactive children were more likely to comply with paternal than maternal requests (Tallmadge & Barkley, 1983).

Barkley (1990b) suggests that children with ADHD are more responsive, less negative, and more attentive with fathers, although it is not clear why this occurs. Barkley suggests that a number of factors may be helpful for understanding these differences: (1) fathers repeat directions less frequently and use punishment more quickly than mothers; (2) fathers spend less time as the primary caretaker of the child, and thus mothers have more responsibility for getting the child to comply; and (3) the size and physical strength of fathers may be intimidating, thus increasing child compliance. Unfortunately, this differential response pattern can create marital discord, particularly if fathers blame mothers for being lax and for using ineffective discipline practices. This dynamic may also be played out in the physician's office, where children with ADHD may be more compliant with male doctors, leading to the notion that mothers create the problem of the child's noncompliance.

Conflictual parent–child relationships have negative effects on parents as well as children (Weiss & Hechtman, 1993). Mothers lack confidence in their parenting skills and report high levels of stress, isolation, and depression (Mash & Johnston, 1983). Mothers tend to blame themselves for their child's problems and also tend to spend lots of time and energy explaining their child's behaviors to others and protecting the child from rejection (Taylor, 1994).

Although parenting styles do not produce ADHD disorders in children, they may have an impact on the development of secondary conduct-related problems during middle childhood and are thus a target of intervention, particularly with aggressive children. Parental psychopathology also affects the parent's ability to cope with a difficult child and may further exacerbate the child's problems.

Parental Psychopathology. Parental psychopathology often leads to other behavioral disturbances in children with hyperactivity, including conduct disorders. Mothers of children with conduct disorders, whether or not they also have ADHD, are likely to present with an "antisocial triad" that includes antisocial personality disorders, substance abuse, and somatization disorders, whereas fathers display antisocial and substance abuse disorders (Biederman, Munir, & Knee, 1987; Lahey, Piacentini, et al., 1988; Schaughency, Vannatta, & Mauro, 1993). Weiss and Hechtman (1993) suggest that parental psychopathology, especially antisocial disorders, increases the likelihood of a co-diagnosis of conduct disorder in hyperactive children.

Parental psychopathology is not typical for children with ADHD who do not possess coexisting conduct and/or oppositional disorders (Schaughency et al., 1993). However, numerous studies have reported maternal depression in mothers of children with ADHD (Beck, Young,

& Tarnowski, 1990; Befera & Barkley, 1985; Biederman, Faraone, Keenan, Knee, & Tsuang, 1990). It has been found that mothers of children with pervasive hyperactivity seem more depressed than mothers of children with situational ADHD (Beck et al., 1990). Depression also appears more frequently in parents of children with ADHD compared to parents of children with learning disabilities and other clinical problems, including anxiety, affective, developmental, or Tourette's disorders (Biederman et al., 1990).

Relatives of children with ADHD also appear to have high rates of ADHD themselves (Biederman et al., 1990). This relationship holds true when comparing biological and adoptive parents; biological parents often have ADHD symptoms similar to their child's (Alberts-Corush, Firestone, & Goodman, 1986). Schaughency et al. (1993) points out that clinicians should consider parental psychopathology when working with families who have children with ADHD because parental depression, antisocial disorders, or substance abuse may interfere with treatment plans.

Parental Emotional Stress. Taylor (1994) suggests that parents experience a variety of emotional reactions to their child's ADHD. Initial feelings of being misunderstood and criticized for their child's difficulties are replaced by feelings of guilt and inadequacy because they cannot fix the problem. These emotions give way to the need to protect and serve the child in an effort to compensate for their feelings of guilt which are balanced with a legitimate concern for the child's well-being. Overinvolvement and enmeshment in the child's problems may take various forms, including overprotecting, nagging, spoiling, pitying, and babying (Taylor, 1994). These behavioral patterns are not healthy for either the child or the parent. Feelings of anger may also emerge because of the stress parents experience when raising ADHD children. Taylor (1994) suggests that parental anger grows out of feelings of hurt and stress.

Finally, parents may become emotionally bankrupt if they feel "completely defeated, drained, and at the end of their rope" (Taylor, 1994, p. 213). Emotional bankruptcy occurs when parents come to believe that nothing they do makes a difference, when their daily lives are constantly in turmoil, when their relationships with spouses and other family members are severely affected, when they are routinely criticized by others, and when they deplete all their options for making things better. These parental feelings often result in an emotional withdrawal from the child, which in turn increases the risk for emotional, verbal, physical, and sexual abuse. Withholding love, criticizing and belittling, hitting, kicking, excessive spanking, and even sexual molestation of the child may occur in extreme situations. The dysfunctional pattern of emotional bankruptcy is easier to prevent than to reverse (Taylor, 1994). Obviously, parental psychopathology and emotional stress may increase the likelihood of child abuse and needs to be considered in conjunction with the child's presenting problems.

Family Status and Emotional Climate

Research investigating marital status and divorce rates in parents of children with ADHD shows mixed results (Schaughency et al., 1993). Some studies report higher rates of divorce and separation in these families (Brown & Pacini, 1989), whereas others report that childhood aggression, not ADHD, increases the occurrence of these outcomes (McGee, Silva, & Williams, 1984). Furthermore, marital discord is associated with behavior problems in boys (Breen & Barkley, 1988). Family discord may be highest for children with antisocial behavior problems rather than with ADHD alone.

Research describing the emotional climate of families who have children with ADHD is also mixed (Schaughency et al., 1993). When investigating positive versus negative family interactions, Hechtman (1981) found that the emotional climate was worse in homes with hyperactive children. Although McGee et al. (1984) found poor familial interactions, Cunningham, Benness, and Siegel (1988) did not find this pattern in families of children with ADHD. Once again, negative family relations may be more frequent in homes where children have antisocial problems rather than ADHD alone.

It is important to point out that having a family with a positive home climate, clear and consistent discipline, and love and support will not guarantee that all children will outgrow their problems—some children are disturbed in spite of these positive conditions (Campbell, 1990a). However, the interaction between parent and child is important because it affects how ADHD is managed. Wenar (1994) suggests that "family factors probably do not cause ADHD but exacerbate and maintain it in vulnerable children, while the children's deviant behavior increases family discord and disruption" (p. 171).

Parental Reactions to School Performance

Parents may experience a great deal of frustration and stress related to their child's school adjustment problems. Parents often encounter school personnel who are not sympathetic to their difficulties, who are not knowledgeable about ADHD, or who are unwilling to make accommodations in the classroom for their child with ADHD. So what already may be a stressful, conflictual relationship between the parent and child is exacerbated by educational professionals who blame parents for the child's noncompliance in school and/or his/her inability to complete assignments and to get along with others.

Parents may spend an inordinate amount of time coercing or bribing their children to do homework, or even in some cases doing the assignments themselves. A project that might take 30 to 45 minutes for other children to complete may take 2 to 3 hours for a child with ADHD. The nightly arguments over homework can be destructive to the already fragile parent–child relationship. Parents are often asked to accomplish what educational experts are unable to do—get their child to complete an assignment in a timely fashion. When children are unsuccessful in completing homework assignments, parents are often blamed for these failings. Criticisms aimed at parents can initiate the cycle of negative parental feelings described by Taylor (1994).

Longitudinal Studies: Families with ADHD Children

It appears that parents' perceptions of their children with ADHD undergo changes at different developmental stages. Weiss and Hechtman (1993) reported the results of a longitudinal study of families at initial time of referral (preschool) and at both 5-year (elementary age) and 10-year (adolescence) follow-up points. At the 5-year point, parents reported that their children in middle childhood and adolescence were significantly worse on almost every assessment criteria than they had been during preschool. Parents' concerns shifted from medical problems and activity levels in preschool to social concerns at the elementary and high school stages. Furthermore, there were no differences in parental concerns about school performance and emotional and intellectual adjustment across the three stages, although parents did seek more assistance during the elementary period.

There were some changes noted in the child's behavior over specific time frames; according to parents, their children became less restless with age (Weiss & Hechtman, 1993). Ratings for conduct-related problems (i.e., stealing and lying) did not differ from middle childhood to adolescence, nor were there clear differences in school functioning. Although children in middle childhood were more frequently rated as liking school, adolescents were rated as more independent and better behaved in school. At every stage, parents of hyperactive children reported problems one measures of social, academic, and activity levels, especially during middle childhood and adolescence. Parents did report improvements in some behaviors (activity levels), although they were less sensitive to increases in antisocial problems (lying and stealing) from middle childhood to adolescence. Weiss and Hechtman (1993) suggest that these behaviors may have started in the home during the middle childhood stage and became problematic in the community during adolescence, so that parents did not distinguish between the two developmental stages. Teenagers may also be more adept at hiding misdeeds from their parents.

Executive Functions: Self-Regulation, Self-Control, and Planning

Executive functions are processes of flexibility, planning, inhibition, and self-monitoring (Teeter & Semrud-Clikeman, 1997), including interference-control processes, effortful organization, and goal-oriented "preparedness to act" (Denckla, 1994, p. 117). Executive functions encompass the regulation, inhibition, and maintenance of behavioral responses as well as problem solving, organization, and reasoning (Teeter & Semrud-Clikeman, 1997). Barkley (1996b, 1997a) emphasizes the relationship between deficits in inhibitory self-control mechanisms and inattention, such that attending to one stimuli requires that competing stimuli be ignored or inhibited. Thus executive control problems are cardinal features of ADHD.

Deficits in executive control mechanisms have been found in children with ADHD in middle childhood (Chelune et al., 1986). Children with ADHD use inappropriate responses and fail to sustain goal-directed behaviors. These deficits have been related to prefrontal lobe activities, and Denckla (1996) suggests that deficits in executive control systems may be the mechanisms that link ADHD and learning disabilities and may explain the high comorbidity of the two disorders. Executive control deficits have also been implicated in other childhood disorders, specifically oppositional and conduct disorders, particularly when ADHD co-occurs with conduct disorder (Moffitt & Silva, 1988; Moffitt & Henry, 1989). Pennington and Bennetto (1993) found that children with conduct disorders who also show impaired verbal language skills and executive processes are at a higher risk for displaying serious aggressive and antisocial behaviors. At present, it does not appear that executive control problems are unique to ADHD, but what seems evident is that a number of childhood disorders share similar behavioral features that include disinhibitory, executive, or self-control problems. Furthermore, it appears that when ADHD is comorbid with other childhood disorders such as learning disabilities and conduct disorder, the presence of executive control deficits may be greater.

Executive control mechanisms appear to have a prolonged developmental course, beginning early in life and extending well into the fourth decade of adulthood (Denckla, 1994). These processes also have broad influences on academic as well as psychosocial functioning in children.

The Developmental Pathway of Executive Control Mechanisms

The developmental course of executive control problems in children with ADHD is not well established. Identifying a developmental pathway for executive functions in general, and specifically for children with ADHD, is complicated by factors related to how we measure these processes. Denckla (1994) discusses these difficulties and suggests that there are two constructs underlying executive controls—a neuroanatomical one and a psychodevelopmental one. The construct of executive control mechanisms is further complicated because they are often described and studied as separate functions, for example, as "attention and inhibition or thought and language," even though the processes are not independent of each other but are parallel and interrelated functions (Denckla, 1994, p. 120). Assessment of executive control processes is further contaminated by the content domains that overlap the function being measured—spatial and language-related tasks.

Attention, Vigilance, and EEG Findings. In a series of studies investigating the relationship between neonate sleep regulation and waking attention, Parmelee et al. (1994) found that infants with "well-integrated state organization and attention are likely to have more successful interactions with their environment, and therefore to be at reduced risk for later developmental problems" (p. 547). Quiet sleep, which is dependent upon brain integrity and development, was related to cognitive development rather than to attention throughout childhood. Active sleep (REM sleep), which is easily disrupted by environmental conditions, was related to vigilant attention at 8 and 12 years of age. Furthermore, indeterminant sleep patterns (poor state organization) in neonatal development was negatively related to cognitive and vigilant attention measures at 8 and 12 years of age.

Using EEG power-spectral analysis, Parmelee et al. (1994) specifically found that neonatal EEG activity in the left frontal regions was correlated with vigilance and speed of information processing in middle childhood (12 years of age). These findings are consistent with other studies demonstrating the role of the frontal areas for regulating attention (Posner & Petersen, 1990). Parmelee et al. (1994) suggest that neonatal state organization (sleep and waking states) serves as a regulatory system "in the development of the biological–environmental interactions of children," although social interactions modulate this relationship (p. 549). "Poor social interactions and general socioeconomic circumstances amplify the negative effects of poor state organization, and good social interactions and socioeconomic circumstances diminish this effect, confirming state organization as important for the biological–environmental interface" (Parmelee et al., 1994, p. 550).

These findings are important for several reasons. First, biological brain systems in neonates appear related to enduring regulating mechanisms that ultimately control attention, arousal, and vigilance in middle childhood. Second, early competency of neurophysiological systems influences later development and affects the biological–environment interactions. Third, social–environmental factors do modulate biological states. Thus biological states do not independently predict later dysfunctions, but social–environmental factors influence the child's overall adjustment. This pattern was depicted in the transactional model described in Chapter 2. Although a number of biogenetic factors place the child at risk, children have natural self-righting mechanisms to counterbalance some biological vulnerabilities (Sameroff & Chandler, 1975). Research that clarifies this complex biological–environment interaction would be particularly helpful in the investigation of ADHD.

EEG Findings: Reasons to Be Cautious. Although early electroencephalographic immaturity has been found in some hyperactive children (Klinderfuss, Lange, Weinberg, & O'Leary, 1965), the relationship between EEG findings and later development is far from clear, and research is contradictory. For example, Weiss and Hechtman (1993) found that EEG abnormalities in young children normalize with age. However, Klein and Mannuzza (1989) reanalyzed data reported by Hechtman, Weiss, and Metrakos (1978) and found that when mild and moderate EEG abnormalities are considered, there is a trend showing a relationship between EEG findings and outcome measures. Klein and Mannuzza (1989) also found a significant relationship between abnormal EEG findings in childhood and DSM-III diagnosis later in life. Even with positive interactions, it should be noted that the application and diagnostic utility of group data is not warranted when investigating individual children because approximately 10–15% of normal children have abnormal EEGs (Weiss & Hechtman, 1993).

Developmental Correlates of Self-Regulatory Mechanisms

Significant age effects have been found on measures sensitive to frontal lobe activity in control groups and in children with ADHD. For example, Boucugnani and Jones (1989) found that children with ADHD and control children between 7 and 10 years of age show similar developmental patterns on tasks measuring self-regulation, inhibition, attention, and planning (e.g., the Wisconsin Card Sort Test, the Stroop Color and Word Test). Although both groups improve with age, children with ADHD routinely showed deficits on these measures when compared to a control group.

Although not all children with ADHD have specific difficulties maintaining a response set (an indication of distractibility), these difficulties do occur to a high degree in some children (Boucugnani & Jones, 1989). On the other hand, perseverative responses and errors are much more common for the ADHD group: children with ADHD have difficulty shifting from one mental set to another, a characteristic consistently found in patients with frontal lobe dysfunction. Children with ADHD react with more distress when given negative feedback about their responses and are unable to alter their response sets. Boucugnani and Jones suggest that a lack of motivation may also be present in some children, which might account for their tendency to respond randomly or to revert to responses that had previously been reinforced. These cognitive factors appear similar to deficits in self-directed and organized attention that were described by Douglas (1983) as core features of ADHD (Boucugnani & Jones, 1989).

In summary, the relationship between executive control dysfunction and ADHD seems to be plausible and may even be explanatory for the numerous difficulties associated with self-control, self-regulation, and problem solving. Neuropsychological assessment of executive control processes in children is still in its infancy, and there are conceptual as well as measurement issues that need to be resolved before this area is fully established. Furthermore, EEG measurement and its relationship to ADHD is controversial, and research is contradictory.

Paradigms relating brain function and behavioral dyscontrol, disinhibition, and inattention are providing insight into some of the core features of ADHD (Barkley, 1990b, 1997a; Teeter & Semrud-Clikeman, 1995, 1997). Even so, brain pathology does not necessarily indicate that specific disorders or deficits can be accounted for by brain dysfunction (Boucugnani & Jones, 1989). See Rutter (1983) and Fletcher and Taylor (1984) for in-depth discussions of the hazards of "argument by analogy." Furthermore, it is not clear whether goal-directed deficits, disinhibition, and reinforcement deficits found in children with ADHD are similar to those found in patients with prefrontal lobe damage or dysfunction. Studies that specifically investigate neuropsychological deficits in frontal lobe functioning in children will inform this dialogue (Boucugnani & Jones, 1989).

Emotional Development

Emotional problems are frequently reported, and the majority of children with ADHD have comorbid disorders that make interventions particularly challenging. A high percentage of children admitted to psychiatric hospitals for serious emotional disturbance require treatment for ADHD compared to children without disabilities or with cognitive or learning disabilities (Singh et al., 1994). In a sample of 1,038 children (ages 5–14 years) with inattentive-hyperactive symptoms, August and Garfinkel (1989) discerned two reliable subtypes of children. The majority of children (80%) were characterized by behavioral symptoms that included inattention, hyperactivity, and impulsivity. This group showed a range of behavioral problems, the most extreme of which were indistinguishable from conduct disorders. The smaller group (20%) was characterized by cognitive problems that included achievement difficulties with inattention, hyperactivity, and impulsivity. Furthermore, the cognitive ADHD subtype showed deficient processing on linguistic tasks, including encoding and retrieval problems.

Defiance and oppositional behaviors at a young age are problematic for a number of reasons. Defiance ratings in middle childhood, independent of hyperactivity, are predictive of serious antisocial behaviors (felony offenses) in adolescence (Satterfield, Swanson, Schell, & Lee, 1994). Clinicians should also be alerted to the fact that arrests for criminal behavior later in life may be frequent in boys with ADHD even without a history of defiance.

Between the ages of 8 and 12 years, children with both ADHD and aggression tend to show increased rates of aggressive behavior under provocation in competitive game situations (Atkins & Stoff, 1993). Although instrumental aggression was higher for groups of ADHD children than for controls, only the children with ADHD and aggression scored higher than the controls on measures of hostile aggression. ADHD appears to place children at increased risk for instrumental aggression.

Socialization and Peer Interactions

The middle-childhood stage is often characterized by relationship problems, as children with ADHD are often rejected by peers, particularly when aggression is present; receive negative attention from teachers (Milich & Landau, 1989); and are described as irritating, annoying, domineering, and rigid in social situations (Whalen & Henker, 1985). Children with ADHD may experience rejection by others as a result of their active, demanding, boisterous and intrusive behaviors (Whalen & Henker, 1985); off-task, disruptive behavior and noncompliance in the classroom (Cunningham, Siegel, & Offord, 1985); achievement problems and/or learning disabilities (Flicek & Landau, 1985); and aggressiveness or conduct problems, particularly if they also have high levels of hyperactivity (Loney & Milich, 1982).

During this stage, children with ADHD often have trouble joining clubs, participating in sports, and engaging in other extracurricular activities (Barkley, 1990b). Although Johnston, Pelham, and Murphy (1985) found that peer problems continue throughout elementary school, Johnston and Pelham (1986) provide some reason to be optimistic in that peer problems appear to improve with age in boys with ADHD who are low in aggression.

Cognitive Development

The relationship between intelligence and ADHD shows that impulsive–hyperactive behaviors interfere with performance on a number of intellectual measures, including working memory, digit span, and arithmetic (Anastopoulos, Spisto, & Maher, 1994). Although verbal IQ appears diminished in children with ADHD (Hinshaw, 1992), Stein, Szumowski, Blondis, and Roizen (1995) suggest that ADHD has a more significant impact on how the child applies his/her intelligence, especially in an adaptive sense.

Language delays are often present in children with ADHD, particularly at a young age. Children with early signs of speech delays (between 2 and 4 years), inattention, and hyperactivity are at risk for a diagnosis of ADHD between the ages of 7 and 14 years (Ornoy, Uriel, & Tennebaum, 1993). Between the ages of 6 and 14 years, children with ADHD also have deficits in organizing events and objects (Zentall, Harper, & Stormont-Spurgin, 1993).

Children with ADHD are more likely to have learning disabilities, to repeat grades, to be in special classes, and to require tutoring than either their siblings or a control group (Faraone, Biederman, Lehman, Spencer, et al., 1993). Although comorbid conduct and depressive disorders are more predictive of school placement than are school failure or IQ scores, even without other disorders children with ADHD have more school failure and lower IQs than controls. On average, children with ADHD score 15 points below their siblings and other control groups on measures of IQ (Fischer, Barkley, Edelbrock, & Smallish, 1990).

Mariani and Barkley (1997) discovered that ADHD also had an impact on readiness and knowledge acquisition even before the child enters first grade. Barkley (1996a) suggests that difficulties in executive functions, particularly working memory, internalized speech, and verbal fluency, affect the acquisition of math, spelling, reading comprehension, and oral/written report skills.

Academic Performance and School Adjustment

Academic problems are present in the majority of children with ADHD during the middle childhood stage because of difficulties in completing classwork and homework, disruptive or noncompliant behavior, and poor peer relations (Barkley, 1989). Academic underachievement (Lambert & Sandoval, 1980), school failure (Barkley, 1990a), learning difficulties (Anderson, Williams, McGee, & Silva, 1987), and learning disabilities (Epstein, Shaywitz, Shaywitz & Woolston, 1992) are common in hyperactive males.

It is likely that by first grade, children with severe ADHD characteristics have already experienced difficulties meeting the expectations of adults in school settings and may have attended more than one program because of their ADHD symptoms. Barkley (1990b) indicates that school adjustment difficulties are more frequent in aggressive or noncompliant children with ADHD. Johnston and Pelham (1986) report that teacher ratings of aggression directed at adults (e.g., rebelliousness), along with peer ratings of dislike, are strong predictors of later adjustment problems for aggressive ADHD children after a 3-year period.·

Children with ADHD appear to have characteristics similar to those of learned helplessness (Milich, 1994). That is, when faced with failure situations, children with ADHD do not persist in their efforts to solve complex puzzles. Although they appear confident when they begin tasks (Milich & Greenwell, 1991; Milich & Okasaki, 1991), they give up more quickly and report greater frustration than children without ADHD (Milich & Okasaki, 1991). This pattern is particularly evident when children with ADHD experience success followed by failure. Milich (1994) further suggests that boys with ADHD show a different pattern of attributional styles than control boys do. Boys with ADHD who gave effort attributions (e.g., "I didn't study hard") were more helpless, whereas externally oriented (e.g., "The test was hard") boys with ADHD were more mastery oriented. Milich (1994) suggests that boys with ADHD may already be putting forth a great deal of effort that does not appear to "pay off" for them; thus the link between effort and success has not been established as it has been in controls. Repeated failure experiences in situations in which boys with ADHD do try hard have taught these children that no matter how hard they try, they will not succeed. Children with ADHD may be used to hearing from parents and teachers that they are not trying, and that is why they give up easily and are not succeeding academically.

Milich (1994) suggests that children with ADHD may be initially optimistic about their potential for success as a means of self-protection, to deflect attention from their own difficulties. However, Hoza, Pelham, Milich, Pillow, and McBride (1993) found that boys with ADHD did not differ from a control group on measures of self-esteem. Milich (1994) states that this finding was unexpected, given that poor self-esteem is a commonly accepted problem associated with the child's failure across academic, social, and behavioral areas. It may be that children with ADHD have limited awareness of their own feelings and problems and thus overestimate their potential for success and their own self-worth. They may also try to protect themselves from these negative feelings and to bolster their own self-appraisals to avoid depressive, self-defeating thinking.

Gender-Related Issues

In a study investigating differences between boys and girls referred for treatment of ADHD in middle childhood, it was found that girls were retained more frequently in school and also evidenced difficulty on spatial memory tests (Brown, Madan-Swain, & Baldwin, 1991). Furthermore, girls were older at the initial referral and showed more severe deficits across a variety of academic, cognitive, and social measures. Carlson et al. (1997) also found that girls with disruptive behavior disorders had more social problems than boys, but boys were more aggressive, inattentive, and inappropriate than girls.

Teacher–Child Relationships

Teachers may experience frustration when dealing with the inconsistent work habits, immaturity, disorganization, and disruptive behaviors often observed in children with ADHD. Teacher–child relationships may suffer as a result, and some teachers may view the child's behaviors as irresponsible and intentional. Teachers may have negative attitudes about children because of the amount of time and energy they spend dealing with low work productivity, noncompliance, and social interaction problems. These attitudes in turn may lead teachers to initiate fewer positive interactions and more commands and eventually to disengage from and give up on the student. Teacher disengagement has negative effects on children's learning, on their attitudes about school, and on their self-esteem.

Initiative and Self-Worth

Low self-esteem can result from the interaction of academic and school adjustment problems and social rejection, a cycle that persists into middle childhood and may subsequently result in serious adult adjustment problems (Wender, 1987). Children often come to realize that they are not meeting the expectations of parents and teachers, and they may be subtly undermined by negative feedback about their competence (Goldstein & Goldstein, 1990). Interventions designed to address problems in middle childhood must be multifaceted and often include efforts to increase the child's feelings of self-worth.

SUMMARY

Children are usually first referred for assessment of ADHD during the first 3 years of school (Weiss & Hechtman, 1986), even though the problems are often no more severe than they were in the preschool years. Weiss and Hechtman (1986) suggest that tolerance on the part of both preschool teachers and parents, along with the hope that the child will outgrow the problem, probably delays the initial referral. These findings may suggest that there is a better "goodness of fit" during the preschool stage, in which the environment is more flexible and able to adjust to the young child's ADHD behaviors. Increased academic demands in elementary school (e.g., learning to read) and the ratio of students to teachers contribute to the need for greater structure, planning, and modifications of assignments to improve the success of children with ADHD during middle childhood. The primary symptoms associated with ADHD make it extremely difficult for the child to adjust to the structure and demands of the classroom without systematic interventions. Social interaction difficulties also interfere witih overall adjustment in middle childhood, and comorbid psychiatric problems are common.

6

Intervention Strategies and Techniques for the Middle Childhood Stage

T *his chapter presents* techniques that have proven effective for treating children between 6 and 12 years of age with ADHD. During the middle childhood stage, intervention programs for children with ADHD are often multifaceted and typically include parent training, behavior management in the classroom, academic interventions for learning problems, social skills training, and pharmacotherapy. Depending on the child's particular profile of strengths and weaknesses, clinicians utilize various strategies that have been found to reduce the negative effects of ADHD on the child's development. The intervention literature is too broad to review thoroughly here, so selected approaches that have proven effective are discussed.

THE NEED FOR MULTIMODAL TREATMENT

During middle childhood, it is critical to investigate the impact that symptoms of ADHD have on family, psychosocial, and academic domains and how these problems ultimately affect the child's self-esteem. As such, careful assessment and diagnosis of the child is crucial and forms the basis of intervention planning. Based on an assessment of the child's assets and deficits, interventions should thus target the multiple domains that are affected by ADHD. Teeter and Semrud-Clikeman

(1995) recommend not only interventions that address multiple problems but also intervention programs that utilize multiple strategies and techniques from different paradigms, including behavioral (for parent training and classroom management), psychosocial and cognitive-behavioral (for academic, emotional, and social problems), and medical–pharmacological approaches (for reducing hyperactivity and increasing attention). These various techniques are frequently used together, and in many instances when used in combination these strategies are most effective.

Interventions during middle childhood continue to focus on primary caregivers, including parents and teachers, in an effort to increase their management and coping skills. This caretaker focus can be met with resistance because parents and teachers often think that the child should be the focus of treatment. In many instances, parents and teachers expect that the clinician will be able to and should modify the child's behaviors by teaching him/her to control impulses, to comply, to listen, and to complete his/her work. These attitudes need to be explored and modified if caretaker interventions are to be successful. It is critical that adults who interact with children understand the important role they themselves play in developing appropriate expectations, using effective reinforcers and consequences for child behaviors, and modifying the environment to increase the compliance, work productivity, and social interaction skills of children with ADHD. Treatment plans that focus solely on the child are rarely effective in isolation; thus there is a need for developing effective parent and teacher management and coping skills.

Other interventions do focus directly on children with ADHD and are designed to facilitate the development of their social interaction, self-management, and academic skills. It is particularly important to address the child's self-esteem and to counteract the negative impact of academic failure, social rejection, and isolation. Strategies to increase self-esteem may include identifying and developing child competencies and may target parent and teacher behaviors (e.g., reinforcing, encouraging, respecting, and affirming the child).

Another important thing to keep in mind is that although techniques initiated in early childhood may have effectively addressed the challenges of the toddler/preschool stage, these interventions rarely produce effects that completely prevent or eliminate problems in middle childhood. There is little research to suggest that interventions in earlier stages serve as inoculations against the stresses and challenges placed on the child at later stages; thus ongoing treatment during each developmental stage is usually necessary. There are several reasons for this. First, it is partly a function of the developmental nature of ADHD; that is, symptoms continue to persist throughout the life span, and the disorder "colors an individual's experiences in every arena of life" (Taylor, 1994, p. 1). Second, although ADHD is a lifelong disorder, the manner in which characteristics affect different age groups depends on the demands and challenges present during each stage. Third, most interventions, including behavior management and medication, lose their potency when discontinued. The inability to generalize the effects of intervention from short to long term has always been a problem for clinicians treating children with ADHD.

TREATMENT GOALS FOR MIDDLE CHILDHOOD

Clinicians may want to consider the following treatment goals when working with ADHD children, their families, and their teachers during the middle childhood stage.

1. Increase effective management skills, improve communication and problem-solving abilities, and enhance healthy parent–child and sibling relations in family systems to decrease the stress and conflict that arises in families who are raising children with ADHD.
2. Increase child compliance, work completion, and work accuracy to decrease the negative impact of ADHD in the classroom.
3. Increase social interaction and problem-solving skills, and appropriate expression of feelings (e.g., anger control) to decrease social isolation and/or rejection in children with ADHD.
4. Increase child's self-esteem by identifying and building competencies and successes.
5. Increase self-control, behavioral disinhibition, and impulse control deficits in children with ADHD by considering medication in combination with other self-management interventions.

Interventions designed to address these treatment goals include parent training, family systems therapy, behavioral management techniques for the classroom, academic interventions, social skills training, and pharmacotherapy.

PARENT AND FAMILY INTERVENTIONS

ADHD affects not only the child but also his/her parents and siblings. Parents often need assistance to develop management strategies for reducing oppositional, defiant, and noncompliant behaviors, and may need support to cope with the social rejection, academic failure, and emotional pain the child experiences as a result of ADHD. Parent and family programs often seek to help parents develop coping mechanisms rather than to change the child's problem behaviors (Whalen & Henker, 1991).

Parent Training

Parent training may be essential during the middle childhood stage of development, especially if the family has not received training in management techniques during the preschool/early childhood stage. Barkley (1987, 1997b), Forehand and McMahon (1981), and Patterson and colleagues (Patterson, 1982; Patterson, Reid, Jones, & Conger, 1975) designed comprehensive parenting programs to reduce problems of noncompliance, defiance, and aggression. These programs are used with parents of children with ADHD because even when a diagnosis of oppositional defiant or conduct disorders is not present, children with ADHD often display the behavioral problems that are targeted by these approaches (Weiss & Hechtman, 1993).

The three major parent training programs incorporate techniques to improve parent–child interactions, to decrease noncompliance, and to facilitate family communication patterns. Goals generally include improving parenting skills and family functioning, developing coping mechanisms, resolving family conflict, and addressing the long-term needs of the family. See Table 6.1 for a summary of the components of each parent training program.

All three parent training programs are behaviorally based and have been shown to be effective for increasing child compliance (Barkley, 1987, 1997b; Barnhardt & Forehand, 1975; Forehand & McMahon, 1981) and for reducing behavior problems in children (Patterson & Fleischman, 1979; Patterson, Reid, Jones, & Conger, 1975).

Barkley's Parent Training Program

Barkley's (1987, 1997b) structured parent training program utilizes behavioral techniques to teach parents how to attend to appropriate child behavior, to use social reinforcement and token economies, and to effectively use time-out and response cost. This program was described in detail in Chapter 4.

Initial research with the Barkley program indicates that children with ADHD do improve on compliance ratings, although they still are more problem-prone than controls following treatment (Barkley, 1987). Newby, Fischer, and Roman (1991) indicate that the "focus of the program is on helping parents cope with the child's problems and

TABLE 6.1. Parent Training Programs for Children with ADHD

Program	Program goals	Training components
Barkley (1987); 8–10 sessions	Improve parental management Increase parent knowledge Improve child compliance	Evaluating child noncompliance and causes of misbehavior Learning to attend/interact appropriately Reinforcing compliance/compliance training Shaping behaviors/independent play Using formal reward system/token economies Using time-out procedures Managing behavior outside the home Planning for future problems Maintenance/booster sessions
Patterson (1976); 5+ sessions	Reduce coercive patterns	Evaluating child's behavior Explaining coercive theory Evaluating nature of noncompliance Identifying compliance/noncompliance patterns Monitoring and recording behaviors Giving effective requests/commands Using Positive Point System Breaking down complex requests/commands Using time-out Using time-out outside home Using maintenance/booster sessions
Forehand & McMahon (1981); 10+ sessions	Increase child compliance Teach social learning theory Shape parental expectations	Evaluating child's behavior Explaining differential attention Using social reinforcement Training in compliance Giving "alpha commands" Using time-out

minimizing the extent to which child noncompliance contributes to these problems and the distress within the family" (p. 257).

Although Weiss and Hechtman (1993) used Barkley's program with weekly individual therapy sessions for a year following parent training, this extended therapy–training phase has not been researched to date. Weiss and Hechtman (1993) caution that parent training is contraindicated when there is severe marital discord, parental psychopathology that requires treatment, and/or comorbid psychopathology in the child (e.g., ADHD with depression). These issues need to be addressed separately before parent training can be effectively utilized.

Patterson's Parent Training Program

Patterson's program for parent intervention (Patterson, Reid, Jones, & Conger, 1975; Patterson, 1976, 1982) was developed to treat families with aggressive, antisocial children. The program explains "coercive theory" to help parents understand how behavior problems are established and maintained. Coercive theory, which evolved from social learning theory, maintains that (1) children learn maladaptive behaviors in the home; (2) both positive and negative reinforcement serve to maintain these problem behaviors; and (3) problem behaviors cannot be decreased without breaking the coercive cycle. The coercive cycle can be seen in the following example. A child whines and/or throws a tantrum to avoid an aversive parental command, such as to turn off the TV and go to bed. The parent withdraws the command to get the child to stop the negative behavior. Finally, the child learns that whining and/or having tantrums is an effective way to avoid future parental commands or requests. The child's behavior eventually becomes coercive—he/she need only threaten a tantrum and parents back down and withdraw requests. One of the major objectives of Patterson's training program is to help parents break this coercive cycle.

Aggressive behaviors are learned and maintained in a similar fashion. Positive consequences of a child's aggression (wherein the child gets his/her way serve to maintain the behavior and strengthen its reoccurrence. Once learned, the child's aggressive behaviors escalate in intensity, and the child becomes exquisitely adept at "reading" situations (e.g., with Mom instead of Dad, with younger sister instead of older brother) in which his/her aggressive behavior will produce the desired effects. These coercive and escalation factors are explained to parents, and techniques for breaking these relationships are introduced.

Patterson and colleagues have conducted years of research with families of antisocial children. In a review of research findings, treatment outcomes appear positive, although the "therapist must be skilled in coping with the resistance to change that characterizes the majority of families referred for treatment" (Patterson, 1982, p. 304). Treating chronic delinquency is more problematic, because families are often "unmotivated and/or extremely resistant to changing their behavior" (Patterson, 1982, p. 306).

The efficacy of Patterson's program for families with ADHD has not been specifically investigated. The extent to which children with ADHD exhibit comorbid aggressive or conduct-related disorders may predict the utility of this particular training program for this group.

Forehand's Parent Training Program

Although not specifically designed for families of children with ADHD, Forehand and McMahon (1981) also developed a comprehensive program for increasing compliance in children. Child compliance is the primary goal, and aspects of the Forehand approach are similar to those of the Barkley and Patterson programs (Newby et al., 1991). Parents are taught to avoid the following pitfalls: (1) the "negative reinforcement trap," in which parents remove commands in light of the child's misbehavior (e.g., whining, having tantrums, fighting); (2) coercive escalation, in which the child threatens to misbehave to avoid compliance in the future; and (3) the "positive reinforcement trap," in which parents pay attention to, talk to, or try to reason with a child when he/she throws a tantrum or misbehaves. Training occurs in parent–child dyads, and parents are taught how to use positive management methods and judicious punishment (time-out).

Research shows that Forehand's program has short-term positive outcomes (Forehand & King, 1974, 1977) and that improvements are sustained over time (Baum & Forehand, 1991). However, although clinic-based treatment appears to generalize to the home, it shows no impact on school behaviors (Briener & Forehand, 1991).

Related Training Programs

Goldstein and Goldstein (1990) describe other training programs for parents and discuss common features for teaching parents how to cope with and manage children with ADHD. In their review, Goldstein and Goldstein suggest that the long-term efficacy of parent training programs is not well established. A combination of training in communication and interaction skills and use of medication does appear to produce positive results. Parent training may need to include family therapy to help parents deal with disappointments, emotional complications, and their own perceptions about their child (Anastopoulos & Barkley, 1990). Principles of social learning theory, attributional styles, and structural systems models are usually incorporated into family systems treatment approaches (Cunningham, 1990).

Family Systems Interventions

Family systems approaches are often incorporated into multimodal treatment plans, particularly when significant stressors and conflicts are present in the families of children with ADHD. Cunningham (1990) describes the dimensions of a structured family systems approach to parent training that include "1) improvements in parenting skills; 2) improvements in family functioning; and, 3) the development of rationales supporting the importance of each of the parenting and family systems skills developed" (p. 434). The structured program is delivered in 15 sessions and followed up in monthly booster sessions.

The program identifies and assesses how parents engage in supportive communication, divide child management responsibilities, and develop solutions to problem behaviors. The assessment phase includes evaluating (1) the alliances that exist between the mother and father; (2) the problem behaviors that are present; (3) the approaches each parent uses to solve these problems; (4) which problem-solving strategies are effective and which are not; (5) the family's strengths and weaknesses; (6) the emotional impact of the problems; (7) the attributions or belief systems of parents; and (8) specific strategies that might be beneficial. Family roles, problem-solving skills, and communication patterns are also investigated.

The family systems program utilizes homework, videotapes, modeling, role playing, and practice sessions with the parent and child in an effort to improve family functioning, child management skills, and communication among family members, and to distribute child management responsibilities. Many of the parenting skills introduced in other parent training programs are also incorporated, including positive attending, rewarding, ignoring, planning ahead for trouble situations, using time-out, and increasing the generalization of skills. The program does offer some unique aspects that may be useful for families, including how to balance parental attention among siblings and how to use "when–then" statements (e.g., "*When* you finish your homework, *then* you can play soccer"). The program includes a child treatment component, in which children are taught prosocial skills, how to follow rules at home, and how to resolve school problems in a group setting.

Little efficacy research is available on this family systems approach, although Cunningham (1990) suggests that parents report improved management techniques and increased self-confidence after completing the program. The family therapy described by Cunningham assumes "that allowing parents to formulate their own solutions to child management problems, enhancing commitment via attributional strategies, and improving key dimensions in family functioning will enhance outcome" (1990, p. 460). These techniques have been found to be effective for distressed and nondistressed families alike (see Brody & Forehand, 1985). Problem solving, communication training, and conflict resolution have been effective strategies for distressed, conflictual families (see Dadds, Schwartz, & Sanders, 1987).

Techniques to Address Other Parent Concerns

Some parents may be quite knowledgeable about basic management principles for gaining compliance and may be more interested in learning techniques to increase their child's independence or self-monitoring skills. Many self-monitoring strategies used in schools can be employed in the home as well. (Techniques for increasing self-management in the classroom are discussed in a subsequent section in this chapter.) Parents may need help in establishing cooperative home–school relationships to address their child's academic problems, such as completing homework assignments or improving classroom behaviors. Parents may need coaching in problem-solving communication and negotiating with teachers, advocating for their child, and working in partnerships with educational and medical professionals.

Parents may need support to deal with their child's social rejection or isolation. During the middle childhood stage, many parents express fears and anxieties about their child's long-term adjustment or prognosis. Parent support groups can be helpful to allay these concerns, and most large communities have established CH.A.D.D. chapters. Participation in parent support groups can be extremely helpful because parents learn how to access resources and to identify professionals in the community who effectively treat children with ADHD.

In some cases in which families experience significant distress or parents have serious emotional problems, individual therapy for parents may be recommended. This is particularly critical in situations in which parents have depressive, alcohol or drug abuse, anger control, antisocial, and/or other significant personal problems that interfere with their functioning as a parent or a spouse. The possibility of spousal abuse and/or child abuse and neglect should not be overlooked in more seriously impaired families.

The child spends long hours in the classroom, and ADHD has a significant impact on adjustment in this setting. So much depends on success in school (e.g., academic and social competence, self-esteem, social relations, adult educational and career outcomes) that school-based interventions are almost always needed. In some cases, children with mild ADHD may not require extensive classroom interventions, and systematic educational modifications may suffice. Gifted children with ADHD may not require elaborate behavior management plans; modifications in workload (i.e., fewer assignments) and/or input and response (e.g., use of a computer for writing assignments) may be all that is needed. Modifications should be specific for each individual child, and plans should be discussed with parents. Some parents may not want the child's workload reduced, particularly if the child is able to complete tasks in a timely fashion, so other options may need to be explored.

CLASSROOM AND EDUCATIONAL INTERVENTIONS

Classroom management and educational planning are among the many challenges facing professionals who design intervention programs for children with ADHD. Specific behaviors that are difficult to ameliorate include concentration difficulties on highly repetitive and boring tasks, noncompliance and failure to follow rules, incomplete work assignments, impulsive responding, and hypersensitivity to the presence or absence of reinforcers.

It has been speculated that children with ADHD have problems responding to the motivational aspects of the environment, especially when consequences are "weak, delayed or unavailable" (Barkley, 1989, p. 53). Zentall (1985) achieved positive behavioral change by reducing task complexity and increasing the novelty and stimulus properties of the task. Other contingency management techniques include token economy, time-out, and self-monitoring.

Guidelines for Implementing Classroom Management Programs

A number of guiding principles should be considered when designing classroom-based management systems.

1. Reinforcements should be given frequently and consistently for appropriate behaviors.
2. Reinforcements must be administered close to the time the behavior occurs. The longer the latency between the behavior and the consequence, the weaker the association.
3. Response cost and other punishment techniques (e.g., time out) should be utilized strategically but infrequently.
4. Response cost and punishments should only be utilized in "reinforcement-rich" environments. Programs in which children receive few or no rewards or in which punishments outweigh opportunities for rewards are almost always doomed to failure.
5. For severe problems (e.g., little or no compliance or work completion), reinforcement targets may be set at levels so that the child receives credit for small successes (e.g., blurting out only twice in a

morning session or completing four out of ten math problems). Once the child is responding more consistently, expectations can be raised. Setting expectations that are too high or outside the child's behavioral repertoire is one of the biggest reasons why management systems do not work.

6. Provide children the opportunity to earn back points or lost privileges contingent upon compliance or work completion. Management systems should not be used as punishment or as a method to document misbehavior or noncompliance. Remember that increased self-control, effort, and work completion are the goals—not perfection.

Classroom Management Practices

Behavioral techniques have been shown to be effective in increasing on-task behavior (DuPaul, Guevremont, & Barkley, 1991), reducing aggression (Abikoff & Gittelman, 1984), and improving academic and behavioral performance (Pfiffner, Rosen, & O'Leary, 1985). Table 6.2 summarizes selected behavioral techniques for classroom problems.

Behavior management techniques have been shown to be highly effective for reducing disruptive behaviors and for increasing work completion in the classroom. Although disruptive problems may be more likely to occur in children with ADD with hyperactivity (ADD/H) than

TABLE 6.2. Classroom Management Techniques for Reducing Problems of ADHD

Problem behaviors	Techniques	Reference
Work productivity	Classroom token economies	Pfiffner & O'Leary (1987)
	Home-based contingencies	Pfiffner & Barkley (1990)
	Peer-mediated reinforcers	Carden-Smith & Fowler (1984)
Disruptive behaviors	Nonexclusionary time-out	Pfiffner & Barkley (1990)
	Response cost	Rapport, Murphy, & Bailey (1982)
	Negative consequences with positive reinforcement	Pfiffner & O'Leary (1987)
Off-task behaviors	Reinforce academic products	DuPaul & Stoner (1994)
	Token economies for task completion	DuPaul, Guevremont, & Barkley, (1991)
	Direct, short reprimands with positive reinforcers	Abramowitz & O'Leary (1991)
	Reinforce number of completed assignments	Robinson, Newby, & Ganzell (1981)

in children with ADD without hyperactivity (ADD/WO), both may have compliance and work completion problems. Token economies (Pfiffner & O'Leary, 1987), home-based contingencies (Pfiffner & Barkley, 1990), and peer-mediated reinforcement (Carden-Smith & Fowler, 1984) are useful for increasing work productivity; and nonexclusionary time-out from positive reinforcement (Pfiffner & Barkley, 1990), response cost (Rapport, Murphy, & Bailey, 1982), and negative consequences (Pfiffner & O'Leary, 1987) are generally incorporated into management programs for reducing undesirable behaviors. Direct, short, calm, firm, and consistent reprimands reduce off-task and disruptive behaviors in the classroom and are more effective than praise alone for some particularly persistent problems (Abramowitz & O'Leary, 1991). However, Pfiffner and Barkley (1990) caution that response cost, time-out, and other consequences or punishments should be implemented within a reinforcement-rich environment. It is necessary to provide reinforcers more frequently (Douglas, 1983) and to change rewards more often because children with ADHD habituate to reinforcers quickly. Habituation to or infrequent application of rewards have caused many otherwise well-planned management systems to fail.

Other behavioral techniques have worked effectively by modifying the characteristics of the environment or the task. Some of these are (1) using informal settings in which choice among a variety of educational activities is available and group memberships are monitored by the teacher (Jacob, O'Leary, & Rosenblad, 1978); (2) changing seating arrangements (Abramowitz & O'Leary, 1991); (3) allowing self-paced versus other-paced activities (Whalen et al., 1978); (4) increasing stimulation and novelty of the task (Zentall & Dywer, 1988; Zentall, Falkenberg, & Smith, 1985; Zentall & Zentall, 1983); (5) using work chunking and time intervals (Allyon & Rosenbaum, 1977); and (6) decreasing noise levels in the classroom when children are learning new tasks (Zentall & Shaw, 1980).

Classroom behaviors of children with ADHD are positively influenced when teachers are energetic, when children are allowed to select activities, and when activities are self-paced (Teeter & Semrud-Clikeman, 1995). Douglas (1983) also found that schedules of reinforcement can be manipulated to improve behaviors and that children with ADHD respond in a manner similar to non-ADHD peers under conditions of continuous reinforcement. Although aggression can be reduced with intensive intervention, behavioral techniques do not normalize the classroom behavior of hyperactive children (Abikoff & Gittelman, 1984). Inattention, high activity levels, and impulsivity are not markedly improved by behavioral interventions, although pharmacotherapy is extremely effective for these behaviors.

When treating hyperactive children, clinicians must consider not only academic performance but also other nonacademic classroom behaviors, like activity level and attentional problems, that may interfere with adjustment in the classroom. Behavioral interventions affect these target behaviors differently.

Manipulating Consequences

Positive versus Negative Reinforcement. Research has shown that, when used in isolation, praise and teacher attention do not produce systematic and consistent change in the classroom behavior of children with ADHD (DuPaul, Guevremont, & Barkley, 1991). Rosen, O'Leary, Joyce, Conway, and Pfiffner (1984) found that removal of positive reinforcers (e.g., teacher praise, approval, or other privileges) did not improve children's behavior unless negative consequences (e.g., loss of privileges) were also employed as part of the plan. The nature of the negative consequences was also important, and this study found that prudent reprimands from the teacher, time-out, and loss of privileges were most effective. When imprudent negative consequences were used (e.g., reprimands given late, inconsistently, or nonspecifically), classroom disruption increased. When positive reinforcers were used without prudent negative consequences, on-task and academic productivity decreased in this same group. Although these authors do not suggest that teachers should avoid using positive reinforcement, Rosen et al. (1984) indicate that the use of negative consequences may be essential for behavioral change in children with ADHD. However, caution is necessary when using negative feedback. Worland (1976) reported that although negative feedback (e.g., a burglar alarm or horn) increased on-task behavior for children with ADHD, it also resulted in a reduction in the accuracy of their spelling work. Furthermore, Carlson (1997) reported that response cost conditions decreased motivation whereas reward conditions increased interest in the task. If the goal is to increase intrinsic motivation, reinforcements may be more powerful in the long run.

Abramowitz, O'Leary, and Rosen (1987) studied the effects of teacher encouragement, reprimands, or no feedback for a group of hyperactive and/or learning disabled children. Praise included smiles, hugs, or verbal praise of the child or his work. Encouragement consisted of verbal remarks such as "Try your best," "I know you can do it," "If you are having a problem with one, just go ahead and try the next one," "If you need help, keep on working and I'll help you as soon as I can," and "Keep trying" (Abramowitz et al., 1987, p. 156). Reprimands consisted of commands to stop the undesired behavior, to engage in desired behavior, or both. In this study, off-task behavior was decreased following teacher reprimands, whereas encouraging remarks for on-task behavior alone did not consistently improve behavior. Although some children did seem to respond to encouragement, they also tended to have higher off-task behaviors and they seemed more susceptible to poorly controlled environments.

Abramowitz, O'Leary, and Futtersak (1988) suggest that long reprimands are less effective than short reprimands. Abramowitz and O'Leary (1991) summarize the conditions under which reprimands are most effective: short versus long; prudent (calm, firm, consistent) versus imprudent (overemotional, inconsistent); and timely versus delayed (by two minutes or more). Finally, it is important to note that an increase in on-task behavior does not always result in improved academic performance. Studies consistently report that an increase in academic performance results when the amount and accuracy of work is directly reinforced; decreased off-task behavior is often an added side effect (Allyon, Layman, & Kandel, 1975; Marholin & Steinman, 1977).

Token Systems. Token systems have been utilized with hyperactive children because praise alone is not sufficient to increase on-task behavior (Barkley, 1989; DuPaul, Guevremont, & Barkley, 1991; Pfiffner & Barkley, 1990). Token systems are arranged so that the child earns points or tokens contingent for appropriate behavior (e.g., on-task, compliance, etc.). Tokens are later turned in for privileges, free time, or tangible reinforcers.

Robinson, Newby, and Ganzell (1981) used a token system to increase the academic performance of a class of children with hyperactivity. In a design similar to a study conducted by Allyon and Roberts (1974) with disruptive children, Robinson et al. (1981) used a token system to reinforce reading abilities rather than to decrease disruptive behaviors. The academic tasks were broken down into 10 manageable learning units. For example, in each unit the child had to learn four new words, to review three previously learned words, and to learn one randomly selected word. The child then had to arrange a sentence incorporating the unit words. Students received tokens for completing unit work and for tutoring each other on unit words. The teacher administered the unit tests and the tokens. The class completed nine times as many lessons on the token system as they did after the token system was removed. The class also passed more standardized vocabulary tests under the token system, and they responded to a variety of reinforcers (e.g., electric ping-pong table and pinball machine, which was replaced with time with the teacher and class outings).

Rapport, Tucker, DuPaul, Merlo, and Stoner (1986) studied the effects of frustration tolerance on a group of children with hyperactivity. In this study, children were given math problems, and conditions of reinforcement delay were tested. During Trial A, children were asked to work for their second favorite space toy after completing 14 of 15 math problems correctly (short active delay). Children were then asked to select from a menu specifying the number of problems necessary to earn more toys. For example, the child could choose to work up to 5 more problems and earn one or two more toys, or the child could decide to solve 15 to 25 more problems and earn three or four more toys. Children choosing to earn three or four toys had to wait 2 days for the toys (long passive delay). The hyperactive males (94%) chose the immediate reinforcement (short delay condition) more frequently than the control group did (31%), whereas the control group chose the long delay (69%) more often than the hyperactive group did (6%). These authors concluded that token systems are effective but that hyperactive children do have difficulty delaying gratification and have low frustration tolerance.

Despite positive outcomes following the use of token economies, there are problems associated with these programs. Although generalization of behaviors outside the reinforced environment has not been adequately studied (Abramowitz & O'Leary, 1991; Barkley, 1989), some researchers have found disappointing effects after reinforcement systems have been discontinued. Furthermore, Barkley, Copeland, and Sivage (1980) found that a combined cognitive-behavioral and contingency management program did not produce lasting effects once treatment was terminated. These are important findings because teachers often discontinue token systems and need to be encouraged to reinstate these programs if child misbehavior and/or work completion problems and noncompliance reappear. Teaching the child to self-monitor and self-reward may prove helpful for maintaining gains in token economy programs. See Stokes and Osnes (1989) for other strategies to increase generalization and maintenance.

As previously noted, studies have consistently found that positive reinforcers alone do not produce consistent behavioral changes in children with ADHD (Abramowitz et al., 1987; Pfiffner & O'Leary, 1987; Pfiffner et al., 1985; Rosen et al., 1984). Barkley (1989) also states that when treating children with ADHD, response cost (e.g., loss of privileges) with token reinforcement is more effective than reinforcement alone. Again these reductive/punishment techniques can be introduced only in reinforcement-rich environments in which the child receives significantly more praise and rewards than punishment.

Response Cost. Response cost programs that are built into reinforcement systems are highly effective for reducing off-task behaviors, incomplete work assignments, and inattention (Fiore, Becker, & Nero, 1993). Abramowitz and O'Leary (1991) suggest that token systems for children with ADHD should incorporate some reductive measure or response cost for undesirable (e.g., aggressive or off-task) behavior; however, they caution that if the child starts to lose more points than he/she is earning, the system should be modified. It may be necessary to reduce expectancies for a short period of time; intervals for reinforcement may need to be shorter; or reinforcers may need to be changed. Abramowitz and O'Leary (1991) also suggest that another form of punishment may be used instead of a loss of points. Time-out may be useful in some circumstances.

Children who are more aggressive and hyperactive also appear to respond favorably to response cost techniques. In a study investigating the effects of reward only versus response cost, Sullivan and O'Leary (1990) found that children showed positive gains (i.e., work productivity and on-task behavior) under both programs. However, children who were more aggressive and hyperactive sustained their behavioral gains for a longer period of time after the programs were discontinued if they had initially been on the response cost program.

Use of electronic devices that credit children with points as part of a program in which teachers can reduce points have proven effective with behavior-disordered boys in a self-contained classroom (DuPaul, Guervremont, & Barkley, 1992). Behaviors that were positively affected included on-task behavior, level of hyperactivity and attentional control. Similar results were reported by Gordon, Thomason, Cooper, and Ivers (1991), although behavioral gains were quickly lost when the program was discontinued. Although the devices facilitate response cost programs in the classroom, Fiore et al. (1993) caution that more research is needed to determine how children with ADHD and their classmates accept electronically based devices.

Besides the use of negative consequences and response cost, other reductive methods have proven effective in the treatment of children with ADHD, particularly time-out from positive reinforcement.

Time-Out Procedures. Time-out from positive reinforcement is commonly used in behavioral therapy (Kazdin, 1980) and has been shown to be effective with retarded youngsters (Foxx & Shapiro, 1978), and emotionally disturbed children (Drabman, Spitalnik, & O'Leary, 1973). Barkley (1987, 1997b) incorporated time-out procedures in his training program for parents of children with ADHD. Although time-out seems like a simple procedure to implement, teachers and parents most likely will need training in the proper use of time-out procedures.

Although the efficacy of time-out has been well established, its potential for abuse or misuse continues to be of concern. The extent of periods of seclusion, the place of seclusion, and the monitoring of seclusion are all areas where abuse could occur. Because of these and other ethical concerns over the use of punishment, many time-out procedures employ nonexclusionary strategies in which the child remains in the classroom but is denied access to reinforcers for a specified period of time.

DuPaul, Guevremont, and Barkley (1991) and DuPaul and Stoner (1994) provide the following guidelines for implementing time-out procedures in the classroom: time-out for misbehavior must be delivered quickly; the teacher must determine when time-out is finished; once time-out is over, the child should correct or compensate for his/her misbehavior; response cost should follow if the child leaves time-out before the specified time; a time-out chair should be used instead of such areas as hallways, closets, or boxes; and time-out procedures should be used in conjunction with rewards.

It is important to use time-out sparingly, particularly for children who have low self-esteem or poor adult–child bonding or who are often rejected by peers. Time-out may serve to further isolate and alienate a disengaged, emotionally fragile child, or it may further damage a tenuous, poorly formed adult–child bond. Time-out should be used to remove the child from a volatile or emotionally charged situation, to allow the child to regain control (or to think about his/her misbehavior), and to reenter the learning or social situation by behaving appropriately. It should not be used as a means to get rid of or humiliate an annoying or demanding child.

In summary, teacher-based classroom management practices are effective for reducing a variety of behavioral problems and for increasing work productivity and accuracy. Because of the problems inherent in generalization and maintenance of behavioral gains once management programs are suspended, some research has focused on methods of increasing the child's ability to monitor him/herself.

Self-Management Techniques

Self-management techniques have become popular for treating classroom problems associated with ADHD (Shapiro & Cole, 1994), despite the fact that their efficacy is largely unsubstantiated (Abikoff, 1985, 1987, 1991). Teachers and parents become increasingly concerned about encouraging responsibility and independence in children with ADHD, so their interest in using self-management techniques is usually quite high. Self-management techniques are attractive because of their ease of use, particularly if the child has been on other management schedules that required teachers and parents to monitor behaviors for extended periods of time. These schedules can create significant problems; teachers and parents may have trouble sustaining effective behavior management programs because they can be time-consuming.

Self-management interventions typically include self-instruction, self-monitoring, and self-reinforcement (Barkley, 1987; DuPaul & Stoner, 1994). These techniques generally fall into the general category of cognitive-behavioral training.

Cognitive-Behavioral Techniques

The use of cognitive-behavioral techniques for treating children with ADHD is appealing because of the impulse control problems hyperactive children display. Increased performance following self-instruction has been documented in a number of studies with hyperactive children, especially on experimental tasks like the Porteus Mazes (Palkes, Stewart, & Kahana, 1968) and the Kagan Matching Familiar Figures Test (Michenbaum, 1976). Other findings are equivocal. Some studies suggest that the academic functioning of nonmedicated children with ADHD does not systematically improve (Abikoff, 1985), whereas others suggest that self-instruction training improves performance both on the experimental task itself and in other classroom behaviors as well (Bornstein & Quevillon, 1976).

Self-instructional programs typically include teaching the child to use self-statements, originally modeled by the teacher, and to self-reinforce when responses are correct. Abikoff et al. (1988) distinguish between specific skill deficits that many children with ADHD have and an impulsive response style to tasks that often results in inaccurate work. Academic improvement must focus on both aspects of the problem. In an effort to determine the effects of self-instruction on academic tasks, Abikoff et al. (1988) designed an elaborate treatment program for 34 children with ADHD. Children were assigned to one of three conditions: an academic cognitive training program with medication; a remedial tutoring program with medication; and a medication alone condition.

The academic cognitive training program consisted of self-instruction, self-reinforcement, self-monitoring, and attack strategy training. The program was individualized to address the academic deficit area of each child (i.e., math or reading). Comprehensive self-instructional procedures were implemented for the academic cognitive training group, including teaching children what to do; how to find directions apart from other information; how to find "doing" words; how to attend to sample items; how to restate directions; and how to self-monitor and self-reinforce. Further training was given to teach children to be careful, to be accurate, and to develop a strategy before starting their work. In the remedial tutoring group, self-instructional procedures were not employed. Both the tutoring and the self-instructional groups had a training and a mastery segment, and points were given for accuracy in carrying out program steps.

After 16 weeks, the cognitive-training-with-medication group did not differ on academic measures, teacher reports, parent reports, or child ratings from the tutoring-with-medication and the medication-alone groups. When scores were calculated on individuals in each group, the cognitive-training-with-medication and the tutoring-with-medication groups showed higher initial academic gains than the medication-alone group. However, six-month follow-up revealed positive academic gains in all three groups. Abikoff et al. (1988) suggest that the problem-solving cognitive approach did not differentially improve academic performance when compared to tutoring-with-medication and to medication alone. Abikoff and Gittelman (1985) also did not find improved home or school behaviors in medicated children when a cognitive training program was added to enhance social skills and strategy building skills in hyperactive children. In general, Abikoff et al. (1988) indicate that the long-term positive effects of medication should be reconsidered given these findings (Goldstein & Goldstein, 1990).

Studies that have shown positive effects for self-reinforcement techniques in children with ADHD still have problems showing generalization of effects once the program is no longer in place. Barkley, Copeland, and Sivage (1980) used four steps in a self-instruction program to teach children with ADHD to listen to directions, to repeat the directions, to repeat the problem in their own words, and to reward themselves for a correct answer. Children were taught to monitor their own behavior using the following five rules: "(1) stay in your seat, (2) work quietly, (3) don't bug others, (4) don't space out (daydream), and (5) raise your hand if you need help" (Barkley et al., 1980, p. 79). Misbehaving during individual seat work was reduced under the self-monitoring and self-reward condition, and on-task behavior increased during individual seat work under the self-control condition. However, there was no change in the activity level (measured by wrist and ankle actometer), nor was there a decrease in inappropriate behaviors in the large-group setting.

The Barkley et al. (1980) study did support the use of self-control and self-reward procedures for managing the behavior of children with ADHD during individual classwork. The program seemed to be most effective when self-monitoring schedules were short (1 to 1.5 minutes) compared to longer intervals (3 to 5 minutes). However, it is important to note that the on-task behavior did not generalize outside the intervention setting. Although some success has been reported, self-instructional programs have not routinely produced improvements that generalize to the classroom or to social situations for children with ADHD.

Self-recording and self-reward programs do show some promise. For example, Bowers, Clement, Fantuzzo, and Sorensen (1985) investigated differences between teacher-administered and self-administered reinforcers for children with ADHD. In this study, children were reinforced for attending to and accurately completing their work. Although reinforcers delivered by the teacher and by the child both resulted in increased attention, self-administered reinforcers strengthened the attending of the children. Although children were as accurate as their teacher when rewarding behaviors, Gross and Wojnilower (1984) stress that non-contingent reinforcement must be followed by a negative consequence or children will reward themselves regardless of whether or not they are engaging in the target behavior.

Correspondence Training

Using a technique that is similar to cognitive-behavioral strategies, Pangiagua (1992) and Pangiagua, Morrison, and Black (1990) modified the behavior of hospitalized children with ADHD using correspondence training. Correspondence training involves teaching children the relationship between verbal and nonverbal behaviors. Children were taught to decrease inappropriate behaviors by promising not to engage in the behavior, by following through with their promise, and by accurately reporting their behaviors. Children showed improvements on observations of inattention, hyperactivity, and conduct-related behaviors after training and reinforcement. Fiore, Becker, and Nero (1993) suggest that correspondence training may be a "practical" technique for school-based interventions as well.

In summary, self-monitoring, child-administered reinforcement, and correspondence training programs can all be incorporated into treatment plans. It has been my experience that self-monitoring programs are most effective with children who have been successful with teacher-based management programs, who have developed basic organizational skills, and who are not too young (8 years and older). Children with low self-esteem may prefer self-monitoring techniques to avoid being singled out for teacher-administered or token systems, particularly if he/she is the only child in the classroom who has a management program.

Home-Based Contingency Programs

Home-based contingency programs are incorporated into treatment programs for many children with ADHD. This method, which provides for daily, direct contact between the classroom teacher (or teachers) and the parent(s), has a number of advantages over school-based programs. Abramowitz and O'Leary (1991) summarize these advantages. Home-based contingencies require daily notes between teacher and parent; they require fewer changes in teacher behaviors and less teacher time; they call less attention to the child; they allow the parent to provide a wider variety of reinforcers; they may result in better parent–child relationships, more effective child management practices by the parent, and increased self-esteem in the child; and they may allow wider generalization because children are learning to delay gratification.

Pfiffner and Barkley (1990) provide a detailed example of a home-based contingency program in which children earn points for improved classroom behavior and are reinforced by the parent at the end of the day. Studies have shown that praise alone is less effective than praise with privileges (Schumaker, Hovell, & Sherman, 1977) and that coupling positive reinforcement with response cost is more potent than reinforcement alone (Rosen, Gabardi, Miller, & Miller, 1990; Abramowitz & O'Leary, 1991). On the other hand, Carlson (1997) reported a decrease in motivation with response cost conditions alone, so high reward conditions should be part of the plan.

Abramowitz and O'Leary (1991) provide guidelines for using home-based systems. (1) Teachers and parents must be well trained in behavioral management techniques. (2) The identification of and rotation of reinforcers, the use of response cost, and contingent reinforcement must be carefully implemented. (3) The ability of parents to conduct the program must be analyzed. (4) Care must be taken to guard against abuse when children do poorly on daily reports. (5) Parents with punitive management styles need prior training in more effective techniques before using this program. (6) Teacher commitment is still essential. To be effective, parents and teachers must collaborate and work in partnerships to monitor and modify programs depending on how the child responds.

Even when problem behaviors are under control, a number of children with ADHD have other difficulties that interfere with academic achievement. Specific interventions have been created to deal with learning and academic difficulties. Many of these techniques are taken from literature addressing learning disabilities, whereas others specifically emphasize problems associated with ADHD. Given that learning problems or disabilities and ADHD overlap, these strategies may be appropriate for both groups. A number of educational experts advise that classroom-wide, teacher-monitored systems can alleviate some of the problems associated with ADHD.

ACADEMIC AND LEARNING STRATEGIES

Efforts should be made to reduce academic and learning problems by teaching the child organizational and study skills. Children may also need extra instructional opportunities or tutoring in specific subject areas, and specific teaching strategies for children with learning disabilities may also be beneficial. See Scruggs and Wong (1990) and Wong (1991) for suggestions for addressing specific learning and academic problems. When academic tasks are the focus of intervention, a number of strategies appear promising, including decreasing the length of tasks, reducing the amount of work, increasing novelty and task interest, increasing opportunities for active participation, varying the presentation of information, and allowing for self-directed or computer-assisted activities.

There are several models of classroom-based interventions available for use with children with ADHD (see Jones, 1989; Goldstein & Goldstein, 1990; Zentall, 1995). Jones (1989) emphasizes the need to modify tasks and classrooms with the following in mind: (1) brevity—use brief lessons, shorter assignments, and smaller chunks of information to increase sustained attention and effort; (2) variety—decrease the amount of repetition as much as possible, infuse assignments with interesting activities, and allow for choice to increase effort and motivation; and (3) structure/routine—plan a highly organized, "focused environment" with well-planned activities and transitions. Goldstein and Goldstein (1990) emphasize the need to change the cognitions of children with the purpose of increasing self-management, and to provide managed environments to increase success. Zentall (1995) describes a model that allows children to move more frequently, to talk and actively question in class, and to learn through novel and interesting assignments. See Goldstein and Jones (1998) for more details.

Classroom Environments

The efficacy of behavioral interventions in the classroom has been the focus of numerous research efforts, and studies investigating the characteristics of the environment and the task have proven useful. Jacob et al. (1978) investigated two classroom environments, formal and informal, to determine the relationship of the setting to the behavior of children with ADHD. The formal classroom setting was described as one that required children to remain in their seats, to complete assigned classwork, and to listen to class presentations. The informal setting was described as one that allowed children to choose tasks, many of which were educational games requiring groups of children to cooperate together. Children were selected using rigid criteria for hyperactivity. They were between 9 and 10 years of age and were of average intelligence.

The children were given remedial math classes. The informal and formal settings were 30 minutes in length and were separated by a 5-minute break. The different conditions were arranged in various parts of the same classroom. The activities for the informal setting included numerous games (e.g., flash cards, dice game, Math Quizmo, and Concentration) or crossword puzzles, treasure maps, measurement tools, or other math problems. Children were allowed to select one or two of the activities with occasional prompts from the teacher. The activities in the formal setting included completing math problems on worksheets or listening to instruction from the teacher.

Although children with ADHD were more active than a control group in both settings, behaviors of the ADHD group were more similar to the control group in the informal, open-classroom setting. Although these results might support an open-classroom approach, the authors suggest caution for several reasons. First, different measures may result in different outcomes. In fact, measures of daydreaming were higher for the hyperactives in the formal setting than in the informal setting. Also, similarities between the control group and the ADHD group in the informal setting were largely a result of an increase in "change of position" (e.g., walking around, standing or leaving seat) measures for the control group. Whether a change in the control group in the informal setting was viewed as positive or negative could not be ascertained because academic performance was not specifically measured. Allowing for increased movement in the classroom may have some benefit when it can be monitored and directed toward academic projects or learning stations.

Others have shown that classroom seating arrangements produce changes in the behavior of hyperactive children. Abramowitz and O'Leary (1991) summarized the findings of several studies and indicated that social interaction was increased in cluster seating arrangements (i.e., several children at a table or desks facing each other), whereas on-task behavior for independent work was not facilitated. On-task behavior seemed to be positively affected when children were placed in a circle for teacher presentations and open discussions. On-task independent work seemed to be enhanced when children were seated in rows of desks.

Task-by-Environment Interaction

Whalen et al. (1978) found that characteristics of the environment and the task have an impact on the behaviors of boys with hyperactivity. Two experimental conditions were tested in a summer school program in which self- versus other-paced and easy versus difficult conditions were compared. Medication and placebo conditions for the boys with hyperactivity were compared to a control group. The medicated group did not differ from the control group, whereas the placebo group showed higher rates of hyperactive, noisy, disruptive, off-task, and inappropriate behaviors compared to the controls. The placebo group showed particularly low rates of attention under other-paced, difficult task conditions. Inappropriate behaviors were highest for the placebo group under other-paced conditions.

Task Characteristics

Task characteristics were altered in several studies by Zentall and her colleagues in an effort to test an "optimal arousal" theory. Zentall (1985) argues that hyperactive children have low tolerance for conditions in which arousal is minimal and that they satiate to stimuli faster than do controls, especially under repetitive conditions (Zentall & Zentall, 1983). Adding novelty and providing stimulating instructional techniques may prove extremely effective for ADHD children (Fiore et al., 1993; Zentall, 1995).

Stimulation and Novelty

Zentall, Falkenberg, and Smith (1985) studied the effects of color added to letters in a handwriting exercise. Under the color condition, fewer errors were made by the hyperactive but not by the control children. Zentall and Dwyer (1988) also found that activity levels were lower for hyperactive children when color was added to a task requiring attention and concentration. Although activity levels improved, the error rate was unchanged. Zentall and Dwyer (1988) conclude that whereas color addition may improve attention and may reduce impulsive responding, noninformational color addition does not increase strategy training. Educators are advised to use color to increase focused and sustained attention and to teach other strategies to improve response accuracy. Zentall's findings suggest that children with ADHD may respond best to stimulation and novelty (e.g., color addition) when tasks are easy and repetitive but that they may interfere with performance when tasks are new or difficult.

Zentall and Shaw (1980) found that hyperactive children were more active and completed fewer math problems correctly under a high-noise condition compared to a low-noise condition when noise was presented through earphones. A control group showed less activity and higher accuracy rates under the high-noise condition. A similar pattern was revealed on another task in which children were asked to circle a series of letters in alphabetical order from a mixed array. In this experiment, the noise conditions were delivered freely into the classroom from a tape recording. Hyperactive children made more errors of commission under the high-noise condition, whereas the control group was able to perform better. Task difficulty interacted in the performance of both groups. Both hyperactive and control children were less accurate in high-noise conditions when the tasks were new or difficult. Noise levels did not adversely affect the performance of hyperactive children when tasks were well practiced. In fact, both groups may actually benefit from classroom noise on tasks that are overlearned, whereas both are distracted by high noise when new learning is required.

Improved performance has also been demonstrated in situations in which children are provided opportunities to move and to be actively involved in the learning process. Zentall and Meyer (1987) found that when motor responses were added to rote memory activities, children engaged in fewer attention-getting behaviors and made fewer errors. Active response conditions channel excessive activity in appropriate, nondisruptive ways and may increase academic task engagement.

Amount of Work

Allyon and Rosenbaum (1977) suggest that matching the amount of work to the child's attention level may be helpful for children with ADHD. Chunking work and using short time intervals for work completion increased academic success in this group. As a group, these studies indicate that positive behavioral changes can be achieved when the environment and task characteristics are modified for children with ADHD.

Teacher Characteristics/Teaching Styles

Zentall (1985) suggests that teaching styles may also affect the classroom behavior of the child with ADHD. Classrooms where children are allowed to move about and to actively participate in learning tasks produce positive outcomes. Teachers who are energetic, who move about, and who engage children frequently also seem to make a difference.

In summary, techniques for managing children in the classroom, for altering the classroom environment, and for introducing novelty and stimulation into the classroom have proven effective for increasing work completion and reducing negative behaviors in children with ADHD. A number of strategies for systems-level modifications focus on modifying the classroom or the educational settings.

PROMISING CLASSROOM-LEVEL INTERVENTIONS

Sandra Reif: How to Teach Children with ADHD

In an effort to meet the educational needs of children with ADHD, Sandra Reif and her colleagues in the San Diego school system employed classroom-wide interventions first introduced by Jones (1989, 1994). Table 6.3 summarizes strategies outlined by Jones (1989, 1994) and Reif (1993), including techniques for getting attention, focusing attention, maintaining attention, reducing distraction, increasing organizational

TABLE 6.3.   Techniques for Teaching Children with ADHD

Problem area	Suggested strategies
Getting attention	Use signals such as turning lights on/off, ringing a bell, and so forth Give commands such as "Listen!" "Ready!" "Freeze!" Make eye contact when giving directions Be enthusiastic and excited about teaching Use theatrics, humor, and interesting props Use mystery box to introduce a new topic: bring a prop in a box and have class guess what is inside
Focusing attention	Use multisensory strategies when giving instructions Use visual aids, pictures, and overhead projectors Use color coding to highlight key words, phrases, problem-solving steps Use finger, flashlight, or other pointer to help child focus on relevant information Use demonstrations and active presentations
Maintaining attention	Be clear, use a quick pace, be prepared Use pairs and cooperative groups to increase participation Use questioning techniques to encourage thinking and reasoning Call on all students; do not ignore anyone Vary method of picking children to respond (e.g., use a deck of cards with student's name)
Reducing distraction	Use unison responding Use individual chalkboards so child can write down answers Use point/tap technique (for example, point to word on chalkboard; teach class to read the word you point to and say word out loud when you tap) Use green card/red card
Organizational skills	Assign a "buddy" to check that homework assignments are written correctly Use assignment calendars and homework notebooks Use a daily action list, "things-to-do" list Provide time at end of class to double-check homework assignments and supplies needed for homework Make a plan between home and school Use "Skills for Success"[a] to emphasize quality work Use heavy paper that will not tear easily
Increasing time-management skills	Use clock face at the desk—set movable hands at important times of day (e.g., specials or pull-out sessions) Use timers (10 or 15 minutes)—reinforce for work completion and accuracy

(*continued*)

TABLE 6.3. cont.

Increasing reading skills	Use storyboards; have child draw pictures of stories Use story charts outlining main characters, main ideas, etc. Use plot profiles to identify important story events Use character webs; put character's name in web and fill in important characteristics Use prediction charts; ask what will happen next in the story Use directed reading/thinking activity (e.g., predict what story will be about, check hypothesis after reading with peers/teachers) Use metacognitive journals (What did I learn?/What did I expect to learn?) Use K-W-L columns (What did I Know? What do I Want to learn? What did I Learn?) Use retelling Use literature, dialogue, and drama
Increasing writing skills	Use prewriting exercise to get child ready to write (e.g., discuss topic ahead of time) Use revising, editing, rearranging, and deleting Use advanced organizing skills to plan paper ahead of time Use and teach metaphors Use brainstorming Use alternatives to overused words Use writing journals for quick writes and sustained, ongoing writing Use draft writing and creative writing to generate ideas, then revise Use word processors and computers
Increasing math skills	Use computers for drill and practice Use math portfolios for reasoning and thinking Use PYBOP ("Put brains on paper") for journals Use graph paper to align columns and rows Use estimation activities Reduce the number of problems Avoid timed tests of basic facts Use color to highlight operational signs Give assignments one sheet or row at a time; go to next sheet when student finishes

Note. For other strategies see Jones (1989, 1994) and Reif (1993).
[a]Archer & Gleason (1990).

skills, developing time-management skills, and increasing reading, math, and written language abilities.

Jones's (1989, 1994) and Reif's (1993) techniques focus on modifying teaching strategies and classroom environments to increase the overall adjustment and academic performance of children with ADHD. Efforts are made to decrease the occurrence of behavioral problems by structuring the classroom for success, by providing options for various learning styles (e.g., using multisensory and visual aids), by changing work areas (e.g., study carrels for privacy), by organizing assignments (e.g., daily action lists and "study buddies"), and by employing active participation in the learning process (e.g., unison responding). These techniques can be used routinely for all children, and teachers are encouraged to restructure and modify teaching strategies rather than trying to fit the child into a "one-size-fits-all" classroom. Although these techniques have not been systematically researched, specific strategies (e.g., color-coding and reinforcement techniques) have been shown to be effective. Jones and Reif describe methods for structuring the learning environment that could be easily evaluated with individual or small groups of children using ABAB designs (i.e., obtain baseline data, implement the intervention/modification, withdraw the intervention, and reinstate the intervention) in order to assess the efficacy of specific approaches.

Mel Levine: Educational Care

Another promising paradigm for reducing problems in the classroom and in the home was developed by Mel Levine. Levine (1993) describes developmental functions that influence the child's learning process, including attention and inattention, simultaneous and sequential processing, production, memory, language, higher order cognition, motor implementation, and social ability. Variations in normal development can produce a variety of attentional and learning problems in children. Levine (1993) argues for the need to modify and to restructure learning environments for children with special needs. For example:

> The more we involve ourselves with disappointing children, the more we understand the risks they must take during childhood. As students, they suffer for their variations. They are at risk not just for prolonged suffering during years that should be marked by the gratifying pleasures of discovery and growth, but for more long-standing loss of self-esteem and identity. . . . Their lives bear the scars of unjust accusation, chronic feelings of inadequacy, and shamelessly untapped talent. Understanding developmental variation, characterizing it without oversimplifying it, and intervening vigorously on behalf of developing humans experiencing inordinate failure—these are urgent needs. (1993, p. 11)

Levine (1993, 1994) developed a paradigm to explain attentional-learning difficulties in children and to explore numerous intervention techniques that address these problems. Table 6.4 summarizes the strategies outlined by Levine (1993, 1994). For each major problem,

TABLE 6.4. Selected Summary of Educational Techniques for Reducing Learning Problems

Observable phenomena	Strategies
Weak mental energy	Give small amounts of work with brief breaks
	Use private signaling to attend (e.g., tap on shoulder)
	Allow child to stand, stretch, and walk around
	Keep hands busy (e.g., doodling)
	Understand inconsistency is not willful; offer encouragement
	Signal when something important is coming up
Weak processing	Prioritize tasks
	Do not call on child who is not attending (causes stress)
	Emphasize important points using summarizing, paraphrasing, finding main idea, etc.
	Use verbal redirection for visual distractibility
	Repeat instructions for auditory distractibility
	Use reminder cards
	Self-monitor own level of distractibility
	Use short and direct instructions; make eye contact
Weak production	Stress previewing, planning ahead, advanced organizers
	Stress estimation skills (e.g., "How many people live in _____?")
	Ask "What if?" questions
	Review alternative strategies before starting a task
	Have child estimate how long it will take to complete a task and then check to see how accurate the estimation was
	Teach child to become aware of actions ("What led up to behavior, how did you feel, what could you have done differently?")
	Encourage daily self-assessments ("Which behaviors are being assessed? How am I doing?"), reward child for success

(continued)

178

Short-term memory	Sit child close to teacher Repeat instructions Teach child to paraphrase material
Active working memory	Allow slow workers more time on tests or give fewer items Jot down main idea, key events, and so forth before writing assignment Use calculators and word processors
Long-term memory	Give advanced warnings before calling child in class Allow more time on tests Ask open-ended questions so more than one answer can be correct Use other ways of demonstrating knowledge than test taking (e.g., write a report) Sustain child's motivation and enjoyment of learning (i.e., teach child how to take exams) Be selective in what child has to remember
Language processing	Avoid embarrassing child in class when he/she misunderstands Repeat directions using intonations and emphasis Use diagrams on board when explaining Teach child to envision directions in their minds Use phonological awareness activities (e.g., music/rhyme)
Concept formation	Make sure child understands Have child describe process before and during activity Use conceptual maps (e.g., concept → critical features → other features → good examples → possible examples, etc.) Make use of child's strongest modality Use tutors
Visual processing	Give verbal explanations with visual material Enhance visualization through artwork Encourage child to describe what he/she sees

(continued)

TABLE 6.4. (*cont.*)

Slow data processing	Use concise instructions
	Be aware of when child becomes overwhelmed; help or reassure him/her
	Use visual aids with verbal presentations (e.g., models)
	Break task into smaller units
	Stress important points
	Use tape recorder for lectures
Excessive top-down or bottom-up processing	Help top-down processors with facts after reading (e.g., underline or list critical events, etc.)
	Encourage bottom-up processors in creative, expansive thinking
Language production	Let child know before calling on him/her
	Use nonlinguistic ways to help child experience success
	Encourage, build on expertise or interests of child
	Delay or waive foreign language
Motor performance	Avoid criticizing in physical education
	Avoid potentially embarrassing situations
	Understand why child may not want to dress for gym
	Use adaptive physical education and occupational or physical therapy
	Encourage child to manage team, assist coach, or report sports
	Use ongoing portfolio to show child's progress
Organization failure	Do not humiliate child in public
	Remind child what to do for homework
	Use color-coded notebooks
	Use home–school communication for assignments
	Teach time-management skills
	Teach child how to prepare for a test or organize a report
	Allow collaboration on projects

Note. For specific details on strategies, see Levine (1994).

Levine (1994) describes specific methods for reducing the effects of attentional-learning dysfunctions (e.g., poor memory, distractibility, etc.) for use in the home and in the classroom, and he stresses the need to provide interventions in both settings.

Levine (1993, 1994) emphasizes the need to help children understand, cope with, and maximize their particular attentional-learning strengths and weaknesses. "Demystification" is an intervention process in which clinicians help children become knowledgeable about their learning problems as well as their strengths (Levine, 1994). Therapists help children understand their difficulties and help them develop a vocabulary for expressing what they are experiencing. When employing strategies for demystification, therapists should incorporate statements that reflect their understanding of the challenges and struggles that the child faces. For example, the therapist might say to a child, "Your mind does not hold on to language too well in class. That makes it hard for you to take notes because you keep forgetting what the teacher just said" (Levine, 1994, p. 79). Demystification is essential to Levine's attentional-learning paradigm for helping children to understand their problems and for teaching them coping mechanisms to deal with their challenges in the school setting.

Children appear responsive to demystification techniques, and they can readily relate to statements that show that adults understand their difficulties and will not blame, humiliate, and/or categorize them because of their unique learning characteristics. Levine's techniques stress the importance of capitalizing on the child's strengths, finding areas where the child excels, and encouraging interests and talents in the child. In effect, the teacher and the parent are encouraged to and shown how to become allies with the child in his/her struggle to be successful in school and at home. Although these techniques have general appeal, they are in need of systematic research to determine their efficacy and long-term impact.

PROMISING EDUCATIONAL PRACTICES

In 1991, Congress allocated funds to the Office of Special Education Programs of the Department of Education to produce a synthesis of current knowledge on effective practices for children with ADD (U.S. Department of Education, 1993). Five ADD Research Centers were funded to conduct extensive literature reviews on educational practices, assessment research, and intervention practices, including medication. In the initial reports from these centers, 26 promising practices were identified throughout the nation. Two systems-level interventions that were identified as "promising" are described here.

The University of California–Irvine: Professional Training Model

James Swanson and colleagues at the University of California–Irvine Child Development Center (UCI; Swanson, 1992) developed a three-model school-based intervention program for ADHD children in elementary school that includes a parallel teaching model, a paraprofessional teaching model, and a multicomponent model (Fowler, 1992). The program was developed for children with varying degrees of severity of ADHD and incorporates different delivery strategies depending on the level of the child's inclusion in regular education classrooms.

The Kenosha ADD Project: Teacher Training/Structured Curriculum

Another promising practice cited by the ADD Research Centers is a structured teacher training curriculum developed by Kathy Hubbard at the Kenosha ADD Project.

Hubbard developed the Kenosha ADD Trainer's Manual, which is a structured curriculum that is available for clinicians and other professionals who are interested in helping teachers understand the nature of ADHD, the educational correlates of the disorder, and empirically based intervention strategies (Hubbard, unpublished materials). The structured teacher training model was created as the cornerstone of the Wisconsin ADD Project, which was funded by the state in an effort to better prepare teachers in effective educational strategies. The program was identified as a "promising practice" by the U.S. Department of Education Office of Special Education and Rehabilitative Services (U.S. Department of Education, 1993).

The Kenosha ADD Program includes materials and activities for a 16-hour teacher training program divided into five training modules. Module 1 provides an overview of the core symptoms of ADHD, differentiating ADD with and without hyperactivity, and presents preliminary strategies for educational interventions. Module 2 contains methods for distinguishing ADHD from other childhood disorders, identifying the causes of ADHD and family correlates of the disorder. Module 3 provides methods for educating inattentive children, for working with parents, and for developing teaching strategies. Medication efficacy and potential side effects are also discussed. Module 4 contains behavioral strategies to increase self-esteem in children and to identify potential reinforcers. Methods for writing formal educational plans are also described in this session. Finally, Module 5 presents a historical perspective of ADHD, including the legal mandates requiring educational services for children with ADHD.

Participants are provided with a select number of resources and references summarizing major research on ADHD. Case studies are presented, and teachers are provided guided opportunities to develop appropriate interventions for children with various behavioral, academic, and psychosocial problems. The materials developed by the Kenosha Project are well organized and detailed, with accurate and useful information for conducting teacher training sessions.

SOCIAL SKILLS TRAINING

The psychosocial functioning of children with ADHD is of particular concern to teachers and parents. Children with ADHD often suffer from high rates of social interaction problems, rejection, and other forms of emotional problems (e.g., depression and/or conduct-related disorders). Treatment efficacy for these problems is less well documented than are those for classroom and behavioral management methods; however, some interventions have either proven efficacious or show some potential for success for children with ADHD (see Sheridan, 1995).

Interventions have been designed to improve social competency and to reduce peer relation difficulties that many children with ADHD encounter (Teeter, 1993; Sheridan, 1995). Behavioral and cognitive-behavioral techniques, including modeling, rehearsal, and corrective feedback, have been employed to teach social entry, conversation, anger control, and conflict resolution skills (Guevremont, 1990). Research investigating the efficacy of these techniques has produced inconclusive and/or disappointing results. Although studies suggest that some improvement is noted after social skills training, the social behavior of children with ADHD often does not approach normal levels (Pelham & Bender, 1982). Generalizing skills from training sessions to natural settings such as the classroom or playground remains a problem. However, Bierman and Furman (1984) were successful in altering the social status of children with ADHD when peers were included in training sessions.

Efficacy of Social Skills Training

Social skills training has been advocated for children with ADHD, although research findings are not overwhelmingly positive in terms of outcome. Pelham and Bender (1982) found that, when used in isolation, social skills training and a token reinforcement system did not significantly improve the social skills of children with hyperactivity; however, when these interventions were combined, peer relationships did improve. Medication seemed to play an important role in producing these effects, and when moderate doses of methylphenidate (Ritalin) were discontinued, improvements seen under behavioral contingency plans were negated (Pelham & Bender, 1982). Response cost procedures may facilitate learning, and high rates of reinforcement may be necessary to produce positive social outcomes (Landau & Moore, 1991).

Effects of Medication on Social Skills

Although stimulant medication has been shown to decrease inappropriate verbal interchanges, children on medication appear to be somewhat dysphoric (Whalen et al., 1979). Other studies have reported decreased aggression in children on stimulant medication (Hinshaw, Henker, Whalen, Erhardt, & Dunnington, 1989) and improved interactions during baseball games (Pelham et al., 1990). Despite behavioral improvements, prosocial behavior is not always forthcoming (Hinshaw et al., 1989), and medicated children may still be ignored by peers (Wallander, Schroeder, Michelli, & Gualtiere, 1987). Although intuitively encouraging, cognitive-behavioral techniques have not shown outstanding results (Landau & Moore, 1991). However in conflict situations, children receiving cognitive-behavioral training combined with medication are able to control their anger under provocation and to use self-control strategies. Although generalization remains a critical issue, techniques designed to address social skills problems provide evidence that combining cognitive and skill-building approaches with medication may produce the best results.

Issues of self-esteem also need to be addressed during the middle childhood stage, and this may be accomplished by increasing the academic and social competencies of children with ADHD. When other comorbid emotional or psychological problems are present, individual and group therapy may also be beneficial.

PSYCHOPHARMACOLOGICAL INTERVENTIONS

"It may surprise educators to know that there are far more studies documenting the short-term efficacy of pharmacotherapy for ADHD than there are studies documenting the effects of educational and behavioral treatments for the disorder" (Pelham, 1993a, p. 201). Stimulant medication for children with ADHD has been the focus of more research than any other treatment approaches for childhood disorders; it has been effective for improving sustained attention, impulse control, activity level, disruptive behavior, compliance, work completion, and work accuracy (Barkley, 1990b). Although stimulants are the first-line medications for ADHD, physicians also administer other medications when these are not effective or when comorbid disorders (e.g., depression, aggression) are present.

Medication Options for ADHD

Medications for neuropsychiatric disorders of childhood generally fall into the following five categories: (1) stimulants (e.g., methylphenidate [Ritalin], dextroamphetamine [Dexedrine], and pemoline [Cylert]); (2) antipsychotics (e.g., haloperidol [Haldol] and thioridazine [Mellaril]); (3) tricyclic antidepressants (e.g., desimpramine [Norpramin] and imipramine [Tofranil]); (4) monoamine oxidase inhibitors (MAOIs; e.g., bupropion [Wellbutrin]); and (5) antihypertensives (clonidine [Catapres]). Table 6.5 summarizes the benefits and potential side effects of these medications.

Stimulants are typically sufficient for reducing the major symptoms of ADHD, although antipsychotics, antidepressants, and MAOIs may be prescribed in cases where children have other comorbid disorders or when stimulants are not effective. Stimulants (Ritalin and Dexedrine) increase the availability of neurotransmitters, whereas antidepressants (Norpramin and Tofranil) prevent the reuptake of transmitters at the synapse (Teeter & Semrud-Clikeman, 1997).

Effects of Medication on ADHD

Psychostimulants

The use of stimulant medication for the treatment of ADHD has generated a lot of controversy. News media and popular magazines periodically suggest that hyperactive children are being overmedicated; one article even referred to Ritalin as "kiddie cocaine." Cocaine is an illegal street drug taken for pleasure and cannot be compared to stimulant medication prescribed by a physician to control impulsive, disinhibited disorders. Although concerns about the misuse and/or potential side effects of stimulant medications are legitimate on an individual basis, inaccurate and alarmist information is not. Overzealous tabloids are meant to be provocative, not thought-provoking. They rarely present scientific literature on the effects of stimulant medications because it does not sell magazines. Journalists may find cases in which a child has been given a questionable diagnosis of ADHD or in which parents are concerned about or have been pressured into medicating their child "against their will." However, ethical, knowledgeable ADHD experts do not engage in these practices. Furthermore, as Comings (1990) also points out, the same parents who are adamantly opposed to Ritalin will pressure their pediatricians to prescribe penicillin for their

TABLE 6.5. Common Uses, Benefits, and Side Effects of Medications for ADHD and Other Neuropsychiatric Disorders of Childhood

Drugs	Common use	Manifestations	Side effects
		Stimulants	
Methylphenidate (Ritalin)	ADHD	Effective in 75% of children Decreased motor activity, impulsivity, and disruptive behaviors Increased attention Improved socialization Improved ratings (teacher, physician, parent) Increased work completion and accuracy Improved test scores (mazes, Performance IQ, and visual memory)	Insomnia, appetite loss, nausea, vomiting, abdominal pains, thirst, headaches Tachycardia, change in blood pressure Irritability, moodiness Rebound effects Growth suppression (can be monitored) Lower seizure threshold Exacerbation of preexisting tics
Dextroamphetamine (Dexedrine)	ADHD	Similar to methylphenidate Subdued emotional response Increased reflectivity and ability to monitor self Increased interest level Improved school performance Improved parent ratings (conduct, impulsivity, immaturity, antisocial behaviors, and hyperactivity)	Similar to methylphenidate Hallucinations, seizures drug-induced psychosis (rare occurrences)
Magnesium pemoline (Cylert)	ADHD	Similar to methylphenidate Improved teacher ratings (defiance, inattention, and hyperactivity) Improved parent ratings (conduct, impulsivity, and antisocial behaviors) Improved test scores (mazes, Performance IQ, and visual memory)	Similar to methylphenidate

(continued)

Antipsychotics

Drug	Indications	Effects and side effects
Haloperidol (Haldol)	Psychosis Tourette's Autism Pervasive developmental disorder ADHD with conduct disorder	Reduces aggression, hostility, negativity, and hyperactivity Reduces psychotic symptoms Reduces Tourette's symptoms Reduces fixations, withdrawal stereotypies, anger, and fidgetiness in autism Increases social responsivity and reality testing in pervasive developmental disorder	Behavioral toxicity with preexisting disorders Dystonia, loss of tone in tongue and trunk) Parkinsonian symptoms (tremors, mask face, and drooling) Dyskinesis (mouth, tongue, and jaw) Dose reduction decreases motor side effects Intellectual dulling and disorganized thoughts
Thioridazine (Mellaril)	Psychosis Severe behavior disorders (extreme)	Reduces hyperactivity Improves schizophrenic symptoms Similar to thorazine	Similar to Haldol Sedation, cognitive dulling and impaired arousal

Tricyclic antidepressants

Drug	Indications	Effects and side effects
Imipramine hydrochloride (Tofranil)	Depression Enuresis ADHD School phobia	Improves (less severe) depression Inhibits bladder muscles Reduces hyperactivity Reduces separation anxiety Improves sleep disorders	Potentially-life threatening cardiovascular problems Central nervous system symptoms (EEG changes, confusion, lower seizure threshold, uncoordination, drowsiness, delusions, and psychosis) Blurred vision, dry mouth, and constipation
Nortriptyline hydrochloride (Pamelor)	Depression	Low rate of clinical improvement in children and adolescents	Withdrawal symptoms

(continued)

TABLE 6.5. (cont.)

Drugs	Common use	Manifestations	Side effects
Desipramine hydrochloride (Norpramin)	ADHD ADHD with tics	Improved ratings (Conners Parents & Teachers Rating Scale) Clinical improvement	Dry mouth, decreased appetite, tiredness, dizziness, insomnia EEG changes at high doses
Clomipramine hydrochloride (Anafranil)	Obsessive–compulsive disorder Severe ADHD Enuresis School phobia	Reduces obsessions Reduces school phobia/anxiety Reduces aggression, impulsivity, and depressive/affective symptoms	Withdrawal symptoms Seizures Somnolence, tremors, dizziness, headaches, sweating, sleep disorder, gastrointestinal problems, cardiovascular effects, anorexia, and fatigue
		Monoamine oxidase inhibitors	
Fluoxetine hydrochloride (Prozac)	Depression Obsessive–compulsive disorder	Effective for adults Clinical improvement for OCD	Nausea, weight loss, anxiety, nervousness, sweating, sleep disorder
Bupropion hydrochloride (Wellbutrin)	Depression ADHD	Adolescents and 18+ improve Improved global ratings (not Conners Rating Scale)	Seizures, agitation, dry mouth, insomnia, nausea, constipation, tremors

Note. From Teeter & Semrud-Clikeman (1997). Copyright 1997 by Allyn & Bacon. Reprinted by permission.

child's cold. "Penicillin can cause anaphylactic shock and is potentially a far more dangerous drug than Ritalin and related medications used to treat ADHD" (Comings, 1990, p. 567).

The use of medication is substantiated by thousands of studies investigating the short-term efficacy of stimulants for reducing ADHD symptoms in children. Specifically, Swanson (1993) found over 9,000 original articles and more than 300 review articles spanning 55 years of research; and Barkley (1990b) asserts that more research has been conducted on the effects of stimulant medications on the functioning of children with ADHD than on any other treatment approach for any other childhood disorder.

At one of the ADD Research Centers funded in 1991 by the U.S. Department of Education, Swanson, McBurnett, et al. (1993) reviewed the literature on the effects of stimulant medications on ADHD and summarized the major findings in a "Review of Reviews" on stimulant medications as follows:

1. About 70% of children with ADHD responded positively to stimulant medication, regardless of how the diagnostic criteria for the disorder has changed during the 55-year period over which the research was conducted.
2. Ninety-seven percent of the articles reviewed reported temporary improvement in the symptoms of ADHD (e.g., decreased hyperactivity, impulsivity, and inattention) with increased concentration and goal-directness.
3. Ninety-four percent of studies that looked for other associated outcomes reported improvements in deviant behaviors, aggression, social interactions, and academic productivity.
4. Ninety-nine percent of studies reported minor (appetite suppression and insomnia) or more serious (tics) side effects, suggesting the need to monitor these difficulties.
5. Eighty-eight percent of studies indicate that long-term effects on social adjustment or academic achievement have not been demonstrated.
6. Seventy-eight percent of studies did not find paradoxical effects when investigating normal children and children with ADHD.
7. Although some studies reported positive effects on complex higher order skills (e.g., reading and learning) and on simple tasks (e.g., rote memory and monitoring of repetitive tasks), 72% did not find beneficial effects on complex skills.
8. Sixty-eight percent of the studies indicated that behavioral, cognitive and neuropsychological test measures do not efficiently predict who will be a positive responder.

9. Many reviews recommended combining medication with psychosocial interventions, although there was little empirical data
to support the recommendations that were made.

In general, this research review demonstrates the strengths, as well
as the limitations, of stimulant medications for treating ADHD. Specific
studies have focused on the efficacy of Ritalin, Dexedrine, and Cylert.

Efficacy of Methylphenidate (Ritalin). The positive effects of methylphenidate (Ritalin) have been documented since the 1970s, according to
Klein and Abikoff (1989). In a review of 28 studies, Klein and Abikoff
report that Ritalin treatment for children with ADHD decreases hyperkinesis in the classroom, increases social interaction with peers, and
improves mother–child interactions. In specific studies, Ritalin appears
to improve attention span and impulse control (Abikoff & Gittelman,
1985; Rapport, Stoner, DuPaul, Birmingham, & Tucker, 1985), aggressive behavior, particularly in natural settings (Hinshaw et al., 1989),
social behavior in groups (Pelham & Hoza, 1987), and trained and
incidental learning of complex visual tasks (Vyse & Rapport, 1989).

Comings (1990) indicates that Ritalin increases motor coordination and improves handwriting. Although they do not increase the IQ
of children with ADHD, stimulants "simply allow a child's native
abilities to be utilized without interference of distractibility and inability to pay attention" (Comings, 1990, p. 570). Academic performance
in the classroom is improved, as Ritalin increases "output, accuracy,
efficiency, learning, reading comprehension, spelling, word acquisition,
and on-task and self-correcting behavior for children" (Comings, 1990,
p. 570).

Pelham et al. (1993) found that the social behaviors of children on
Ritalin were significantly improved and were similar to those of normal
children when interacting with peers and adults. Pelham et al. (1990)
reported that children treated with Ritalin also showed more on-task
behaviors and improved "game-awareness" on the baseball field. Because stimulants did not improve performance during the game, systematic coaching in athletic skills was viewed as an important adjunct to
medication.

Despite positive findings, controversy has arisen concerning the
effects of Ritalin on learning. Two studies found an inverse relationship
between the dosage level of Ritalin and optimal learning, such that levels
that produced the best learning did not affect hyperactive behavior
(reported by Klein and Abikoff, 1989). Levels of Ritalin that produced
the best effects on hyperkinesis decreased learning. According to Klein
and Abikoff (1989), these results have not been replicated in nine
subsequent studies. It must also be noted that direct remediation in the

area of the academic deficit is needed when specific skills deficits (e.g., reading or language disorders) are present.

Some research has suggested that medication may lead to a causal attributional style whereby children credit successes to medication rather than to effort or ability (Henker & Whalen, 1980). However, in studies with careful controls, children on medication made more "effort" attributions than "medication" attributions (Carlson, Pelham, Milich, & Hoza, 1993; Milich, Licht, Murphy, & Pelham, 1989). Pelham et al. (1992) found that distinctions between attributions for success and failure conditions exist in some cases. For example, children made "significantly more effort and ability attributions on positive daily report (success) days and significantly more pill attributions on negative daily report (failure) days" (Pelham et al., 1992, p. 289). In this study, the researchers did not find that stimulants produce debilitating attributional thinking in boys with ADHD. Furthermore, a positive attributional style may be beneficial in reducing depression in this group.

Finally, another interesting finding that dispels popular conceptions is that Ritalin does not produce a paradoxical effect on children with ADHD. Normal children and adults also show signs of decreased motor activity and increased vigilance on reaction tasks while on Ritalin (Comings, 1990; Rapoport, 1983); however, children who have ADHD show the most dramatic improvement on Ritalin. On medication, boys with ADHD appear similar to normal boys on activity measures. It is important to emphasize that moderate dosages of stimulants do not produce a drug "high" or "euphoria." Ritalin should not be characterized as a "street" drug. It is a medication that "corrects a chemical imbalance in the brain and allows ADHD children to be less distractible, less hyperactive, and to concentrate better . . . they cut the strings of the genetically induced chemical straight jacket that ADHD children are locked into" (Comings, 1990, p. 567.)

Potential Side Effects of Ritalin. The negative side effects of Ritalin have been discussed in detail in Barkley (1990b), Comings (1990), Copeland and Copps (1994), Klein, Gittelman, Quitkin, and Rifkin (1980), and Klein (1993). First, with moderately high dosages, a small percentage of children will develop tachycardia (increased heart rate). In instances in which this has been reported, the use of Ritalin is contraindicated. Second, decreased appetite and sleeping disorders may occur in about 15–20% of children. Third, changes in mood, including sadness, touchiness, and interpersonal difficulties, may occur. These last two effects decrease when the child is off medication and can be controlled with lower dosages and "drug holidays." Fourth, one of the most serious concerns about Ritalin therapy has been decreased growth observed in children following prolonged usage (4 years; Mattes & Gittelman,

1983). Gittelman (1983) found that growth effects are related to initial measures (height and weight) and can be very pronounced in some children. However, these decrements do not appear to persist after the child has been taken off medication. Comings (1990) suggests that few or no problems with growth are reported except when dosage levels are high and that acceleration of growth occurs when medications are stopped during summer months. Although other nonphysical risks have been discussed, including learned helplessness, state dependent learning, and substance abuse, these risks have not been substantiated for the most part (Gittelman, 1983).

Efficacy of Dextroamphetamine (Dexedrine). Dexedrine has proven effective in decreasing activity levels and improving vigilance, motor coordination, handwriting skills, and reaction time, and it has many of the same benefits reported for Ritalin (Copeland & Copps, 1995). However, Ritalin and Dexedrine may act differently on neurotransmitters (Shaywitz, Shaywitz, Anderson, et al., 1988), so that if a child is not responsive to one medication, he/she may benefit from the other stimulant or from another class of medications (cited in Copeland & Copps, 1995).

Copeland and Copps (1995) provide useful guidelines for deciding which stimulant to use for treating ADHD. In controlled studies, about 96% of children with ADHD and ADD without hyperactivity respond favorably to either Ritalin or Dexedrine, so a trial on both medications may be warranted. Choosing the medication with the most positive effects and the fewest side effects after titrating each at wide dosage levels is recommended (Calis, Grothe, & Elia, 1990).

Potential Side Effects of Dexedrine. Dexedrine has many of the same side effects as does Ritalin (Copeland & Copps, 1995). Appetite suppression may be more obvious, and the abuse potential for dexedrine is greater than with Ritalin. Copeland and Copps (1995) suggest that Cylert may be more appropriate if abuse is a possibility and indicate that psychiatric facilities often avoid using Dexedrine with adolescents, particularly with teens who have a history of "street drug" experimentation.

Efficacy of Pemoline (Cylert). Cylert is the newest stimulant and does not always have the same positive benefits as Ritalin and Dexedrine; thus it is often considered a third or fourth choice medication for ADHD (Copeland & Copps, 1995). Cylert requires ongoing monitoring to assess its long-term benefits and safety. Cylert is typically contraindicated for individuals with liver disease, Tourette's disorder, and seizure disorders (Copeland & Copps, 1995). Comings (1990) cautions that

Cylert is more likely to produce tics than other stimulants and that it is only rarely used with individuals who have ADHD and Tourette's disorder. Furthermore, frequent blood tests are recommended, which can place an undue burden on the child and family.

Tricyclic Antidepressants

In rare cases when stimulants do not work, antidepressants may be appropriate. Antidepressants are often used for a variety of disorders, although as a class these medications affect neurotransmitters differentially—tricyclic antidepressants affect norepinephrine and dopamine, whereas Prozac and MAO inhibitors affect serotonin (Copeland & Copps, 1995). Tricyclics (imipramine [Tofranil] and desipramine [Norpramin]) are considered to be the best second-line treatments for attentional problems when stimulants are not indicated because of negative side effects or a lack of responsivity.

Efficacy of Imipramine. Historically, antidepressants (tricyclics) have been used with success for the treatment of depression and enuresis. Because children with ADHD often have comorbid depression, imipramine has been viewed as an appealing option. Copeland and Copps (1995) suggest that children, adolescents, and adults described as "irritable, moody and prone to highs and lows may especially benefit" and that those who have a history of depression and/or bipolar disorder may benefit from using imipramine rather than stimulants (p. 212).

The effectiveness of antidepressants with hyperactive/attention disorders, especially for improving restless and antisocial behavior, has been demonstrated in several studies. In studies reviewed by Rapoport (1986), positive effects of drug treatment on hyperactive–aggressive behavior were documented when imipramine was compared with a placebo. Although behaviors improved with imipramine, Ritalin was more effective. Rapoport (1983) found that long-term use of imipramine for ADHD is not warranted and that there may be a "wear-off" effect with this drug at the point at which its therapeutic effects might expected to be the highest. Therefore, Rapoport (1983, p. 399) concludes that "while of great theoretical appeal, tricyclics are not likely to play an important role in the treatment of the hyperkinetic syndrome."

Efficacy of Desipramine. Riddle, Hardin, Cho, Woolston, and Leckman (1988) found that desipramine reduces symptoms of ADHD without the side effects of tics. However, three clinical cases have resulted in the sudden deaths of children, which calls into question its usefulness for children under 12 years of age (Riddle, Nelson, Kleinman, & Cohen,

1991). As a result, physicians do not routinely administer desipramine, and when they do, it is highly monitored.

Monoamine Oxidase Inhibitors (MAOIs)

Although attempts have been made to isolate the neurotransmitter systems involved in ADHD and to study the effects of various classes of drugs on these mechanisms, Copeland and Copps (1995) suggest that "our use of medications at this time might well be described as a 'shot-gun' approach" (p. 231). MAOIs apparently inhibit the breakdown of serotonin, dopamine, and norepinephrine at the synapse. Although MAOIs have utility for treating children with severe ADHD, "it is typically a medication of last resort" because of its interaction with other drugs and foods (Copeland & Copps, 1995, p. 233). Interaction with foods such as pickled herring, liver, smoked or aged sausage or meat, cheese, chocolate, alcohol, and caffeine have been reported; thus the risks of using MAOIs often outweigh the potential benefits.

Antihypertensives

Responsivity to medication remains highly individualized and requires careful monitoring (DuPaul, Barkley, & McMurray, 1991). Children with high levels of hyperactivity and attentional deficits tend to respond quite well to stimulant medication (Barkley, 1989, 1990b). In contrast, children who are overaroused, with high impulsivity and aggression, respond well to clonidine, an antihypertensive agent (Hunt, Mandl, et al., 1991).

Clonidine is the best known of the antihypertensives that are used for some children with ADHD. Children tend to respond well to clonidine if they are highly aroused and nonresponsive to stimulants; aggressive, explosive, conduct-disordered, or oppositional; poor responders to other medications; prone to tic disorders or Tourette's in reaction to stimulants; and overfocused (Copeland & Copps, 1995). Clonidine has been used to treat posttraumatic stress disorder, school phobia, panic and anxiety disorders, hyperarousal, obsessive–compulsive disorders, and Tourette's disorder (Copeland & Copps, 1995). Clonidine causes drowsiness, which may make it difficult for a child to get out of bed and to get through the morning.

Clonidine appears to reduce neuronal activity in the locus ceruleus in the brainstem region. The ceruleus produces over 70% of the norepinephrine in the brain, and clonidine appears to inhibit the release of norepinephrine (Comings, 1990). Comings (1990) suggests that norepinephrine affects serotonin, which in turn acts as the "great inhibitor" for controlling behavior. Serotonin is widely spread throughout the brain, including the prefrontal lobes, the limbic system, and other regions that play a critical role in modulating behavior. Serotonin deficiency is related to a variety of disorders, including impulsivity, aggression, and depression (Traskman, Asberg, Bertilisson, & Sjostrand, 1981).

Deciding When to Medicate and Monitoring Medication

Pediatricians and psychiatrists may use more than one medication for children with comorbid disorders. See Biederman, Baldessarini, Wright, Knee, and Harmatz (1989) and Wilens, Biederman, Geist, Steingard, and Spencer (1993) for a more in-depth discussion of medications for comorbid disorders with ADHD. The decision to medicate should be considered carefully and the benefits and negative side effects weighed. Once medication is administered, ongoing monitoring is necessary.

Medicating a child with ADHD is a complex decision that should be made by the child's parents in consultation with their physician. It is important to obtain information from the school to determine the extent to which ADHD interferes with classroom, academic, and psychosocial adjustment prior to a medication trial. Although there may be cases in which parents and physicians choose not to involve or inform school professionals about the use of medication, this is not a recommended practice. School professionals can often provide valuable information that will assist in this decision, and once medication is initiated, they are in a position to help monitor medication efficacy and potential side effects.

Barkley (1990b) and DuPaul and Stoner (1994) enumerate the following considerations in deciding when to medicate a child with ADHD: (1) the severity of the child's ADHD symptoms and disruptive behaviors; (2) a history of limited success with other interventions; (3) the presence of other comorbid disorders (e.g., depression and/or anxiety); (4) parents who are informed about the research on medication and who are in agreement with the decision; (5) the availability of adequate medication monitoring and adult supervision; and (6) a positive attitude on the part of the child. Psychosocial and behavioral interventions should be in place prior to medication trials (Pelham, 1993b; Teeter, 1991).

The decision to medicate typically involves assessing the benefit-to-risk ratio (Copeland & Copps, 1995). This process involves determining whether the risks of side effects outweigh the probable negative consequences of ADHD on the child's daily life (social, academic, and emotional). Once the decision to medicate has been made, several other important questions need to be explored: Which medication should be used? Which dosage is appropriate? When should medication be taken? The existence of comorbid disorders and a history of seizures, tics, or other medical problems generally influence the decision of which medication to use. Physicians may use more than one medication when treating severe and/or complex cases or when high dosages of medication produce unacceptable side effects.

It is important to note that responsivity to medication remains highly individualized, so dosage levels must be carefully titrated and risks and benefits should be assessed at various dosage levels for each child (DuPaul, Barkley, & McMurray, 1991; Pelham, 1993a). Medication should be monitored when dosage levels are first established and periodically thereafter to ensure optimal effects. The Academy of Pediatrics recommends a follow-up every 3 to 4 months (Copeland & Copps, 1995). The question of medicating the child during nonschool times may depend on the philosophy of the attending physician (Copeland & Copps, 1995). It is important to assess both the extent to which ADHD symptoms are affecting the child's psychosocial adjustment and the negative impact of the child's symptoms on the family. These issues should be carefully assessed with the family to determine the individual environmental and the child and family contextual factors that might affect the decision to medicate outside school hours.

Summary of Medication Findings

Research consistently shows that medication improves sustained attention, impulse control, activity level, disruptive behavior, compliance, work completion, and work accuracy (Barkley, 1989, 1990a; Swanson, McBurnett, et al., 1993). Although medication responsivity remains highly individualized, children with higher levels of hyperactivity and attentional deficits tend to respond well to stimulant medication (Barkley, 1989, 1990a; DuPaul, Barkley, & McMurray, 1991). Although most children with ADHD and ADD without hyperactivity respond favorably to methylphenidate, lower dosages are found to be effective for children with ADD without hyperactivity compared to ADHD. Medication has also been shown to have a positive effect on parent–child interactions (Barkley, Karlsson, Strzelecki, & Murphy, 1984), teacher–child interactions (Whalen, Henker, & Dotemoto, 1980), and child–peer interactions (Whalen et al., 1989).

Cautions and Future Research Directions

When investigating articles that were written for the general public, Swanson, McBurnett, et al. (1993) found that these authors (journalists rather than specialized scholars) generally were more critical of the use of medications. These articles were generally written in an attempt to expose the "myth" of ADHD, and they argued for the abandonment of present diagnostic and medication trends. Other reviews, written for clinicians and scholars, also advocate greater caution when medicating children and more restrained use of stimulant treatment (Jacobvitz, Sroufe, Stewart, & Leffert, 1990).

Despite positive findings, particularly for stimulant medications, no single treatment is sufficient for producing significant, long-lasting behavioral changes in children with ADHD (DuPaul, Barkley, & McMurray, 1991). Thus when medication is administered, other management techniques are frequently recommended to improve classroom behaviors and psychosocial adjustment.

COMBINED INTERVENTIONS

The absence of long-term effects of behavioral interventions and concerns over the side effects of medications suggest the need for multimodal interventions that combine behavioral interventions with medication (DuPaul, Barkley, & McMurray, 1991). Behavioral programs typically target conduct-related problems (e.g., compliance), academic difficulties (e.g., work completion and accuracy), and peer relation problems (Pfiffner & Barkley, 1990). Pelham (1993a) advises that medication trials be initiated after behavior management, parent training, and psychosocial approaches have been tried and found unsuccessful. Furthermore, the shortcomings of either behavioral or pharmacological approaches can be reduced when these two approaches are combined (Pelham, 1993a).

Rutter (1989) stated that "although stimulant medication is the most effective short term treatment, long term management requires a combination of treatment strategies of which medication is only one" (p. 17). Rutter indicates that medication produces positive effects in the parent–child relationship, and, as such, clinicians should capitalize on this initial effect when establishing a therapeutic plan. However, this effect does not imply that medication can be administered for a short time period to get the child "ready" for other therapeutic interventions (Pelham, 1993a). Combined medication, behavioral, and psychosocial interventions are most likely required to improve the long-term outcome for individuals with ADHD.

Medication with Psychosocial Interventions

In a comparative analysis, Whalen and Henker (1991) concluded that medication, although effective, has limitations due to side effects and the inability to predict responders and nonresponders prior to drug trials.

Behavioral and cognitive-behavioral interventions also share limitations a fact which further supports the need for treatment plans that integrate approaches and methods from the various biomedical, behavioral, and psychosocial paradigms. Whalen and Henker declare:

> The nonpharmacologic treatments considered here teach problem solving and coping skills not only to ADHD children but also to those who interact with the child on a regular basis. Psychological approaches treat ADHD in its interpersonal context, recruiting the child's family and caretakers as partners and equipping the team with resources for managing a challenging and persistent disorder. (1991, p. 135)

Pelham (1993a) found that when psychosocial and behavioral interventions (e.g., home–school notes and work completion monitoring) are in place, lower dosages of medication produce positive results similar to those found in conditions in which higher medication dosages have been used. Although Pelham et al. (1993) advocate combined behavioral and psychosocial therapy approaches, they found that the addition of medication to a behavioral treatment program benefited 78% of boys, whereas 41% benefited from the addition of a behavior management program to medication intervention. Medication improved compliance with teacher requests, increased work productivity in the classroom, and reduced disruptive behavior and aggressive interactions with peers. Pelham et al. (1993) support the combined use of long-term psychosocial and behavioral interventions for children with ADHD on medication.

Medication with Behavior Management

When behavior therapy is combined with stimulant medication, children show superior adjustment compared to children on Ritalin alone on teacher ratings but not on measures of attention or conduct problems (Klein & Abikoff, 1989). Klein and Abikoff (1989, p. 171) argue that the question is not whether behavior management should be an "alternative treatment strategy to methylphenidate, but whether the addition of behavior therapy to medication leads to accrued improvement." They conclude that behavior therapy improves some behaviors, but it is not always superior to drug therapy alone. "Therefore, the results suggest that behavior therapy cannot be recommended routinely for children receiving methylphenidate, but should be considered among those who continue to have residual behavior problems while receiving medication" (Klein & Abikoff, 1989, p. 171).

Pelham et al. (1988) investigated the effects of adding medication to behavioral interventions (e.g., parent training/management with teacher-implemented classroom interventions). In this study, 80% of the children who received a combined approach were "normalized," compared to only 30% of the children who received a management system alone. Although these results show an impressive effect for medication, adding a behavior management program to the treatment regimen reduced the need for higher dosages of medication (Carlson, Pelham, Milich, & Dixon, 1992). Pelham, Carlson, et al. (1993) also found that the effect size of medication was twice as high as that of the behavioral treatment alone. However, it must be noted that the increased effects of combined approaches do not persist if either approach is withdrawn (Pelham, Carlson, et al., 1993).

When designing an intervention program, Pelham (1993a, 1993b) suggests establishing a baseline for classroom work and compliance, monitoring the effects using a home–school daily report system, then adding medication in a double-blind control paradigm. This process allows one to systematically determine whether medication adds anything to a behavior management program for treating children with ADHD and to measure which dosage levels are most effective.

As previously discussed, the efficacy of Ritalin for reducing many of the problem behaviors associated with ADHD has been well established. Klein and Abikoff (1989) report that "a fair appraisal of the drug's efficacy is that many but not all aspects of symptomatic behaviors are normalized by stimulant treatment" (p. 168). Interventions that increase skills in social areas have been investigated, including behavior therapy and cognitive training, in an effort to find the best combination for treatment.

Medication with Cognitive-Behavioral Techniques

The idea that cognitive training approaches might promote better social adjustment and academic progress in children with ADHD has also been investigated. Abikoff and Gittelman (1985) found that self-instructional techniques did not add to treatment efficacy when compared to Ritalin alone and actually decreased performance on some measures (i.e., speed of response, which lowered Performance IQ). Klein and Abikoff (1989) conclude that behavior and cognitive therapies are not superior to medication. Behavior therapy should be considered when medication does not clearly reduce behavior problems for children, but there is little value in using cognitive training for managing hyperactive children, according to Abikoff and Gittelman (1989). Furthermore, generalization of gains made in self-instructional training is still a problem. Abikoff (1991) goes so far as to say that "none of the studies has generated results to indicate, or even suggest, that cognitive training is a competitor to stimulants, or that it enhances their beneficial effects" (p. 208).

SUMMARY

This chapter presented a number of behavioral procedures that have been effective in reducing problems in the classroom for children with ADHD. Positive outcomes have been documented when teachers are energetic and engaging and when children are able to select activities and to actively participate in learning tasks. Self-paced activities also produce higher on-task behaviors than teacher-paced ones. The use of negative consequences seems essential for producing positive effects in management systems, especially the use of prudent and timely reprimands. Although generalization is still a problem, token systems have been successful. To date, cognitive-behavioral approaches have not been shown to be systematically effective due to problems in generalization.

Stimulant medication produces a positive effect in the majority of children with ADHD, although it does not normalize behaviors. Behavioral techniques appear to be most effective for increasing academic performance, especially when concepts and skills are taught directly, whereas medication seems to produce better effects on activity and attentional levels.

In summary, interventions are designed to:

1. Improve parent–child relationships and child compliance in the home using family therapy and parent training strategies;
2. Increase work completion and compliance in the classroom by using teacher training, behavior management, token economy, and self-monitoring techniques, and by modifying assignments and classroom environments;
3. Increase social interaction skills by incorporating "normal" peers into training programs and reinforcing skills in natural settings (i.e., classroom and playground);
4. Decrease impulsivity, inattention, and hyperactivity using medication in combination with behavior management and psychosocial interventions (i.e., home–school notes).

7

Developmental Challenges of the Adolescent Stage: The Impact of ADHD on Normal Development

T his chapter reviews developmental challenges of the adolescent stage and discusses the impact of ADHD on this process. Adolescence is a particularly expansive developmental stage, where physical, cognitive, and psychosocial changes are dramatic and highly interdependent. Adolescence is a psychological phenomenon that is not universal across cultures, although it does mark a biological period starting in puberty and continuing into adulthood (LeFrancois, 1995). Puberty begins in late childhood or early adolescence and signals major sexual and physical development. The age span of adolescence is arbitrary but typically ranges from 12 to 20 years of age, although age 12 is generally viewed as an approximation of the beginning of adolescence.

Normal developmental challenges in adolescence can be pronounced, such that even well-adjusted youngsters undergo a highly charged and sometimes confusing metamorphosis during this time. Although the majority of teens are well adjusted, about 15% of adolescents describe themselves as anxious, confused, sad, and psychologically empty (Offer, Ostrov, & Howard, 1984). Frequently, the degree of success in handling earlier developmental challenges sets the stage for adolescent adjustment, particularly for those youth with various psychiatric, psychosocial, and/or behavioral disorders. As such, early effective interventions and support can be the best strategy for alleviating or coping with the additional problems that teens with ADHD face.

Some of the normal milestones and developmental variables that are important in the adolescent stage include: (1) physical and sexual maturation; (2) cognitive–intellectual growth into formal operations; (3) developing executive controls for self-regulation and self-control; (4) self-identity; (5) psychosocial development; and (6) academic and career planning.

The extent to which normal developmental challenges interact with ADHD is of interest to clinicians, parents, educational professionals, and the teenager him- or herself. The fact that even well-adjusted youth may find the adolescent stage to be one of great turmoil only adds to the complex picture of how ADHD affects the adolescent.

NORMAL DEVELOPMENTAL CHALLENGES

It is important that clinicians place the effects of ADHD within the context of normal adolescent development—the context of the appearance of new feelings, insights, and experiences that can be both exhilarating and unnerving. Offer and Offer (1975) found that about one-fourth of adolescents experience turmoil and conflict (tumultuous growth), whereas one-third are relatively adjusted (urgent growth) with only transient periods of negativity marked by anger, defiance, and immaturity. Another one-fourth of the age group progress through the stage with a sense of purpose and well-being and maintain good relations with their parents, whereas the remaining are not easily classified. The amount of turmoil and conflict that teenagers experience is highly individual (Sroufe & Cooper, 1988).

Physical and Sexual Maturation

Physical development during adolescence is marked by rapid changes in both primary and secondary sexual characteristics (LeFrancois, 1995). Primary sexual development includes changes in the ovaries of females and the testes of males whereby both organs become functional for reproduction (e.g., producing ova and sperm). With the maturation of sexual organs, the adolescent body undergoes secondary changes in appearance (e.g., development of breasts, voice changes, growth of pubic and facial hair). There is a great deal of variability as to when these changes occur in individuals, and early or late maturation may have its own distinct challenges depending on the sex of the adolescent.

Early maturing males tend to be larger and stronger and thus they may have an advantage in athletic ability due to increased strength, speed, and agility. Because athletic ability is so highly prized by peers and society alike, early maturing males suffer fewer psychological problems than those who mature later (LeFrancois, 1995). Early maturing boys tend to be well liked by their peers, more confident in themselves, and more successful in their relationships with girls (Crockett & Jones, 1987). Later maturing males appear more anxious, more restless, and less confident, have more trouble with self-esteem, and engage in attention-seeking behaviors. These differences tend to be less obvious in adulthood, although they do affect the male's adjustment, popularity, and leadership during adolescence (LeFrancois, 1995).

On the other hand, the picture for early maturing girls is more complex and varied. Some studies suggest that early maturation in girls may actually be a disadvantage because of higher rates of precocious sexual behavior that often violates the norms of later maturing girls (Stattin & Magnusson, 1990). Early maturation may be more deleterious if it occurs while the female is quite young, particularly if it results in social exclusion. In general, girls mature about two years ahead of boys, so early maturing girls may be 3 to 4 years ahead of their male age-mates. LeFrancois (1995) suggests that this differential in itself may create some of the social problems that early maturing girls encounter. Similar to male patterns of development, these differences also tend to disappear in later stages.

Physical Changes within a Social Context

The consequences of early maturation can become problematic if changes place the teenager at odds with his/her age-mates or when the changes are deemed undesirable (Petersen, 1988). So for boys, early maturation may be a plus for interpersonal relationships; the opposite may be true for girls. Parental relationships can also be affected by early maturational patterns, with early development favoring boys but not girls (Savin-Williams & Small, 1986). Thus from a transactional, ecological perspective, the developmental changes occurring within the teenager interact with how others (peers and parents) perceive these changes and/or how these changes affect interactions with these important people.

The physical changes occurring in this stage present teens with numerous issues of appearance, and adolescents worry about their hair, skin (e.g., blemishes, freckles, birth marks), weight, and facial features (e.g., size of the nose, lips, chin; LeFrancois, 1995). Harter (1990) suggests that adolescents' physical appearance may be the most significant factor affecting their self-worth. Moreover, the relationship between self-esteem and physical appearance is exacerbated in the presence of eating disorders (e.g., obesity and/or anorexia nervosa). For example, obesity is associated with low self-esteem and poor school performance and presents a host of stressors for the adolescent. Obesity has been estimated to be extremely high in North America and may affect as many as 25% of the adolescent population (Whitney & Hamilton, 1984).

On the other extreme, eating habits of teens can also be influenced by a desire to have the "ideal" body weight, which can trigger significant weight loss. Anorexia nervosa (i.e., significant weight loss, fear of gaining weight, and distortions of body image) and bulimia (i.e., recurrent binge eating episodes with self-induced vomiting) are two serious eating disorders that affect a large number of teenagers and young adults (LeFrancois, 1995). Depending upon the definition one uses, rates of eating disorders can be quite high, ranging from 1% to 4.2% for anorexia and 6.5% to 18% for bulimia (Pope et al., 1984). When eating attitudes of athletes are measured, data are even more alarming, with 4.6% of boys and 10.6% of girls scoring in the anorexic range (Stoutjesdyk & Jevne, 1993). Furthermore, the percentage of girls indicating that they significantly restrict their diet is as high as 13%, according to some studies (Lachenmeyer & Muni-Brander, 1988).

Today's society places a great deal of emphasis on appearance and portrays the "perfect body image" for women in mainly unrealistic proportions (e.g., large breasts with small waists and hips), so it is no surprise that teens are extremely "body conscious" and are often dissatisfied with their own figures. The influence of the media cannot be overlooked, as the messages teens receive from television, movies, and music videos all personify beauty as the "Barbie Doll" body that is for the most part unattainable for typical adolescents. Thus teens can develop a "fear of fat" and an assortment of eating disorders. Although these idealizations may challenge the body images of people in all age groups, teenagers are particularly prone to internalizing negative messages if their bodies do not fit the latest fashion model figure or popular look of the time.

The extent to which teenagers can "survive" this stage with a modicum of self-esteem when their bodies are undergoing rapid outward as well as inward (hormonal) changes probably depends on a number of factors. Teens do learn to value themselves not only by how they look but also by what they can accomplish in academics and in other creative pursuits. Success in building and maintaining friendships can also play an important role in this process, as friendships influence how the teen thinks, behaves, and feels about him/herself.

Sexual Behavior and Intimacy

"Sex is an area of profound preoccupation with adolescents, an area that consumes a great deal of their time and energy and to which they sometimes devote themselves with rarely equaled ardor" (LeFrancois, 1995, p. 566). However, Olson, Huszti, and Youll (1995) suggest that health care professionals have limited data available on the sexual activity of youth because of the political pressure that has ended funding for national surveys. This fact seriously impedes efforts at pregnancy and disease prevention. As it is, the call for teenagers to practice abstinence comes into conflict with efforts to reduce problems (i.e., teen pregnancy and sexually transmitted diseases) associated with premarital sexual activity.

Sexual beliefs, attitudes, and behaviors have radically changed (Zani, 1991), during which we have seen progressively younger teens engaged in more premarital sexual relations than in previous generations. Perhaps one of the most dramatic changes may be the decline of the "double standard," as sexual activity has become more socially acceptable for both males and females alike. Whereas in the past females tended to be less sexually active than their male age-mates, these differences were virtually erased by the 1980s (Darling, Kallen, & Van Dusen, 1984). However, casual sexual activity is not condoned, and most teens see the need to be in a caring relationship before sex is acceptable (Roche & Ramsbay, 1993).

Another change in teenage sexual behavior has been the decrease in age of initial sexual experience (LeFrancois, 1995). Some researchers have found that as many as one-third of girls and one-fourth of boys report having had intercourse by 15 years of age (Zani, 1991). This trend has disturbing consequences including increases in teen pregnancy and sexually transmitted diseases.

Teen Pregnancy. The National Center for Health Statistics (1990) reported that teen pregnancy has been on the rise since 1988. The statistics are alarming: (1) over 50% of all pregnancies are unplanned and about one-third of these result in abortion (Harlap, Kost, & Forrest, 1991); (2) about 50% of unplanned pregnancies occur in the first six months after initiation of sexual activity, with one-fifth occurring in the first month (Zabin, Hirsch, Smith, Street, & Hardy, 1986); and (3) about one-third of births to unmarried women in 1988 were to girls between 15 to 19 years of age (Williams & Pratt, 1990).

The United States has one of the highest teen pregnancy rates in the world, and the cost of public funds to support unmarried mothers and their infants reached $30 billion in 1993 (Olson et al., 1995). The personal cost to adolescents has also been high. "Teenage parents are more likely to drop out of school, to require public assistance, or to be able to hold only menial jobs with little hope of advancement" (Olson et al. 1995, p. 328). Although not all teenaged mothers are economically disadvantaged or have troubled children (Furstenberg, Brooks-Gunn, & Chase-Landale, 1989), females who have later pregnancies do appear to fare better than those who do not (Roosa, 1991). Teenage pregnancy is considered a major problem for society and has a sobering impact on the long term outcome of the teenager and her offspring.

Sexually Transmitted Diseases. With the increased frequency of sexual activity in teens has come a corresponding increase in the number of serious sexually transmitted diseases as well. In fact, teenage females (15–19 years of age) have the highest rates of some sexually transmitted diseases (e.g., gonorrhea, cytomegalovirus, chlamydia, cervicitis, and pelvic inflammation), except for prostitutes and homosexual males (Cates & Rauh, 1985).

There has also been an increase in AIDS in young adults (aged 20 to 29), many of whom likely contracted the virus in adolescence (Centers for Disease Control, 1993). Unfortunately, research into the number of teens who are engaging in risky behaviors (e.g., unprotected sex, sexual relations with multiple partners, intravenous drug use) has been limited, so we do not know the relationship between age of initial sexual activity, patterns of condom use, and other factors that may influence the transmission of HIV/AIDS.

Factors That Influence Sexual Behaviors. A number of issues appear to influence the decision to become sexually active, including religious beliefs, parenting style and family status, peer group behaviors and pressures, and educational and cognitive abilities. First, teens who attend church regularly have more conservative views (Roche & Ramsbay, 1993) and appear less likely to engage in sexual activity (White & DeBlassie, 1992). However, if they do choose to be sexually active, they may be somewhat less interested in obtaining contraceptive information.

Second, parenting style and family cohesion appear to be strong factors influencing the sexual activity of teens. Parents who provide more supervision and are moderately strict are more likely to have teenage children who are more sexually responsible (Miller, McCoy, Olsen, & Wallace, 1986). Close parental supervision is a significant factor because most teens report having sex in the home when parents are not present. This may help to explain why an absent father or a single-parent family is such a strong predictor of early sexual intercourse (Newcomer & Udry, 1987). Teens in these situations may have more unsupervised time.

Parent–teen relationships may also be an important factor in this decision, as Brooks-Gunn and Furstenberg (1989) report that good mother–daughter relationships tend to delay early sexual activity.

Third, an alarming number of pregnant teens report that they have been the victims of rape, attempted rape, or sexual abuse (Boyer & Fine, 1992).

> As a result of their research, Boyer and Fine identified several factors contributing to adolescent pregnancy: pregnancy as a result of the sexual offense itself; family dynamics that support incestuous role patterns; self-worth based on sexuality; lowered self-esteem and related emotional needs; pregnancy as a way of escape from an abusive situation, and the effects of sexual trauma on the developmental process. (Olson et al., 1995, p. 330)

These facts certainly suggest that teen pregnancy is more than a problem of sexually permissive youth and indicate the need to take a broader ecological perspective when looking for solutions to the problem.

Fourth, peer influences often exert pressure on teens to become sexually active. It should be noted that teens often overestimate the number of their friends who are engaging in sexual activity. However, early physically maturing teens may serve as a visual stimuli for others to initiate early sexual advances (Olson et al., 1995). Furthermore, Brooks-Gunn and Furstenberg (1989) indicate that biological factors (i.e., hormonal changes) have a greater effect in males than in females.

Finally, a lack of educational investment in school is related to sexual activity for females but less so for males (Ohannessian & Crockett, 1993). Educational goal setting, grades, and participation in school activities all appear to suffer when a student is sexually active. Teens who do poorly in school are at a high risk for early sexual activity, but it is difficult to determine the causal path of this relationship (Brooks-Gunn & Furstenberg, 1989). That is, does early school failure increase the likelihood of disengagement, which then leads to increased interest in sexual activity? Or does interest in sexual relationships and thoughts of marriage and a family interfere with academic performance? The answers are probably different for individual teens. However, because of the adverse economic effects of early pregnancies, efforts have been made to keep pregnant teens in school for as long as possible. Interventions for school-related problems should be rigorous, and efforts should be made to increase the academic self-esteem of young people, particularly girls, because boys at least superficially appear to be less seriously affected by teen pregnancy. Further research is needed to shed light on these issues.

The extent to which accomplishments and successes serve as a buffer for teens through this developmental stage often depends on cognitive–intellectual abilities and academic skills acquired earlier in childhood. Adolescents experience cognitive-developmental changes that take them to the brink of adult performance on many standard measures of intelligence and that afford the adolescent a means to work through some of the challenges of this developmental period in ways that were not possible in younger childhood.

Cognitive–Intellectual Development

Cognitive–intellectual development relates to other domains, including social and academic areas, and provides many resources for dealing with the changes inherent in this stage.

Cognitive Maturity/Formal Operations

With the advent of formal operational thinking, the adolescent is able to consider a range of possibilities through hypothesis building and propositional thinking. This developmental milestone allows the teen to engage in abstract thinking and to arrive at solutions that can be deduced rather than experienced first hand or concretely. Although not all adolescents or adults reach the formal operational stage (Kohlberg & Gilligan, 1971), thought processes take on dimensions not observed in younger stages of cognitive–intellectual development. Teens are capable of contemplating things in a qualitatively different manner than they could earlier, and they are often idealistic in their thinking. Interest in philosophy and the meaning of life are commonplace. Issues of humanity and/or man's lack of humanity often serve for lively debates on what the world "should" be like versus what it is like.

Although earlier stages center on the child's ability to understand and adjust to what *is,* the adolescent stage is marked by possibilities of "what could be" (Papalia & Olds, 1992). Teens are able to analyze moral dilemmas and to appreciate that some situations don't have necessarily right or correct answers. The teen often feels strongly and is emotionally attached to his/her opinions, such that thoughts and feelings become connected. The soul searching, idealism, and passions that arise in adolescence often are the major motivators that drive lifelong pursuits and interests.

Although some suggest that Piaget overestimated the degree to which individuals reach formal operations (Kohlberg & Gilligan, 1971; Papalia, 1972), other cognitive psychologists point to significant changes in cognition from an information-processing perspective (LeFrancois,

1995). The acquisition and application of a knowledge base, the deliberate process of learning, and an awareness of this process mark this period of cognitive development. Adolescents become active in the process of knowing and remembering and are aware of the self as an "information processor" (Flavell, 1985). They come to understand the role they play in learning, to analyze their own performance, to predict ahead of time how they will do, and to change learning strategies to effect a different outcome from their predictions. These metacognitive abilities are powerful tools for developing academic as well as interpersonal problem solving.

Cognitive changes in adolescence correspond to neurodevelopmental maturation, as well as to social–environmental factors (Papalia & Olds, 1992). The world of the adolescent is greatly expanded, with increased opportunities to experience and to experiment. Cultural, as well as educational, experiences play an important role in the development of formal reasoning, and teens can be guided toward rational thinking by adults. However, other forces may compete with adult guidance, including the teen's own egocentrism and the influence of his/her peer group.

Adolescent Egocentrism. Although formal operations and rational thinking are possible during this stage, adolescent egocentrism presents some interesting challenges. Egocentrism "involves a failure to distinguish one's own point of view from a more objective conception of reality" (Sroufe & Cooper, 1985, p. 524), and is characterized by "an inability to differentiate between objects and concerns of others and those of concern to the adolescent" (LeFrancois, 1995, p. 523). Adolescent egocentrism is often manifested by the teen's inability to understand that other people's views of what is important may not be the same as that of the adolescent. This orientation often leads the adolescent to believe that everyone is watching him or her and that everyone is consumed by the same concerns.

Elkind (1967, 1984) pioneered research into adolescent egocentrism and described some of the behaviors associated with this stage of thinking, including the imaginary audience and the personal fable.

Imaginary Audience. The extreme self-consciousness that teens often feel can best be understood in terms of the "imaginary audience," or the notion that everyone is watching everything that the adolescent does. The myriad of physical changes the adolescent undergoes may leave him/her feeling awkward and self-conscious, hence the concern about how others view him/her (Sroufe & Cooper, 1985). These feelings may cause the teen to seek privacy as a method for escaping the negative judgments of the "imaginary audience," which is made up of friends, parents, teachers, and coaches.

Elkind and Bowen (1979) developed a scale to measure the extent to which adolescents feel that other people are watching them. The scale is a measure of self-consciousness and attempts to differentiate permanent from transitory states. The extent to which adolescents feel that they are being watched and judged by peers may be related to their concern with how they look. The intense scrutiny teens feel may be founded in this concept: teens may engage in destructive, delinquent, sexual, or other risk-taking behaviors (e.g., drugs and alcohol) in part because of how they think the "imaginary audience" will view them.

The imaginary audience remains a part of our psyche even into adulthood, but its importance diminishes as we begin to realize that others are not as concerned about us as we once thought. Because teens are especially self-conscious and can suffer greatly from criticism, Elkind (1984) admonishes adults to avoid publicly criticizing teens to reduce the level of despair and pain teens may already feel.

Personal Fable. Another aspect of egocentrism during this stage is described as the "personal fable" (Elkind, 1984). This aspect of egocentrism refers to the teen's belief that he/she is unique, that no one else shares the same experiences (Sroufe & Cooper, 1985). The perceptions that "I'm the only one who feels this way," or "you just don't know how it feels," leave the teenager feeling alone and isolated. Once he/she begins to share these private thoughts with friends, the notion of uniqueness is replaced with the realization that "other people feel the way I do." This understanding can be reassuring and helps the teen overcome the loneliness of "being the only one." This exploration and sharing with peers is often very personal, which may explain the need for privacy that also seems so important to the adolescent.

Egocentrism may lead teenagers to think that the rules of nature do not apply to them (LeFrancois, 1995). The common belief that "It can't happen to me" may place the teen in an especially vulnerable position. This thought pattern may lead to a lot of self-destructive behaviors because the adolescent may feel that he cannot be killed or that she will not get pregnant or that experimenting with drugs will not hurt (Papalia & Olds, 1992). Empirical evidence does not appear to support these notions and suggests that teens, as well as adults, have an optimistic bias and that adults may be even more optimistic in this regard (Millstein, 1993; Quadrel, Fischhoff, & Davis, 1993). So it may not be a sense of invulnerability that leads to engagement in risky behaviors but an underestimation of the danger in these behaviors that is the real problem (Arnett, 1992).

Risk-Taking Behaviors. High accident rates can occur from risk-taking behaviors, such as speeding and reckless driving or driving after having had a few drinks. Teens may deliberately underestimate the danger of their actions (Arnett, 1992), and it appears that they may even overestimate the benefits of some risky behaviors such as smoking, sex, and drinking (Benthin, Slovic, & Severson, 1993). Thus the underestimation of the potential risks in certain behaviors, coupled with the idea that "it won't happen to me," leaves the teen particularly vulnerable to serious and negative consequences of their choices. Teens do not always anticipate and take necessary precautions that would protect them from high-risk behaviors.

Pressure to engage in risk-taking behaviors also arises from the fact that teens frequently overestimate the number of their friends who engage in risky behaviors. A teenager may have the sense that he/she is the only 16-year-old on the face of the earth who has not done whatever it is that he/she feels compelled to do. Only later do they realize that they were not the only ones who did not sneak out after curfew or did not have sex with their boyfriends, or did not smoke marijuana. Decisions to engage in risk-taking behaviors have serious consequences, including teen pregnancy and/or substance abuse problems.

Moral Development

Moral development is generally discussed within the context of cognitive development. However, moral development influences social development and adjustment as well.

Morality refers to "behaviors and judgments relating to broad issues of human justice, such as the value of human life, the ethics of causing harm to others or to their property, and the placement of trust and responsibility" (LeFrancois, 1995, p. 528). As such, morality interacts with the teen's ethics and values, sense of trust, and understanding of the rights of others.

Moral and cognitive development appear related, and may occur in stages. Although there are a number of theories of moral development (e.g., Piaget), Kohlberg's stages of morality have been empirically tested. In an effort to study moral development, Kohlberg presented children with stories that posed a moral dilemma for the story character. A formal stage theory was developed based on how subjects responded to these dilemmas.

Kohlberg (1969) originally identified three levels and six stages of moral development, but in subsequent revisions he deemphasized stage 6 (LeFrancois, 1995). The levels of morality are: Level I, Preconventional; Level II, Conventional; and Level III, Postconventional. At the preconventional level, the young child believes that bad behavior will be punished, and thus obedience is an attempt to avoid punishment, not an evaluation of "right" or "wrong." Later in the preconventional stage, the child begins to evaluate situations based on how he/she will bene- fit—instrumental hedonism. At this stage, the child will do something "good" if he/she can see a potential benefit in the action.

At Level II, society and peer groups influence the child's conformity (LeFrancois, 1995). During this stage, the child behaves in a certain manner to maintain friendships or good relations. In this instance, the child seeks approval from a variety of people, including significant adults (e.g., parents and teachers) as well as friends. Conformance at this stage is a means to obtain approval from others. Finally, at Level III the individual begins to view morality on the basis of human rights, principles, and ideals rather than as a means to win approval.

The extent to which stages of moral development are predictable and correlated with cognitive development has been investigated with some promising findings. Colby and Kohlberg (1984) showed that children progressed through these stages slowly, such that most young adolescents were between stages 1 (morality as self-serving) and 2 (emphasis on being "good" and doing what is expected), whereas stage 3 development was evident in older adolescents between the ages of 16 and 18. Walker (1988) also found that individuals generally progress from one level to another and do not regress to earlier levels.

Others have criticized Kohlberg's work on a number of grounds, including the fact that the questions/stories are complex and abstract. Children and adolescents show higher levels of moral reasoning when questions are less complex and when they are observed in more natural situations (Darley & Shultz, 1990). Moderator variables, including the intention of the transgressor, characteristics of cruelty and kindness, outcomes or consequences, and interpersonal relations, affect the way an individual makes a moral judgment (Tisak, 1993).

Gender Differences in Moral Development. Gilligan also criticized Kohlberg's theory of moral development on the grounds that he did not investigate morality in females and that the moral dilemmas he presented to his subjects did not reflect situations that were relevant to teens (LeFrancois, 1995). In order to address these limitations, Gilligan devel- oped a model to test moral development in females, using scenarios more typical and realistic for teens.

Three stages of moral development were described by Gilligan (1982) based on her research with females. In the first stage, females act in ways that are motivated by selfish concerns or "What is best for me?" In the next stage, females begin to make judgments based on responsibilities to others. Finally, a nonviolent stage appears that incorporates what is good for the self as well as what is good for others.

LeFrancois (1995) contrasts research investigating males and females based on differences in Kohlberg's and Gilligan's stages. Given these two perspectives, males progress from principles of hedonism (pain–pleasure) to conventional, rule-governed principles. Males appear to be concerned about law and order, whereas females appear more concerned about caring and responsibility. For females, morality is less abstract and more personal (Stander & Jensen, 1993). As such, females may feel more obligated to fulfill responsibilities that reflect caring and responsibility to other situations that are open-ended and extensive in their scope (Nunner-Winkler, 1984). However, studies that contrast males and females on dimensions of altruism, cooperation, justice orientation, and prosocial behavior do not report significant gender differences (Muuss, 1988; Walker & De Vries, 1985; Walker, de Vries, & Trevethan, 1987). Although males and females may not differ, the motivations behind their actions may.

Moral Reasoning. Moral reasoning and judgment refer to decision making about the " 'proper' thing to do in a particular situation" (Sroufe & Cooper, 1985, p. 527). Cognitive psychologists argue that moral reasoning develops as a direct consequence of cognitive development and social experiences. Adolescents are able to consider their own moral viewpoints as well as those of others and begin to develop moral rules that guide their behaviors. Interactions with peers also play an important role in the development of moral reasoning. Lower levels of moral reasoning (e.g., hedonistic) are found in delinquents (Gibbs, 1987), whereas individuals with higher levels of morality tend to be honest and behave in more prosocial ways (Kohlberg & Candee, 1984).

Executive Controls: Self-Regulation and Self-Control

It is important to consider the development of executive controls, especially when trying to understand adjustment in adolescents. Older children and adolescents begin to value self-control, and it is viewed as an important part of self-concept (Berk, 1989). Chandler (1981) found that older children and adolescents describe self attributes in terms of how well they control their anger and how well they apply themselves. On the other hand, about one-third of adolescents mentioned having self-control problems (Rosenberg, 1979). Berk (1989) indicates that as children make the transition from childhood to adolescence, "self-control starts to become an internalized value of considerable importance—a matter of personal commitment and responsibility" (p. 546).

There appears to be a group of adolescents who have been described as "undercontrolled" or "disinhibited" (Gorenstein & Newman, 1980). "Disinhibited" youth are more likely to be impulsive, both cognitively and behaviorally. In adolescence, inadequate self-control can be manifested as acting out, aggression, and/or delinquency problems or as overcontrol problems such as anxiety and/or obsessive–compulsive disorders (Wenar, 1994). Eating disorders may also represent forms of under- or overcontrol (e.g., obesity or anorexia). ADHD has been conceptualized as a disorder of executive controls, in which disinhibition (i.e., inability to inhibit responding) may be a prominent factor. The concept of "disinhibition" will be explored in more detail in the discussion of how ADHD interferes with normal development in adolescence.

Psychosocial Development and Self-Identity

Psychosocial development is an ongoing process that undergoes marked changes in adolescence, and raises issues involving self-worth, self-identity, and peer and family relations. Although most adolescents are well adjusted, some turmoil issues, such as delinquency and drug/alcohol use and/or abuse, do affect a small portion of youth.

Development of Self

Adolescence is marked by development of the concept of "self," which is defined as the "essence of a person" (LeFrancois, 1995, p. 546). Young children use descriptors that focus on external aspects of self, such as "I have brown hair and brown eyes, and I'm good at baseball." With age, children begin to employ general phrases describing internal psychological dispositions, such as "I'm a real loyal friend. My friends and I like the same music, go to the same movies, and we laugh at the same jokes. We all have a weird sense of humor, which helps us get along." According to Berk (1989), the teen begins to use more specific details about his/her own psychological characteristics, such as "I'm generally a very optimistic person but sometimes world events get me down. It's really hard not to get upset when the news shows kids killing each other. It makes me angry that we don't care more about each other, and that we can't stop the violence. I guess I'm just too idealistic." This progression shows how the adolescent view of self develops and demonstrates the complex interaction of psychological characteristics and how they are influenced by situational factors.

Although earlier stages of development mark the beginnings of initiation, self-reliance, and progressive differentiation, the development of personal or self identity may be one of the biggest developmental challenges of adolescence. Adolescents undergo qualitative changes in their understanding of "self" that are marked by a more cohesive, integrated view of self, an understanding of past actions, an anticipation of the future, an ability to self-reflect, and an awareness of how others view them (Sroufe & Cooper, 1988). These changes can be far-reaching, so increased self-awareness and sensitivity to what other people think is pronounced during the adolescent stage (Elkind, 1971). Self-consciousness is "largely absent in childhood," but the adolescent engages in a considerable amount of "self-watching" and "self-evaluation" in respect to how others perceive them (Elkind, 1971, p. 111).

Even when things are going well, teens are often acutely aware of what others think, what they value, and how they behave. As such, the development of personal identity is dependent upon how the teen has been judged in past as well as present evaluative situations (e.g., "How did I fit in?" "Did others think I was cool [smart, pretty, or good at sports]?" "Was I accepted for who I am?"). Again, the idea of the imaginary audience may be involved in this process.

Sroufe and Cooper (1988) indicate that adolescents undergo two stages or subphases of development in how they view "self." In early adolescence (13 to 15 years), teens do have an advanced understanding of self compared to elementary-aged children; however, older adolescents (17 to 18 years) experience even greater changes in their understanding. Older adolescents become aware of differences in conscious and unconscious levels of thinking and feeling (Selman, 1980) and understand how thoughts, judgments, and decision-making processes control physical activity (Broughton, 1978). Although young teens begin to understand how past and future concepts of self are related (Secord & Peevers, 1974), it is not until later adolescence that teens can fully appreciate and rectify contradictory aspects of self (Bernstein, 1980). Sroufe and Cooper (1988) indicate that with an increased awareness and understanding of self, older adolescents begin to lose extreme feelings of self-consciousness.

Feelings of Self-Worth

There are many ways in which to describe self-worth, but it often includes the individual's self-concept or self-appraisal. When an individual thinks highly of him/herself, a positive self-concept is implied, whereas a negative self-concept appears to exist when the individual does not think well of him/herself (LeFrancois, 1995). Self-worth may also be referred to as self-appraisal or self-esteem.

There may be separate areas in which the child evaluates him/herself that add up to feelings of global self-worth. Harter (1987) described at least five areas, including scholastic competence, athletic competence, social acceptance, behavioral conduct, and physical appearance. In earlier stages, the area of behavioral conduct outweighs other dimensions for self-appraisals by young children (grades 1–3), whereas physical appearance and social acceptance are more heavily weighted for older children (grades 6–8). At later stages, self-evaluation becomes more cognitive and less emotional, and adolescents begin to evaluate themselves in specific activities, such as writing essays, calculating math problems, playing tennis, and so forth (Byrne & Shavelson, 1987). So older teens make self-appraisals about how competent they are across these various areas, and global self-concept then may comprise all these inferences.

According to Offer, Ostrov, Howard, and Atkinson (1988), the concept of self-image may comprise a number of facets that can be evaluated separately. These facets are similar to those described by Harter. These facets include the psychological self, the social self, the sexual self, the familial self, and the coping self.

The psychological self comprises the adolescent's feelings, dreams, and fantasies. Emotions and body image are important to this facet of self. The social self consists of how the teen views his/her social relations and includes morals, goals, and aspirations. The sexual self encompasses attitudes and feelings about sexual behavior. Familial self involves attitudes and feelings about parents and siblings. Finally, the coping self includes awareness of one's psychological adjustment, emotional well-being, and coping skills and mastery over challenges.

In a cross-cultural study of teens from 10 different countries, Offer et al. (1988) found that some universal or common characteristics were related to the various facets of self-image. These universal findings suggest that teens around the world do have positive images of self and that they view themselves as relatively well adjusted across these areas. There were some culturally specific findings that were related to contextual variables, including the availability of economic, medical, and vocational opportunities. In situations in which poverty and safety were of concern, adolescents tended to view themselves as more vulnerable, sad, and fearful.

Relationships with Parents

Parent–teen relationships are most strained during early puberty, before parents and families can adjust (Paikoff & Brooks-Gunn, 1991). Parents constantly hear the following comments from their teenage children: "Everyone else is doing it"; "Adam's dad let him have a beer"; "Tracy's mom said she could go to the party even though Scott's parents are out of town. If Tracy can do it, why can't I?"

Conflicts tend to center on issues of control on the part of the parents and increased independence on the part of the teen. As peers become more important, this too may cause turmoil in the family (Bibby & Posterski, 1992). Freedom and friendships are ranked as the most important values for teens, with family life ranked significantly below these issues.

Tensions between parents and teens often focus on everyday events. These points of conflict have not changed for 50 years. Arguments over doing homework, getting chores done, getting home on time, and appropriate style of clothing all can create havoc in families, whereas more serious discussions about drugs and sexual behaviors may not occur (LeFrancois, 1995). Teens often complain that their parents are too intrusive when it comes to their social lives, overbearing about schoolwork and getting good grades, and critical of their friends (Sebald, 1984). Money, such as allowances, can also be another source of conflict.

Teenagers seek more independence, which can be threatening to the parents' control and authority. Parents may react by becoming more strict or unreasonable, which in turn increases the likelihood of rebellion. Baumrind (1989) described three parenting styles that are characterized by varying degrees of control. Authoritarian parenting styles often are rigid and unyielding; the teen is allowed little autonomy or decision-making power. Control rather than reasoning dominates the relationship. On the other hand, permissive parents are nondirective and place few demands on the teen. Punishment is not forthcoming for rule infractions, and the teen is basically left alone to make his/her own decisions. Both of these parenting styles can create special problems for the parent–child relationship at any stage of development but can be particularly damaging during the adolescent stage. The authoritarian style may produce angry, rebellious teenagers, whereas the permissive style may produce teens who lack moral and ethical judgment.

A third parenting style—the authoritative—falls between the two extremes. In this style, parents have clear but high standards. Although values are important, the parent allows the teen to make decisions based on the standards of the home (e.g., religious, ethical, moral). Reasoning and problem solving may be the mode of communication between parents and teens in these households. Baumrind (1977) found that firm, directive parents tended to raise socially responsible children, and she advocates the use of an authoritative parenting style (e.g., firm yet reasonable, demanding yet loving). Other research supports the finding that authoritative parenting is related to positive child outcomes (Bronstein, Clauson, Stoll, & Abrams, 1993)

In general, parent–teen interaction patterns can be either a buffer and protective factor for teens or they can serve as the foundation for serious social and psychological problems. When disrupted, parent–teen relationships appear to be indicators of much adolescent psychopathology, as well as academic difficulties. Coercive parent–child interactions form the basis of conduct-related disorders and reinforce the development of aggressive, antisocial behaviors in children (Patterson, 1986). Furthermore, children who are school bullies are known to come from homes that are characterized as punitive with high rates of physical discipline, with parents who are described as hostile, rejecting, inconsistent, and ineffective problem solvers (see Batsche & Knoff, 1994). So a number of adolescent adjustment problems are related to impaired parent–teen interactions.

Some adolescents have been described as "extremely critical (especially of authority figures), argumentative, self-conscious, self-centered, indecisive, and apparently hypocritical—characteristics that still reflect some egocentrism" (Papalia & Olds, 1992, p. 326). The ability to envision or imagine an ideal world leaves the adolescent open to disappointments when individuals that were once admired disappoint or do not live up to expectations (Papalia & Olds, 1992). Fault-finding and criticism are commonplace, and the teen is often likely to be quite adept at pointing out the little things that are wrong with something or someone else. By practicing this newfound skill of identifying subtle nuances, teens can become embroiled in arguments with adults that strain the relationship. Teens can also be just as blind when it comes to seeing their own faults, which can also frustrate the parent–teen relationship.

Peer Relationships

Peer relations take on a special status as adolescents make the transition into adulthood. Friends are a source of comfort and provide a means for satisfying emotional and social needs. Peer groups change during this period, become more central to the life of the teenager, and exert a great deal of influence on him/her. Intimacy increases and friendships deepen as teens open up to each other in an effort to explore and resolve their issues, concerns, and problems. Teens tend to associate with same-age peers (Hartup, 1978) and to move from same-sex peer groups to male–female pairings with age (Dunphy, 1963). Older adolescents particularly seem to prefer the company of their age mates and are rarely seen with their parents or younger children (Montemayor & Van Komen, 1980).

Status within the peer group is of great importance during adolescence. Being well liked is associated with many positive characteristics, including being sociable, fun, happy and cheerful, and outgoing (LeFrancois, 1995). On the other hand, children who are not well liked are more likely to become school dropouts (Gronlund & Holmlund, 1958), although the causal relationship between these two factors is difficult to discern (LeFrancois, 1995). LeFrancois (1995) suggests that it is difficult to know whether peer rejection leads to adolescent maladjustment (e.g., school dropout, delinquency) or whether the problems (e.g., hostility, withdrawal, antisocial) that are responsible for the maladjustment are the very reason for the rejection. Parker and Asher (1987) found that peer rejection and aggressiveness at a young age are powerful predictors of poor adolescent outcome. Dishion, Patterson, Stoolmiller, and Skinner (1991) also found that peer rejection with academic failure at the age of 10 years was related to antisocial peer-group affiliation in early adolescence.

The ability to understand and empathize with another person typically matures in adolescence. Although children can understand and verbalize these differences at earlier ages, according to Selman (1980) children appear to progress in stages from egocentric (up to age 6) to social–informational (6 to 8 years) to self-reflective (8 to 10 years) to mutual (10 to 12 years) and to social and conventional at adolescence (12 to 15+ years). This progression is marked by more principled, ideological, and value-based thinking in the adolescent. Through a better understanding of the feelings, thoughts, and beliefs of others, adolescents demonstrate more empathy, support, and allegiance to others.

Issues Causing Turmoil in Social Development

For the majority of teens, adolescence is a time of challenges that culminate in growth and increased independence; for others, there are some major pitfalls that can dramatically affect overall adjustment. Issues such as juvenile delinquency and drug and alcohol use and abuse are important because of the concern that ADHD youth might be more susceptible to these problems than the normal teen.

Juvenile Delinquency. Delinquency is a legal term referring to actions or behaviors that break conventional state or federal laws (LeFrancois, 1995). At present, delinquency is considered to be a major problem because there are more illegal acts committed by teenagers and young adults than by individuals over 25 years of age (U.S. Bureau of the Census, 1992). Teens tend to be arrested for truancy, sexual promiscuity, underage drinking, driving without a license, and running away from home (U.S. Bureau of the Census, 1992). The number of arrests is not as high as the actual number of transgressions that go undetected by police, and some estimate that as many as 80% of adolescents admit to breaking the law (Hindelang, 1981). Males tend to be more at risk for delinquency, particularly when it comes to violent crime (LeFrancois, 1995). Violent crimes are on the rise, and the emergence of gangs is a reality in many of our communities.

There are a number of factors that seem to increase adolescents' risk for juvenile delinquency. In general, delinquents tend to have lower IQs than nonoffenders (Binder, 1988), particularly in the verbal domain. Verbal reasoning and language deficits have also been found in young people with significant conduct-related disorders and chronic emotional disturbance (Teeter & Smith, 1993). In fact, reasoning, problem solving, and verbal IQ abilities were significantly delayed in emotionally disturbed youth compared to a control group of adolescents in an urban school setting. The extent to which verbal language and reasoning problems form the basis of poor social interaction and achievement potential needs further investigation in this population. These cognitive factors do place the child at risk for school failure, trouble in the classroom, and identification with other less successful, alienated teens.

Although peer influences play a part in gang-related and violent activities, the role of the family, particularly the father, is also extremely important. Delinquent males are more likely to have fathers with serious emotional as well as legal problems, including a history of alcoholism and of antisocial and criminal activities, a severe punitive and rejecting parenting style, and drug abuse (Biller, 1982). Other researchers have shown that gang activities among culturally diverse students are related to high levels of family stress; parental joblessness and economic strain; bicultural family stress as a result of assimilation difficulties; low self-esteem; high rates of domestic violence; high rates of alcohol and drug abuse; poor parent–teacher communication or school involvement; and multigenerational gang involvement (Kreft & Soriano, 1993). (See Soriano, Soriano, & Jimenez [1994] for an in-depth discussion of these and other factors related to youth violence in culturally diverse youth.)

Another major factor that appears related to delinquency is the adolescent's overall academic and school adjustment. Aggression and severe emotional disturbance have been found in teenagers who are chronically truant, academically deficient, and behaviorally disordered (Teeter & Smith, 1993). However, some elements of a student's school experience may be considered risk factors for increased school violence, including school climate, school environment, and school organizations (Morrison, Furlong, & Morrison, 1994). Claes and Simard (1992) also found that delinquent adolescents befriend individuals outside of school at higher rates than nondelinquent adolescents do. Antisocial activities tend to occur within this nonschool group. One of the strongest predictors of deviant adolescent behavior is association with a deviant peer group (Elliott, Huisinga, & Menard, 1989).

From this brief review, it is easy to see that adolescent characteristics interact in important ways with family, peer, and school variables to produce delinquency and violent behavior in young people. It also suggests the need for multifaceted interventions to deal with these problems. It should be noted that even young people without ADHD are at risk for conduct-related problems and delinquent activities, although it will be shown that when ADHD is present these problems are exacerbated.

Drug and Alcohol Use and Abuse. Although there has been a decrease in drug use since 1971 (U.S. Bureau of the Census, 1992), the United States has the highest rates of drug use among comparable industrialized countries (Newcome & Bentler, 1988). In a longitudinal study investigating personality factors associated with drug use, Shedler and Block (1990) found that 18-year-old "drug experimenters" were better adjusted than non-drug users. On the other hand, "drug abusers" were more impulsive and had higher levels of emotional problems than the other two groups. Adolescents who did not experiment were found to be somewhat more tense, controlled, and socially isolated. Shedler and Block (1990) showed that youth who frequently abused drugs had emotional problems as early as age 7 that included poor self-esteem, low moral development, and impulsivity. By age 11, signs of inattention, poor cooperation, poor coping skills, and continued emotional problems were evident. This longitudinal study demonstrates that young people who develop drug problems showed chronic emotional problems early in life.

In another study conducted on a large sample of urban youth, Farrell, Danish, and Howard (1992) found that adolescent behavioral problems are interrelated and that there may be a "single common factor" that underlies these difficulties (p. 709). The majority (90%) of participants in the study were African-American; one-half lived in single-parent homes and one-third lived with both parents. Between one-third of 9th graders and one-half of 7th graders of the group received free lunches. "Measures of the frequency of cigarette use, alcohol use, marijuana use, delinquency, and sexual intercourse were positively correlated with each other and negatively correlated with measures of conventional behavior, including school attendance and grade point average" (Farrell et al., 1992, p. 709). Furthermore, the presence of one problem suggests the need to screen for other risk behaviors as well (Farrell et al., 1992). Rather than programs that focus on one problem behavior, these authors recommend broad-based interventions that work on prevention, skill building, positive attitudes, and life skills.

Peer influence appears as a strong factor affecting initial drug use. In fact, the selection of a particular drug is highly dependent on whether a friend also used the drug (Dinges & Oetting, 1993; Swaim, Oetting, Thurman, Beauvais, & Edwards, 1993). Poor self-esteem, parental alcoholism and drug use, child neglect and/or abuse, poverty, and poor school adjustment have been found to be contributing factors for drug misuse (Franklin, 1985). Given this context, peer pressure may be more difficult to overcome and poor judgment may ensue, particularly when family and school problems also exist. Parents should be aware of these risk factors. Even if their teenager might be considered at low risk, relative ease of access to drugs and peer influences suggest the need for parent–teen communication about these issues.

Although drug experimentation is not necessarily an indication of pathology, some drugs (cocaine and heroin) have strong addictive qualities that make experimentation highly risky (LeFrancois, 1995). Genetic factors may also play a role in an individual's response to drugs. Drug use/abuse by other family members certainly increases both opportunity and access to drugs.

Academic Achievement

Academic achievement appears related to a number of positive adolescent outcomes and, when significantly impaired, correlates with teen pregnancy, alcohol and drug use and abuse, and school dropout. Research to date is often hard-pressed to determine whether poor school achievement predisposes a teenager to these behavioral problems or whether these behaviors interfere with academic productivity and success. Nonetheless, academic achievement and behavioral problems are so highly interdependent that they must be considered together to understand the effects of one on the other and to undertake preventive efforts to break negative patterns.

A number of factors, including family and parental support and peer group association, affect student success in high school. Research has long shown the relationship between parental involvement with their child and the child's academic success (e.g., high grade point average and graduation rates). Of particular interest is the finding that paternal involvement is especially important in a student's success and that less involvement by the father is related to lower grades (National Center for Educational Statistics, 1987).

In a large cross-sectional study of adolescents (15–19 years of age), Brown, Mounts, Lamborn, and Sternberg (1993) found that parental support, including encouragement for academic success, monitoring, and joint decision making (allowing the teenager to have input as opposed to unilateral parental or teen decision making), had a positive influence on adolescents' academic achievement, self-reliance, and drug avoidance. These factors in turn influenced group membership (e.g., popular, "jock," "brain," "normal," "druggie," or outcast), which was also a significant factor in the school success equation. Brown et al. (1993) found a low correlation between socioeconomic status and group affiliation, with the school community exerting a greater influence. Furthermore, group affiliation was not likely to

> countermand parental influences . . . to lead an adolescent into deviant behavior despite parents' efforts to orient the child toward prosocial values and behaviors. Instead, peer group norms serve to reinforce behaviors and predispositions to which parents (through parenting strategies and/or family background characteristics) have already contributed. (Brown et al., 1993, p. 479)

This study has important implications for educators and parents alike and suggests that attempts to increase achievement outcome for at risk students should consider the interaction of peer group affiliation, early social skills, and parenting strategies with academic achievement.

Socioeconomic status (e.g., family income and parental occupation and education) has a weak correlation with academic achievement that decreases with age (Papalia & Olds, 1992). The success that schools have in providing enriching opportunities, coupled with high dropout rates among low-achieving students, probably accounts for some of this decrease. It has been found that school dropout rates are higher among young people from single-parent households or in families with poorly educated parents (National Center for Educational Statistics, 1987). Other factors related to school dropout are poor or failing grades, repeating a grade, working more than 15 hours a week, teen pregnancy and/or marriage, and other antisocial behavioral problems (e.g., suspensions, expulsions, probation, or illegal activities).

Career Planning

The quest to understand the meaning of one's existence, to develop an appreciation of "who I am," and to discover oneself is an important task of the adolescent stage. Young people often begin to develop a strong sense of who they want to be, what they want to accomplish, and the type of work or career they want to pursue. Erik Erikson (1968) first introduced the term "identity" to describe the process by which adolescents come to understand these aspects of self and posited that the concept of identity included the move toward self-discovery (Sroufe & Cooper, 1988).

The Adolescent Crisis: Identity versus Identity Diffusion

During adolescence, young people begin to develop a personal identity that integrates their past and present experiences and includes an awareness of society's expectations for their future. The challenges the adolescent undertakes in this process are referred to as an "identity crisis" by Erikson; when the crisis is resolved, the adolescent emerges with a coherent and consistent view of self (Sroufe & Cooper, 1988). When unresolved, the adolescent is confused about sex roles and may be unsure of which occupational choices to pursue. When investigating gender differences, Streitmatter et al. (1993) found that males and females did not differ in terms of their identity development. Although Erikson's theory appears to be supported by these data, further exploration into methods for measuring and defining identity development would be helpful.

Although Erikson's work is largely theoretical, Marcia (1980) found that adolescents do demonstrate individual differences in identity formation and can be classified into the following categories: foreclosure, identity diffusion, moratorium, and identity achievement. In foreclosure, the adolescent retreats from exploring various options and instead selects a role that is prescribed by others—typically the parent—thereby bypassing the identity crisis. Marcia (1980) views this commitment as a "pseudo identity" because it is built on an unquestioning acceptance of someone else's view and is not autonomous self-assessment. Identity diffusion results from being overwhelmed by the various possibilities. The adolescent changes roles, makes few commitments, and shows no long-term plans. Thus the identity crisis is unresolved. An adolescent in moratorium status is still in the midst of identity formation and has not made a definitive decision. These individuals are in the middle of the crisis and may need time to identify their major life goal. This is considered to be a healthy process by which to attain identity formation.

Finally, identity achievement is marked by a conscious choice, made after an autonomous decision-making process. The individual is confident in his/her occupational choice and committed to achieving his/her plans.

Well-Adjusted Youth

Although adolescence generally marks a period of increased risk behaviors, the majority of teenagers are not reckless, out of control, or amoral

(LeFrancois, 1995). Data gathered by the U.S. Bureau of the Census (1992) reveals that a majority of teens are handling the pressures of adolescence in mature, functional ways. Specifically, these data showed the following: (1) 5.6 million adolescents between the ages of 16 and 19 held jobs, and more than 14 million were in school; (2) 87% of 12- to 17-year-olds had not used marijuana and 97.6% had never used cocaine or stimulants (U.S. Bureau of the Census, 1992; cited in LeFrancois, 1995). Thus it is important to note that for the most part young people are coping with the stresses of adolescence in a productive manner.

Summary

LeFrancois (1995) suggests that although early theories considered adolescence to be a period of storm and stress, "adolescence throughout the world is predominantly a positive, nonturbulent, energetic, growth-filled period" (p. 550). When things do not go well, contextual variables play a large role in the adjustment process and significantly affect the moods and behaviors of teenagers.

A review of normal development sets the stage for a better understanding of the impact of ADHD in the adolescent stage. Although this is not necessarily a tumultuous period for the majority of teens, adolescents undergo changes that are nonetheless remarkable. When ADHD is added to these normal developmental issues, the adolescent stage can be quite a challenge.

EFFECTS OF ADHD IN THE ADOLESCENT STAGE

Perhaps one of the more disturbing findings is that for the majority of individuals, ADHD persists into adolescence and adulthood. Although early conceptualizations suggested that ADHD diminished in adolescence (Laufer, Denhoff, & Solomons, 1957), longitudinal research shows that the symptoms persist. Table 7.1 summarizes research showing the characteristics and problems associated with ADHD during the adolescent stage.

In general, the relatively few studies that have been completed consistently report that although the characteristics of ADHD persist over time, the problems change from childhood to adolescence. Wender (1987) indicates that some characteristics, such as hyperactivity per se, diminish, whereas self-control problems linger. Self-control deficits might manifest in various ways such that empathy and awareness of how one's behavior affects others may be lacking and thrill-seeking behaviors may be quite high.

TABLE 7.1. Characteristics of ADHD in the Adolescent Stage

Source	Adolescent characteristics
Barkley (1989)	Inability to follow rules and assume responsibility
Barkley, Fischer, Edelbrock, & Smallish (1990)	In 8-year follow-up: 71% had ADHD; 59%, oppositional defiant disorder (DSM-III-R); 43%, conduct disorder (DSM-III-R); 10% were dropouts; those with ADHD were more likely to fail a grade and to be expelled
Blouin et al. (1978)	Teens with ADD and other problems: more conduct problems, impulsivity, hyperactivity; higher scores on self-injury scale and use of alcohol; behaviors normalized for majority (60%) between ages 16–21 years; 31% full syndrome symptoms; 9% still show difficulties since childhood Teens with ADD symptoms without other problems: 48% antisocial; 32% substance abuse (drugs), antisocial behaviors precede drug abuse Teens without ADD symptoms but with other problems: 13% antisocial; 10% substance abuse, same as controls; early aggression in childhood predicts later antisocial problems (especially when mean, calculated, and deliberate)
Mendelson, Johnson, & Stewart (1971)	13-year-olds who were identified between 8 and 10 years of age: 25% in special education; 2% in training schools; 2% in psychiatric hospitals; 70–80% restless and distractible; 26% with history of antisocial problems; 17% in juvenile court
Schachar, Rutter, & Smith (1981)	Pervasive hyperactivity predicts persistent psychiatric disorders for 9- to 14-year-olds
Taylor (1986)	Pervasive hyperactivity may increase risk for conduct disorder and academic failure
Weiss & Hechtman (1993)	Original symptoms diminish, replaced by antisocial, school, and social problems; repeated antisocial behavior varies (between 10% and 45%), including serious crimes (assault with a deadly weapon); primary social learning deficit combined with impaired parent–teen relationship
Wender (1987)	Inability to experience pleasure normally—possibly high thrill-seeking behaviors; self-control problems; lack of empathy and awareness of others' reactions; 50% outgrow symptoms; symptoms diminish/other symptoms persist in 25–30%; mixed, unclear outcome for 10–25%

There is not a great deal of research specifically investigating ADHD in adolescence or, for that matter, in adulthood. The studies that have been conducted are either retrospective or prospective in nature (Weiss & Hechtman, 1993). Retrospective studies attempt to describe the disorder by looking into past medical and clinic records that are typically several years old, whereas in prospective studies children are first diagnosed and then are periodically tested to determine developmental changes over time. Prospective studies are considered the stronger of the two research designs from a methodological perspective.

Adolescent Outcome Data

Retrospective Research

In one of the early studies investigating hyperactivity in older children who had been previously seen in a psychiatric clinic, the following characteristics and symptoms were found in adolescents: (1) 70–80% continued to show signs of restlessness and distractibility; (2) 26% showed chronic antisocial behaviors; (3) 17% had been in juvenile court; (4) 25% had been in special education classes; and (5) 2% had required psychiatric hospitalization at some time in their childhoods (Mendelson, Johnson, & Stewart, 1971). Although these findings are important because this was one of the first systematic follow-up studies on hyperactivity, the retrospective nature of the design is somewhat problematic (Weiss & Hechtman, 1986, 1993).

In general, retrospective studies can be problematic because it is difficult to use history taken from medical or school charts to make diagnoses based on current diagnostic criteria. However, this study showed that the majority of children with ADHD did not outgrow the disorder, and it stimulated other longitudinal studies that have subsequently followed young children into adolescence.

The prospective longitudinal studies that are discussed next collected data beginning when young children were first diagnosed, then again in adolescence and in adulthood.

Prospective Longitudinal Research

Weiss and Colleagues. In a series of reports that began in the early 1960s, Weiss and her colleagues conducted a 5-year follow-up on adolescents aged 11 to 16 years, with a mean age of 13.4 years (Minde et al., 1972; Weiss et al., 1971). The adolescents had been diagnosed as pervasively hyperactive when they were between the ages of 6 and 12 years of age. Although DSM-III was not in use at the time, Weiss and her colleagues did indicate that all subjects were ADHD and that the majority had conduct-related problems.

Weiss and Hechtman (1993) reported (1) decreases in major symptoms of ADHD (i.e., hyperactivity, distractibility, impulsivity, and aggression), although scores were still elevated compared to a control group; (2) signs of immaturity, problems setting goals, and sad affect when discussing past failures and future plans; (3) low self-esteem; (4) higher failure/retention rates and poorer grades in school compared to classmates; (5) impulsive response style on cognitive tasks; and (6) decreased motor skills (Cohen, Weiss, & Minde, 1972; Minde et al., 1972; Weiss et al., 1971). The hyperactive teens had significantly elevated scores on a measure of psychopathy compared to normals, and 25% had antisocial behavioral problems. It is important to note that this group also had signs of conduct-related problems, and it has been shown that conduct disorders with ADHD may represent a more serious disorder than either ADHD or conduct disorder alone. Weiss and Hechtman (1993) followed this same group of subjects into adulthood, and outcome data are reviewed in Chapter 9.

Barkley and Colleagues. In the most recent longitudinal study of adolescents between 12 and 20 years of age who were diagnosed with ADHD in childhood (4–12 years), Barkley, Fischer, et al. (1990) reported the following data, taken after an 8-year interval: 71% met criteria for a diagnosis of ADHD using DSM-III-R (1987); 59% had oppositional defiant disorder (compared to 11% of the control group); and 43% had conduct disorders (compared to 1.6% of the control group). Of the most problematic behaviors, inattention and difficulty following instructions were associated with ADHD symptoms and arguing and irritability were associated with oppositional symptoms and with all conduct-disorder symptoms (with the exception of four items). Other findings from these studies are reported in subsequent sections that discuss cognitive, academic, and psychosocial problems in teens with ADHD.

A rather disturbing pattern was revealed in that problems persisted for teens with ADHD even after rather extensive intervention. As a group, they had had an average of 3 years of medication, 16 months of individual psychotherapy, 7 months of family therapy, and between 40 and 65 months of special education for learning, speech, and behavioral disorders (Barkley, Fischer, et al., 1990). Other research suggests that a multimodal treatment program can alter the negative prognosis of ADHD for adolescents (Satterfield, Satterfield, & Cantwell, 1980, 1981). Further research is needed to determine the long-term effects of early interventions for ADHD in childhood.

Summary of Major Longitudinal Studies. Weiss and Hechtman (1993) summarized findings across various longitudinal studies and reported that (1) syndrome symptoms diminished in most adolescents; (2) school performance, self-esteem, and peer relation problems were consistently reported; and (3) major differences were found across studies in the frequency of antisocial behavior problems (from 10% to 45%). This later finding may be related to the degree of overlap with ADHD and conduct disorders and to the study site (e.g., conducted their study in Los Angeles; Satterfeld et al., 1982).

The following sections review available research across developmental domains to show the specific impact of ADHD on cognitive, academic, and social areas. Because there is such a paucity of research for ADHD in adolescents, data from the longitudinal studies that were not previously summarized are included here, as well as discussions of issues related to ADHD with other comorbid disorders (e.g., conduct disorder, depression, and anxiety).

Cognitive and Neuropsychological Performance

In a longitudinal study of adolescents, Fischer, Barkley, Edelbrock, and Smallish (1990) investigated attentional, neuropsychological, and academic problems in a group of adolescents with ADHD. Sustained attention and impulse control problems persisted in teenagers with hyperactivity, although they were not significantly different from the control group on distractibility. Fischer et al. (1990) found that when tasks were sufficiently long, tedious, and unsupervised, sustained attention (measured by the Gordon Continuous Performance Test) was most vulnerable. There was a definite improvement for the older (mean age 16.5 years) hyperactive youth over the younger group (mean age 12.9 years) on some of the measures (Fischer et al., 1990). In general, older adolescents made fewer omission errors and were less off-task on distractibility measures. Furthermore, fewer commission errors were made, and the older adolescents were less likely to play with objects during testing. Thus, younger adolescents appeared more impulsive and had more problems with behavioral disinhibition, which improved in the older adolescent hyperactive group.

The hyperactive group did not show significant problems on select neuropsychological tests measuring verbal fluency (such as the Controlled Oral Word Association Test) or verbal memory (the Selective Reminding Test). The literature shows conflicting findings when verbal fluency, verbal learning, and verbal memory are measured. Fischer et al. (1990) suggest that differences across studies may be a function of the presence of coexisting learning disabilities in some subjects with ADHD.

Other studies do report signs of neuropsychological weaknesses in preteens and young adults (9- to 20-year-olds) with ADHD. Seidman et al. (1995) found that youth with ADHD did have impaired performance on neuropsychological measures even in the absence of other coexisting problems or a family history of ADHD. Furthermore, an ADHD group with learning disabilities specifically showed slow reading rates and reduced dominance on motor tasks. Signs of frontal lobe weaknesses and alterations in motor dominance were found in the ADHD group irrespective of the existence of comorbid problems compared to a control group.

Abnormalities were found in a study investigating brain metabolism in the frontal cortex of female adolescents with ADHD. Ernst et al. (1994) measured cerebral glucose metabolism rates using positron emission tomography (PET scans). Although adolescents with ADHD did not differ from a control group in global or regional glucose flow, when gender differences were analyzed, there were significant findings. Females with ADHD showed significantly abnormal (19.6% lower) global glucose metabolism compared to normal girls. However, males with ADHD did not show this pattern of low cerebral glucose metabolism. The authors conclude that these findings suggest that more attention needs to be directed toward females with ADHD. In general, females with ADHD may be underdiagnosed and may remain untreated into adolescence and adulthood. These issues will be explored in Chapter 9, on adults with ADHD.

Finally, in a preliminary study conducted by Becker, Doane, and Wexler (1993), there were signs of perceptual asymmetry in young people with ADHD. When words with neutral, negative, or positive emotional tones were presented on tape in a dichotic-listening experiment, teens with ADHD differed from normals. Under positive-emotion conditions, non-ADHD subjects showed a right ear advantage, indicating that processing was mediated by left hemisphere regions. This was not the case for the teens with ADHD, who showed a lower right ear advantage and left hemisphere processing when words were positive. Although these results are considered preliminary because of the small sample size, the authors indicate that these findings demonstrate support for the theory that ADHD individuals have a "reward system dysfunction" due to abnormalities in the brain mechanisms responsible for processing emotionally charged stimuli. The degree to which these findings are related to other problems in interpersonal, academic, and behavioral areas needs further investigation. However, this study utilized a research protocol that might prove useful in future studies.

Frontal lobe functioning, as measured by the Wisconsin Card Sorting Test, was found to be comparable between hyperactives and a control group. McGee, Williams, Moffitt, and Anderson (1989) also reported similar findings with a group of 13-year-old learning disabled, ADD, and control participants. This was not entirely expected, given that younger ADHD children have shown deficits on the Wisconsin Card Sorting Test (Chelune, Ferguson, Koon, & Dickey, 1986). Fischer et al. (1990) caution that these findings do not necessarily imply frontal lobe efficiency. Adolescents did show deficits on other measures of frontal lobe functioning, particularly in vigilance and reaction time for complex tasks (i.e., the Gordon Continuous Performance Test). Fischer et al. (1990) hypothesize that "behavioral disinhibition may be less likely to emerge on tasks of dorso-lateral frontal lobe functions, such as card sorting or verbal fluency, but more likely to appear on measures of disinhibition, such as commission errors on a vigilance task" (p. 587), the latter of which seem to be mediated by different cortical and subcortical regions (i.e., orbital frontal and subcortical striatal regions).

It may be too soon to draw definitive conclusions about the presence of global or specific neuropsychological deficits in adolescents with ADHD. However, emerging research does suggest that there are signs that cerebral metabolism rates are low in females with ADHD. Deficits were reported on other measures of cerebral dominance and perceptual asymmetry. The question of deficits on frontally-mediated tasks is still equivocal, with conflicting data being reported.

Academic and School Adjustment Difficulties

To date, outcome data suggest that school-related problems persist into adolescence. Teens with ADHD are at risk of grade retention, of dropping out of high school (10% compared to 0% of the control group), and of failing to pursue college or university training (Barkley et al., 1990). When other school variables are investigated, ADHD teens show high rates of special education placement for learning disabilities (32.5%), behavior disorders (35.8%), and speech–language therapy (16.3%; Barkley et al., 1990).

Although suspension and dropout rates were high for teens with ADHD, the added diagnosis of conduct disorder increased these problems including expulsion rates. Compared to a control group, hyperactive adolescents were significantly deficient on measures of reading recognition, spelling, and mathematics calculation (Fischer et al., 1990). As a group, hyperactive teens scored 0.5 to 1 standard deviations from lower than their age-mates and had significantly more school-related problems, including higher retention, expulsions, suspensions, and dropout rates. Based on a 15-minute clinic observation, scores from the Restricted Academic Situation scale did reveal significant differences between the hyperactive and control groups, with increased reports of off-task, fidgety, noisy, and out-of-seat behaviors in the hyperactive group (Fischer et al., 1990). Again, younger teens had more problems than the older hyperactive teens, who showed more restraint and more self-control than the younger group.

Family Relations and Conflicts

Family problems generally center on the adolescent's difficulty obeying rules, solving problems, and being responsible and trustworthy (Barkley, 1989). Parents do report high rates of oppositional defiant problems (e.g., argues, defies requests, deliberately annoys others, is easily annoyed by others, angry and resentful) in teens with ADHD (Barkley, Anastopoulos, Guevremont, & Fletcher, 1991). Rebelliousness, conduct disorders, and family conflict are major issues that may characterize family relations during this period (Barkley et al., 1991; Robin, 1990; Weiss & Hechtman, 1993).

Parents describe interactions with their adolescents as conflictual, angry, and negative (Barkley et al., 1991). Robin, Kraus, Koepke, and Robin (1987) found that families seeking clinic-based services have difficulty communicating and have poor problem-solving skills, adolescents make negative and malicious parent attributions, and teens and parents alike show disengagement. Robin and Foster (1989) indicate that the normal adolescent rebellious and independence-seeking behaviors are intensified by the symptoms and characteristics of ADHD.

When summarizing the major problems of adolescents, Barkley (1990a, p. 122) indicates that parents seek clinical services for their teenagers because of "poor schoolwork, social difficulties with peers, [and] problems related to authority (especially at school)." Based on clinical experience, Robin (1990) also suggests that parent–teen conflicts often provide the impetus for families to seek professional help.

Social and Behavioral Problems

Social difficulties continue to be a major concern to parents of teenagers with ADHD (Barkley, 1990a). Drug, alcohol, and delinquency problems tend to be part of the adolescent profile for many hyperactive adolescents.

Drug and Alcohol Problems

Although drug and alcohol problems have been found in adolescents with ADHD, controversy surrounds the issue of whether teens with ADHD are more at risk than are their peers without the disorder

(Barkley, 1989, 1990a). Inconsistencies may result from a lack of standardized definitions utilized in studies that were conducted in the 1970s prior to the adoption of diagnostic criteria for ADHD established by DSM-III or DSM-III-R (Barkley, 1990a).

In an attempt to understand how hyperactivity affected adolescents, Blouin, Bornstein, and Trites (1978) compared teens who had ADHD with and without other behavioral or conduct problems to a control group. Hyperactive teens with other problems showed more drinking, self-injury, impulsivity, and conduct problems than the other two groups. Many of these problems subsided between ages 16 and 21 for the majority of hyperactive youth. Adolescents with ADHD but no other problems did have antisocial problems (48%) and substance abuse problems (10%); however, the antisocial disorders preceded the drug use in this group. Although not trouble-free, the control group showed fewer problems than both clinical groups, in which 13% had antisocial disorders and 10% showed substance abuse problems. The Blouin et al. (1978) study shows that ADHD alone does not necessarily place a teenager at higher risk for substance abuse, but it does show the relationship between substance abuse and antisocial behavioral problems.

Higher-than-normal rates of alcohol or drug problems may occur more frequently in adolescents with conduct disorders than with ADHD alone (Barkley, 1990a; Gittelman, Mannuzza, Shenker, & Bonagura, 1985). The social-behavioral consequences of disinhibition may prove to be an important factor that helps show how these disorders are related. The long-term and serious consequences of disinhibition are also reviewed in Chapter 9.

In a longitudinal study of 870 adolescents, Bates and Labouvie (1995) found that drinking habits are a function of person–environment interactions. Specifically, impulsivity, disinhibition, and affiliation with a deviant peer group were found to be high-risk factors for problem drinking in adolescents. To a lesser extent, low parental control was also found to be a significant factor in this equation. Although teens in this study were not identified as ADHD, disinhibition and impulsivity are symptoms that may place a teenager at risk for increased alcohol use. The extent to which disinhibition and impulsivity influence the selection of friends and affiliation with other adolescents who have problems is of interest and warrants further study.

Arrest and Juvenile Delinquency

The relationship between criminal behavior, juvenile delinquency, and ADHD has been the focus of investigation. In a study of 42 incarcerated youth, Forehand, Wierson, Frame, Kempton, and Armistead (1991) found that the majority (71%) of these adolescents met criteria for conduct disorder, whereas 29% met criteria for both conduct disorder and ADHD. Also, teens with conduct disorder and ADHD were a more seriously disturbed group of youth who were more likely to be arrested at an earlier age and had more total arrests. The added element of ADHD appears to have serious consequences for the development and maintenance of juvenile delinquency. However, it is important to note that ADHD alone was not found to be a significant factor.

These initial findings offer reasons to be optimistic about adolescents with ADHD but without conduct disorder, but concerns about the comorbidity of these disorders are also warranted. The findings also suggest the need to develop early and intensive intervention programs for children identified with ADHD and conduct disorder in order to avoid delinquency problems in later life.

There are some characteristics that predict which young people with ADHD are at highest risk for delinquency. Satterfield, Swanson, Schell, and Lee (1994) did find that aggression/defiance ratings in childhood were related to negative outcome measures. Teen arrest records were significantly related to high scores on measures of defiance. Although high defiance scores were associated with high rates of felony offenses, adolescents with low defiance scores also had higher rates for minor antisocial offenses compared to a control group. This suggests that even without significant defiance problems, teens with ADHD often make poor decisions that get them into trouble.

This problem is illustrated in the case histories of several families with whom I have worked with over the years. In one instance, the teenager with ADHD was arrested for petty theft while working as a caddie at a golf course, and in another case a teenager was arrested for tearing hood ornaments off luxury cars in the neighborhood. In general, adolescents with ADHD are prone to risk-taking behaviors, particularly in situations in which problems of disinhibition, poor impulse control, and poor social reasoning and judgment interfere with good decision making.

In an earlier prospective study, Satterfield, Hoppe, and Schell (1982) investigated the arrest and delinquency rates of young people living in the Los Angeles area. Hyperactive males between the ages of 13 and 21 years of age had higher arrest rates and were incarcerated for delinquency more often than those in a control group. The arrests were for serious crimes; minor offenses (e.g., running away from home, petty theft, underage drinking, and possession of less than 1 ounce of marijuana) were not included. Arrest rates were high across all socioeconomic levels in the ADHD group, with 58% coming from lower levels, 36% from middle-class levels, and 52% from upper-class levels. In the control group, the rate of arrests was highest for youth in lower socioeconomic levels (11%) and showed a steady decline in middle-class (9%) and upper-class (2%) levels. Although problems of self-control and behavioral disinhibition are common across all socioeconomic groups, it is unclear why no decrease appears in the middle and upper socioeconomic levels among teens with ADHD similar to the decrease found in the control group. Do these differences suggest intense parent–child conflict or perhaps higher risk-taking behaviors in teens with ADHD who come from higher socioeconomic levels?

Further research into the relationship between socioeconomic status and criminal activity in hyperactive adolescents is needed to answer these questions. These relationships may provide important information for determining the primary treatment goals. In the case of intense parent–teen conflicts, family therapy and conflict resolution might be the primary focus of treatment, whereas high risk-taking behaviors suggest the need for individual and/or group therapy to increase impulse control and prosocial behaviors.

Other Risk Behaviors

In their longitudinal study, Weiss and Hechtman (1986) found that adolescents with ADHD were likely to have more automobile accidents than other adolescents. Barkley, Guevremont, Anastopoulos, DuPaul, and Shelton (1993) also investigated the driving habits of teenagers and young adults with ADHD. The study compared the driving records of 35 ADHD participants to 36 control participants between the ages of 16 and 22 years of age. In general, teens with ADHD were less careful drivers on almost all measures, as they showed a higher number of crashes and more bodily injury resulting from auto accidents and were more often "at fault" for these incidents. Traffic citations were also higher in the ADHD group, and speeding was a particular problem.

In an attempt to determine the effects of coexisting disorders on these data, Barkley et al. (1993) also measured the impact of oppositional defiant and conduct disorders. A subgroup of teens with comorbid disorders (ADHD + oppositional defiant disorder or ADHD + conduct disorder) did have worse records and more driving-related problems. These results suggest the need to discuss driving with care and other problem solving strategies with parents and teens who have ADHD when designing treatment programs for this age group.

COMORBIDITY: ADHD WITH OTHER DISORDERS OF ADOLESCENCE

ADHD presents a myriad of adjustment problems for adolescents, but when combined with other psychiatric and behavioral problems, a very guarded outcome is likely. There appears to be a group of adolescents who have been described as "undercontrolled" or as "disinhibited" (Gorenstein & Newman, 1980). Disinhibited youth are more likely to be impulsive cognitively as well as behaviorally. The concept of disinhibition has been used to describe a number of problems, including conduct disorders, antisocial personality disorders, and ADHD.

Conduct Disorder with ADHD

In general, behavioral, emotional, and social adjustment problems appear to be common for adolescents with ADHD. In studies investigating the relationship between ADHD and other conduct-related problems, the incidence of comorbidity was high. This relationship was found in young children (see Biederman et al., 1992), as well as in teenagers. Barkley, Anastopoulos, Guevremont, and Fletcher (1991) reported that teens with ADHD were more likely to have major adjustment problems compared to a control group. The incidence of oppositional defiant disorder was 68%, and 39% of the ADHD group also had conduct disorder. Parents reported problems in social competence and in behavioral, emotional, and school adjustment. Difficulties were demonstrated on clinical measures of vigilance and verbal learning as well. High rates of ADHD symptoms were also observed in adolescents while they were completing a math task.

Taylor (1986) suggests that pervasive hyperactivity may increase the risk for conduct disorder as well as for academic failure. Others suggest that antisocial behavior problems in adolescence are related to early aggression, especially when young children are mean, calculated, and deliberate in their actions (Blouin, Bornstein, & Trites, 1978). The possibility of conduct or delinquent problems increases during adolescence, particularly for those teens who have ADHD with early aggressive or antisocial behaviors.

The occurrence of antisocial behavioral problems with ADHD appears to be high (Barkley, 1996a; Hinshaw & Anderson, 1996); as many as 43% of hyperactive adolescents have also been diagnosed with conduct disorder (Barkley et al., 1990). The combination of ADHD and conduct disorder increases the rate of coexisting alcohol and drug problems (Gittelman, Mannuzza, Shenker, & Bonagura, 1985), academic failure and school adjustment problems (Fischer et al., 1990), and antisocial and criminal behaviors (Klein & Mannuzza, 1991) in adolescents.

The developmental trajectory of comorbidity suggests that ADHD increases the risk for the development of conduct disorder or oppositional defiant disorder, although determining whether ADHD or early aggression is most powerful in this equation is still difficult (Hinshaw & Anderson, 1996). Loeber (1990) found that comorbid ADHD with oppositional defiant/conduct disorder did predict a treatment-resistant group that showed early and persistent signs of psychopathology. Early onset and a life course of antisocial problems appears related to the presence of ADHD in young children (Moffitt, 1993).

> Furthermore, Moffitt's (1990) investigation points to the complexity of developmental trajectories for the subgroup of aggressive–hyperactive children. Early attention problems display statistical interactions with (1) family adversity and (2) low verbal IQ in predicting adolescent antisocial patterns, signifying that cognitive functioning and psychosocial variables propel the risk for poor outcome among comorbid youth. (Hinshaw & Anderson, 1996, p. 133)

This developmental course also points to the interaction of impulsivity with other cognitive, psychosocial, and family factors in producing guarded adolescent outcome, as proposed in the Teeter and Semrud-Clikeman (1997) transactional, neurodevelopmental model of ADHD.

Depression and Bipolar Disorders with ADHD

A significant number of adolescents with ADHD also have symptoms of depression (Biederman, Faraone, et al. 1991; Biederman, Faraone, et al., 1992). Recently there has also been some question about whether adolescents with bipolar disorders are misdiagnosed as ADHD. Isaac (1992) studied a group of 12 adolescents diagnosed with ADHD and conduct disorder who were in a special-education treatment facility. These teenagers were the most resistant to treatment and appeared to be crisis-prone. Following a 6-month observation and intensive reevaluation, eight of the adolescents met diagnostic criteria for bipolar disorder, and three showed significant symptoms but did not meet all the DSM-III-R criteria for the full syndrome. This study may provide important insight into adolescents who are highly treatment-resistant and who require special education and/or outpatient treatment because of serious emotional disturbance. The study also points to the need for clinicians to reassess and to conduct ongoing, long-term observation for the most accurate diagnosis of psychiatric disorders in adolescents. By this means, a working diagnostic hypothesis can be verified or discarded after considerable observation and intensive treatment or a diagnosis of comorbid psychopathology may be made.

SUMMARY

There is clear evidence that for a majority of adolescents ADHD symptoms persist and increase their chances of having other academic, behavioral, and psychosocial adjustment problems. The conceptualization and emphasis on executive control problems as the basis for a variety of disorders is gaining recognition and may eventually provide a unifying theory for understanding and treating childhood, adolescent, and adult psychopathologies. Careful documentation of comorbid disorders is also important, given that the presence of these disorders predicts a more persistent, severe, and treatment-resistant group, especially when ADHD is combined with oppositional defiant/conduct disorder.

8

Intervention Strategies and Techniques for the Adolescent Stage

*P*roviding *therapeutic* interventions for adolescents can be a challenge for clinicians for a number of reasons. First, teens with ADHD have a history of difficulties and may have already had either positive or negative therapy experiences with professionals at an earlier age. "Their patterns of interaction with the environment are frequently entrenched. They are often unwilling to accept responsibility for their problems and are resistant to treatment. In treatment, the initial hurdle with ADHD adolescents is convincing them to be active, as opposed to passive, participants" (Goldstein & Goldstein, 1990, pp. 24–25).

Second, unlike the middle childhood stage, intervention research with adolescents with ADHD is scant, even though many of the difficulties of childhood (e.g., with social relations, academic progress, self-control, and behavioral adjustment) continue into adolescence. Unfortunately, the consequences of disinhibition, poor self-control, and impulsivity can have a serious impact on the adolescent because unresolved problems set the stage for adjustment problems in early adulthood (e.g., educational attainment, career success, and solid interpersonal relationships).

This chapter reviews some therapeutic methods and approaches for addressing adolescent challenges, including (1) family therapy; (2) academic interventions; (3) self-control and self-management techniques; (4) individual and group therapy; (5) medication issues; and (6) career planning. The limited number of empirical studies that have been conducted are discussed first, followed by descriptions of promising interventions that require verification through controlled studies.

RESEARCH ON EMPIRICALLY BASED INTERVENTIONS

Research identifying effective therapies and intervention approaches has started to focus on the adolescent with ADHD. Studies have addressed only a few of the major problems facing adolescents, including family therapy and psychopharmacology; however, some trends toward prevention are emerging.

Family Therapy

Family therapy is frequently necessary to address the conflictual parent–adolescent relationships that are common during this stage. Barkley, Guevremont, Anastopoulos, and Fletcher (1992) investigated the efficacy of three therapy programs that were designed to reduce conflicts and to increase positive parent–teen relationships. Participants in the study were 64 adolescents and their mothers, who completed at least eight therapy sessions and provided pre- and posttreatment data.

Behavioral management, problem solving and communication training, and structural family strategies produced significant decreases in the number of and intensity of conflicts in parent–adolescent interactions.

Behavior Management Training

This program utilizes techniques developed by Barkley (1987, 1997b) for parents with defiant, noncompliant children. (See Chapter 6 for a detailed description.) Parents are taught to use positive attention, to isolate or ground teenagers in the home, to use point systems, to anticipate problem situations, and to develop plans before problems occur (Barkley et al., 1991). Parents are expected to complete homework assignments and to practice skills outside therapy sessions.

Problem-Solving Communication Training

Portions of the problem-solving training techniques were developed by Robin and Foster (1989). Parents are taught how to use a five-step problem-solving program, to substitute effective communication strategies in conflict situations, and to modify negative parental attributions directed at their son or daughter. Homework assignments and critiques of videotaped home conflict situations are also included in the treatment.

Structural Family Therapy

Techniques developed by Minuchin were adapted for study (Barkley, Guevremont, Anastopoulos, & Fletcher, 1992). A family systems process is used to identify and alter maladaptive interactions. (See the description of transgenerational coalitions and triangulations in the discussion of Robin and Foster's program later in this chapter.) Families are taught to realign, refocus, and restructure problematic dynamics and systems. Homework targeting ineffective family interactions is incorporated into the program.

Research Findings

Although the three approaches did not differ in overall therapeutic effect, some interesting findings on measures of change are noteworthy. First, the percentages of families showing significant improvement on the number of conflicts was 10% with behavior management training, 24% with problem solving communication training, and 10% with structured family therapy, whereas percentages of participants defined as "recovered" were 5% with behavior management training, 19% with problem solving communication training, and 10% with structured family therapy. Second, on measures of anger frequency and intensity, decreases of 20% with behavior management training, 29% with problem solving communication training, and 5% with structured family therapy were shown. Third, 10% of the BMT group actually showed clinical deterioration during treatment. Finally, 20% of the behavior management training group, 19% of the problem solving communication training group, and 5% of the SFT group showed "clinically significant improvement." Mothers in all treatment groups rated adolescent improvements on internalizing and externalizing problems, as well as school adjustment. Mothers' self-reports also showed decreased depression.

There were some other differences among the groups: (1) therapists rated families receiving problem solving communication training low on cooperation, but no differences were noted between the other two groups; and (2) the SFT program had more participation from fathers. According to Barkley, Guevremont, Anastopoulos, and Fletcher (1992), low cooperation levels within the PSCT group may be a function of the program's high demands for acquiring and practicing new skills, for homework assignments, and for teen participation rather than of low motivation from this group. Also, attributions and negative beliefs about adolescent compliance actually worsened in mothers receiving problem solving communication training. Barkley, Guevremont, Anastopoulos, and Fletcher (1992) suggest that focusing on family conflicts worsened attributions. It is also possible that these negative attitudes, which are directly targeted in treatment, become more obvious to parents and simply require more time to resolve. Further research would be helpful to clarify these possibilities.

Although there is reason to be optimistic about treatment effects for some families, the overall outcome data are rather discouraging. The number of families considered "clinically recovered" was still low, with only 5–20% showing change and only 5–30% showing improvements in the number of conflicts and frequency and intensity of the anger during conflicts after family therapy. Barkley, Guevremont, Anastopoulos, and Fletcher (1992) note that these findings are similar to other studies addressing short-term, single modality treatments for adolescents with hyperactivity and aggression. The data are also consistent with longitudinal studies showing the number of adolescents who continue to demonstrate problems after treatment (Barkley, Fischer, et al., 1990). Furthermore, the authors called for "multimodal, long-term, joint pharmacological–psychological interventions," particularly for adolescents with ADHD plus oppositional defiant disorders (Barkley, Guevremont, Anastopoulos, & Fletcher 1992, p. 460).

Psychopharmacotherapy

Efficacy research with adolescents is sparse compared to research with preadolescent populations and is difficult to conduct due to a lack of cooperation from older children (Klein, 1993). In fact, in the not-too-distant past "the clinical wisdom regarding the use of stimulants with ADHD adolescents has been variable. For a long time it was thought that stimulant medication should not be used for adolescents" (Evans & Pelham, 1991, p. 538). This practice was influenced by the belief that stimulants had a paradoxical effect on children that was no longer effective in adolescents. These earlier conceptions of stimulant action have not been empirically proven, and research suggests that medication can be an effective component for treating adolescents with ADHD.

Medication Research

Initial research with teens shows that stimulant medications reduce scores on parent and teacher rating scales (Varley, 1983; Klorman, Brumaghim, Fitzpatrick, & Borgstedt, 1990) and increase social behavior, on-task behaviors, and academic performance in a highly structured educational setting in a summer clinic monitored with a response cost management system (Pelham & Hoza, 1987). Social behaviors improved in both recreational and academic settings. The clinic classroom did not represent the average high school classroom that most teens encounter, in which independent work is at a high premium; so generalization to school-based classrooms cannot be made.

In a double-blind, placebo-controlled study, Evans and Pelham (1991) found that stimulants had a significant effect on nine junior high school students with ADHD. In this study, an "ecologically valid" set of measures was employed in a real-life, natural classroom setting (e.g., performance on quizzes and tests; behaviors during lectures and study hall). Improvement was noted on the following measures: scores on quizzes and tests; observations of student attention and behavioral control during lectures; teacher rating scales; and accuracy on assignments during study hall.

The majority (66%) of the adolescents showed a positive response rate to medication, with some individual variations in effect size (Evans & Pelham, 1991). Data for six of the adolescents showed large effect size and uniform improvements on classroom measures. One participant showed an adverse effect outside the classroom, and three displayed minimal to adverse effects in the classroom. In one case, a teenager who did not show positive changes in the classroom did evidence significant improvements on peer and adult ratings of negative social behaviors in nonacademic settings, so medication was considered a viable intervention. Lower dosages of medication (mean dose 9.75 mg) were recommended for all teens who had been on medication prior to the summer program, suggesting the additive effects of other psychosocial and behavioral interventions in conjunction with medication. The range of effective doses was also highly individual (from 0.15 mg/kg to 0.3 mg/kg). In another case, a participant previously on a high dose was taken off medication because of adverse rebound effects in the evening (e.g., aversive and confrontational parent–teen interactions at home), in spite of a positive daytime response.

The Evans and Pelham (1991) study is important for a number of reasons. First, positive medication effects were shown in a classroom designed to replicate a more naturalistic setting typical of junior high school, with minimal behavior management and teacher-imposed structure. Adolescents were able to perform better on medication in more independent academic settings (e.g., study hall) and in recreational periods. Second, although medication effects were shown for the majority of teens, responsivity was highly variable. A decision on whether to medicate must consider the social as well as the academic benefits and should be made only after systematic monitoring of medication effects in naturalistic environments. In some cases, the social benefits may outweigh the academic benefits, and in others, the opposite may be the case. Data should be gathered to determine the positive and negative impact of medication for each individual.

In a review of effects of medication on ADHD children, Swanson, Cantwell, Lerner, McBurnett, and Hanna (1993) suggest that the decision to medicate should be based on unfavorable response patterns rather than on favorable effects. Adverse effects may overshadow the positive outcomes and should be heavily weighed when deciding to medicate. More research with larger sample sizes is needed to further expand our knowledge of medication effects and cautions for adolescents with ADHD.

Nonstimulant Medication Options

Psychostimulants are the "first line" medications for treating ADHD; however, in a small number of cases these have not proven effective (Wilens, Biederman, Geist, Steingard, & Spencer, 1993). As such, tricyclic antidepressants have been used as an alternative treatment or "second-choice" category for individuals who do not respond positively to stimulants (Biederman et al., 1989). In a retrospective analysis of medical charts, Wilens et al. (1993) determined the effects of nortriptyline in a group of children ($N = 37$) and adolescents ($N = 21$), the majority of whom (97%) had been previously found to be nonresponders to stimulants. Results showed that a large percentage (76%) of the group showed moderate to marked improvement and that almost half (48%) of the nortriptyline responders demonstrated a marked improvement. A slight but not significant increased effect was found for adolescents (90%) compared to the younger group (68%).

The participant pool in this study did have high rates of comorbid disorders (49%), including mood disorders (34%), oppositional defiant (18%) and conduct disorders (5%), anxiety disorder (5%), developmental learning disorder (5%), and pervasive developmental disorder (4%). Nortriptyline was effective within a 2- to 4-week period and showed sustained effectiveness (mean of 15 months). The authors suggest that nortriptyline may be a viable option for individuals who are treatment-resistant, particularly those resistant to stimulants. Although caution is warranted due to the shortcomings of using extant data gathered from medical files, the findings are promising, particularly for adolescents who have not improved on stimulants. The study does not address the question of whether nortriptyline is more effective than stimulants for all individuals with ADHD, but it does give evidence that other medications may be effective when stimulants are not. Another factor that must be considered is that 50% of the participants were also treated with other medications. When participants receiving other medications were compared to those with nortriptyline alone, there were no significant differences on ADHD symptoms. In the future, research into single and multidrug combinations may be helpful for adolescents with significant problems who are nonresponders to stimulant medications.

In another study, Steingard, Biederman, Spencer, Wilens, and Gonzalez (1993) investigated the use of clonidine in children and adolescents (3–18 years) with ADHD or ADHD with comorbid tic disorders. Results indicated that 72% of the ADHD group showed moderate behavioral improvement, whereas 96% of the group having ADHD with tic disorders responded more favorably. These results are consistent with studies of younger children that have also shown the efficacy of clonidine for ADHD and tics (Hunt, Minderaa, & Cohen, 1985), and they further suggest that clonidine may be an even more viable option when ADHD and tic disorders coincide.

Finally, Spencer, Biederman, Kerman, Steingard, and Wilens (1993) determined the effects of desipramine on a group of children and adolescents with ADHD and comorbid chronic tic disorders or Tourette's disorder. In a 16-month follow-up, desipramine was found to substantially improve symptoms of both disorders. Desipramine may be a viable alternative to stimulants when tics are present, particularly when ADHD coexists with chronic tic disorders, because neuroleptics do not decrease ADHD symptoms. Furthermore, stimulants have not proven helpful because even though they do decrease ADHD symptoms, they increase tics. Spencer et al. (1993) suggest that these effects may also occur when using bupropion, which is a stimulant-like antidepressant. Although these findings are promising, caution is warranted, and further research is still necessary due to the cardiotoxic risks of desipramine and other tricyclic antidepressants in young children.

Medication Compliance

Compliance with medication interventions can be a serious problem because adolescents often discontinue medication, particularly when they "do not perceive it to be helpful" (Copeland & Copps, 1995, p. 150). Taylor (1994) suggests that adolescents stop taking medication for the following reasons: (1) a belief that medication no longer produces positive results; (2) unwanted and unpleasant side effects (e.g., stomachaches, appetite loss, etc.); (3) perceived change in self when medicated (e.g., feeling strange, different from peers, etc.); and (4) improper dosages (e.g., overdosage, leading to numb or lethargic feelings). These issues need to be addressed by the prescribing physician.

Compliance can be increased through interventions. Careful monitoring and fine-tuning of dosage levels may alleviate the problems
associated with a lack of medication efficacy and undue side effects from
overmedication (Taylor, 1994). Systematic monitoring helps verify medication effects on academic, social, and behavioral functioning and thus
provides more reliable information than relying on the adolescent's
perceptions as the sole source of information for determining dosage
changes. Such data provide a good starting point from which the
physician and the teen can discuss and explore other concerns and
impressions.

Educating both the parent and the adolescent on medication effects,
side effects, and benefits has proven beneficial in increasing medication
compliance (Copeland & Copps, 1995). Adolescents need to understand
why they are on medication and that taking medication is not a sign of
being dumb, bad, or stupid. They must learn to make realistic attributions about medication (e.g., that it helps them control themselves but
is not responsible for their good behavior). They must also understand
that ADHD is not an excuse for unacceptable behavior, that it is a
manageable problem that can be controlled, and that ADHD has many
advantages and that individuals with ADHD have many positive traits
(Copeland & Copps, 1995).

Forgetfulness and disorganization may also be an issue interfering
with compliance. When these problems are present, other techniques
may prove helpful. Copeland and Copps (1995) suggest that watch
alarms are helpful reminders, particularly when medication schedules are
variable. Parents should monitor medication compliance and should
work with their physician and psychologist when noncompliance is a
problem.

Increased Risk for Drug and Alcohol Abuse

Some parents fear that a decision to medicate will make their teenage
child more susceptible to increased risk of drug and/or alcohol abuse.
Copeland and Copps (1995) suggest that these are legitimate concerns
but that in making the decision, parents should weigh the potential risks
and benefits of medication against those of leaving the problem untreated. "The risk of not treating ADHD and ADD are, in my opinion,
often greater than the risks of the medicines used to treat them"
(Copeland & Copps, 1995, p. 187). It is important to note that teens
receiving medication for ADHD do not feel euphoric and that the
medication does not produce withdrawal symptoms.

Research investigating drug and alcohol abuse in teens with ADHD
is somewhat equivocal; however, in studies that show higher substance

abuse in teens with ADHD than in controls, comorbid conduct disorders (ADHD plus conduct disorder) have also been present (Barkley, Fischer, et al., 1990; Gittelman, Mannuzza, Shenker, & Bonagura, 1985). When Barkley, Fischer, et al. (1990) controlled for conduct disorders, substance abuse was not significantly higher in teenagers with ADHD than in controls.

Furthermore, Copeland and Copps (1995) suggest that substance abuse may be higher in untreated adolescents with ADHD and adults because of the many unresolved problems they experience (e.g., anger, poor self-esteem due to chronic failure, low frustration tolerance). These unresolved problems place teens with ADHD at risk for substance abuse. It has been shown that teens referred to clinics for substance abuse problems do have high rates of ADHD, impulsivity, and hyperactivity (21%); however, this population also had an even greater incidence of conduct disorders (42%; DeMilio, 1989). Again we see the overlap of substance abuse problems with conduct disorders, although we should not ignore the rates of substance abuse found in adolescents in general, with or without ADHD. Many clinicians believe that these figures are unacceptably high and that the problem requires more aggressive treatment than is presently available.

Copeland and Copps (1995) caution that drug or alcohol experimentation may bring some relief of symptoms for adolescents and adults with ADHD and that individuals may continue to "self-medicate." Another dangerous cycle can ensue in which tranquilizers and sleeping pills are used. It is these "downers," not the stimulants, that may then become addictive. So care should be taken when deciding whether to use stimulant medication for teens, especially in view of the fact that failing to medicate can have serious consequences: ADHD symptoms left unchecked can create problems of their own.

Medication Abuse

Early studies investigating stimulant effects on treated adolescents have found that medicated teens do not show signs of drug addiction or abuse (Safer & Allen, 1976; Varley, 1983; Weiss & Hechtman, 1993). Unfortunately, research findings do not always counterbalance the histrionic media coverage that sometimes occurs in the rare cases in which abuse is reported. Furthermore, the number of teens who do abuse medication is overgeneralized and overestimated. Stories of stimulant abuse that do appear in local and national newspapers, magazines, nightly TV news and other talk shows, or "news-oriented" TV programs often imply that taking stimulant medications is the first step to serious drug abuse in adolescents. These scare tactics can be quite harmful when the media neglect to also report on scientific research, especially if parents refuse to consider medication because their fears about drug abuse are piqued by sensational, biased media coverage.

There are little if any data to suggest that teens treated with stimulants abuse medications, and in cases in which this does occur, there appear to be other contributing problems (e.g., alcohol/drug abuse problems with significant academic difficulties). In one case in which abuse was reported, Jaffe (1991) found that an adolescent with ADHD who had coexisting alcohol/substance abuse problems was also misusing methylphenidate. The teen developed intranasal abuse of Ritalin while he was being monitored for other drug usage. The author cautions that although this is a rare case, professionals should be alert to the possibility of abuse of Ritalin in adolescents who are in settings where high numbers of teens are treated with the medication (e.g., private schools for troubled youth). This case suggests the need for special schools to be especially vigilant when monitoring medication.

Although Ritalin is considered a relatively safe medication, it is a controlled substance and needs to be carefully monitored by responsible adults. Careful monitoring by parents, school personnel, and physicians is important. In closing, Copeland and Copps (1995) remark:

> In assessing the risk, it is also important to remember that ADHD and ADD are physiological problems and not behavioral or learning problems. The attentional centers are not being stimulated properly and, thus, are not organizing and integrating information efficiently. Medication alerts the attention system so that it functions effectively. If medication is taken by a child, adolescent or adult without ADHD/ADD, it will overstimulate the attentional system and produce tension and overfocused behavior, not pleasure and euphoria. To achieve pleasant effects one must use the drugs I.V. or escalate the dosage sometimes a hundred times as much as a normal dose to receive the "drug" effect. (p. 188)

To date, research does not show this to be a problem for the majority of teens taking stimulants for ADHD.

Long-Term Effects of Psychopharmacotherapy

Despite positive short-term effects, stimulant treatment has not shown long-term improvements on behavioral, academic, and psychosocial functioning (Jacobvitz et al., 1990; Weiss & Hechtman, 1993), even when symptom levels are controlled (Weiss, Kruger, & Danielson, 1975). Fischer et al. (1993) also found that duration of stimulant therapy was not a factor predictive of adolescent outcome. The reasons for these findings are not well known at this point, but they may be related to the finding that parents often fail to renew prescriptions for medication after 1 month (Sherman & Hertzig, 1991).

There may also be a number of problems that have not been adequately addressed in the studies that have been conducted, such as: flawed study designs, including nonrandom assignment of participants, the criteria used to judge clinical improvement; dose-response variations that depend on the domain of functioning under study (e.g., learning versus behavioral); the presence of state-dependent learning, particularly in high-dosage studies; an interaction of stimulant benefits with mental age or IQ; high rates of comorbidity across ADHD samples; differences in dextroamphetamines and methylphenidate; maladaptive cognitive styles of medicated children; medication response that covaries with other biological, neuropsychological, or nutritional factors; and a history of prior medication use (see Richters et al., 1995, for a review). In short, long-term medication effects have not been adequately studied (Swanson, McBurnett, et al., 1993).

The lack of evidence for long-term medication efficacy has prompted researchers to investigate combined therapies for individuals with ADHD. Although psychopharmacology studies investigating short-term effects frequently show that the primary characteristics of ADHD improve (e.g., hyperactivity, impulsivity), other secondary characteristics (e.g., academic and social) may be unaffected. Thus combined treatment approaches have been of interest to researchers and clinicians.

Medication with Other Interventions

In a study investigating the effects of medication alone compared to medication with psychological and educational interventions, Swanson (1988) reported that a majority of adolescents treated with a combination of interventions are better off than those treated with medication alone. Adolescents in the medication-only group were essentially indistinguishable from a group who received no treatment at all. This finding is particularly important given the complexities of treating adolescents with ADHD. Medication compliance is a problem, but apparently it may be worth the effort to get adolescents to cooperate in their treatment programs.

At present, there are six research projects funded by the National Institute of Mental Health. These projects are investigating the relative contributions of medication, medication with psychosocial interventions, and psychosocial interventions alone in an attempt to more thoroughly answer the question of which interventions are most effective in the treatment of ADHD (Richters et al., 1995).

PROMISING INTERVENTION TECHNIQUES

Other efficacy research has been done on problem-solving communication training (PSCT) with families. Although this training has proven effective in families with troubled adolescents, these techniques are considered promising because they have not been sufficiently evaluated for families who have adolescents with ADHD. Initial research (see Barkley, Guevremont, et al., 1992) shows that problem-solving communication training is effective for reducing anger frequency and intensity in parent–adolescent interactions, and about one-fourth of families do improve following treatment. The following sections describe some strategies for dealing with dysfunctional communication using behavioral family systems techniques.

Robin and Foster: Problem-Solving Communication for Families and Teens

Robin and Foster (1989) developed an extensive intervention program for families with parent–adolescent conflicts. The program provides activities to increase family engagement, address medication issues, restore parental control, improve school performance, teach problem solving and communication, and restructure unrealistic or faulty beliefs. This program also provides individual therapy sessions for teens who are experiencing anger, depression, or self-esteem problems.

Behavioral, problem-solving, and communication techniques are the foundation of this family therapy. The primary goals are to improve parent–adolescent communications and to teach conflict resolution.

Components of Behavioral Family Systems Therapy

PSCT incorporates a number of interrelated techniques, including training in problem-solving and communication skills. Cognitive restructuring to help parents think differently about their child's problems is also provided to some families, depending on whether their beliefs and attitudes are interfering with healthy communication patterns. In severely distressed families, techniques are employed to address dysfunctional systems. PSCT utilizes assessment, problem-solving training, communication training, and cognitive restructuring along with functional structural changes to improve family interactions and problem-solving patterns.

Assessment and Analysis of Family Conflicts. The comprehensive family training program begins with an in-depth assessment and analysis of the presenting, as well as underlying, problems that the family is struggling with. Robin and Foster (1989) provide a detailed description of how to conduct a behavioral interview, how to set the stage for the therapeutic process, how to handle challenging problems that arise in the interview, and how to ask questions that elicit potentially sensitive but clinically rich information about family conflicts, communication style, problem-solving habits, and coalition patterns.

Interviews must be comprehensive, and it is advised that two sessions be used to gather all pertinent information before planning family therapy sessions. Rather than conducting an initial family interview, the clinician may want to interview the parents and adolescent separately. This allows everyone the opportunity to discuss issues and problems that might be stifled in a larger family discussion. Teens may be more willing to talk under these circumstances, and parents may feel more open to discuss marital stress or strain that might also be a factor. A decision to proceed with individual interviews has its drawbacks. It may set a secretive or separate alliance dynamic between the parents and the adolescent that ultimately undermines therapy goals. Issues of confidentiality become paramount in these situations, and the therapist needs to communicate the parameters of confidentiality in the first interview.

Robin and Foster (1989) provide some options for handling confidentiality. One option is to leave disclosure of information from individual sessions up to the therapist, who must first obtain written or oral consent. Another option, one the authors seem to prefer, is to tell family members that information will be shared with other family members at the discretion of the therapist. Secrecy will be honored unless it is interfering with the therapeutic process. The individual's wishes will be considered when making this determination and advanced discussions of disclosure will be done beforehand. Another option is to have the individual tell the therapist what information he/she would like to have kept confidential. These wishes will be honored unless there are disclosure exclusions (e.g., suspected abuse), in which case state laws and professional practice guidelines must be followed.

During the interview, content-focused questions are employed, such as "What do you like [dislike] about your family [mother, father, son, daughter]?" (Robin & Foster, 1989, p. 50). Process-focused questions are used to elicit information about how the family functions. These may include such questions as, "I'd like to get a general picture of what your family life is like. Could you describe a typical day? Start from the time you get up, and tell me about when you see each other, the kinds of things you do, and so forth" (Robin & Foster, 1989, p. 50). The authors provide helpful guidelines for what to look for during the family interview (e.g., Who listens? When do interruptions occur? What happens? Who intervenes when conflicts arise? Does the teen interfere with the parent–parent or the therapist–parent discussions?).

After the family treatment strategies are outlined, a therapy contract is signed. The contract includes goals of the treatment plan, specifics about family (attendance; fees; compliance on homework; providing assessment information) and therapist responsibilities (who will provide treatment; confidentiality), and other important details about the treatment plan (e.g., length and location of sessions, length of therapy, etc.). Robin and Foster (1989) provide excellent methods for keeping the conversation on track, getting everyone talking, building rapport, and remaining neutral.

Families should be screened before therapy begins. The PSCT approach would not be appropriate for families in which: (1) the parent–child relationship is good, but the adolescent is experiencing more problems outside the family (in school or with peer groups)—these can be addressed in individual designed sessions; (2) conflicts are primarily a result of marital problems or parental psychopathology—these problems should be addressed in individual sessions or combined with family work; (3) older adolescents are resisting leaving home, and conflicts arise from the approaching departure (e.g., over living independently, taking drugs, etc.)—these issues can be treated with a strategic–structural approach in which parents are reestablished as the disciplinarians, who then work to get the teen to comply; (4) the adolescent refuses to cooperate or participate and actively sabotages sessions—individual work with the parents or family therapy specifically designed to deal with disruptions may be helpful here (Robin & Foster, 1989). It is also important to determine whether individual or marital therapy is advised prior to embarking on problem-solving communication therapy.

Other observational techniques and questionnaires are utilized to gather information about the problems of individual family members and in the family system. Questionnaires that measure family satisfaction, beliefs, conflict resolution skills, adaptability and cohesiveness, marital satisfaction/stress, structural interactions, and communication patterns are described by Robin and Foster (1989). The Child Behavior Checklist serves as a valuable tool for assessing the extent and nature of the teen's problems. Interview, observational, and rating scale data are integrated to develop a comprehensive picture of the family, including both strengths and areas of conflict or weakness. Themes and interlocking patterns of interactions are noted. This functional analysis serves as a guide for understanding the problems and for structuring therapy sessions.

Problem-Solving Training. The problem-solving model employs four basic steps that follow a framework developed by D'Zurilla and Goldfried (cited in Robin & Foster, 1989): (1) defining the problem; (2) generating alternative solutions; (3) decision making, and (4) planning and implementing the solution. Negotiation skills may also be taught. Family members are taught how to use problem-solving communication to solve pressing conflicts and problems. Opportunities to practice are provided in the therapy sessions, and homework assignments are given. Family members learn how to identify the basic problems, to generate reasonable alternatives that will solve the conflicts, to make decisions that include negotiation and compromise, and to develop and implement plans for solving conflicts.

Communication Training. Communication training is another major focus of Robin and Foster's (1989) behavioral family systems therapy. Families are taught to identify problematic communication behaviors (e.g., accusing, blaming, being defensive, overgeneralizing, lecturing, preaching) and are taught alternative strategies (e.g., accepting responsibility, making "I" statements, making tentative statements). The therapist points out problematic communication patterns in sessions and models statements that are more functional (e.g., descriptive vs. accusatory, direct vs. rambling). Other strategies and techniques are used that teach family members to communicate with each other rather than through a "third party." For example, parents are asked to speak directly to their son or laugher rather than to the therapist when discussing their concerns. So when the father identifies a problem behavior and says to the therapist, "The problem is that Chris shows no respect for curfew rules," the therapist asks the father, "Please tell Chris the problem, and I'll listen." The goal here is to define the problem for Chris and to begin a parent–teen dialogue to which the therapist can listen and provide feedback in sessions.

Parents are also taught to avoid using accusatory remarks, and teenagers are taught how to assume responsibility for their behaviors. Interrupting and talking over each other is discouraged. Parents and teens are shown how to analyze and modify nonverbal communication behaviors (e.g., avoiding eye contact, shrugging shoulders, turning eyes toward the ceiling, etc.) that impede good communication.

Cognitive Restructuring. Perceptions, attitudes, beliefs, and attributions may contribute to poor communication habits in families and thus are the target of intervention in this phase of therapy. Overgeneralization, rigid negative beliefs, inaccurate inferences, and other misattributions are approached using Ellis's rational–emotive techniques. Techniques are employed for helping family members to reframe situations and to correct misattributions by getting verification from others.

Robin and Foster (1989) give numerous examples of how to use cognitive restructuring, and they provide rich dialogue demonstrating positive therapy practice. Homework assignments are utilized in the process, and parents and teens are taught to analyze unreasonable thoughts, to identify rational reevaluations, and to develop action plans. Rehearsal and use of "pretend interactions" are all part of the techniques used in this phase.

Functional and Structural Techniques. This portion of therapy focuses on dysfunctional family systems that create and sustain problems in the family. Five major problems are addressed: "(1) weak parental coalitions, (2) cross-generational coalitions, (3) triangulations, (4) adolescent misbehavior preventing parental conflict, and (5) the overprotective–rebellion escalator" (Robin & Foster, 1989, p. 174). Weak parental coalitions can be seen in families in which a "spoiled, omnipotent adolescent manipulates two parents who can't reach an agreement with the other about discipline, and achieves his/her way or escapes discipline with regularity" (Robin & Foster, 1989, p. 174). The goal in this situation is to break the coercive cycle in which teen misbehavior is negatively reinforced. One parent's attempt to reduce this aversive interaction with a disciplinary action leads to another aversive interchange between parents who disagree on a course of action. The teen takes advantage of this interaction, continues to misbehave, and thereby forces parents to continue using ineffective discipline. Parents give up trying, the teen does what he/she wants, and parents are no longer in control. Giving up allows parents an escape from conflictual and frustrating interchanges with their child and with each other—hence the term "weak parental coalition." In this situation, parents are unable to take an agreed upon and effective course of action to handle an out-of-control adolescent. A similar cycle was described in earlier discussions about aggressive children.

This cycle is a particularly common pattern in households with out-of-control adolescents. The dynamic creates a lot of hostility, leading to physical or verbal fighting, and weakens positive bonds among all members. Because of the negative consequences, this pattern is an important one to modify, although a difficult one to change. The therapist helps parents to become aware of this cycle, to talk through their differences of opinion, to agree upon a solution they both can accept, to practice giving support, to follow through in therapy, and to try the techniques at home.

Cross-generational coalitions refer to situations in which one parent sides with the adolescent against the other parent. Manipulation of this sort is not uncommon in healthy families (e.g., the child approaches each parent independently, then complies with the more lenient parent) and is considered problematic only if it divides the parents and creates a breakdown in effective parental disciplinary actions (Robin & Foster, 1989). Techniques to strength the mother–father coalition are practiced in sessions, using problem-solving and communication strategies.

Triangulation refers to situations where two family members disagree and lobby a third party for support. The third party is inconsistent in giving support and may switch from one family member to another. This pattern may be common in blended families, in which the natural parent is caught between the adolescent and his/her stepparent or other natural parent. By explaining this pattern and correcting it using problem-solving strategies, the therapist helps families overcome these interchanges.

Another problem Robin and Foster (1989) tackle in their therapy approach is the situation on which the adolescent is misbehaving to take the focus off a troubled marriage. Teens may rebel so that parents will join together to discipline or to help their child rather than argue, separate, or divorce. In essence, the teen attempts to shift the focus to his/her own problems and may even escalate misbehavior (e.g., drugs or alcohol) to keep the family together. These are difficult conflicts to handle in therapy and often require indirect measures to avoid resistance from parents. Functional family systems techniques have been found useful, in which the teen's behaviors are analyzed in terms of the functional payoff; that is, considering what the misbehavior achieves. Although therapists do not try to change these functions, they do attempt to teach less aversive mechanisms and behaviors to achieve the relationship outcomes that are desired (Robin & Foster, 1989). Cognitive restructuring and problem-solving strategies can be helpful in this process.

The overprotective–rebellion cycle is the last functional/structural problem that may be addressed in therapy. In this instance, parents in supportive relationships may overreact to initial signs of teen rebellion by becoming authoritarian; the misbehaviors then escalate, leading to further parental restrictions and even more teen rebellion. Again, an aversive reciprocal interaction ensues in these situations whereby increased parental punishment creates more coercive and higher risk misbehaviors on the part of the adolescent. This cycle is often played out in high-stakes behaviors such as teenage alcohol and drug use, sexual experimentation, or illegal activity or in deviant friendship alliances and neglect of curfews.

Cognitive restructuring techniques are used to help parents confront distorted beliefs. Such distortions often suggest that giving freedom will inevitably lead to disastrous consequences. Unrealistic fears about negative consequences are also addressed in therapy. One of two courses of action might be taken. Parents agree to use less restrictive controls if the teen agrees to be responsible (e.g., "We'll let you go to the concert if you promise you won't drink"). The teen must also comply with parental requests made with the promise that the parents will be less restrictive ("If I promise not to drink, then you will let me go to the football game with my friends"). Robin and Foster (1989) suggest starting out with small steps first, a "try it for a week" experiment.

Research Findings

Robin (1975) compared 22 families that underwent problem-solving training with 22 mother–adolescent dyads that received no treatment. The study showed that the problem-solving techniques were learned; however, participants did not report changes in disputes or communication patterns in the home. Although the findings were not positive, some questions were raised about the instruments that were used to measure efficacy.

Using more psychometrically sound measures, Foster (1978) investigated the effectiveness of problem-solving training. In this study, fathers were included in the training, and real conflict areas were the target of intervention. A group receiving problem solving communication training and a group receiving problem solving with generalization training were compared to a control group of people on a waiting list for therapy. Results of the study showed the following: (1) maternal negative feelings improved in the generalization group versus the control group; (2) maternal anger levels also improved for both the problem-solving communication training and the problem-solving communication training with generalization training groups on a measure of conflict intensity; (3) fathers showed lower intensity scores only for the problem-solving communication training with generalization training; (4) adolescents in the problem-solving communication training had better relationships with their mothers than those in the other two groups; and (5) participants in both therapy groups obtained higher goal-attainment scores than the control group.

The Foster (1978) study showed that the problem-solving communication approach to therapy was effective. However, gains were also reported for the no-treatment group, a result which has also been found in other therapy studies. In this instance, gains were attributable to end-of-the-school-year improvements that may have reduced the number of problem areas. Another interesting finding was noteworthy at follow-up. The problem-solving communication training with generalization training group actually showed deterioration on some measures, which suggests that the generalization training was an impediment to long-term adjustment.

In a subsequent study, Robin (1981) compared a problem-solving communication training with generalization training group who received cognitive restructuring training to an alternative family therapy group (i.e., family systems, eclectic, or psychodynamic). Although anger-intensity measures improved for both therapy groups, the group with cognitive restructuring training did show higher scores on measures of problem solving and positive communication, and parents in the problem-solving communication training with generalization training group were generally more satisfied than the alternative family therapy group. Some deterioration was found on follow-up measures of anger-intensity, although parents in both groups reported that the number of problematic issues decreased.

Stern (1984) also investigated the effects of problem-solving communication on parent–teen dyads, with a problem-solving communication training only group and a problem-solving communication training group with stress control and anger management training. Positive behavioral changes in teens and reduced negativity in parents were observed in both treatment groups. The additional stress control and anger management features did not appear to add appreciably to outcome data. There were no follow-up data reported for this study.

Cautions about Using Problem-Solving Communication Training

Although there are many questions that need to be answered, problem solving communication training has demonstrated efficacy in more than one-half to two-thirds of families receiving therapy (Robin & Foster, 1989). Communication and problem-solving skills improved in discussions of real-life problems under observation, and there were fewer conflicts reported in the home. The studies reviewed were conducted with families seeking clinic services whose adolescent children had few juvenile offenses, and further study is needed to determine how useful problem-solving communication will be in families who have teens with ADHD. However, Barkley, Guevremont, et al. (1992) did assess aspects of the problem-solving communication training approach and found that it was fairly effective for parents of teens with ADHD.

Other Parenting Techniques

Other parenting techniques for dealing with difficult adolescents are described by Alexander-Roberts (1995) and Phelan (1993). Both of these approaches provide practical tips for avoiding and negotiating conflict situations between parents and teens with ADHD. Alexander-Roberts (1995) outlines a number of promising techniques for positive discipline, including ideas about how to: (1) "let-go" in small steps by increasing responsibility in the teen; (2) negotiate rules and consequences for rule breaking with several pointers on problem solving; (3) organize family meetings to discuss important issues; (4) use grounding effectively (e.g., short time periods) after rules and consequences have been established; (5) provide choices to avoid power struggles; (6) write and implement a behavioral contract with response cost and removal of privileges; (7) use logical consequences; and (8) use other effective parenting techniques (e.g., using praise without put-downs; allowing for mistakes). There are also good examples of techniques to avoid traps parents often fall into including being manipulated, being rigid (e.g., "Our way or no way"), giving unwanted advice, dwelling on past mistakes, and being pessimistic, as well as techniques for communicating nondefensively, without hostility. When using behavior management or contracting methods, reinforcers need to be carefully selected with a great deal of input from the teen. Money and other privileges (e.g., later curfew on a Friday after the football game) serve as powerful incentives for many teens.

Phelan (1993) takes a different approach but gives tips on how to avoid some cardinal sins of parenting. The tips include (1) eliminating spontaneous problem discussions as much as possible by having the parent tell the teen ahead of time that they need to discuss an issue, then setting a time for the talk; (2) reducing nagging; (3) doing away with parental lectures; and (4) never arguing. Phelan also describes ways to improve parent–teen communication by using active listening, avoiding judgmental questions, rephrasing feelings, and using checks and summarizing statements. Other ideas for improving relationships include sharing, doing fun things together and using positive reinforcers. The discussion of major and minor system infractions is instructive, as are the guidelines for deciding when to seek professional help and the practical techniques given for solving specific problems (e.g., phone privileges, household chores, curfews, church attendance, appearance/hair/jewelry/clothes, drugs/drinking, and friends/dating).

In general, Alexander-Roberts (1995) and Phelan (1993) provide useful parenting tips for improving relationships and communication patterns, avoiding problems, and solving conflicts. Techniques to help parents disengage from ineffective strategies and to consider other parenting options are often clinically insightful. Although these techniques have not been empirically tested to determine their efficacy in resolving parent–teen problems, many of these strategies have been used successfully in clinical settings.

ACADEMIC AND SCHOOL-BASED INTERVENTIONS: "PROMISING PRACTICES"

During the adolescent stage, interventions to improve academic competencies should be continued, and tutoring or remedial classes may be necessary. Despite this need, there is very little research investigating which strategies are effective for school-related problems for teens with ADHD. Thus the interventions to be discussed are considered "promising" and need further verification.

Although many behavioral problems associated with ADHD do have an impact on classroom and academic performance, including work completion and difficulties in organization, there have been few studies investigating specific interventions for adolescents. Furthermore, the majority of adolescents with ADHD are likely to receive treatment through medical and/or clinic-based mental health centers (Barkley, 1990b). Although clinic-based treatment may be useful, school-based interventions should also be considered as an adjunct (DuPaul & Stoner, 1994; Power, Atkins, Osbourne, & Blum, 1994; Shapiro, DuPaul, Bradley, & Bailey, 1996).

School-based services are particularly important given that adolescents with ADHD face numerous challenges from the increased educational demands placed on them at this stage (e.g., class changes every 45–50 minutes; multiple teachers; longer lectures requiring increased note-taking and listening and advanced organizational skills; Shapiro et al., 1996). Parents and teachers also have higher expectations for teenagers to accomplish things independently. Unfortunately, many teens with ADHD still struggle with organization and planning, and they do not function very independently or productively without a lot of assistance.

Several promising school-based programs provide guidelines for selecting academic interventions for adolescents with ADHD.

Elmbrook ADD Project: Problem-Solving Communication

In an effort to develop an ethos of educational "best practices," the Elmbrook ADD Project developed a Problem-Solving Communication

Model for teachers and other educational professionals (i.e., psychologists, social workers, and nurses), parents, and physicians. The Elmbrook ADD project was funded in 1993 by the Wisconsin Department of Public Instruction with federal funds and is part of the Wisconsin ADD Project. The Wisconsin ADD Project is a statewide consortium of six school districts. The Wisconsin ADD Project was designed to improve educational services for children and adolescents with ADHD.

The major goals of the Elmbrook ADD Problem-Solving Communication Project were as follows:

1. To educate teachers and parents about educational "best practices" for school-based interventions for ADHD children and adolescents.
2. To organize consultation teams in the schools to design and implement effective intervention strategies.
3. To develop a standardized assessment protocol for the educational diagnosis of ADHD.
4. To establish a link among mental health professionals, medical practitioners, and educational professionals to address systems-level and institutional barriers to educational best practices.
5. To provide parent support to families with children and adolescents with ADHD.
6. To build partnerships between teachers, parents, and physicians to meet the needs of children and adolescents with ADHD.

Two major efforts of the Elmbrook ADD Project, Problem-Solving Communication and Differentiated Instruction, have been utilized to improve the academic and behavioral outcome of children and adolescents with ADHD.

Elmbrook Problem-Solving Communication

A problem-solving communication model was developed for use with teachers and parents to find solutions to academic and behavioral problems encountered by children and adolescents with ADHD (Teeter & Stewart, 1996, 1997). The program incorporates basic problem-solving steps similar to those described by Robin and Foster (1989) and utilizes communication, negotiation, compromise, and monitoring techniques to improve the educational outcome of students with ADHD.

The problem-solving communication model provides a format for parents and teachers to identify major problems and concerns, identify potential solutions, build consensus (to arrive at agreed-upon solutions), negotiate and compromise when consensus is not reached, put a plan into action, and provide ongoing monitoring and modification of the plan. The problem-solving communication model has been used for case consultation, crisis intervention (e.g., disciplinary actions), individual educational plans or Section 504 plans, and/or ongoing management of problems that occur in the home or school. This model has been used to resolve tense, conflictual parent–teacher situations and to "successfully" resolve difficult expulsion and suspension hearings.

The problem-solving communication model increases home–school partnerships, attempts to alleviate conflicts between parents and teachers, and mediates conflicts when they do occur. Initial evaluations indicate that parents and teachers were "extremely satisfied" with the process and that the meetings were beneficial in facilitating problem solving; selecting appropriate accommodations or strategies; providing resource information; advocating for the student; and supporting the teacher, the parent, and the student (Teeter & Stewart, 1996). Participants endorsed descriptors of their feelings during the process, such as "included," "respected," and "reassured," and did not report feeling "intimidated," "threatened," "rushed," or "angry" during the meeting. The problem-solving communication model provides a format for problem solving with difficult issues that confront teachers and parents working with ADHD students and appears to be a positive mechanism for decision making in case conferences. Further evaluation of its efficacy is needed to determine whether the long-term outcome for students is positive, whether the process alters or changes teacher practices and whether parents and teachers observe positive changes in teens with ADHD.

Differentiated Instruction Model for Adolescents

A districtwide initiative for differentiated instruction to meet the educational needs of at-risk students has been used for students with ADHD. The school district of Elmbrook adopted differentiated instruction as one of its major goals, and schools developed a plan for implementing it in every classroom. A districtwide planning committee defined differentiated instruction as follows:

> Differentiated instruction is using multiple teaching approaches to deliver the curriculum so that students have a variety of options in the classroom for taking in information, making sense of ideas, and expressing what they learn.
>
> When differentiated instruction is occurring, all students are actively engaged in learning processes in an environment designed to increase the likelihood of their individual success in achieving high standards of performance.

> While individualized instruction for every learner is not implied by this definition, differentiated instruction for several kinds of learning styles and abilities within the classroom is the essence of the definition. (Teeter & Stewart, 1997)

In an effort to facilitate the understanding and use of differentiated instruction, the district planning committee also identified a list of teacher beliefs and behaviors that enhance (see Table 8.1) or impede (see Table 8.2) differentiated instruction, indicators that differentiated instruction is not occurring in a classroom (see Table 8.3), and signs that differentiated instruction is occurring (see Table 8.4). Specific strategies for implementing differentiated instruction in the classroom are also the focus of teacher planning and in-service training.

At present, the district is implementing and evaluating differentiated instruction practices in the high schools. A number of complimentary strategies are being used to accomplish the goal of differentiated instruc-

TABLE 8.1. Teacher Beliefs and Behaviors That Encourage and Facilitate Differentiated Instruction for High School Classrooms

- Students need to believe that school and work are relevant to them.
- Expectations must remain high.
- Differentiation is not helter-skelter but organized.
- Students should be allowed/encouraged to take risks.
- Flexibility is based within a rubric.
- Time can be used more creatively (e.g., block 2-hour periods).
- Time management can be taught.
- Periodic student conferences should be held to check on progress on projects.
- Differentiation works.
- All students can be successful and are talented in some areas.
- Multiple types of intelligence are acknowledged and are fostered.
- Students have different learning styles.
- Students, not content, should be taught.
- Classroom starts with a community.
- Quality is more important that quantity.
- Teachers are a community of learners who need ongoing teacher education.
- Learning is lifelong.
- Learning is best done through themes, connections, patterns, and so forth.
- Learning can come through (student) learning.
- Activities do not have to be text-driven.
- Meaningful experiences for learning can be provided.
- Success breeds success.
- Ideas for planning, assessing, and so forth can be solicited from students.
- A teacher's job is to help kids learn.
- Differentiation is not going to affect standardized test scores in a negative way.
- "There is time to do this"—time limits should not be discouraging.

Note. Ideas generated from districtwide efforts to improve educational strategies, Elmbrook School District. See Teeter & Stewart (1997).

TABLE 8.2. Teacher Beliefs and Behaviors that Discourage and Impede Differentiated Instruction in High School Classrooms

- Differentiated instruction will lower standards.
- Differentiated instruction takes too much time.
- Differentiated instruction is too expensive.
- Differentiated instruction requires too much planning.
- Differentiated instruction forces personal involvement with students.
- Differentiated instruction is too hard to manage.
- Differentiated instruction is a fad—this too will pass.
- Differentiated instruction focuses too much on extremes.
- Differentiated instruction raises grading and reporting questions.
- Instruction should focus on content and textbooks.
- Students are already too coddled.
- Students should be grouped on ability levels—separate classrooms for separate abilities.
- Not all students can learn or succeed.
- Students have a right to fail—life lesson all kids should have.
- Successful students in traditional system will be annoyed or threatened.
- We keep forgetting the average student.
- This is a waste of time (student's perspective).
- What's enough? How do I know when I'm done?
- This is not what college or the workplace will be like.
- It is too expensive to do staff development.
- They aren't doing this in other districts.
- Teachers don't teach (kids).
- Been there—done that—did not work the first time.
- It will reduce learning to lowest common denominator.
- Different assignments will create hostility and a sense of unfairness among students.
- Parents and public will never support this.
- Why change what's not broken?
- Where is the data to support this?
- Differentiation is unfair.

Note. Ideas generated from districtwide efforts to improve educational strategies, Elmbrook School District. See Teeter & Stewart (1997).

tion. First, teachers are receiving intensive training on various topics, including: the impact of brain-related behavior disorders in the classroom (e.g., ADHD; executive control dysfunction; disinhibition); methods and strategies for modifying curricula to meet the individual learning styles of high school students; ways to engage and motivate the disinterested adolescent; self-management and self-instructional strategies for the adolescent at-risk learner (e.g., impulse control and disorganization problems); and increasing the responsibility and success of at-risk teens. Second, teachers are provided ongoing consultation from a professional knowledgeable about ADHD and educational best practices. Third, peer coaching and collegial study groups have been established for interested faculty. Fourth, collaborative efforts within and across various departments are facilitated through teacher planning days throughout the school.

TABLE 8.3. Indicators That Little or No Differentiation Is Taking Place in High School Classrooms

- Everyone is on the same page, same textbook.
- Same instructional strategy (teaching the same) whether it works or not.
- No student engagement.
- One kind of assessment.
- High absenteeism.
- Lots of extra credit in place of choices.
- Sterile room.
- Quiet (little interaction) or out-of-control room.
- Sleeping.
- No windows.
- Angry student.
- Not personable.
- Rote homework—isolating.
- Late homework/no homework.
- Students afraid or unwilling to ask or answer questions or ask for help.
- Teacher-centered classroom—"It's my way or no way!"
- Blaming students for bad grades.
- Lack of mutual respect.
- Tardiness.
- Constant requests to leave room (go to nurse, go to bathroom).
- No concern for learning styles.
- Tests every Friday, movie every Monday.
- Heavy reliance on textbook-guided instruction, guides, and instruction.
- Teacher is center of all knowledge.
- Students cannot pass tests.
- Confusion about learning or learning objectives.
- Angry parent conferences.
- Teachers discipline through threats and put-downs.
- Little student responsibility.
- "You should already know this"—constant review.
- "No more questions."
- Saying it again *slower* and *louder.*
- Teacher does not go through test corrections.
- Little use of technology.
- Pop quizzes.
- Backlog of uncorrected work.
- Teacher angry about special learning needs of students.
- A lack of teacher-to-teacher consistency.
- Whole class discipline.
- Teachers stand and wait for silence, or not even speaking.
- No two-way communication on how to do things.
- Substitution of "buddy" for teacher because of strained student–teacher interactions.
- Sending kids to office and abdicating responsibility.
- No rewards for jobs well done.
- Discipline with detentions (threats).
- Only grades are used as evaluation.
- No humor.
- Only using tests or basing grades on tests.
- Emotionless teachers—"robotic teacher."
- Competition.

Note. Ideas generated from districtwide efforts to improve educational strategies, Elmbrook School District. See Teeter & Stewart (1997).

TABLE 8.4. Indicators of Full Differentiation in High School Classrooms

- Demonstrating what has been learned.
- Enrichment activity center/learning labs.
- Student input into learning choices.
- More reliance on outside sources.
- All kids *actively* involved.
- Use of technology without eliminating books.
- Address both learning strengths and weaknesses.
- Career and daily living relevance.
- Evidence that kids are taught about what they learn.
- Varies assignments.
- Tiered assignments.
- Compacting curriculum.
- Focus on applying knowledge and skills.
- Students choosing higher level thinking activities.
- Students' products become models for other students.
- Shared resource file in the content area.
- Pretesting to avoid "repeats."
- Flexible grouping for instructing.
- Independent study.
- Self-pacing within reason.
- Criteria for *quality* work is evident.
- Success is possible for everyone.
- Creativity to promote interest.
- More conversation and input with variety in schedule and lessons.
- Acceptance of alternative answers.
- Students know purpose of work.
- The audience for student products may be outside the classroom, other than teacher or classmates.
- Balance between cooperation and competition.
- Expectation for basic skills mastery.
- Balance between learning groups and individual work.
- Nonthreatening but productive atmosphere.

Note. Ideas generated from districtwide efforts to improve educational strategies, Elmbrook School District. See Teeter & Stewart (1997).

The Lehigh University–Consulting Center for Adolescents with Attention Deficit Disorders (LU-CCAADD)

This program was established through a grant funded by the U.S. Department of Education. The focus of the LU-CCAADD project was to provide a behavioral consultation model for students with ADHD in middle and junior high schools (Shapiro et al., 1996). The project has features similar to the Elmbrook ADD Project, with three basic levels of services: (1) in-service training for educational staff in assessment, school-based interventions, parent training, collaboration with community, and peer-relationship interventions; (2) behavioral consultation for identifying students with ADHD, designing treatment plans, communicating with physicians, and assisting in implementation of parent, social skills, self-management, and program evaluation services; and (3) advanced knowledge, dissemination, and consultation to educational staff (Shapiro et al., 1996).

Initial outcome data from the LU-CCAADD project found that teachers increased their knowledge about ADHD; were satisfied with the services provided; were still implementing the strategies developed in consultation; adapted strategies for new students who were not part of the initial consultation; and for the most part were interested in obtaining more information about ADHD (Shapiro et al., 1996). These are impressive outcomes, although the authors caution that student outcome data must be collected in order to make a more thorough evaluation of the program. There were a number of factors that appeared related to the outcome of the consultation process, including receiving administrative support, appointing a district contact person who attended consultation meetings, having motivated teacher participants, and selecting of appropriate strategies (Shapiro et al., 1996).

The Elmbrook and the LU-CCAADD projects provide guidelines for developing a school-based model that can be replicated in other regions. These programs appear to be promising practices for school-based interventions.

School-Based Strategies for Adolescents: DuPaul and Stoner Guidelines

DuPaul and Stoner (1994) provide the following strategies to address the academic skill deficits, organization problems, and difficulties in self-directedness found in many adolescents with ADHD. These suggestions are:

1. Basic instruction in study and test-taking skills should be ongoing, and students should be provided with opportunities for supervised practice.
2. Homework should be organized in an assignment workbook that includes short-term and long-term projects. Teacher–parent communication, starting with daily or weekly check-in procedures (e.g., initial assignments or home–school notes), is recommended. Reinforcers are made available to the student for compliance in keeping the log and can be phased out as he/she takes on more responsibility.
3. Allow the student to tape-record lectures as a way to compensate for attentional and/or organizational difficulties. This may be a useful tool when the student is first learning to take notes, and it remains under the supervision of the teacher. Another set of

books should be made available to keep at home to avoid the problem of "forgetting."

4. Continued use of self-instruction and self-monitoring techniques for assignments, note-taking, and organizational skills is recommended.

Although these techniques have not been systematically evaluated with adolescents with ADHD, similar strategies have been proven effective with younger children.

Self-Management Techniques

In a case study design, Shapiro, DuPaul, and Bradley (in press) found that a self-management program was helpful for two 12-year-old boys in sixth grade. The children had problems getting organized, completing homework, and working independently. A five-phase program was implemented using procedures described by Rhode, Morgan, and Young (1983). Phase 1 involved gathering baseline data to determine the nature of the behavioral problems, the frequency and conditions of the problems, and the overall quality of the student's performance. In Phase 2, the student was made aware of the teacher ratings gathered in phase 1, and a management system was utilized. During Phase 3, the student was asked to rate his/her own behavior; these self-ratings were compared to teacher ratings for the same time period. If there was a student–teacher match, the student was reinforced. In Phase 4, teacher ratings were gradually reduced while student management was increased. In Phase 5, independent self-management was completed.

One student showed steady improvement across the teacher-management and matching phases of the treatment (i.e., 75% to 100% on task behavior and improved ratings on impulsivity and inattention). The other subject also showed improvements from baseline for on-task behaviors, attention to task, and improved academic performance. Some cautionary notes are appropriate, as Shapiro et al. (in press) suggest that teachers first need to understand why the procedure is being implemented because they may question the usefulness and practicality of the technique. Second, teacher management techniques should be discussed ahead of time to help the teacher ward off arguments with students if disagreements occur during the matching phase. Third, the techniques should not be implemented without using other strategies. Fourth, other controlled studies are needed given the inconsistent findings for self-control techniques reported by Abikoff (1985, 1991). However, initial clinical case studies offer some reason to be optimistic about self-management and its usefulness for some target behaviors (Shapiro et al., in press).

Techniques for Increasing Academic Outcomes

Techniques that teach study and organizational skills and time management may prove to be effective for increasing the overall academic performance of adolescents with ADHD. Teaching methods that use direct step-by-step procedures with concrete examples and activities and provide an opportunity to practice under supervision may prove most effective. Behavioral and home–school contracts might help reinforce these skills (Pfiffner & Barkley, 1990). Many of the same academic accommodations described for the middle childhood stage may also be required for the adolescent. Accommodations such as reduced homework or in-class assignments (e.g., assigning fewer problems), tutoring, providing access to computers with printers, and daily home–school notes may be implemented to assist in work completion.

Even though computer-assisted instruction (CAI) has not been studied for adolescents with ADHD, there is evidence that it increases achievement in students from elementary school through college (Khalli & Shashaani, 1994). There are several advantages to using CAI with academically at-risk students, including self-paced learning, opportunities for immediate feedback, simulation activities, and increased novelty. There are a number of systems available: (1) speech recognition for oral-language input that can be combined with written output; (2) speech synthesis that reads text aloud; (3) hypermedia, hypertext, and responsive systems for interactive, self-directed lessons; and (4) optimal character recognition, with which text can be scanned and combined with speech synthesis for read-aloud text (McCullough, 1995). Programs for word processing, reading recognition and comprehension, and spelling and vocabulary development can be combined with classroom instruction to increase academic skills in difficult-to-teach students.

In one study, Warren and Rosebery (1988) created a computer game, RACER, to increase accuracy and speed of decoding skills. Low achieving high school students showed improvement in reading speed, automatic phonological decoding, and decoding accuracy after 24 sessions using the RACER program. DuPaul and Stoner (1994) suggest that CAI can be successfully incorporated into an intervention plan for students with ADHD with the following provisions: give the student a keyboard to increase sustained attention and motivation for the task; select educational programs that are stimulating and interesting and that provide frequent, immediate student feedback; use CAI to increase math and language skills and to plan for generalization of skills in authentic settings; integrate CAI into classroom instruction and provide teacher supervision and feedback; and define educational outcomes before implementing CAI, and document the outcome of instruction.

CAREER PLANNING

Parents of adolescents with ADHD have reason to be concerned about their teenager's future success and adjustment in college and his or her ultimate career attainment. It is important for the clinician to deal with these fears and to engage in realistic and strategic planning. These concerns can be addressed in family sessions, although individual sessions with the parent and with the teen may also be needed.

Setting realistic goals for academic success should begin early in high school, so that the student can be sure to take the right courses and credits to get into college. It is necessary to work in collaboration with the school for the best results. School counselors and high school teachers may need to be apprised of the adolescent's cognitive and academic abilities, as well as his/her ADHD. The talents of teens with ADHD are often overshadowed by their difficulties getting assignments done, and their intellectual abilities may be underestimated because they appear scattered and unfocused. Bright students with ADHD may be underchallenged and may be inadvertently counseled away from the more demanding high school curricula. This is a major loss for both the adolescent and the school. With proper accommodations and differentiated instructional techniques, teens with ADHD can successfully pursue academically rigorous college and university programs that lead to stimulating and rewarding careers.

In order to ensure that realistic academic goals are established and appropriate support is provided, developing a 504 Educational Plan may be essential. These educational plans specify academic goals and reasonable classroom accommodations (e.g., amount of classwork and homework, use of tape recorders, extra time for tests, alternative test formats, etc.) and provide details on how to monitor and measure the efficacy of the plan. In clinical work with schools, we have found that collaborative problem solving between the home and school can be extremely helpful to the overall adjustment of the high school student with ADHD (Teeter & Stewart, 1996).

Finding an appropriate college or university is an important task. For some teens with ADHD, finding a school that offers special programs for learning disabled adults may be best. In other instances, special campuses may not be necessary, because most colleges have learning centers that provide assistance for students with special needs. Access to university services usually requires a current psychological report verifying that the student has a handicapping condition, describing the nature of the problem, and providing recommendations for accommodations and interventions. Universities typically provide a variety of accommodations to students that may include note takers for lectures; access to professor's notes; extra time on examinations; and alternative methods for completing tests and assignments using computers or other technologies. Counselors and advisors often encourage the student to advocate for him- or herself and aid in the development of this important life skill.

It is important to note that parents may need therapy and support during the career-planning phase. Many parents go through a grieving process similar to the one they experienced when their child was first diagnosed with ADHD. Parents may need to alter their career expectations for their son or daughter. Parents may feel a sense of loss because their child may not get into the college of their choice or may not be able to pursue the career of their dreams. They may worry about their son's or daughter's ability to fend for him/herself in a competitive job market. These disappointments and anxieties may interfere with parent–teen relationships and may be the cause of arguments, tension, disengagement, and disapproval or enmeshment and overprotection. If this is the case, these problems need to be addressed in family therapy.

Family therapy may also facilitate the home and school planning processes. We have found that regardless of whether therapy is a part of the intervention plan or not, school professionals need to be aware of the anxiety parents feel. These worries may be expressed as anger or frustration toward the school, when in fact these are misplaced anxieties. In other instances, parents may pressure teachers to do more so their child can be successful, or they may blame the teachers for their teenager's failures. By understanding and respecting the feelings and concerns parents have about their child's success, teachers and educational professionals can avoid conflictual home–school relationships. This is a critical intervention link that can either facilitate or impede home–school collaboration and ultimately the student's academic success.

INDIVIDUAL AND GROUP PSYCHOTHERAPY

Adolescent concerns with dating, sexual behavior, and peer pressure to experiment with drugs and/or alcohol may be paramount during this stage. Poor self-esteem and peer relationship difficulties may also result in depression and withdrawal. Despite the need for therapy, there is no evidence that psychotherapy when used in isolation is an effective tool for alleviating these problems. There is some evidence that psychotherapy can be helpful for children with ADHD if it is part of a multicomponent program (Satterfield, Satterfield, & Cantwell, 1981). The extent to which these findings can be generalized to adolescents with ADHD has not been studied.

There is reason to be optimistic that, with proper dosages of medication and compliance, therapy may be helpful for adolescents. Alexander-Roberts (1995) suggests that life skills and habits may be the focus of therapy. Helping teens develop skills that may have been missed in early developmental stages may be useful (e.g., goal attainment, self-discipline, organizational, and listening skills).

When serious conduct problems are present, more intensive anger control techniques may be appropriate. See Goldstein, Harootunian, and Conoley (1994) for therapeutic strategies for conduct-related and severe aggressive disorders. Patterson (1982) also describes a family-based intervention that has proven effective for reducing aggressive, antisocial, and delinquent behaviors in children and adolescents. Patterson's work raises a serious question about whether anger, conduct disorder, and severe antisocial behaviors in children and adolescents can be controlled without a family-based therapy program.

Cognitive-Behavioral and Self-Control Techniques

The area of self-management has been of great interest to clinicians and researchers alike. Cognitive-behavioral techniques that teach teens with ADHD to manage and regulate their own behaviors seem intuitively justified. Cognitive-behavioral techniques may include modeling, role playing, response cost, social skills training, self-reinforcement matched to an external criterion, attribution retraining, and coping skills (Whalen & Henker, 1991).

After a decade or more of carefully controlled studies, either alone or in combination with other treatments, cognitive-behavioral training has not proven effective for youngsters with ADHD (Abikoff, 1991). In a comprehensive review of studies, Abikoff (1991) states:

> The belief, especially in early studies, that the development of internal-ized self-regulation skills would facilitate generalization and mainte-nance effects has not been realized. . . . Moreover, none of the studies has generated results to indicate, or even suggest, that cognitive training is a competitor to stimulants, or that it enhances their beneficial effect. (p. 208)

Abikoff (1987) found that cognitive-behavioral training does not im-prove social, attentional, or cognitive competencies.

Whalen and Henker also indicate that "At present, [cognitive-behavioral training] is neither as pervasive nor as scientifically justified as either stimulant or behavioral treatments for ADHD" (1991, p. 126). In an analysis of therapies, Whalen and Henker (1991) suggest that comparative studies, usually contrasting medication and behavioral and cognitive-behavioral approaches, are difficult to conduct because different domains are often targeted. For example, cognitive-behavioral training therapists may focus on what the child thinks and how he/she acts, which involves new learning, whereas behavioral approaches might focus on a specific targeted behavior.

In summary, research on cognitive-behavioral training approaches has shown that the time, effort, and cost that are involved are not justified. Pfiffner and Barkley (1990) suggest that cognitive-behavioral techniques may be more helpful for parents and teachers in their daily interactions with students with ADHD.

Social Skills Building

Parents are often concerned about improving social reasoning and judgment skills and about significant isolation and withdrawal and/or antisocial deficits in their adolescents. On the other hand, teens may or may not view poor social reasoning and judgment as major problems but may express feeling depressed because of a lack of friends. Goldstein and Goldstein (1990) indicate that "parents and teachers tend to focus primarily on social skills that facilitate compliance and self-control while children and adolescents are more interested in the quality of their relationships with others" (p. 332).

There are a number of structured programs available for adolescents with social skills deficits. *Skillstreaming the Adolescent: A Structured Learning Approach to Teaching Prosocial Skills* (Goldstein, Sprafkin, Gershaw, & Klein, 1980) provides 50 sessions on various prosocial skills. The program includes a detailed checklist for determining which social skills should be a focus of training. Social skills are taught using modeling, role playing, and corrective feedback during practice activities. Homework assignments, behavioral contracts, and self-reinforcement techniques are utilized outside of sessions to increase maintenance and transfer of training to natural settings.

There are helpful tips on how to handle problem behaviors that interfere with the group-format process (e.g., inattentiveness, isolation, negativism, apathy, verbal inadequacies, and lack of self-confidence). The tips cover behavioral management (e.g., use of reinforcers and shaping behaviors), instructional (e.g., correcting deficient behaviors using extinction and punishment), and relationship-based techniques (e.g., using empathic encouragement and eliciting peer support). The handbook also provides much clinically useful information (e.g., transcripts for sessions), and a videotape has been developed as well (Goldstein & McGinnis, 1988).

The *Walker Social Skills Curriculum: The ACCESS Program* (Walker, Todis, Holmes, & Horton, 1988) is also available for use with adolescents. Many of the same principles are utilized in both programs, and a number of the skills are similar. The ACCESS program uses a problem-solving focus in which students are taught to assess and amend problem behaviors. Both of the programs can be used in either a classroom or a therapy setting.

To date, research on the efficacy of social skills training with adolescents with ADHD has not been reported. Many of the shortcomings of social skill development described in Chapter 6 may also apply here. Research has not been conducted to date, so efficacy, maintenance, and generalization issues are unknown. Furthermore, there may be problems that are unique to teens with social skills and friendship problems that need to addressed.

PREDICTING AND PREVENTING PROBLEMS IN ADOLESCENTS WITH ADHD

ADHD is a disorder that can be managed but not cured. As such, clinicians are on the lookout for strategies and interventions that reduce the negative impact of disinhibition, impulsivity, and hyperactivity. When assessing which interventions to employ, factors that have found to be protective or predictive of positive outcomes are also considered.

Protective Factors

One of the important results of the longitudinal studies that have been conducted has been the identification of factors that appear to have some protective function for adolescents and that, when present, help to predict outcomes for this group. Barkley (1990b) indicates that it is a combination of factors rather than an isolated factor that appear related to positive outcomes. The clinician has no control over some of these factors, whereas others may be affected by effective interventions.

Similar to outcome data for other disorders (e.g., conduct disorders), these studies show that the socioeconomic status and stability of the family are correlated with positive outcomes, including academic achievement, educational attainment, and level of adult employment for individuals with ADHD (Barkley, 1990b). Specifically, Fischer et al. (1993) found that parental competencies (i.e., greater education in mothers and fewer antisocial problems in fathers) were more powerful predictors of parent ratings of social adjustment in adolescents than were early child characteristics or behaviors (e.g., hyperactivity, conduct disorders, and preschool adjustment). Teacher ratings of social incompetence were predicted by high rates of family instability, whereas teen ratings were predicted by the amount of the therapy the teenagers received. Also of interest was the finding that the amount of time spent in special education was predictive of increased rates of emotional problems in adolescents, based on parent, teacher, and self-report ratings (Fischer et al., 1993).

A number of other factors that were predictive of negative outcome include the presence of oppositional defiant disorders; the overlap of conduct disorder with ADHD; the presence of early aggression; high rates of defiance in early mother–child interactions; and the adolescent's cognitive–intellectual abilities (Fischer et al., 1993). Adolescent delinquency, antisocial acts, and number of arrests were related to the level of child noncompliance in early mother–child relations but not to early levels of hyperactivity in the child. Furthermore, antisocial behaviors were related to maternal mental health problems and job instability in fathers, high rates of family moves, and the educational status of the mother rather than to child characteristics (Fisher et al., 1993). In short, economic and family stability were related to poor adolescent outcome, particularly for increased antisocial and delinquent problems.

The power of family problems in predicting adolescent outcome suggests the need to consider family-based interventions in the therapy plan. Fischer et al. (1993) suggest that efforts to increase family stability, routine and structure, and personal adjustment and competencies in parents and to provide marital therapy may be helpful. Early and effective interventions to improve parent–child interactions and to reduce child aggressive and oppositional-defiance symptoms should be considered.

Impediments to Treatment Efficacy

Some of the major impediments to effective intervention for this group include the adolescent's lack of compliance when on medication, a desire not to be singled out as different, secondary emotional and self-esteem issues due to chronic school failure, and feelings of helplessness and inadequacy (Pfiffner & Barkley, 1990). These attitudes usually need to be addressed separately in order to increase cooperation and participation in therapy for adolescents with ADHD. Behavioral contracts, explicit reinforcement, and contingency management may be helpful to increase cooperation in therapy and medication management.

SUMMARY

To be most effective, intervention programs for children with ADHD must be designed to address problems specific to each developmental stage. Programs should be multidimensional in nature, addressing behavioral, academic, and psychosocial features of ADHD. Intervention must be long-term and include parent training and family systems interventions, behavioral management in the classroom, academic tutoring or special education, medication, and social skills building. The following goals and strategies may be helpful for adolescents with ADHD.

1. Improve academic performance by providing differentiated instruction that matches student learning characteristics, peer tutoring, and computer-assisted instruction by teaching study and organization skills.
2. Increase self-control and independence by teaching self-management and self-monitoring skills.
3. Decrease ADHD symptoms by using medication with other psychosocial intervention and by providing medication monitoring for compliance.
4. Increase psychosocial adjustment by providing family, individual, and/or group therapy and career planning.

9

Developmental Challenges of Adulthood: The Impact of ADHD on Normal Development and Intervention Options

*A*DHD *was once* considered a disorder of childhood that was outgrown and had little impact on adult functioning. Research has recently shown that this is far from the case and that a majority of children with ADHD continue to experience the effects of disinhibition, impulsivity, inattention, disorganization, and emotionality lability throughout their lives. This chapter reviews developmental challenges in adulthood and summarizes longitudinal research showing how ADHD affects adult adjustment. Strategies and interventions for adults with ADHD are also presented.

It is beyond the scope of this review to explore the entire adult lifespan; thus salient milestones in early and middle adulthood are discussed, including college, career, work, and intimate relationships (e.g., marriage and family). Although later adulthood presents its own unique challenges, there is virtually no research on the impact of ADHD into later phases of life.

Developmental psychologists typically identify the following milestones in adulthood: (1) cognitive–intellectual development; (2) college and/or postsecondary education; (3) career and work adjustment; and (4) intimate relationships (e.g., marriage and family).

NORMAL DEVELOPMENTAL CHALLENGES OF ADULTHOOD

Cognitive–Intellectual Development

For decades cognitive psychologists have been interested in intellectual development throughout the life span. Although several theories of cognitive development in adults have been advanced, Sternberg's (1980, 1985) triarchic theory was selected because it has potential for explaining the impact of ADHD on various aspects of adult functioning. This theory of intelligence has relevance for other developmental stages as well. Three aspects of intelligence are proposed: the componential, the experiential, and the contextual. The componential aspect of intelligence relates to the internal world of the individual; the experiential level relates to both internal and external elements; and the contextual level relates to the external world (Kolligan & Sternberg, 1987). ADHD may affect various aspects of intelligence differentially, and as such this theory may shed light on how the disorder affects intellectual functioning and adult adjustment.

According to Sternberg (1985), the first aspect of intelligence, the *componential* element, determines how efficiently an individual processes and analyzes information. The componential aspect is critical in problem solving, analysis, monitoring, and evaluating information. Componential intelligence is that measured by most standardized intelligence tests and represents critical, analytic abilities.

Kolligan and Sternberg (1987) further delineate three basic kinds of components that comprise componential intelligence: metacomponents, performance components, and knowledge-acquisition components. Metacomponents encompass higher order executive functions that involve defining the nature of tasks; selecting the lower level processes needed to accomplish tasks; selecting and combining strategies; allocating mental resources to complete tasks; and monitoring and evaluating performance. Kolligan and Sternberg (1987) hypothesize that metacomponential deficits are present in individuals with learning disabilities and are primarily manifested as "working memory" problems. An individual with metacomponential deficits might continue to use ineffective strategies or ignore relevant information that might be helpful for effective problem solving. Speed of component execution may also be impaired, resulting in cognitive sluggishness (suboptimal use of memory) or impulsivity (execution too quickly). Sternberg (1987) differentiates this aspect from Kagan's (1965) model of reflectivity–impulsivity and emphasizes an individual's ability to selectively utilize reflective or impulsive style depending on the characteristics of the task. Cognitive flexibility is thus viewed as optimal. Although deficits in metacomponents remain controversial in the field of learning disabilities, deficits in executive functions have been shown in some studies of ADHD populations (Pennington & Ozonoff, 1996).

The second aspect of intelligence, the *experiential* element, determines how individuals approach new or familiar tasks. Although the experiential element relies on automatic skills and operations (e.g., word recognition), this level of intelligence involves a comparison of new with old information and allows original configurations or insights to develop. Creativity and insight characterizes this element, which is rarely measured by traditional intelligence tests.

The experiential aspect of intelligence can be viewed on an experiential continuum, from complete novelty to automatization of information processing (Kolligan & Sternberg, 1987). Automatic processing does not require conscious direction, whereas controlled information processing is purposeful and requires a great deal of effort and attention. Learning disabled individuals have been shown to have trouble with automaticity, which may result from difficulty constructing mental representations, difficulty recoding certain information for higher order memory, an aversion to some types of mental operations (e.g., mathematics), low motivation for subject matter, or specific neuropsychological deficits (Kolligan & Sternberg, 1987). Motivation plays an important role in the process of automatization, and repeated failure may reduce achievement efforts and task motivation. Difficulty remaining optimistic and motivated to achieve or work harder in the face of habitual failure may be a significant problem for adults with ADHD. Although individuals with ADHD are often creative and utilize unique problem-solving strategies, they may experience difficulties with the experiential element of intellectual functioning even if other basic componential skills are intact, particularly when memory problems interfere with accessing previously learned information.

The *contextual* element of intelligence determines how an individual deals with the environment—it includes the practical or real-world elements of intelligence (Sternberg, 1985). The contextual or practical element of intelligence is important in adulthood; it is made up of the ability to analyze and decide what to do in a situation, to adapt to the situation, or to alter the situation. Adaptation is a key factor whereby one modifies thoughts, feelings, and behaviors in order to match one's goals, needs, and motives to the environment. This element allows the individual to change the old environment, to find a new environment, or to effect some change in both (Kolligan & Sternberg, 1987). In essence, the contextually intelligent individual judges problems and adapts to or shapes the environment to find the "best fit." Individuals with an ability to read situations, to take effective courses of action, and to work around environmental barriers might be quite successful and may be able to overcome obstacles that arise from weaknesses in other facets of their intelligence.

Tacit knowledge is an important component of contextual intelligence and represents information that is not formally taught or expressly stated but nonetheless is important to such goals as success on the job. Aspects of tacit knowledge that are important to job performance include skills in self-management (i.e., motivation; organization of time and energy), management of tasks, and management of others. An otherwise intelligent adult who cannot manage his/her schedule, cannot muster his/her energies, and cannot pick up the subtle nuances (e.g., unwritten office rules or company policies) may struggle in trying to keep up or get ahead. The histories of adults with ADHD are replete with examples of difficulties in these areas.

Recently a 50-year-old self-employed contractor with ADHD reported:

> "I have plenty of good ideas and dreams but I can't seem to put them into action. I'm better as the idea man—big plans but I have trouble getting things started and getting everything to run smoothly. I can't seem to keep up with the kind of schedule that it takes to be really successful. I'm two hours late for appointments in the morning because I'm exhausted from working late the night before. I often work 7 days a week and late into the night on weekdays—9:00 or 10:00 P.M. quitting time is not unusual for me. I'm always missing appointments or getting there late because I've overbooked myself and haven't given myself enough time to get between jobs. I sometimes get sidetracked by talking with my customers and time slips away from me. My clients get frustrated with me, and it creates a great deal of stress for me and my family. I can't even begin to tell you what my accounting procedures look like. I'm always late with my billings so I get behind in payments to my suppliers. Also my business is cyclical so when there is down time, I get easily bored. Then every summer when it's time for vacation, I'm overcommitted and have to hold up the family when it's time to get away."

It is easy to see how an adult with ADHD struggles with managing time and developing a productive schedule.

To date, Sternberg's triarchic theory of intelligence has not been empirically tested, but it is supported by inferential means and shows promise for researchers and clinicians alike. Determining the extent to which strengths or deficits in componential, experiential, and contextual intelligence affect performance may help us better understand learning disabilities in general and ADHD in particular. Clinicians might help adults figure out how ADHD is affecting these aspects of intellectual functioning. It is possible that adults with ADHD might be highly functional on one or two levels (e.g., the contextual level—able to adapt to one's environment) but may struggle with another area (e.g., the componential element—unable to make, monitor, or execute plans). With this knowledge, the therapist and adult with ADHD can develop strategies to capitalize on intellectual strengths and plan ways to compensate for weaknesses.

Subsequent sections of this chapter summarize the impact of ADHD on cognitive–intellectual functioning, particularly within college and work environments.

College and Postsecondary Education

Today's complex, multimedia, computer-driven society has increased the need for a college degree or postsecondary education. College experiences may consist of a 2-year program at a junior college, a vocationally oriented technical college, or a traditional 4-year university or small liberal arts school (Papalia & Olds, 1992). For many individuals, college marks a transition period between adolescence and adulthood and as such involves numerous developmental challenges. Many assumptions, values, attitudes, and life-style habits are challenged and expanded by an increased exposure to people from different cultural, economic, and racial backgrounds. A new adult identity often emerges during this period, formed by these experiences.

College provides a myriad of intellectual, moral, and social challenges, dilemmas, and opportunities. Depending on how an individual copes with these experiences, self-discovery and skill acquisition results in healthy development; or, if coping skills are ineffective, then adult adjustment problems ensue. Attitudes and behaviors toward drinking, taking drugs, and sexual activity may create stress that ultimately results in an identity crisis; or these stresses may be resolved with the development of healthy adult patterns.

The college experience provides an opportunity to develop career choices and to expand intellectual pursuits that shape vocational and career opportunities for young and middle-aged adults. Academic success and social-emotional adjustment during this period have long-term effects on the individual and set the stage for financial as well as personal satisfaction (i.e., a sense of accomplishment and contentment with career choice). This stage of development is not easily defined by age; college students may be adolescents straight out of high school, young adults who dropped out of or never attended college, or adults changing careers in middle or late adulthood. Unlike at any other time in the post-World War II era, a college or postsecondary education now determines amount of money earned, promotion and career advancement opportunities, and even the ability to be gainfully employed at all. Consequently, successful completion of advanced educational training may be essential for long-term career adjustment. In later sections, we will investigate how ADHD symptoms create unique challenges for adults in college or other vocational training programs.

Career and Work Adjustment

An interesting phenomenon has occurred over the past 50 years concerning job and career satisfaction. Specifically, adults under 40 are less satisfied and less involved with their jobs and are more likely to switch jobs than are adults over 60 (Papalia & Olds, 1992). Although the reasons for these differences are difficult to discern, younger adults appear to be concerned about how interesting their jobs are, their ability to develop skills on the job, and the chance to be upwardly mobile.

Another trend that affects adults is the increasing number of women in the work force and the number of dual-earner families. A major shift has occurred in which both men and women are likely to work outside the home (Papalia & Olds, 1992). The percentage of women in the workforce has dramatically increased; in 1987 approximately 56% of women worked outside the home, compared to 33.9% in 1950 (Matthews & Rodin, 1989). Whereas women in the 1950s were primarily stay-at-home mothers, traditional home life has radically changed. The trend has affected both the husband–wife relationship and the parent–child relationship, because more children now require day care outside of the home than at any other time in history. A working couple raising children already face daunting challenges in balancing the demands of work and family. If either spouse or if a parent and a child experience the effects of ADHD, we can be sure to find a stressful, hectic family life. Quality-of-life issues are often overlooked when treating adults with ADHD, but they may be essential to achieving mental health and well-being. Clinicians should investigate the impact of ADHD on the work, school, family, and personal lives of their clients before developing an appropriate intervention program.

Intimate Relationships

Divorce rates in the United States have dramatically increased over the past 2 decades, although these trends have leveled off since 1980 (Martin & Bumpass, 1989). In fact, the divorce rate in the United States is the highest in the world (U.S. Bureau of the Census, 1989). One of the consequences of the increased divorce rate is the rise in single-parent families (Papalia & Olds, 1992). The marriage rate of young adults aged 20–39 is also lower than in previous years (U.S. Bureau of the Census, 1989). It is hard to measure the real impact of ADHD on adult social adjustment against this social backdrop because, in general, young adults appear to be waiting longer to get married, may be raising families alone, or may be living alone following divorce. These trends may be a result of a better educated population that is pursuing career opportunities, greater mobility and freedom, and self-fulfillment. Young adults may also fear divorce and may postpone marriage in order to avoid these problems.

Erikson (1985) describes the major developmental challenge of adulthood (from 20 to 40 years) as a resolution of the conflict of "intimacy versus isolation." Young adults who achieve intimacy and are able to make a commitment to another person achieve a sense of identity, the quest for which begins in adolescence. Through a loving relationship, adults learn to compromise, adapt, and resolve conflicts.

In a longitudinal study of healthy young males, Vaillant and Vaillant (1990) found that adulthood was marked by a series of experiences that change and develop over time and that high-quality, sustained relationships help shape these events and even set the stage for mental health. The establishment of adulthood usually occurs somewhere between ages 20 and 30 and is marked by marriage and starting a family. Young adults begin a new phase of autonomy from their own parents during this phase (Vaillant, 1977). The adaptive model includes a period (from age 25 to 35) in which adults focus on their careers (career consolidation stage). This stage may threaten a marriage or may be a stressful time if the husband and wife are "out of sync"; that is, stress can be introduced into a marriage if partners are on different career paths. The career consolidation stage is usually marked by a period in which fathers devote themselves to their careers and families, play by the rules, and strive for promotions and advancement. A transition stage occurs around age 40, where middle-aged adults become less compulsive in their career pursuits and begin to look inward for self-fulfillment. Men who use adaptive mechanisms tend to experience happiness during these stages and are physically and mentally better adjusted than those with less effective adaptive styles (immature, psychotic, or neurotic). See Vaillant and Vaillant (1990) for more details.

Levinson (1986) also describes changes that occur in early adulthood, between the ages of 17 and 45 years. Choosing a career or occupation, establishing a home and family, and making connections to a community are typical between the ages of 22 and 28, whereas reassessment of work and family patterns may occur between 28 and 33 (Levinson, 1986). From ages 33 to 45, adults make deeper commitments to careers and families, set goals, and establish their niche in society. In later phases, adults may become more independent, becoming "one's own person." Levinson (cited in Papalia & Olds, 1992) also believes that women experience the same stages as men but that they may experience more stress and conflicts throughout these stages. Career and family priorities shift around age 30 for women, who up to this time were able to deal with conflicting achievement and relationship goals. Many women begin to make greater demands on their marriages and families when they pursue careers. Women who have both families and careers often become more disciplined, focused, hard-working, and confident than women who have neither of these avenues of expression.

The extent to which handling both career and family commitments places undue stress on both women and men warrants further investigation. Working couples are the norm rather than the exception today, and one does not have to venture far to observe the stress experienced by those who are negotiating a marriage, raising children, and establishing and maintaining successful careers. The long days, unruly schedules, fast pace of life, and unending demands can be seen everywhere in families today. The burdens of meeting these normal challenges will of course be more difficult in families in which one or both parents have ADHD or if one or more children have ADHD.

THE IMPACT OF ADHD ON ADULT DEVELOPMENT

Longitudinal research shows that ADHD persists into adulthood and continues to be problematic for a majority of individuals diagnosed in childhood (Barkley, Fischer, et al., 1990; Wender, 1995; Weiss & Hechtman, 1993). Most individuals do not outgrow ADHD in adulthood, and many of the symptoms of the disorder continue. Specifically, 66% of adults report at least one symptom (i.e., restlessness, poor concentration, impulsivity, explosiveness) of the syndrome; 64% complain of being restless and 44% are observably restless during clinical interviews (Weiss & Hechtman, 1993). The following sections summarize the major effects of ADHD on adult adjustment and illustrate how signs and symptoms differ from childhood to adulthood.

The Characteristics and Symptoms of Adult ADHD

Although characteristics of ADHD in adulthood can be problematic, there are some differences in how these symptoms are manifested in children and in adults. See Table 1.1 in Chapter 1 for a summary of major correlates of ADHD in children and adults based on clinical and empirical work cited by Wender (1995). Attentional difficulties, motor problems, impulsivity, disorganization, altered responses to social reinforcement, stress intolerance, emotionality and mood shifts, and possible impaired interpersonal relations characterize ADHD.

Wender (1995) states that "in many instances ADHD in adults is a continuation of the same childhood disorder in which many symptoms persist without diminution; the patient copes with the resultant problems in an age-specific way but is still handicapped" (p. 8). This statement emphasizes two important aspects of adult ADHD. First, many symptoms persist into adulthood. Second, adults employ coping strategies in response to these problems but still continue to be handicapped by the disorder. The mechanisms adults use to cope with ADHD can either be helpful (e.g., self-management, medication, therapy), harmful (e.g., substance abuse), or chaotic (e.g., multiple divorces and/or job changes).

The manner in which adults cope with or compensate for ADHD has a significant impact on their overall personal and professional work adjustment. Adult adjustment is also heavily influenced by the cooccurrence of other adult psychiatric disorders, including antisocial personality disorder, alcohol and substance abuse, and residual learning difficulties. Wender (1995) argues that ADHD in adults is biologically mediated and genetically transmitted and probably results from decreased monoaminergic (i.e., dopaminergic) functioning. Although the disorder may be etiologically heterogeneous, Wender (1995) states that it should be treated like other genetically transmitted medical disorders.

Wender (1995) provides a lucid discussion of the concept of "variable penetrance" or "variable expression" of genetic disorders and suggests that the same genetic defect/abnormality may manifest itself differently across individuals because of the influence of other genes or other environmental factors. As such, "the 'simple' genetic errors—such as one in an enzyme regulating the synthesis of a particular neurotransmitter—might produce hyperactivity in one person, impulsivity in a second, inattention in a third, and full ADHD in a fourth" (p.79). A further complication when investigating the genetic basis of ADHD in adulthood is the phenomenon of "pleiotropism," in which one genetic abnormality is responsible for multiple and/or different problems. For example, the D_2 receptor gene for dopamine has been implicated in hereditary alcoholism, Tourette's disorder, autism, and ADHD (Comings, Comings, et al., 1991).

Various complications, including variability in symptom expression and coexisting psychiatric disorders, increase the need for a careful diagnosis using symptom patterns, childhood and adult history, and response to previous treatment efforts. Paradigms of ADHD in adulthood provide evidence of biological and neuropsychological abnormalities.

The Biogenetic and Neurological Basis of ADHD in Adulthood

It is important to point out that even though ADHD has strong genetic linkage and is considered a neurobiological disorder, there is no predictable or inevitable path that individuals follow. Moreover, environmental factors, including family support, a structured work or school setting, family and/or individual therapy, and medication have been shown to be highly effective for alleviating or reducing the impact of many of the problems associated with ADHD. As such, neurobiological influences do not produce negative outcomes in and of themselves but interact with the environment in ways that either enhance or impede adjustment.

Genetic Studies: Familial Patterns of ADHD in Adulthood

Genetic studies show a strong familial basis for the disorder, and many parents of children with ADHD also are diagnosed with ADHD (Quinn, 1995). Numerous studies have shown that ADHD is genetically transmitted (Biederman, Faraone, Keenan, & Tsuang, 1991; Faraone, Biederman, Keenan, & Tsuang, 1991; Faraone et al., 1992; Gillis, Gilger, Pennington, & DeFries, 1992). Biederman and his colleagues found that relatives of children with ADHD, especially immediate family members and near relatives, have high rates of anxiety and depression, suggesting a genetic basis for other psychiatric disorders as well.

Researchers have found an increased rate of antisocial personality disorder and Briquet's syndrome (hysteria) in parents of "hyperactive" children (Morrison, 1980), as well as of alcoholism, sociopathy, and hysteria (Cantwell, 1972). Morrison and Stewart (1971) indicated that childhood hyperactivity was a precursor of parental alcoholism, sociopathy, and hysteria. These results should be interpreted with caution because when hyperactive children are differentiated from those with aggression, phobic neurosis, and aggression with hyperactivity, psychopathology is not found in parents of hyperactive children (Wender, 1995). Antisocial disorders appear highest in relatives of children with

ADHD plus conduct disorders and those with ADHD plus oppositional personality disorders (Faraone et al., 1991). Faraone et al. (1995) discovered that (1) boys had a slightly higher risk for ADHD than girls; (2) maternal ADHD seems to indicate a higher risk for ADHD in children who come from families with antisocial disorders; and (3) families with antisocial disorders in general have more psychopathology, including ADHD, depression, substance abuse, and conduct disorders. These data suggest that the presence of other psychiatric problems (e.g., conduct disorders, oppositional defiant disorders, aggression), increases the likelihood of more serious forms of parental psychopathology.

Rutter (1987) suggests that there is not a direct causal linkage between risk factors that leads to impaired development and poor adult outcome. According to Mash and Dozois (1996),

> early patterns of adaptation influence later adjustment in complex and reciprocal ways. Adverse conditions, early adaptational struggles, and failure to meet developmental tasks do not inevitably lead to a fixed and unmalleable dysfunctional path. Rather, many different factors, including chance events and encounters, can provide turning points whereby success in particular tasks (e.g., educational advances, peer relationships). (p. 20)

However, severe marital discord, dysfunction in the family, low social class standing of the parents, large family size, criminal activity in fathers, mental health disorders in mothers, and foster care placement are among the many adverse factors that can deflect development into maladjustment or psychopathology. This paradigm suggests that it is not simply the presence of risk factors (e.g., familial ADHD) but a constellation or aggregate of problems (e.g., parental psychopathology, substance abuse, family discord, etc.) that interact with the presence or absence of protective factors (e.g., easy temperament, positive parenting) that can affect adjustment in the long run.

Wender (1995) cautions that categorical diagnostic approaches (in which the number of signs or symptoms above some predetermined threshold determines categorical classification) may also mask the prevalence of various disorders in the relatives of children with mild or "subsyndromal" ADHD. For these reasons, Wender (1995) argues that dimensional ratings are useful for understanding milder forms of the disorder because such examinations are based on the hypothesis that the "major disorders occur along a continuum in severity and that there is an increased frequency of milder manifestations in the relatives of individuals with clear-cut instances of the disorder" (p. 90). Wender further argues that "we know that genetic factors play a role in the etiology of ADHD, but we may reasonably expect phenocopies and a large amount of genetic heterogeneity. We can expect to see differences in symptom patterns, in penetrance, and severity, and therefore in familial association" (1995, p. 117).

In summary, there is a strong consensus that ADHD is often transmitted from parent to child. However, ADHD is exacerbated by other adversity factors in the family and environment. Biogenetic and neurobiological factors do place an individual at risk for later problems and must be considered when treating adults with adjustment difficulties, substance abuse, or severe psychopathology.

Neurological Studies

The neurobiological basis of ADHD has been investigated with positron emission tomography (PET) scans and magnetic resonance imaging (MRI) techniques with fairly consistent findings. PET scans have shown that adults with a history of ADHD have the following: (1) lower total rate of cerebral glucose metabolism (8%); (2) slight variations in glucose metabolism in men (6% decrease) compared to women (13% decrease) with ADHD; and (3) 30 of 60 brain sites have lowered metabolism, including lateral, frontal, and parietal regions in both hemispheres, medial frontal regions (cingulate), and subcortical regions (striatum and thalamus; Zametkin et al., 1990). After glucose rates have been normalized, only the premotor and the prefrontal regions in the left hemisphere were considered abnormal. The prefrontal systems are intimately involved in dopaminergic activity; and when neurons entering (from subcortical regions), residing in, or passing though the frontal regions are dysfunctional, hyperactivity, impulsivity, learning and conduct disorders, and other behavioral problems often result (Comings, 1990). ADHD seems associated with decreased dopaminergic activity but may not necessarily be caused by it (Wender, 1995).

The Zametkin et al. (1990) study is still considered preliminary and should be viewed with some caution. Weiss and Hechtman (1993) argue that diagnosis of ADHD was made retrospectively, which may create some weaknesses in the study. Also the total number of statistical comparisons may introduce the possibility of error. With these limitations in mind, the study does hold promise for future research into the neurological mechanisms of ADHD.

In another study, Matochik et al. (1994) investigated the effects of methylphenidate and dextroamphetamine in adults with hyperactivity. The results showed that the methylphenidate affected glucose levels but dextroamphetamine did not. However, methylphenidate increased glucose rates in some areas of the brain and decreased activity in others.

Again, decreased blood flow and cortical underactivation appear as viable neurological hypotheses for ADHD.

Interaction of Neurobiology with Environmental Factors

In a transactional paradigm, basic brain functions serve as the foundation from which to investigate an individual's intellectual, academic, and psychosocial functioning. However, the environment, including both early and later parent–child relationships (e.g., bonding; feelings of being loved and of meeting the expectations of significant others) and school, academic, and work performance (i.e., experiences with success and failure) interact to produce either optimistic, motivated individuals who effectively meet the challenges of adulthood or pessimistic, downhearted individuals who see very little reason to keep up the effort needed to be successful academically, professionally, or even interpersonally. In essence, experiences provide opportunities for a person to develop into either an interesting, creative adult or a troubled, unhappy individual who never quite reaches his/her potential. ADHD is not a straight-line trajectory into disaster and failure. The manner in which the environment shapes, supports, and facilitates individual differences can thus have a profound effect on what an individual becomes, even as he/she must deal with biogenetic vulnerabilities.

Work Adjustment and Employment

"In adulthood, there is far greater tolerance of nonconformity and opportunity for individuals with 'specialized brains' to find vocations that are well suited to their strengths and interests" (Sandler, 1995, p. 66). In one of the major longitudinal studies conducted to date, Manuzza, Klein, Bessler, Malloy, and LaPadula (1993) found that 90% of adults who were identified as having ADHD in childhood were gainfully employed. Of this group, many adults owned their own businesses. Earlier studies also showed that adults with ADHD had a rate of employment similar to that of a control group and were as self-sufficient (Borland & Hechtman, 1976). However, adults with ADHD were more likely to change jobs and often worked two jobs as a means of coping with the feelings of restlessness and nervousness they have when bored or inactive.

Following a 10-year follow-up of 21-year-olds with hyperactivity, Weiss and Hechtman (1993) found that (1) young ADHD adults did not have higher rates of being fired or laid off, changing jobs, or unemployment compared to controls, nor did they spend less time in jobs; and (2) hyperactives generally chose jobs that required more activity. At the

15-year follow-up, employers rated hyperactive adults more negatively on the following dimensions: fulfilling work expectations adequately, working independently, completing tasks, and getting along with supervisors. Employers were also more negative about whether they would hire the employee again (Weiss & Hechtman, 1993). Furthermore, hyperactive adults entered the work force at an earlier age and either quit or were laid off more frequently. Although hyperactive and control adults were not fired at different rates, employers may lay workers off rather than fire them.

When measuring work status, hyperactives did not differ in annual salaries but did differ on the Hollingshead Scale of Work Status (Weiss & Hechtman, 1993). Hyperactive adults did report having difficulty with work tasks more frequently, but they did not report significantly higher problems with concentration. Although hyperactives and controls had similar rates (80%) of preference for "active" versus "sedentary" jobs, hyperactive adults have a greater tendency to enjoy jobs because they like the people they work with.

In summary, Weiss and Hechtman (1993) suggest that the poor work records of hyperactives are likely due to lower educational attainment, effects of previous learning difficulties, and difficulties with impulsivity and characterological problems (e.g., general malaise). The employment news for adults with ADHD is far from dismal, as the majority of adults are employed. Adults also have a greater opportunity to select environments—work and career situations—that are better matched to their particular strengths and weaknesses. Even with this degree of flexibility, a number of adults do experience work adjustment problems that appear related to ADHD symptomology (e.g., impulsivity).

Comorbid Psychopathology

Studies reporting the psychiatric status of adults with ADHD, using either follow-up or prospective designs, indicate that about 50% of adults have a fairly good outcome (Weiss & Hechtman, 1993). However, in their longitudinal study, Weiss and Hechtman (1993) did find that overall psychiatric history was more impaired in the ADHD adult sample compared to controls, and a trend toward higher rates of sexual problems, including homosexuality, premature ejaculation, and occasional impotence, was found. Weiss and Hechtman reported that adults could be divided into groups who were either psychiatrically disturbed or antisocially disturbed, with some overlap between the two. Adults with antisocial or psychiatric problems were more likely to have employment problems, criminal behaviors, suicide attempts, substance abuse, psychiatric hospitalizations, and borderline psychosis (Weiss & Hecht-man, 1993).

Adults with ADHD appear to have high rates of comorbid psycho-pathology, particularly with antisocial behavioral problems (10–40%); as many as 25% meet criteria for antisocial personality disorder (Barkley, 1990a). Weiss and Hechtman (1993) found that minor antiso-cial acts involving heavy drinking, drinking and driving, fighting while drinking, drug abuse, and/or failure to pay debts characterized the antisocial patterns of one-third of adults meeting criteria for antisocial personality disorder. Generally, antisocial behavioral patterns begin in early adolescence and may result in substance abuse disorders in a small but significant number (12%) of adults (Gittelman et al., 1985). Sub-stance abuse, particularly with nonprescription drugs, did decrease with age, although marijuana and alcohol use were higher in adults with ADHD compared to control adults.

In their prospective study, Mannuzza et al. (1993) found that only a small minority of adults (11%) reported significant ADHD symptoms. ADHD symptoms were measured using self-reports, which may under-estimate the prevalence of these signs, according to Wender (1995). Adults with ADHD often underreport the extent of their problems and may be inaccurate in their self-appraisals. Even so, 16% of the groups reported nonalcohol substance abuse problems compared to only 4% of the control group, and 18% of the adults with ADHD were diagnosed with conduct or antisocial personality disorders (Mannuzza et al., 1993). The overall response rate was impressive for the Mannuzza et al. study, with 88% of the ADHD group and 95% of the control group respond-ing.

Longitudinal studies have not reported high rates of comorbid major depression, bipolar disorder, dysthymia, anxiety, and borderline personality disorders, although in individual cases these disorders have been observed in adults with ADHD (Weiss & Hechtman, 1993; Wender, 1995). On the other hand, cross-sectional studies suggest that depression is a serious problem for a number of adults with ADHD. For example, Shekim, Asarnow, Hess, Zaucha, and Wheeler (1990) diag-nosed depression in 10% and dysthymia in 25% of their adult ADHD sample. Tzelepis, Schubiner, and Warbasse (1995) also found that 29% of the adults in their study had lifelong depression and that 19% had dysthymia. Tzelepis et al. (1995) offered some explanations for these differences and indicated that both cross-sectional studies focused on older adults; depression does increase with age. Furthermore, Tzelepis et al. hypothesized that older adults who are referred for ADHD may be a more disabled subgroup.

Regardless of the incidence rates on a group level, coexisting psychiatric disorders should be investigated for adults presenting with ADHD symptoms. Wender (1995) and Weiss and Hechtman (1993) provide extensive discussions of overlapping symptoms and guidelines for making a differential diagnosis. At any rate, comorbid psychiatric disorders appear to place the adult at greater risk for substance abuse, employment difficulties, and overall adjustment problems.

Psychosocial Adjustment, Marital Status, Intimate Relationships, and Family Adjustment

The extent to which ADHD affects adult relationships has also been studied. Although an understanding, supportive spouse may suffer burnout from the constant drama and chaos of living with an ADHD adult, he/she can also be an important part of the intervention plan and should be consulted periodically throughout treatment. Spouses often bear the brunt of disappointments that occur outside the home, at work, or at school and may need support themselves.

> Even if an adult with ADHD has not had educational or occupational problems, or has learned how to cope with educational or occupational demands, social relationships can remain a shadowy frontier, muddled with uncertainty and insecurity, and intimate relationships can be the biggest puzzle of all. (Ratey, Hallowell, & Miller, 1995, p. 218)

This is a theme that has been echoed by other researchers who have investigated the impact of ADHD on adults (Kinsbourne, 1996). Kinsbourne suggests the need for researchers and clinicians to attend to "quality of life" issues when assessing the impact of ADHD and when treating this disorder.

How does ADHD play out in everyday encounters? How do adults interact with colleagues, friends, spouses, and/or significant others? How do they feel about these encounters? Are adults with ADHD constantly too hard on themselves and overly critical about their mistakes? Do they overreact in social situations, or are they oblivious to the subtle nuances of social interchange? Can they control what they say and do in heated, emotional moments? Are they selfish and narcissistic, always needing to be the focus of attention? How do disinhibition, hyperactivity, impulsivity, distractibility, emotional lability, and other neurocognitive deficits affect social relations? These questions all touch on "quality of life" issues. Ratey et al. (1995) refer to these factors as "biology of intimacy" symptoms that include physiological, behavioral, cognitive, and emotional aspects of ADHD.

Ratey et al. (1995) suggests two neurobiological hypotheses related to social adjustment: (1) the catecholamine hypothesis, which describes imbalances of noradrenergic and dopaminergic neurotransmitters (see Chapter 2 for a discussion of the proposed biochemical processes underlying ADHD); and (2) the disinhibition hypothesis, which explains behaviors associated with underactivation of frontal lobes and inhibitory mechanisms. These systems are most likely interactive, as the frontal lobes are rich in catecholamines. Dysfunction of these neurobiological substrates results in difficulties inhibiting inappropriate behaviors, planning future behaviors, learning from past experiences, and modulating or controlling feelings and emotional reactions.

Few controlled studies have been conducted that measure the social impact of ADHD in adulthood. Feldman, Denhoff, and Denhoff (1979) found that adults with hyperactivity scored within the normal range on measures of self-concept but were significantly below those of a control, sibling group. These young adults with ADHD had received extensive treatment in childhood, including medication, individual and family counseling, language and special education, and visual–perceptual training, so they may constitute a group of "treated" ADHD adults that may differ from others who have not received such extensive treatment. However, others have reported that adult hyperactives were not unlike siblings on measures of social functioning and did not differ from siblings on rates of marriage and separation (Borland & Heckman, 1976). Furthermore, this group of adults seemed to recover from earlier social and academic difficulties, lowered self-esteem, and motivational problems in school, and earlier problems did not affect their overall educational attainment as adults.

Longitudinal Studies

Weiss and Hechtman (1993) addressed self-esteem and social adjustment issues in the 10-year follow-up of their longitudinal study and found that only a small number of adults had serious problems in these areas. On measures of oral response to social scenarios, hyperactive adults did differ from a control group but were similar on written response items and on responses simulating a job interview. Adults did not seem to have difficulty assessing social situations from a cognitive perspective, but they had difficulty responding to heterosocial situations and to personal assertion. Self-esteem measures were significantly lower for hyperactives compared to the control group, particularly on items contrasting obedient–disobedient, strong–weak, calm–nervous, nice–awful, careless–careful, attentive–inattentive, disorderly–orderly, and grateful–ungrateful. Specifically, at a 15-year follow-up, hyperactive adults rated themselves as "more nervous and less nice, but also less honest, more foolish, and more indifferent," and they rarely rated themselves better than the control group (Weiss & Hechtman, 1993, p. 161).

At the 15-year mark, Weiss and Hechtman (1993) found that the sample was experiencing more problems than they had at the 10-year follow-up, and virtually all the hyperactives were significantly lower than the control group on measures of social skills and self-esteem. The 10-year report assessed a smaller portion of the sample, which may explain these differences, although Weiss and Hechtman (1993) suggest that older adults may actually experience more difficulties when aspirations are not realized or seem far out of reach. There is some evidence that early and extensive treatment may protect adults from these negative social outcomes (Feldman, Denhoff, & Denhoff, 1979).

Marital Status

High rates of divorce and separation have been reported in several studies of adults with ADHD (Mannuzza et al., 1993; Weiss & Hechtman, 1986). Wilens, Spencer, and Biederman (1995) suggest that the clinical features of ADHD may have an impact on relationships, especially stubbornness, low frustration tolerance, and conflicts in social situations with friends, colleagues, bosses, and spouses. Other associated psychopathology or substance abuse problems also complicate this picture and place added stress on relationships.

Intimate Relationships

Intimacy issues and quality of relationships have not been systematically investigated, but clinical evidence suggests that adults with ADHD often experience stress and conflict in these areas (Ratey et al., 1995). Poor self-esteem, chronic failure, and demoralization may have a negative impact on relationships.

> For some of these adults, intimate relationships are much like college courses, degrees, jobs, or challenges. Once the thrill of the novel and bold passes, some have even become bored and move on. They have had many relationships, some have even had many marriages. And sometimes they withdraw from the fray, forsaking relationships altogether, feeling like they have no capacity for them because of their selfishness, narcissism, or immaturity. (Ratey et al., 1995, p. 219)

Some may put enormous energy and time into fixing relationships, so when they do dissolve, adults with ADHD often feel devastated by the loss.

Physiological, cognitive, and affective barriers put strain on relationships (Ratey et al., 1995). Physical closeness may be uncomfortable for adults who are hypersensitive to touch, and some adults feel trapped or smothered by physical intimacy. Intimate relationships require emotional maturity, including the ability to control and appropriately express emotions, to make plans and to carry them out, to understand the nuances of social interactions, to inhibit or to delay responding, to listen and to pay attention, all or some of which abilities might be compromised by ADHD (Ratey et al., 1995). Impulsivity may play itself out through a string of relationships that are not developed or sustained due to boredom or a lack of persistence. Withdrawal and isolation may characterize other relationships, so that intimacy and closeness are out of reach. Sexual intimacy may be characterized as frenetic, demanding, insensitive, or insatiable, leaving the spouse or partner feeling unloved, used, or unappreciated (Ratey et al., 1995).

Ratey et al. (1995) use the term "cognitive disinhibition" to describe relationship barriers that result from difficulty delaying responses. Quick judgments, hasty conclusions, rigid reasoning, and misreading and/or misinterpreting social cues may all be part of the cognitive features of the disorder. These factors affect communication skills and may impede conflict resolution skills.

Finally, emotional barriers may result from difficulties in controlling and modulating feelings. Adults with ADHD may vacillate from being distant and withdrawn to intense and demanding (Ratey et al., 1995). Ratey et al. (1995) suggest that the dysfunction of limbic structures (amygdala and hippocampus) may influence the temperament of the adult, resulting in "exaggerated temperament" or overreactivity to situations. Temperamental dispositions may manifest differently in adults with attention-deficit disorder without hyperactivity (ADD/WO; shy and withdrawn) compared to those with attention-deficit disorder with hyperactivity (ADD/H). The withdrawn, obsessive–compulsive, sedate temperament may be more characteristic of ADD/WO, whereas emotional outbursts and temper tantrums seem to be found in individuals who are hyperactive, distractible, and emotionally labile (ADD/H).

Although these specific assumptions need further investigation, it is reasonable to conclude that symptoms of ADHD affect intimacy and emotional closeness. At this time, clinical evidence, is more abundant than research evidence but there is good reason to assess these issues when treating adults with ADHD. In fact, difficulty managing interpersonal relationships and a sense of a lack of well-being may drive adults with ADHD to seek out psychological or psychiatric help.

Family Adjustment

Family functioning is an area that appears affected by ADHD symptoms or problems, although the evidence of these difficulties comes from clinical rather than empirical sources. Dixon (1995) suggests that family functioning is affected by factors that often coexist with ADHD, such as comorbid disorders (e.g., depression, alcoholism, learning disabilities, anxiety, and obsessive–compulsive disorders); impaired cognitive functioning; low socioeconomic status; lower stress tolerance; quality of spousal relationship; the number and severity of other stress factors (e.g., job, commuting time, responsibility of caring for one's parents, illness); the number of children and their problems; social support from parents, family, and friends; and early identification and treatment for ADHD problems. It is important to note that ADHD rarely occurs without other associated or comorbid disorders (Shekim et al., 1990).

Dixon (1995) discusses the impact of ADHD on families in such major categories as household organization, parenting, and couple's issues. The household organizational problems generally involve day-to-day management issues such as handling family finances, maintaining and juggling schedules, and completing chores efficiently (e.g., shopping, doing laundry, cleaning, cooking, doing yard work). The primary and/or secondary characteristics of ADHD (e.g., memory problems, attentional and organizational deficits, low frustration tolerance, lack of persistence, restlessness) make these tasks even more difficult, and adults with ADHD often report feeling overwhelmed by these demands. Procrastination may be a big problem, especially with tedious tasks such as balancing the checkbook, paying bills, and taking care of important paperwork (e.g., investments, insurance forms, taxes); thus the probability of missing important deadlines or letting details go unfinished increases. Long-range planning can also be problematic because so much energy is needed to get through the day or because delaying gratification (e.g., saving instead of spending) is so hard. Adults with ADHD are often distracted when carrying out these household tasks and simply fail to get things done in a timely, efficient manner. Disarray, clutter, and chaos are not uncommon in the homes of women with ADHD (Solden, 1995).

A lack of success or difficulty managing the household often leads to feelings of low self-esteem and/or high levels of anxiety and depression. Some adults with ADHD may attempt to put order into their lives by being extremely organized, making lists, and putting structure into every activity. If these attempts are not successful or if things do not go exactly as planned, the adult with ADHD may get upset. Temper outbursts may occur after simple, everyday setbacks (e.g., when the toilet overflows, when the washer breaks down, when the dog has an accident, etc.). Feeling overwhelmed by everyday responsibilities is commonly reported by adults with ADHD.

Many of the same ADHD symptoms described above also interfere with parenting. This is especially the case if an ADHD parent is trying to manage a child with ADHD. This combination may create a situation in which the parent is overly protective and not very demanding of the child because he/she can so readily identify with the problems the child is facing. It may also result in underestimating the nature and severity of the child's problems (e.g., "I was just like that when I was young, and I turned out fine"). The situation in which both parent and child have ADHD may also result in a parent having problems controlling his/her temper when the child gets into trouble at home or at school, yelling at the child to increase compliance, constantly nagging and berating the child when he/she fails, and/or providing little follow-through when the child does not comply. Adults with ADHD may need parent training to handle these challenges.

Finally, couples issues may surface when one spouse is unable to keep up his/her responsibilities. Dixon (1995) advises that understanding the way in which ADHD interferes with the relationship is important. The spouse without ADHD may feel frustrated and resentful because of the chaos, disorganization, emotional outbursts, behavioral variability, irresponsibility, and forgetfulness of the spouse with ADHD. Spouses without ADHD may also experience burnout or may become codependent in the relationship—both patterns must be actively avoided and may require couples therapy to resolve. Although the dual-ADHD marriage may be wrought with difficulties, Dixon (1995) points out that there may be more sympathy and understanding in these marriages. However, mutual blaming must be avoided if these marriages are going to be supportive and family functioning is going to improve (Nadeau, 1991). Communication problems may create other difficulties that interfere with parenting and intimacy issues between spouses. Impatience, poor problem-solving skills, poor listening, inadequate planning, difficulty finishing household projects, and sexual problems have been reported in individual case studies (Weiss & Hechtman, 1993).

Predictive Factors Affecting Adult Outcome and Treatment

In multivariate analyses, Weiss and Hechtman (1993) investigated the interaction among personality factors, social–academic factors, and family parameters and their effects on school performance, work record, criminal behaviors, car accidents, and alcohol and drug abuse in young adults who had been diagnosed with ADHD in childhood. Consistent with the transactional paradigm discussed in Chapter 2, ADHD characteristics interact with other variables to influence overall adult outcome.

School performance was related to IQ, socioeconomic status, and family parameters including child-rearing practices and the emotional climate of the home (Weiss & Hechtman, 1993). Work record was related to relationships with adults and antisocial problems, whereas hyperactivity predicted work adjustment, socioeconomic status, and age at time of first job. The likelihood of being fired was predicted by hyperactivity, IQ, adult relationships, antisocial behavioral problems, and age on entering work force; that of being laid off was predicted by socioeconomic status, adult relationships, and peer relations.

Further analyses revealed that criminal activity was predicted by a combination of factors, including hyperactivity, IQ, emotional instability, peer relations, family socioeconomic status, family mental health status, emotional climate of the home, and child-rearing practices, specifically overprotectiveness (Weiss & Hechtman, 1993). The severity of criminal offenses was related to personal characteristics of aggressiveness, emotional instability, and low frustration tolerance; social parameters, including peer and adult relation difficulties; and family difficulties, including socioeconomic status, mental health status of family members, emotional climate of the home, and child-rearing practices that included lack of control and overprotectiveness. Thus adult criminal behaviors were related to initial emotional instability, family socioeconomic status, mental health status of the family, and child-rearing practices.

Alcohol use was related to personal characteristics (aggression, hyperactivity, and antisocial behaviors) and family parameters (mental health of family members). Marijuana/hashish use was related to IQ, antisocial behaviors, and family mental health, whereas antisocial behavior and emotional climate of the home predicted extensive marijuana use. The use of other drugs (cocaine and heroin) was low, and there were no significant findings for use of these drugs. On the other hand, use of hallucinogens was related to initial antisocial problems; stimulant use was related to IQ and antisocial problems; and use of barbiturates was related to mental health status of family members and to IQ. Although peer relations did not enter any of these multiple regression analyses, this factor was highly related to antisocial behavioral problems.

Weiss and Hechtman (1993) summarize their major outcome data in the following ways.

In summary, even though some initial measures are more important in predicting particular outcome variables—for example, IQ in predicting education completed; socioeconomic status in predicting work, education, and police involvement—generally our findings point to the importance of several factors such as personality characteristics and family and social parameters all acting together cumulatively in predicting outcome. This explains why long-term drug studies have generally not resulted in as positive an outcome as was once hoped for. It also points to the need for a multifaceted approach in treating these children. (Weiss & Hechtman, 1993, p. 272)

Although subtle brain anomalies may place some limits on early successes, the way parents and teachers help individuals make sense of their abilities and limitations can make lasting impressions on adult motivation and self-esteem. In many ways, we are finding that it is not necessarily the original limitation (e.g., neurochemical or biogenetic vulnerabilities in brain function) that has such a negative impact on the adult with ADHD but the subsequent environmental context and framework in which these vulnerabilities are played out. It is not so much the struggle to learn or the extra time that it takes to get things done that can be so devastating as it is the message about who and what we are as we move through these challenges. It is with this knowledge, sensitivity, and appreciation that we can begin to reduce the negative impact of ADHD on adults.

TREATMENT AND INTERVENTIONS FOR ADULTS WITH ADHD

There has been a growing awareness of the need to provide treatment for adults with ADHD over the past decade. Treatment efficacy is not as well documented for adults as it is for children, but many of the same principles apply. Most clinicians and researchers indicate a need for multimodal interventions that may include medication, individual and family therapy, strategies for success in school and work, and methods for increasing personal self-efficacy. Also, as with interventions for children and adolescents, treatment plans for adults with ADHD should be individualized depending on the nature of the problems, the particular profile of the individual's strengths and weaknesses, and the resources available for support (e.g., family members, helpful boss or colleagues, close friends, etc.).

Hallowell and Ratey (1994) describe different ways in which attentional problems may be expressed in individuals:

The vastness of the attentional system partially accounts for the variation of ADD "types." Where one individual needs an oil change, the next needs spark plugs replaced. Where one individual is withdrawn and overwhelmed by stimuli, the next is hyperactive and can't get enough stimuli. When one is frequently anxious, the other is depressed. To compensate, each develops his or her own coping strategies that developmentally add to, or subtract from, the brain's various subsystems. So Mr. A. becomes a stand-up comedian, and manic. Ms. B becomes an architectural wizard with obsessive traits. Their offspring become a sculptor and a stunt pilot. None of them balance their checkbook. All of them wish they had more time in the day. (p. 280)

With this in mind, interventions will by necessity be different for each individual depending on how ADHD is expressed, on differences in coping styles, on academic and work history, on coexisting psychiatric disorders, and on the presence of interpersonal or social networks.

Diagnosis of ADHD in Adults

It might come as a surprise, but many adults receive their first diagnosis of ADHD when they seek psychiatric or psychological help for their troubled child or adolescent. A number of parents become more aware of their own difficulties when providing diagnostic and background history about their child's problems. It is not uncommon for Mom or Dad to say during a clinical interview, "I was just like Matt when I was his age. I almost dropped out of school, but I had a 10th-grade teacher who wouldn't give up on me. I wonder if Matt's ADHD comes from me? What do you think, doctor?" This scene is probably played out in a number of clinics, particularly when the whole family seems to be struggling with a problem child. Is the impact of the child's ADHD made that much worse because one or both parents also suffer from the same or similar problems?

A comprehensive assessment and accurate diagnosis of ADHD serves as the starting point for developing an effective intervention plan for adults. Clinicians treating adults with substance abuse problems should investigate the possibility of coexisting ADHD in their patients. There is reason to suspect that for some individuals, drinking or drug use was initiated at an early age to cope with the primary symptoms of ADHD (e.g., impulsivity, disinhibition) or associated features of the disorder, including school or work failure or social and interpersonal difficulties. Substance abuse problems do occur more frequently in individuals with comorbid conduct-related disorders and ADHD, so other factors increase the complexity of the abuse picture.

Utah Assessment Diagnostic Model

The Utah Assessment Diagnostic Model (Wender, 1995) has been used among clinicians for assessing and diagnosing ADHD in adults. In the initial development of inclusionary criteria, Wender (1995) saw adults who had not been previously seen or treated for ADHD as children. This was not considered unusual at the time (late 1940s, early 1950s) because there was only one psychiatrist in Utah. In order to augment data that came from patient self-reports, a standardized rating scale (the Conners Abbreviated Rating Scale) for parents or parent substitutes was used to assess the adult's pediatric history. Parents were asked to rate their off-spring's behavior between the ages of 6 and 10 years of age. Wender (1995) provides a distribution of scores for adults on this measure. The Wender Utah Rating Scale was also developed, and a distribution of scores for normal adults, ADHD adults, or unipolar depressed adults is available.

Elevated scores on these measures serve as a first step in the diagnostic process, but are not sufficient for a diagnosis; thus the Utah Criteria include childhood history and adult diagnostic criteria (Wender, 1995). These two parts represent a broad-band and narrow-band set of criteria.

Wender (1995) provides guidelines for determining the presence of early conduct and oppositional characteristics that persist into adulthood or are manifested as antisocial personality disorder (about half outgrow these problems). Consequently, it is important to determine whether the adult has persistent symptoms such as antisocial personality disorder, passive–aggressive personality disorder, or oppositional defiant disorder. The etiology and treatment outcomes of combined disorders are not known at present, but due to the high rates of comorbidity, these should be explored.

In the adult diagnostic criteria part of the Utah model, the clinician ascertains the presence of motor activity and attentional problems (both symptoms are required) and two of five other characteristics (i.e., affective lability, hot temper, inability to complete tasks and disorgani-zation, stress intolerance, and impulsivity). The hyperactivity dimension includes restlessness, fidgetiness, finger drumming, hair twisting, inability to relax (described as nervousness), foot tapping, intolerance of or discomfort with inactivity (e.g., watching TV or reading), and feelings of dysphoria when inactive (Wender, 1995). Impaired concentration is described as distractibility (inability to filter out competing stimuli), difficulty attending to conversations, inability to concentrate on task at hand (e.g., when reading), forgetfulness, misplacing or losing things, or having one's "mind frequently somewhere else" (Wender, 1995, p. 127). The Utah Criteria require that both hyperactivity and concentration problems be present for a diagnosis of ADHD to be made in adults. Two of the following characteristics must also be present.

Affective lability is defined as shifts in mood, from depression to mild euphoria or the feeling of being excited or "wired." The feelings of depression become more pronounced with age, and the feelings of "being up" may fade altogether. Adults with ADHD do experience pleasure, particularly when engaging in enjoyable events or activities. However, it can be difficult for them to get started or to initiate activities due to "psychological inertia." These feelings are exacerbated by life events and may improve when things turn for the better with ongoing treatment or when coping strategies are effective.

Temper outbursts, explosive, short-lived loss of control, and being easily provoked or impatient fall into the category of hot temper (Wender, 1995). The characteristic feature of this symptom is "overreactivity." The outburst is usually short-lived but can be a real problem in interpersonal relationships. Inability to complete tasks and disorganization can be seen in the following: lack of organization in the home, while doing school work, or at the job; sloppy work space; inability to complete tasks or frequently interrupting work; switching from one thing to another in a haphazard manner; starting something new before an old task is complete; disorganization in problem solving; poor time management; and a lack of persistence (e.g., giving up easily).

Wender (1995) describes stress intolerance as an inability to handle normal stress; inappropriate reactions such as depression, confusion, uncertainty, anxiety, or anger; becoming easily discouraged; emotional reactions that interfere with affective problem solving; high sensitivity to criticism and pressure; and appearing tense, hassled, flustered and "in crisis" when dealing with routine stress. Finally, impulsivity is characterized as talking before thinking; interrupting; being impatient; acting without thinking about consequences; and impulse buying. Wender (1995) suggests that impulsivity may appear as mania or as an antisocial personality disorder. Wender (1995) suggests that impulsivity can be seen when decisions are made without thinking them through or without needed information (e.g., quitting a job, abruptly ending a relationship, or making foolish business transactions or investments). Driving habits might also be reckless. Furthermore, individuals may actually feel uncomfortable if they have to delay acting (Wender, 1995). Kinsbourne (1996) also describes a feeling of discomfort that individuals with ADHD have when they attempt to control their impulses.

Wender (1995) has defined a set of exclusionary criteria to rule out other symptoms and/or disorders, such as bipolar and depressive disorder; schizophrenia, schizoaffective disorder, and schizotypal personality disorder; select symptoms of borderline personality disorder (i.e., long-standing unstable interpersonal relations, suicidal or mutilating behaviors, identity disturbances, chronic feelings of emptiness, fears of abandonment); antisocial personality disorder; and substance abuse or history of drug abuse (Wender, 1995). The Utah Criteria seeks to identify a homogeneous or "pure" group of hyperactives, which may be "statistically atypical" (Wender, 1995, p. 129). Wender (1995) acknowledges that this model may rule out adults with comorbid disorders, but he provides a strong rationale for these exclusionary criteria. For example, depressive disorders are generally nonresponsive to stimulants; schizophrenic symptoms may be exacerbated by stimulants; borderline disorders are largely unresponsive to medication, and individuals with this disorder may be prone to abuse stimulants; and antisocial personalities are often unreliable and may be at risk for substance abuse. Issues of unreliability play a large role in exclusionary factors particularly in individuals with alcoholism. It should be noted that when treated with stimulants, alcoholics may have reduced urges to drink. Wender (1995) does caution that clinicians still need to treat adults with these presenting problems, and in some cases even "pure" hyperactives may develop subsequent disorders over time. In cases where a dual diagnosis is appropriate, treatments should address different symptoms and typically require combined interventions.

   Although appropriate diagnosis is the beginning point for all effective intervention programs regardless of the developmental stage, clinicians need to begin here with adults who have not had a previous diagnosis of ADHD. Accurate diagnosis is also important for individuals with a childhood history of ADHD in order to determine if a significant number of symptoms remain and if they are severe in nature, and the extent to which these symptoms interfere with the success of the individual in school, work, or interpersonal relations. Other assessment paradigms have broadened the scope of evaluation for adults to include measurement of neurocognitive functioning.

Promising Neuropsychological Models for Assessment

In an overview of the neurodevelopmental variations in adolescents and adults, Sandler (1995) describes an interactive paradigm for understanding learning and attentional problems. The paradigm was developed at the Clinical Center for the Study of Development of Learning at the University of North Carolina at Chapel Hill and might be helpful when learning disabilities and ADHD coexist. In this model, the strengths and weaknesses identified in the adult serve as the fundamental neurocognitive operations that influence one's ability to learn and one's productivity level. Termed "elemental functions," these functions are defined as "subconstructs grouped within well established interdependent neurodevelopmental constructs, which include attention, memory, language, visual–spatial ordering, temporal–sequential ordering, neuromotor/graphomotor function, social cognition, and higher-order cognition" (Sandler, 1995, p. 62). These elemental functions correspond to those described in the Teeter and Semrud-Clikeman (1997) transactional, neurodevelopmental paradigm (see Chapter 2) whereby cognitive, academic, and psychosocial adjustment are ultimately influenced by basic brain functions.

The emphasis on a production component adds a dimension that can be objectively measured (e.g., how does the adult read, comprehend, utilize reading material, learn from reading) and shows how neurodevelopmental strengths and weaknesses affect adult outcome across a variety of areas (e.g., academic and work productivity). This portion of the assessment model is critical for determining how the disorder interferes with or affects the adult. Sandler (1995) uses reading ability to illustrate how essential elemental functions affect production components: (1) selective attention permits attending to the internal structure of words in order to decode them; (2) sustained attention allows resistance of distractions or cognitive fatigue when reading; (3) self-monitoring helps in comprehending what is being read; (4) intentional strategies lead to deciding what and how to read; (5) selective attention, which is related to self-monitoring, facilitates getting started by tuning out multiple competing stimuli; (6) task staging permits sequencing and breaking assignments into stages or chunks that can be managed; and (7) determinants of salience help in prioritizing information being read. For effective reading, adults must employ cognitive functions efficiently and flexibly and must use comprehension monitoring strategies through active dialogue with reading material (What did I just read? What did that mean? How does that fit into what I already know about this topic?).

Other elemental processes that affect production components (e.g., reading skill) include memory functions for sight words and automatic processing and active working memory to keep facts in mind as we read, which allows for discourse processing, or putting things together in a coherent manner. Phonological awareness (appreciating sound–symbol relationships) continues to be important, and metalinguistic strategies (e.g., awareness of comprehension difficulties and use of corrective measures such as rereading to increase comprehension) take on an even greater role for the older, mature learner. Critical-thinking and problem-solving abilities also influence the comprehension process, particularly because reading places greater demands on adults and requires an ability to draw inferences from what is read.

It is easy to see how an adult with weaknesses in these elemental processes will struggle in college or in careers or jobs where reading and the ability to decipher complex reading materials are required. The neurodevelopmental model provides a mechanism whereby clinicians can evaluate discrete elemental processes and measure their impact by assessing production components (e.g., reading or math comprehension).

This model significantly expands more traditional assessment procedures that focus on identifying the symptoms or signs of attentional deficits or learning problems and provides a framework for a more thorough understanding and description of the impact of the symptoms in the everyday life of the adult. This type of evaluation then becomes an important piece of information for increasing self-awareness and developing coping strategies to deal with the basic neurodevelopmental weaknesses that might affect the adult's college or career success, work productivity, work/school adjustment, and overall self-esteem.

Strategies for Increasing Success in College

Successful completion of college is often out of reach for a majority of adults with ADHD. Longitudinal studies report a rather pessimistic figure of only 5% of ADHD children graduating from college, whereas 41% of a control group are successful in this endeavor (Barkley, 1990b). Despite these distressing figures, Richard (1995) suggests that college and university staffs are paying more attention to students with ADHD as a result of a new emphasis on helping students with disabilities become more successful. Richard (1995) indicates that there has been an increase in the number of requests for accommodations on the basis of Section 504 of the Rehabilitation Act of 1973, which provides students with legal rights to support services. (See Table 9.1 for a summary of legal rights of individuals with ADHD.) Many of the interventions that are currently available are similar in nature to those offered to students with learning disabilities.

Universities and colleges are not required to reduce standards for admissions or graduation, nor do they have to waive course requirements that are essential to a program or degree; however, colleges are compelled to "modify requirements so that they do not discriminate against individuals on the basis of disability" (Richard, 1995, p. 285). Access to accommodations in college becomes the responsibility of the student, which reflects a shift from elementary and high school, in which teachers and parents often take the initiative to seek accommodations. It is not the legal responsibility of universities to provide support if the student does not request accommodations. Entering freshmen (and their parents) may be unaware of this shift in responsibility, and students can get into academic trouble quickly if they cannot keep up the pace without support. However, most colleges and universities provide academic assistance through learning centers and student support programs, and these should be investigated prior to enrollment.

The increased need for self-initiated advocacy can be a problem in and of itself. Self-advocacy requires that the student plan ahead and

TABLE 9.1. Legal Statutes Ensuring Rights of Individuals with ADHD

Statute	Specifications/considerations
Rehabilitation Act (RA, 1973)	*Definition of disability*: "An individual who (i) has a physical or mental impairment which substantially limits one or more of such person's major life activities, (ii) has a record of such an impairment, or (iii) is regarded as having such an impairment" (Rehabilitation Act of 1973, 706[8][B])
	Definition of physical or mental impairment: A physical or mental impairment includes "any mental or psychological disorder, such as mental retardation, organic brain syndrome, emotional or mental illness, and specific learning disabilities" (29 CRF 1613.702[b][2]).
	ADHD is recognized as a "mental or psychological disorder."
	Definition of substantial impairment: The disability must be severe and must "substantially limit" activity so that the individual is (i) "unable to perform major life activity that the average person in the general population can perform," or (ii) "significantly restricted as to the condition, manner or duration" of the major life activity.
	The following must be considered when assessing the impact of the individual's limitations: (i) the nature and severity of the disorder and (ii) the duration and long-term impact of the disorder (29 CFR 1630.2[j][2][I]-[iii]).
	For the majority of individuals, ADHD is considered a lifelong disorder. The extent to which ADHD "substantially limits" the individual's performance in the workplace must be determined.
	Major life activities: The disability must substantially limit the individual's ability to care for self, such as performing manual tasks, walking, talking, seeing, breathing, speaking, learning, and working.
	ADHD symptoms (e.g., disinhibition, impulsivity, etc.) may significantly limit all of the above (except for breathing).
	Effects on learning: Requires assessment of actual academic performance. Must impact directly or indirectly because of inappropriate behaviors. An individual with ADHD who has adequate academic performance and who is not disruptive may not be eligible under the learning activity.

(continued)

305

TABLE 9.1. cont.

Statute	Specifications/considerations
	Effects on working: Consider the type/class of job and the types/classes and number of jobs from which the individual is barred. May consider: "(1) academic qualifications, (2) required on-the-job experience, (3) competence in the work itself, (4) general standards of cooperativeness in the work situation, and (5) compliance with 'good citizenship' rule" (Latham & Latham, 1995, p. 340).
	Testing: Tests cannot be used as single criterion for determining hiring, promotion, or firing decisions. There is an exception if and when it can be determined that testing criterion is important to the job or to the educational setting. Institution may decide that alternative testing or accommodations are not appropriate for some positions (e.g., teaching).
Americans with Disabilities Act (ADA)	*Prohibits:* Discrimination against individuals in educational, employment, or public programs.
	For protection all of the following must be shown: (1) The individual has a disability, (2) the person is "otherwise qualified," (3) the person was denied a job (or education or benefits) solely on the basis of the disability, and (4) the institution is covered under ADA or RA.
	Definition of disability: Same as RA.
	Definition of mental or physical impairment: Similar to RA.
Individuals with Disabilities Education Act (IDEA)	*Provides for:* Free and appropriate education at the elementary and secondary level
	Definition of disability: Children with disabilities are defined as " … being mentally retarded, hard of hearing, deaf, speech impaired, visually handicapped, seriously emotionally disturbed, orthopedically impaired, other health impaired, deaf-blind, multihandicapped or as having specific learning disabilities" (Federal Register, 1975, p. 42478).
	ADHD is not recognized as a separate handicapping condition under IDEA but may be considered under one of the other categories.

Note. Information summarized from Latham & Latham (1995).

anticipate the consequences of not seeking support. Furthermore, self-advocacy requires that the student approach four to five new professors a semester to discuss their specific learning and/or attentional problems and to develop appropriate accommodations for each course. Universities with special centers for students do provide a useful mechanism and frequently provide note takers, study skills programs, tutoring, extra time on exams, and writing labs, to name just a few. Access to special services requires current documentation of the disability (usually within last 3 years); in some cases, universities may have an assessment center for diagnosing attentional and learning problems in students.

Unfortunately, there are no studies presently available that have systematically investigated strategies and techniques for helping college students with ADHD. Consequently, the following suggestions are offered as promising practices that need further study to determine efficacy. Also, more research is needed to answer the following questions: Which factors are related to academic success for adults with ADHD? How do comorbid learning disabilities or psychiatric disorders affect overall academic success? How does strategy and study skills instruction affect college performance?

Techniques for how to manage time, how to study, and how to plan and organize are frequently recommended (Nadeau, 1995; Richard, 1995). Table 9.2 summarizes self-help and other strategies that may be useful for both college and work settings.

It is important for the college student to utilize these strategies beginning the first semester. It is not uncommon for students to wait until they are in academic trouble and are failing or falling behind in one or two courses before they seek assistance or before they begin to significantly alter their study skills and manage their time. Students often seek assistance from our assessment and special services center at the University of Wisconsin–Milwaukee after they fail midterms and have lengthy term papers due. Early self-advocacy is important because it is so easy to get lost in the first month of classes. Some entering freshmen are shocked when they realize that college is different from high school and that college requires enormous amounts of self-discipline and self-directed study. So it is not difficult to imagine the extra burden that ADHD brings to this transition period—a time when the academic rules change overnight, independence and self-sufficiency are highly regarded, and competition and expectations can be intense. In my experience, successful college students with ADHD typically are identified early (many prior to college), have developed a set of study strategies, work closely with faculty and/or academic advisors, receive psychological or emotional support from parents and/or therapists, have a tenacious approach to meeting challenges, and have a support group of friends.

TABLE 9.2. Strategies for Success in College

Difficulties	Strategies
Self-advocacy	Request accommodations from college instructors; discuss nature of learning, attentional problems; seek out support services through disabled-student services (e.g., taping services, books on tape, lecture notes prior to class); request alternate test format (e.g., oral vs. written, access to computer for test taking).
Study skills	Plan for longer study time; find a quiet space that is used for studying only (a quiet corner in the library away from all the hustle and bustle); develop a regular routine; when reading or studying use tape recorder to identify important concepts to remember; take frequent breaks; keep up with work and do not wait until the last minute to study; allow extra time for writing assignments and get editing and rewriting tips from writing lab; use available tutors whenever necessary; develop memory techniques (highlighting or color coding important information, write lists and study, then test self on information studied; make up practice essay questions and write for an hour; use active study techniques when reading from text (e.g., read headings before reading chapter, skim chapter to see what comes next, take notes while reading, make up questions using chapter headings, practice answering these questions, recite answers aloud, review major points); use a laptop computer when taking class notes; develop a relationship with each professor and discuss needs with them.
Organizational skills	Keep desk relatively clear of mess; use folders/binders to organize class notes and study notes; leave margins when taking notes to add information from the text; keep track of books and other supplies; check supplies on weekly or bimonthly basis to avoid running out; get books and articles from library before you sit down to write; clear/straighten your desk at the end of every day
Time management skills	Start each day with a list of what needs to be done and prioritize your goals; do not procrastinate, finish daily "to do" list; do not overbook or overschedule; allow extra time for assignments, for reading, and for studying; use breaks between classes to organize and check notes; see professor immediately if anything was missed; take a break between classes, get a snack, walk around in the fresh air, sit and relax for a moment; space studying throughout the day (1-hour sessions) rather than having to spend 3–4 hours in the evening; organize day with some time for breaks, rest, exercise, and social time; do not neglect eating.

(continued)

TABLE 9.2. cont.

Difficulties	Strategies
Planning skills	Use a daily planner to write down all important tasks/activities for the day; stick to the plan and avoid temptations of distracting activities; be realistic about how long things will take and block off study time, lab work, library research, and writing time in the daily planner (block of 2- to 3-hour periods); build in a little extra room (15 minutes) in case things take longer than planned; try to schedule classes carefully (e.g., allow for enough time to get from one part of campus to another; alternate between harder/easier or challenging/less challenging courses; spread class load over 2-3 days (e.g., Mondays, Wednesdays, Friday mornings are heavy, but Tuesdays and Thursdays are lighter) to allow for study and writing time; plan big papers well in advance; meet with your professor to discuss a topic; do a little library research before you make a commitment; make headings/subheadings for paper (outlines serve as a good organizer); plan time for editing, rewriting, and reorganizing; use initial drafts to see what has and has not been covered; use the writing lab for editing and final revisions; make a list of all the components of a task and build these into the daily plan.
Procrastination	Stick to the daily plan; do the things that were put off from the day before; tackle tough assignments early; pick interesting paper assignments to avoid boredom; evaluate choice of major and seek help from advisor or the career center; learn what is motivating to oneself; work before playing; use lots of little rewards throughout the day (coke breaks, snacks, telephone call, visiting a friend); time breaks to avoid letting a 10–15 minute break turn into 30–45 minutes; avoid the TV when studying (use this as a reward for finishing) or plan study time around a TV break, and then get back to the books; give bigger rewards for getting a paper done (weekend away from campus, game away from home, or visiting a girl/boyfriend at a nearby campus).

Note. Information summarized from Nadeau (1975). See Nadeau (1995) for other helpful strategies.

Career and Workplace Adjustments

The wonderful thing about adulthood is the freedom to choose a life style that fits individual talents and to find a work situation that fits one's neurocognitive, psychosocial, and behavioral styles. Adulthood offers more choices and more opportunities to maximize strengths and to minimize weaknesses. Career and work opportunities can be selected to better "fit" a cognitive or personality style that is creative, chaotic, and/or frenetic. On the other hand, the consequences of failure during this stage can have a dramatic impact on self-esteem and adult adjustment (e.g., chronic unemployment or underemployment). As such, the workplace can provide more opportunities for adults with ADHD to match their abilities with a sympathetic or complementary career, or it can be as much a mismatch as some academic settings.

Although job match is important, there are a number of strategies that adults can utilize to solve problems in the workplace. See Nadeau (1995) and Latham and Latham (1995) for a more detailed discussion of strategies and accommodations for the workplace.

A number of psychosocial and behavioral issues may interfere with work adjustment, and Nadeau (1995) describes strategies for the workplace that may be helpful. For example, to reduce excessive activity levels, adults may find a job that allows a lot of movement. Take frequent breaks from a desk job (e.g., get a drink of water every 20–30 minutes), and exercise or take a walk at lunchtime and after work. When considering a job change, the adult with ADHD should look for work that involves contact with other people, allows walking or moving around, or includes travel from job site to job site and should avoid jobs that require long periods of sedentary activities or detailed deskwork (Nadeau, 1995).

Strategies for distractibility may include setting up "no interruption" periods (except for emergencies) throughout the day; explaining the need not to be interrupted to supervisors and office peers; and scheduling intensive work during time-specified periods. Individuals who find internal thoughts and daydreams continuing to disrupt their productivity may need to consider changing careers. People with ADHD can use a notebook to write down flow of ideas or rapid thoughts about a project or to make notes of ideas to be discussed in a meeting to prevent rapid or uncontrolled thoughts from interfering. They can also make an effort to keep workspaces uncluttered and organized (Nadeau, 1995). To help in planning and organization, individuals with ADHD should take time each morning to list and prioritize daily projects, appointments, and "must get done today" lists. If possible, they should work on projects with someone who is organized. Time-management suggestions include using a daily schedule, avoiding overscheduling, breaking big projects into concrete, time-specified pieces, and learning how to say "no."

Difficulties getting along with colleagues and supervisors in the workplace are often overlooked. To reduce interpersonal problems caused by stubbornness, argumentativeness, or hot-temperedness, an individual with ADHD can learn to become more aware of social cues; to use active listening skills to pay attention to conversations (e.g., listening to and understanding what is being said rather than thinking about one's own next comment); to avoid interpersonal confrontations by paying more attention to internal moods and by developing better early warning signs; or to try to find a job that allows for autonomy and freedom (Nadeau, 1995). If these problems persist or are very destructive to work adjustment, individual therapy may be necessary to develop better self-control and problem solving strategies.

One strategy for difficulties in prioritizing is to use an A-B-C paradigm, in which A stands for things that "have to be done today," B is for things one "would like to get done today," and C is for things that one "will do today if all As and Bs are completed" (Nadeau, 1995, p. 331).

Many of the strategies discussed for adults with ADHD are similar to those suggested for adolescents and younger children. That is, whenever possible, modify the task requirements to fit the characteristics of ADHD; develop and use coping strategies to increase success in the workplace; and when necessary seek professional help for more serious adjustment problems.

Psychotherapy as a Means of Managing ADHD

Adults with ADHD may require therapy to learn to cope with their disorder. Adults who were not identified as ADHD in childhood or adolescence may have years of failure, lack of confidence, interpersonal conflicts, and chronic adjustment problems that rob them of their self-esteem. This chronic pattern of failure and of not living up to one's potential may also increase the probability of acquiring other substance abuse or psychiatric problems. When other comorbid disorders are present, they should also be specifically addressed in therapy. There are a number of therapy options for adults with ADHD, including individual or couple/family therapy.

Individual Therapy

There are few studies to date that have investigated the efficacy of individual psychotherapy for adults with ADHD. Despite the lack of research in this area, a number of experts in adult ADHD explicate some conditions under which psychotherapy may be warranted and discuss potential therapy goals (Hallowell, 1995; Wender, 1995).

Adults with ADHD may have already been in psychotherapy or counseling, although Wender declares that for clients seen in his clinic, "by and large it did not help" (1995, p. 190). Wender (1995) does concede that it is likely that those individuals who had success in therapy would not contact his clinic. Nonetheless, many adults seeking help for ADHD may have had a trial with nonstimulant medication but have experienced few successes in their attempts to cope with the disorder. Adults seeking therapy may have more serious problems, such as characteristics of antisocial personality disorder; a parent with ADHD or antisocial personality disorder; a history of alcoholism that increases the likelihood of uncontrolled behaviors; or an alcoholic parent and a history of family dysfunction. Furthermore, Wender (1995) found that 45% of his ADHD patients in a long-term medication study report a history of child abuse and are even more likely to have a history of being criticized by parents and teachers because of their attentional problems, poor work habits, and academic failures. "We are beginning to document that such early childhood traumas may produce lifelong distortions in personality" (Wender, 1995, p. 191).

Wender (1995) describes therapy with adults with ADHD as a process whereby the adult begins to learn about the biological nature of ADHD. Although medication may be sufficient to help some adults to gain a sense of psychological well-being so that they can learn problem-solving strategies, others need assistance in dealing with the consequences of their ADHD symptoms (e.g., difficult relationships with spouse and children). In these cases, therapy may be appropriate, and strategies to improve relationships may be the focus.

Hallowell (1995) recommends that treatment for adults with ADHD should have five basic components: diagnosis, education, structure, psychotherapy, and medication. Hallowell introduces the concept of "therapist as coach" and discusses the need to see the human, emotional aspects as well as the neurobiological problems of people with the disorder. The analogy Hallowell uses suggests that

> the coach keeps the player focused on the tasks at hand and offers encouragement along the way . . . the therapist/coach can help the patient from reverting to old bad habits: habits of procrastination, disorganization, and negative thinking, the latter being the most damaging and pernicious. Treatment begins with hope, with a jump start of the heart. (p. 148)

In essence, Hallowell proposes a form of therapy with ADHD adults that is often more direct than for other adult disorders.

Hallowell (1995) suggests that the therapist ask questions using the initials H-O-P-E. The therapist finds out what kind of HELP the client needs. The therapist then seeks to find out what OBLIGATIONS the adult has in his/her life and what plans the person has to deal with them. The therapist inquires about the client's PLANS or goals. These goals and plans help the person focus and move ahead. Finally, ENCOURAGEMENT is a major part of the therapy in which the "therapist as coach" actively encourages and affirms the client. Hallowell (1995) advocates for interpersonal systems-oriented therapy rather than interpretative therapy. Structure is an important feature of each session, and the therapist keeps the client focused when they get off track. The form of therapy Hallowell suggests differs from insight therapy in which free associations and elaborations are welcomed. Unfocused thoughts impede the progress of adults with ADHD and may reflect inner distractions and difficulty following through with plans.

Group therapy may also be helpful for some adults with ADHD according to Hallowell (1995). Support, empathy, and problem solving can be productive in a group setting. Adults actively practice listening skills and often develop strong group cohesion. Active problem solving and crisis intervention is often the focus of groups.

Family and Couple Therapy

In her discussion on the impact of ADHD on the family, Dixon (1995) offers a number of tips for household management and parenting. The day-to-day workings of the family generally are important issues that must be addressed in family and/or couple therapy. Teaching communication skills and providing a means for working through tense and conflictual issues within the confines of therapy can be helpful. Kelly and Ramundo (1993) suggest that family communication rules are an important feature of the process and recommend the following strategies for family management: avoid screaming or yelling; avoid trying to communicate when engaged in other activities; make plans a week ahead of time to reduce arguments; establish family rituals, and change rules when appropriate. Dixon (1995) suggests that family rules may be difficult for adults with ADHD but that the structure can be helpful.

Adults with ADHD often enter marriages with chronic low self-esteem and other personal problems (e.g., inadequate interpersonal skills, emotional lability and sensitivity, etc.) in conjunction with the primary characteristics of ADHD (Dixon, 1995). Couple therapy frequently focuses on identifying and recognizing how ADHD is affecting the relationship. The therapist helps partners understand how they each contribute to communication and problem-solving difficulties in their relationship.

Although unique issues exist when both adults have ADHD, some therapists suggest that there are positive benefits that can be capitalized on in therapy, including expressing sympathy and understanding, setting reasonable expectations, and forgiving the spouse for his/her problems (Nadeau, 1991). On the other hand, issues of codependency and spousal burnout may present as major problems for marriages when only one partner has ADHD. Weiss (1992) describes techniques for reducing codependency in "mixed" couples whereby the dynamics of codependency are discussed and more effective communication styles are encouraged. Nadeau (1993) also emphasizes the need to address the high levels of stress in these marriages. In her review, Dixon (1995) points out the necessity of focusing on the anger, resentment, unhappiness, and unmet needs of the spouse without ADHD and helping him/her to understand his/her role in the marital imbalance (e.g., assuming too much responsibility). Issues of denial in the spouse with ADHD may also need to be addressed. Other therapy techniques emphasize the need for verbal communication, defining marital responsibilities and roles, and establishing appropriate boundaries (Hallowell, 1993).

To date, there is no research on the efficacy of couple therapy; however, accurate diagnosis of adulthood ADHD is probably necessary in order for couple therapy to have a chance for success. Clinical case studies do show that adults with undiagnosed ADHD often have a history of unsuccessful marital therapy (Weiss & Hechtman, 1993).

Support Groups for Adults with ADHD

In recent years, there has been an increased interest in support groups for adults with ADHD. Local CH.A.D.D. chapters provide an avenue for organizing support groups. These groups can serve as an informal means to gather information about community resources (e.g., ADHD experts, psychiatrists, and psychologists), facts about ADHD, strategies for coping with ADHD, and support for dealing with the frustrations and failures that often accompany the disorder in adulthood. Support group meetings can be motivating and can serve as a network for obtaining current information, resources, and advocacy strategies. A level of support and genuine empathy are essential to the process of self-education and management of ADHD in adulthood.

Psychopharmacology for Adults with ADHD

A review of medication options was reserved for the last section of this chapter in hopes of encouraging psychologists, psychiatrists, and adults with ADHD to consider other adjunctive treatments before deciding on medication. In cases in which the symptoms of ADHD have a severe negative impact on adult adjustment, then medication may be a first step.

The use of medication to treat adults with ADHD is not as well documented as it is with children, and the efficacy results appear more variable. This section reviews various medication options, including studies reporting the long-term effects of medication. Characteristics of adults who appear nonresponsive to medications are also discussed, particularly in light of treatment implications.

Effects of Stimulants on Adults with ADHD

In his review of medication, Wender (1995) reported that stimulants were first administered to adults with ADHD-like symptoms in 1947, and some decrease in symptoms (i.e., aggressiveness, temper control problems, low frustration tolerance, impulsivity, and irritability) was reported. Stimulants were virtually forgotten from 1947 until the 1970s, when the use of dextroamphetamines was reported in clinical case studies.

Stimulants that have been used to treat ADHD include methylphenidate (Ritalin), dextroamphetamine (Dexedrine), and magnesium pemoline (Cylert). Stimulant medications are known to alter the reuptake of dopamine and norepinephrine at the presynapse, an action that has been shown to produce positive effects on ADHD symptoms (Comings, 1990; Copeland & Copps, 1995; Wender, 1995; Wilens, Spencer, & Biederman, 1995). Although all stimulants appear to reduce ADHD symptoms, each may have a different mode of action. Specifically, Ritalin and Dexedrine have similar affects on dopamine, but they appear to differentially affect norepinephrine (Elia et al., 1990). A more in-depth discussion of the various neurotransmitter systems involved in ADHD was presented in Chapter 2. See Table 2.2 for a review of the neurotransmitter circuitry and Table 2.4 for the proposed effects of various medications on these neurotransmitters.

In a review of the six studies that have systematically investigated stimulant medication efficacy, Wilens, Spencer, and Biederman (1995) reported that adults have a variable response to stimulants. In doubleblind placebo studies, between 25% and 78% of adults under study showed positive response rates to medication. Only two studies showed positive effects that approach those for children (73% and 78% response rate), and the remaining studies reported only mild to moderate effects. Although both Ritalin and Cylert have shown these variable results, there have been no controlled studies investigating the use of Dexedrine in adults with ADHD.

In efficacy studies, stimulants appear to produce the following results: decreased hyperactivity (fidgeting and restlessness); improved concentration and attentiveness; improved mood states, with fewer highs and lows, increased initiative, motivation, and interest and less demoralization; fewer anger outbursts, greater control over temper, and increased ability to verbally express angry feelings rather than acting on them; increased organization; a feeling of being less "hassled"; increased planning skills; a decrease in interruptions and better listening skills and improved communication (Wender, 1995). In many cases, adults reported better interpersonal relationships because they had fewer mood swings and more control over temper and were better listeners. These changes affect both work and interpersonal relationships.

Dose-dependent responses (modest response on 0.05 mg/kg with robust results on 1.0 mg/kg) were similar to those found in children, with improvements in cognitive, behavioral, and academic domains occurring in a stepwise fashion as dosages increased (Wilens, Spencer, & Biederman, 1995). Given the small number of available studies, dosage guidelines remain highly individualized. It is important to note the following: (1) side effects were considered mild in nature (e.g., insomnia, edginess, appetite suppression, altered mood, headaches); (2) there were no cases of medication-induced psychosis; and (3) there were no reports of medication abuse despite the addictive potential of stimulants (Wilens, Spencer, & Biederman, 1995). Wender (1995) also notes that euphoria does not occur when stimulants are taken orally at prescribed dosage levels but may occur in large dosages or when taken intravenously or snorted. Cylert does not appear to have the same potential for abuse as the other two stimulants.

Controlling for Potential Stimulant Abuse. The potential abuse of Ritalin and Dexedrine and the recreational use and abuse of these medications create a dilemma for prescribing physicians (Wender, 1995). These concerns may be further exaggerated in a population in which conduct and antisocial personality disorders are relatively high; these individuals appear most at risk for abuse. Wender (1995) also acknowledges that physicians with large numbers of clients on Schedule II (controlled substances, e.g., stimulants) drugs may be investigated by state licensing boards. These factors weigh into the decision of whether or not to medicate adults.

For the most part, when medicating adults, physicians consider the adult's level of responsibility and the absence of a history of alcohol or drug abuse or a period in which the adult is drug and alcohol-free (Wender, 1995; Wilens, Spencer, & Biederman, 1995). Copeland and Copps (1995) also caution physicians to be aware of " 'doctor-shopping' by parents to obtain more Ritalin presumably for themselves" (p. 171). In cases in which potential for abuse is high, Wender (1995) recommends using pemoline or MAOIs and bupropion. At any rate, careful monitoring by the physician is imperative when prescribing stimulants.

Adults may also find it difficult to find physicians who are willing to consider prescribing stimulant medication for ADHD. These adults may be advised to seek assistance from one of the major research or medical facilities across the country who specialize in adult ADHD issues. These centers offer diagnosis and treatment and may help locate knowledgeable physicians locally. The issue of medical insurance may also be a problem for many people in health maintenance organizations or other managed-health programs. Adults, and children for that matter, with complex problems may have trouble getting appropriate insurance coverage, particularly when long-term treatment is required. This can create a lot of stress and frustration for the person seeking professional assistance. Physicians also report that clients with ADHD can be a financial drain on a medical practice, and, in a few cases, some physicians have been asked to leave practices where the amount of billable hours are tightly controlled.

Adult Outcome after Long-Term Stimulant Use in Childhood. Weiss and Hechtman (1993) conducted one of the few studies that looked at outcome for adults who began long-term medication stimulant use in childhood. Adults who had been medicated for 3 to 5 years as children were compared to a group of adults with ADHD who did not receive medication in childhood and to a control group. In an extensive investigation across a variety of areas, the medicated group did show significant differences compared to the other two groups. Compared to nonmedicated hyperactive individuals, hyperactives who had received medication had fewer car accidents, more positive attitudes about their childhoods, fewer instances of stealing in childhood, better social skills, and higher self-esteem. Aggression levels were lower in the medicated group, and they required less psychiatric care. "Stimulant treatment in childhood may not eliminate educational, work and life difficulties, but it may result in less social ostracism, with subsequent better feeling towards others and themselves" (Weiss & Hechtman, 1993, p. 255).

It is also important to note that the three groups did not differ on physiological measures (e.g., blood pressure, pulse, height, and weight); serious psychopathology; antisocial behavior; and adult alcohol use (Weiss & Hechtman, 1993). Medicated hyperactives did have a history of more marijuana and cocaine use than the control group, and non-medicated hyperactives had more heroin use. The number of medicated hyperactives who currently and in the past used drugs and alcohol was not judged to be significant in the overall usage patterns.

Klein and Mannuzza (1988) also found that young adults treated with stimulants did not show growth suppression over time. There were no differences in height between the medicated group and the general population. In cases in which there was some initial slow growth in childhood, a growth rebound occurred once medication was stopped.

Second-Line Medications

The antidepressants (e.g., tricyclic antidepressants [TCAs], Prozac, and monoamine oxidase inhibitors [MAOIs]) are considered to be the most effective second-line treatment for ADHD when stimulants are not effective or when they are counterindicated (Copeland & Copps, 1995).

TCAs affect the action and availability of dopamine and norepinephrine, whereas Prozac and MAOIs affect the activity of serotonin.

Although the efficacy of TCAs has been investigated in children and adolescents, there have been no prospective, controlled studies in adults (Wilens, Spencer, & Biederman, 1995). In their clinical use of TCAs, Wilens, Biederman, Mick, and Spencer (1995) found that a majority (68%) of adults with hyperactivity have a good response to desipramine and nortriptyline, with more than half (52%) showing marked improvement.

Other stimulant-like antidepressants (such as bupropion [Wellbutrin]) have been shown effective (Wender, 1995; Wender & Reimherr, 1990). Bupropion has been found to be helpful for adults with ADHD who also have mood instability or cardiac abnormalities (see Wilens, Biederman, Mick, Spencer, et al., 1995 for a review). Wender and Reimherr (1990) did find that 71% of adults showed moderate to marked improvement and that bupropion was better for controlling affective lability including depression, when compared to stimulants. However, stimulants were better for control of hyperactivity, overreactivity, disorganization, and impulsivity—the classic features of ADHD. Wender (1995) also recommends bupropion over other antidepressants (selective serotonin reuptake inhibitors such as fluoxetine [Prozac]) for ADHD adults who experience chronic major depression.

The MAOIs (i.e., pargyline and deprenyl—not available in the United States) may have some utility for adults with comorbid depression and/or anxiety, according to Wilens, Spencer, and Biederman (1995). Compliance may be a problem due to dietary restrictions (low tyramine diets), and medication- or diet-induced hypertension may also be a problem when using MAOIs. Other side effects, including weight gain, lethargy or agitation, hypotension, sexual dysfunction, and sleep disturbance may interfere with compliance issues and are often very unpleasant for the patient.

Adults Who Appear Resistant to Medications

There are a number of adults who do not respond favorably to medications. In these cases, careful study of the individual symptoms and a new course of action should be considered. Wilens, Spencer, and Biederman (1995) provide excellent detailed outlines for addressing various changes in medication. For example, for adults whose symptoms worsen on medication, the clinician may consider the following: increasing the dose of medication, changing the time medication is taken, using another stimulant, using multidrug treatment for other symptoms (e.g., depression), or adding conjunctive therapy (e.g., cognitive-behavioral). Other suggestions include discontinuing stimulants, adding another dosage of medication, or evaluating for comorbid disorders when symptoms such as psychosis, depression, or dysphoria or rebound effects emerge.

Medication appears to have a positive effect on many adults with ADHD. However, careful monitoring and adjunctive therapy is often recommended. Stimulants are still the first-order medications for ADHD in adulthood, and comorbid disorders may also require multidrug treatment. The physician and client need to work closely together to make these important determinations and to evaluate the efficacy of medication and other treatments that are being used.

SUMMARY

It is important for clinicians working with adults who have significant problems with self-esteem, interpersonal conflicts, underemployment or chronic job adjustment difficulties, and other psychological disorders (e.g., substance abuse; antisocial traits) to explore the potential for undiagnosed ADHD. Although the efficacy of adult interventions has not been systematically investigated, clinical case studies suggest that these and other interventions have promise.

1. The first step for effective interventions is an accurate diagnosis of ADHD. Look for a history of academic, psychosocial, and interpersonal problems and previous unsuccessful therapy attempts in childhood. For those adults who have been diagnosed with ADHD in childhood, continued treatment may be necessary.
2. To increase success in college, teach time management, organizational and planning skills, self-advocacy, and coping and problem-solving skills.
3. Increase work adjustment by providing accommodations such as allowing frequent breaks, increasing movement or exercise after long work periods, and setting up "no interruption" periods for intensive work. It is important to find a job with requirements that fit ADHD symptoms.
4. To improve psychosocial adjustment, consider individual, family, and/or couple therapy.
5. To reduce ADHD symptoms, consider stimulant medication in cases in which hyperactivity, inattention, or impulsivity significantly interfere with work and/or psychosocial adjustment.

10

Future Research Trends

*T*here are a number of fronts in which research will undoubtedly advance our understanding and treatment of ADHD in the coming years. Researchers will continue to investigate the biogenetic basis of the disorder, the subtle brain anomalies associated with the disorder (using neuroimaging techniques), and the effectiveness of multimodal treatment paradigms. The degree to which research informs assessment and treatment planning is critical for establishing and implementing scientifically based approaches for ADHD. Finally, causal models of ADHD need to be investigated to get a better understanding of how biogenetic vulnerabilities affect brain function and subsequent adjustment across a variety of domains and how moderator variables reduce the negative impact of these vulnerabilities.

BIOGENETIC STUDIES

Genetic research provides evidence that ADHD is a biogenetic disorder that occurs in families. Further refinement in genetic research protocols may help to isolate which traits or behaviors (e.g., disinhibition) are passed from parent to child and to determine how various traits are manifested across generations.

The search for genetic markers is ongoing, and particular attention is being paid to dopamine receptor genes. Although most researchers believe that ADHD is not likely caused by a single gene but most likely occurs because of the interaction of multiple genes in some predictable patterns, the dopamine receptor genes offer a promising area for investigation. The dopamine receptor site seems promising because medications that influence the action of dopamine at the neurotransmitter site are particularly effective for the treatment of ADHD symptoms (i.e., methylphenidate, dextroamphetamine, pemoline, and bupropion). Although various medications affect dopamine differentially (e.g., blocking reuptake at the presynapse or facilitating the reuptake of dopamine in the presynapse), they all seem to produce positive behavioral changes.

Further genetic investigations may help us to identify dopamine receptor transport actions that can then be used to refine classification of children on the basis of etiology (i.e., family history of ADHD); increase our understanding of medication efficacy and other potential biological interventions; and increase our understanding of gene–environment interactions (Cook & Stein, 1996). Although genetic research may ultimately help in the diagnosis and treatment of ADHD, there are still limitations on the information that is gathered from this line of inquiry. Even if we can identify a genetic predisposition, we cannot predict with certainty whether a child will have ADHD, nor can we know how the disorder will be manifested. However, biogenetic research may be helpful in identifying children who are at risk because of familial ADHD so that preventive treatments (e.g., parent training and classroom management) can be implemented early in the child's life to reduce the negative impact of difficult, challenging behaviors. Early parent support and training may also help the child and family to adapt and to learn compensatory and coping skills before secondary self-esteem and conduct-related disorders emerge.

NEUROIMAGING STUDIES

Neuroscience research has experienced phenomenal advances in recent years. New technologies such as magnetic resonance imaging (MRI) and functional magnetic resonance imaging (fMRI) allow for more direct measures of brain structure and activity that at one time were indirectly inferred from neuropsychological measures. Research findings are in many ways confirming some of the neuropsychological and cognitive theories of ADHD, but they also show that the complexity of the brain–behavior relationship is such that different models for explaining impulsivity, hyperactivity, and attentional deficits are called for. The prefrontal lobes are emerging as major structural features of ADHD that, when underactivated appear associated with disinhibition, poor impulse control, and impaired planning and execution of complex behavioral sequences.

Although the prefrontal lobes appear to be a critical site for investigation, a feedback loop between the basal ganglia and the prefrontal cortex is also of great interest to neuroscientists. At a functional level, the basal ganglia appear to play a role in context recognition; that is, the ability to determine when to do something, when to delay, and how to interpret information based on the context. Subtle structural differences have been found in the basal ganglia–prefrontal loop in children with ADHD: (1) the frontal lobes appear smaller; (2) asymmetry of the basal ganglia appears less frequently (normally right is larger than left); and (3) the total volume of the basal ganglia, the caudate nucleus, and the globus pallidus, which are all part of the basal ganglia–frontal feedback loop, is smaller (Rapoport, 1996).

Neuroimaging research may also show how other frontal lobe connections to the basal ganglia, limbic system, thalamus, and other posterior regions are associated with ADHD and other childhood psychopathologies (Pennington & Ozonoff, 1996). It may be that different developmental disorders (e.g., autism and ADHD) are caused by (neurochemical, metabolic, or structural changes or disturbances) in various parts of the prefrontal cortex or its interrelated systems.

Neuroimaging research has found other isolated anomalies in individuals with ADHD, including differences in the cerebellar region. Although the cerebellum has long been know to play a role in the execution of highly routinized and complex motor sequences (Teeter & Semrud-Clikeman, 1997), the cerebellum also seems to be involved in aspects of cognition and intentionality. The extent to which cerebellar activity will add to our understanding of ADHD may or may not prove great, but it warrants further investigation, particularly as this line of research may help us to understand the heterogeneity of the disorder. The cerebellum does have connections to the prefrontal–basal ganglia loop, and it may be helpful to identify whether abnormal structures or functions along this feedback loop are related to various subtypes or behavioral patterns and whether different structural anomalies respond differentially to various treatments (e.g., medications, self-instruction, etc.).

Whereas MRI scans measure structural brain differences, fMRI technology provides a direct way of measuring brain activity while an individual is engaged in a cognitive task. This technology is more favorable than positron emission tomography (PET) scans because it does not require the use of radioactive isotopes. As studies begin to utilize fMRI scans with children and adults with ADHD, we may develop stronger models for understanding how various brain areas are involved in the control, planning, and execution of complex behaviors (e.g., inhibition, attentional control, memory skills, and other learning-related abilities). It may be possible to develop better models for understanding the mechanisms underlying ADHD alone, as well as ADHD with other psychiatric disorders (e.g., depression, obsessive compulsive disorders), with language and learning disorders, and with other low-incidence problems (e.g., Tourette's disorder). Finally, models of right hemisphere frontal–striatal dysfunction advanced by Heilman, Voeller, and Nadeau (1991) and models of executive control dysfunction advanced by Barkley (1996a, 1997b), Pennington and Ozonoff (1996), and Teeter and Semrud (1995, 1997) can also be more directly investigated.

In summary, neuroimaging research may eventually shed light on meaningful subtypes of ADHD and may help us better understand the neurodevelopmental course of ADHD. These will be important scientific discoveries that may eventually aid in assessing and planning treatment for children, adolescents, and adults with ADHD. This is a very exciting time for neuroscientists, as technology is providing a means to study subtle brain anomalies, as well as structural and functional differences in the brains of individuals with ADHD.

CAUSAL MODELS OF ADHD

Several causal models can be tested to determine the interaction of brain function and behavior. Barkley (1996a, 1997b) articulates a frontal, executive control model, whereas Teeter and Semrud-Clikeman (1995, 1997) describe a transactional, neurodevelopmental model for ADHD. Each of these models provides a theoretical perspective that can be empirically tested. Research in the future needs to be theory-driven, particularly when theories incorporate the current research base as a starting point. These models can then be used to determine which factors are causal, and thus explanatory, and which are not. We are at a position in our search to understand and treat ADHD at which these neurocognitive models can move us into a more integrated, comprehensive view of the interaction of brain function and human behavior, and to better understand the effects on cognitive, perceptual, attentional, memory, or psychosocial functioning.

MULTIMODAL TREATMENT STUDIES

At present, the National Institute of Mental Health has funded a collaborative multisite, multimodal treatment study of children with ADHD. Six sites are conducting a 5-year study to determine under what circumstances (comorbid conditions, age, gender, family background) do which treatment combinations (medication, behavior therapy, parent training, school-based interventions) have what impacts (improvement, stasis, deterioration) on what domains of child functioning (cognitive, academic, behavioral, physical, peer relations, family relations), for how long (short- versus long-term), to what extent (effect sizes, normal versus pathological range), and why (processes underlying change). (Richters et al., 1995, p. 996)

The results of this multisite investigation should shed light on the additive effects of medication with psychosocial interventions and interactions among treatment options and may help to refine decision-making rules concerning who should receive what kind of intervention.

The extent to which protective and/or resiliency factors come into play are also of importance. As scientists further address treatment approaches, the extent to which moderator variables (e.g., cognitive abilities, family adjustment, access to health and mental health treatment, and educational accommodations) protect children with ADHD can be more systematically investigated. The degree to which clinicians, educators, and parents can have a positive effect by altering or influencing these factors deserves further study. In effect, this book has argued for multimodal treatment approaches to reduce the negative impact of this biogenetically based disorder.

In essence, "ADHD is not an excuse, it is an explanation" (Stewart, 1997, personal communication). It is an explanation that should guide educators, psychologists, physicians, parents, and the individual with ADHD to seek ways to modify the environment and to increase coping strategies for better adjustment. Biogenetic vulnerability does not necessarily lead to psychopathology or major adjustment disorders. It is a sign that, when handled properly, biogenetic vulnerabilities or various risk factors can presage the need for early intervention, appropriate parent training, classroom management and accommodations, and medication, depending on the individual and his/her sociocultural and environmental context.

References

Abikoff, H. (1985). Efficacy of cognitive training intervention in hyperactive children: A critical review. *Clinical Psychology Review, 5,* 479–512.

Abikoff, H. (1987). An evaluation of cognitive behavioral therapy for hyperactive children. In B. Lahey & A. Kazdin (Eds.), *Advances in clinical child psychology* (Vol. 10, pp. 171–216). New York: Plenum Press.

Abikoff, H. (1991). Cognitive training in ADHD children: Less to it than meets the eye. *Journal of Learning Disabilities, 24,* 205–209.

Abikoff, H., Ganeles, D., Reiter, G., Blum, C., Foley, C., & Klein, R. G. (1988). Cognitive training in academically deficient ADHD boys receiving stimulant medication. *Journal of Abnormal Child Psychology, 16,* 411–432.

Abikoff, H., & Gittelman, R. (1984). Does behavior therapy normalize the classroom behavior of hyperactive children? *Archives of General Psychiatry, 41,* 449–454.

Abikoff, H., & Gittelman, R. (1985). Hyperactive children treated with stimulants: Is cognitive training a useful adjunct? *Archives of General Psychiatry, 42,* 953–961.

Abramowitz, A. J., & O'Leary, S. G. (1991). Behavioral interventions for the classroom: Implications for students with ADHD. *School Psychology Review, 20,* 220–234.

Abramowitz, A. J., O'Leary, S. G., & Futtersak, M. W. (1988). The relative impact of short reprimands on children's off-task behavior in the classroom. *Behavior Therapy, 19,* 243–247.

Abramowitz, A. J., O'Leary, S. G., & Rosen, L. A. (1987). Reducing off-task behavior in the classroom: A comparison of encouragement and reprimands. *Journal of Abnormal Child Psychology, 15,* 153–163.

Achenbach, T. M., & Edelbrock, C. S. (1983). *Manual for the Child Behavior Checklist and Revised Child Behavior Profile.* Burlington: University of Vermont, Department of Psychiatry.

Ainsworth, M. D. S. (1979). Infant–mother attachment. *American Psychologist, 34,* 932–937.

Ainsworth, M. D. S., & Bell, S. (1974). Mother–infant interaction and the development of competence. In K. Connolly & J. Bruner (Eds.), *The growth of competency.* New York: Academic Press.

Alberts-Corush, J., Firestone, P., & Goodman, J. T. (1986). Attention and impulsivity characteristics of biological and adoptive parents of hyperactive and normal control children. *American Journal of Orthopsychiatry, 56,* 413–423.

Alexander-Roberts, C. (1995). *A parent's guide to making it through the tough years: ADHD and teens: Proven techniques for handling emotional, academic, and behavioral problems.* Dallas: Taylor.

Alesandri, S. M. (1992). Attention, play, and social behavior in ADHD preschoolers. *Journal of Abnormal Child Psychology, 20,* 289–302.

Alesandri, S. M., & Schramm, K. (1991). Effects of dextroamphetamine on the cognitive and social play of a preschooler with ADHD. *Journal of the American Academy of Child and Adolescent Psychiatry, 30,* 768–772.

Allyon, T., Layman, D., & Kandel, H. J. (1975). A behavioral-educational alternative to drug control of hyperactive children. *Journal of Applied Behavior Analysis, 8,* 137–146.

Allyon, T., & Roberts, M. D. (1974). Eliminating discipline problems by strengthening academic performance. *Journal of Applied Behavior Analysis, 7,* 71–76.

Allyon, T., & Rosenbaum, M. (1977). The behavioral treatment disruption and hyperactivity in school settings. In B. Lahey & A. Kazdin (Eds.), *Advances in clinical and child psychology* (Vol. 1, pp. 83–118). New York: Plenum Press.

Alvarez, W. F. (1985). The meaning of maternal employment for mothers and their perceptions of their three-year-old children. *Child Development, 56,* 350–360.

Amen, D. G., Paldi, J. H., & Thisted, R. A. (1993). Brain SPECT imaging. *Journal of the American Academy of Child and Adolescent Psychiatry, 32,* 1080–1081.

American Psychiatric Association. (1987). *Diagnostic and statistical manual of mental disorders* (3rd ed., rev.). Washington, DC: Author.

American Psychiatric Association. (1994). *Diagnostic and statistical manual of mental disorders* (4th ed.). Washington, DC: Author.

Anastopoulos, A., & Barkley, R. A. (1990). Counseling and training parents. In R. Barkley, *Attention-deficit hyperactivity disorder: A handbook for diagnosis and treatment* (pp. 397–431). New York: Guilford Press.

Anastopoulos, A. D., Spisto, M. A., & Maher, M. C. (1994). The WISC-III Freedom from Distractibility factor: Its utility in identifying children with attention deficit hyperactivity disorder. *Psychological Assessment, 6,* 368–371.

Anderson, D. R., & Levin, S. (1976). Young children's attention to *Sesame Street. Child Development, 47,* 806–811.

Anderson, D. R., Long, A., Leathers, E., Denny, B., & Hilliard, D. (1981).

Documentation of change in problem behaviors among anxious and hostile–aggressive children enrolled in a therapeutic preschool program. *Child Psychiatry and Human Development, 11,* 232–240.

Anderson, J. C., Williams, S., McGee, R., & Silva, P. A. (1987). *DSM-III* disorders in preadolescent children. *Archives of General Psychiatry, 44,* 69–76.

Anderson, J. A. (1983). Television literacy and the critical viewer. In J. Bryant & D. R. Anderson (Eds.), *Children's understanding of television: Research on attention and comprehension* (pp. 297–327). New York: Academic Press.

Arnett, J. (1992). Reckless behavior in adolescence: Recent advances and future directions. *Developmental Review, 12,* 339–373.

Atkins, M. S., Pelham, W. E., & White, K. J. (1989). Hyperactivity and attention deficit disorders. In M. Hersen (Ed.), *Psychological aspects of developmental and physical disabilities: A casebook* (pp.137–157). Newbury Park, CA: Sage.

Atkins, M. S., & Stoff, D. M. (1993). Instrumental and hostile aggression in childhood disruptive behavior disorder. *Journal of Abnormal Child Psychology, 21,* 165–178.

August, G. J., & Garfinkel, G. D. (1989). Behavioral and cognitive subtypes of ADHD. *Journal of the American Academy of Child and Adolescent Psychiatry, 28,* 739–748.

Baker, L., & Cantwell, D. P. (1987). A prospective psychiatric follow-up of children with speech/language disorders. *Journal of the American Academy of Child and Adolescent Psychiatry, 26,* 546–553.

Bandura, A. (1989). Self-regulation of cognitive processes through perceived self-efficacy. *Developmental Psychology, 25,* 729–735.

Barkley, R. A. (1976). Predicting the response of hyperkinetic children to stimulant drugs: A review. *Journal of Abnormal Child Psychology, 4,* 327–348.

Barkley, R. A. (1981). *Hyperactive children: A handbook for diagnosis and treatment.* New York: Guilford Press.

Barkley, R. A. (1982). Specific guidelines for defining hyperactivity in children (Attention Deficit Disorder with Hyperactivity). In B. Lahey & A. Kazdin (Eds.), *Advances in clinical child psychology* (Vol. 5, pp. 137–180). New York: Plenum Press.

Barkley, R. A. (1988). The effects of methylphenidate on the interactions of preschool ADHD children with their mothers. *Journal of the American Academy of Child and Adolescent Psychiatry, 27,* 336–341.

Barkley, R. A. (1987). *Defiant children: A clinician's manual for parent training.* New York: Guilford Press.

Barkley, R. A. (1989). Attention-deficit hyperactivity disorder. In E. J. Mash & R. A. Barkley (Eds.), *Treatment of childhood disorders* (pp. 39–72). New York: Guilford Press.

Barkley, R. A. (1990a). Attention-deficit disorders: History, definition and diagnosis. In M. Lewis & S. Miller (Eds.), *Handbook of developmental psychopathology* (pp. 65–76). New York: Plenum Press.

Barkley, R. A. (1990b). *Attention-deficit hyperactivity disorder: A handbook for diagnosis and treatment.* New York: Guilford Press.

Barkley, R. A. (1996a). Attention-deficit/hyperactivity disorder. In E. J. Mash & R. A. Barkley (Eds.), *Child psychopathology* (pp. 63–112). New York: Guilford Press.

Barkley, R. A. (1996b). Critical issues in research on attention. In G. R. Lyon & N. A. Krasnegor (Eds.), *Attention, memory and executive function* (pp. 45–56). Baltimore: Brookes.

Barkley, R. A. (1997a). *ADHD and the nature of self-control.* New York: Guilford Press.

Barkley, R. A. (1997b). *Defiant children: A clinician's manual for assessment and parent training* (2nd ed.). New York: Guilford Press.

Barkley, R. A., Anastopoulos, A. D., Guevremont, D. C., & Fletcher, K. E. (1991). Attention-deficit hyperactivity disorder in adolescents: Mother–adolescent interactions, family beliefs and conflicts, and maternal psychopathology. *Journal of Abnormal Child Psychology, 20,* 263–288.

Barkley, R. A., Copeland, A. P., & Sivage, C. (1980). A self-control classroom for hyperactive children. *Journal of Autism and Developmental Disorders, 10,* 75–89.

Barkley, R. A., & Cunningham, C. E. (1979). The effects of methylphenidate on the mother–child interactions of hyperactive children. *Archives of General Psychiatry, 36,* 201–208.

Barkley, R. A., & Cunningham, C. E. (1980). The parent–child interactions of hyperactive children and their modification by stimulant drugs. In R. Knights & D. Bakker (Eds.), *Treatment of hyperactive and learning disabled children* (pp. 219–236). Baltimore: University Park Press.

Barkley, R. A., DuPaul, G., & McMurray, M. B. (1990). A comprehensive evaluation of attention deficit disorder with and without hyperactivity as defined by research criteria. *Journal of Consulting and Clinical Psychology, 58,* 775–789.

Barkley, R. A., Fischer, M., Edelbrock, C. S., & Smallish, L. (1990). The adolescent outcome of hyperactive children diagnosed by research criteria: I. An 8-year prospective follow-up study. *Journal of the American Academy of Child and Adolescent Psychiatry, 29,* 546–557.

Barkley, R. A., Grodzinsky, G., & DuPaul, G. J. (1992). Frontal lobe functions in attention deficit disorder with or without hyperactivity: A review and research report. *Journal of Abnormal Child Psychology, 17,* 14–24.

Barkley, R. A., Karlsson, J., & Pollard, S. (1985). Effects of age on the mother–child interactions of hyperactive children. *Journal of Abnormal Child Psychology, 13,* 631–638.

Barkley, R., Guevremont, D. C., Anastopoulos, A. D., DuPaul, G. J., & Shelton, T. L. (1992). Driving-related risks and outcomes of attention deficit hyperactivity disorder in adolescents and young adults. *Pediatrics, 92,* 212–218.

Barkley, R. A., Guevremont, D. C., Anastopoulos, A. D., & Fletcher, K. E. (1992). A comparison of three family therapy programs for treating family conflicts in adolescents with attention-deficit hyperactivity disorder. *Journal of Consulting and Clinical Psychology, 60,* 450–462.

Barkley, R. A., Karlsson, J., Strzelecki, E., & Murphy, J. (1984). Effects of age and Ritalin dosage on the mother–child interactions of hyperactive children. *Journal of Consulting and Clinical Psychology, 52,* 750–758.

Barkley, R. A., & Ullman, D. G. (1975). A comparison of objective measures of activity and distractibility in hyperactive and nonhyperactive children. *Journal of Abnormal Child Psychology, 3,* 213–244.

Barnhardt, A. J., & Forehand, R. (1975). The effects of labeled and unlabeled praise upon lower and middle class children. *Journal of Experimental Child Psychology, 19,* 536–543.

Baruch, G. K., & Barnett, R. C. (1986). Father's participation in family work and children's sex-role attitudes. *Child Development, 57,* 1210–1223.

Bates, J. E. (1987). Temperament in infancy. In J. Osofsy (Ed.), *Handbook of infant development* (2nd ed.). New York: Wiley.

Bates, J. E., Maslin, C., & Frankel, K. (1985). Attachment security, mother–child interaction, and temperament as predictors of behavior problem ratings at age three years. In I. Bretherton & E. Waters (Eds.), Growing points of attachment theory and research. *Monographs of the Society for Research in Child Development, 29* (Serial No. 97).

Bates, M. E., & Labouvie, E. W. (1995). Personality–environment constellations and alcohol use: A process-oriented study of intraindividual change during adolescence. *Psychology of Addictive Behaviors, 9,* 23–35.

Batsche, G. M., & Knoff, H. M. (1994). Bullies and their victims: Understanding a pervasive problem in the schools. *School Psychology Review, 23,* 165–174.

Battle, E. S., & Lacey, B. A. (1972). A context for hyperactivity in children over time. *Child Development, 43,* 757–773.

Baum, C., & Forehand, R. (1991). Long term follow-up assessment of parent training by use of multiple outcome measures. *Behavior Therapy, 12,* 643–652.

Baumrind, D. (1968). Authoritarian vs. authoritative control. *Adolescence, 3,* 255–272.

Baumrind, D. (1971). Harmonious parents and their preschool children. *Developmental Psychology, 41,* 92–102.

Baumrind, D. (1977). Some thoughts about childrearing. In S. Cohen & T. Chomisky (Eds.), *Child development: Contemporary perspectives.* Itasca, IL: Peacock.

Baumrind, D. (1989). Rearing competent children. In D. Damon (Ed.), *Child development today and tomorrow.* San Francisco: Jossey-Bass.

Beck, S. J., Young, G. H., & Tarnowski, H. (1990). Maternal characteristics and perceptions of pervasive and situational hyperactives and normal controls. *Journal of the American Academy of Child and Adolescent Psychiatry, 29,* 558–565.

Becker, D. F., Doane, J. A., & Wexler, B. E. (1993). Effects of emotion on perceptual asymmetry in adolescent inpatients with attention-deficit hyperactivity disorder. *Journal of the American Academy of Child and Adolescent Psychiatry, 32,* 318–321.

Befera, M., & Barkley, R. A. (1985). Hyperactive and normal boys and girls:

Mother–child interaction, parent psychiatric status, and child psychopathology. *Journal of Child Psychology and Psychiatry, 26,* 439–452.

Bell, R. Q., & Harper, L. (1977). *Child effects on adults.* New York: Wiley.

Benasich, A. A., Curtiss, S., & Tallal, P. (1993). Language, learning, and behavioral disturbances in childhood: A longitudinal perspective. *Journal of the American Academy of Child and Adolescent Psychiatry, 32,* 585–594.

Beninger, R. J. (1989). Dopamine and learning: Implications for attention-deficit disorder and hyperkinetic syndrome. In T. Sagvolden & T. Archer (Eds.), *Attention-deficit disorder: Clinical and basic research* (pp. 323–338). Hillsdale, NJ: Erlbaum.

Benthin, A., Slovic, P., & Severson, H. (1993). A psychometric study of adolescent risk perception. *Journal of Adolescence, 16,* 153–168.

Berk, L. E. (1989). *Child development.* Boston: Allyn & Bacon.

Bernstein, R. (1980). The development of the self system during adolescence. *Journal of Genetic Psychology, 136,* 231–245.

Bibby, R. W., & Posterski, D. C. (1992). *Teen trends: A nation in motion.* Toronto: Stoddart.

Biederman, J., Baldessarini, R. J., Wright, V., Knee, D., & Harmatz, J. (1989). A double-blind placebo-controlled study of desipramine in the treatment of ADHD: I. Efficacy. *Journal of the American Academy of Child and Adolescent Psychiatry, 28,* 777–784.

Biederman, J., Faraone, S. V., Keenan, K., Benjamin, J., & Krifcher, B. (1992). Further evidence for family–genetic risk factors in attention-deficit disorder: Patterns of comorbidity in probands and relatives in psychiatrically and pediatrically referred samples. *Archives of General Psychiatry, 49,* 728–738.

Biederman, J., Faraone, S. V., Keenan, K., Knee, D., & Tsuang, M. T. (1990). Family–genetic and psychosocial risk factors in *DSM-III* attention-deficit disorder. *Journal of the American Academy of Child and Adolescent Psychiatry, 29,* 526–533.

Biederman, J., Faraone, S. V., Keenan, K., & Tsuang, M. T. (1991). Evidence of familial association between attention deficit hyperactivity disorder and major affective disorder. *Archives of General Psychiatry, 48,* 633–642.

Biederman, J., Faraone, S. V., Mick, E., Spencer, T., Wilens, T., Kiely, K., Guite, J., Ablon, J. S., Reed, E., & Warburton, R. (1995). High risk for attention deficit hyperactivity disorder among children of parents with childhood onset of the disorder: A pilot study. *American Journal of Psychiatry, 152,* 431–435.

Biederman, J., Faraone, S. V., Spencer, T., Wilens, T. E., Norman, D., Lapey, K. A., Mick, E., Lehman, B., & Doyle, A. (1993). Patterns of psychiatric comorbidity, cognition, and psychosocial functioning in adults with attention deficit hyperactivity disorder. *American Journal of Psychiatry, 150,* 1792–1798.

Biederman, J., Munir, K., & Knee, D. (1987). High rates of affective disorders in probands with attention deficit disorder and in their relatives: A controlled family study. *American Journal of Psychiatry, 144,* 330–333.

Biederman, J., Newcome, J., & Sprich, S. (1991). Comorbidity of attention-deficit hyperactivity disorder with conduct, depressive, anxiety, and other disorders. *American Journal of Psychiatry, 148,* 564–577.

Biederman, J., & Steingard, R. (1987). Attention-deficit hyperactivity disorder in adolescents. *Psychiatric Annals, 19,* 587–596.

Bierman, K., & Furman, W. (1984). The effects of social skills training and peer involvement on the social adjustment of preadolescents. *Child Development, 57,* 230–240.

Biller, H. B. (1982). Fatherhood: Implications for child and adult development. In B. B. Wolman (Ed.), *Handbook of developmental psychology.* Englewood Cliffs, NJ: Prentice-Hall.

Binder, A. (1988). Juvenile delinquency. *Annual Review of Psychology, 39,* 253–282.

Bjorklund, D. F., & Jacobs, J. W., III. (1985). Associative and categorical processes in children's memory: The role of automaticity in the development of organization in free recall. *Journal of Experimental Child Psychology, 39,* 599–617.

Blackman, J. A., Westervelt, V. D., Stevenson, R., & Welsch, A. (1991). Management of preschool children with attention-deficit hyperactivity disorder. *Topics of Early Childhood Special Education, 11,* 91–104.

Blouin, A. B., Bornstein, R., & Trites, R. (1978). Teenage alcohol use among hyperactive children: A 5-year follow-up study. *Journal of Pediatric Psychology, 3,* 188–194.

Borchgrevink, H. M. (1989). Cerebral processes underlying neuropsychological and neuromotor impairment in children with ADD/MBD. In T. Sagvolden & T. Archer (Eds.), *Attention-deficit disorder: Clinical and basic research* (pp. 105–130). Hillsdale, NJ: Erlbaum.

Borland, B. L., & Heckman, H. K. (1976). Hyperactive boys and their brothers: A 25-year follow-up study. *Archives of Clinical Psychiatry, 33,* 669–675.

Bornstein, P., & Quevillon, R. (1976). The effects of a self-instructional package on overactive preschool boys. *Journal of Applied Behavior Analysis, 9,* 179–188.

Boucugnani, L., & Jones, R. W. (1989). Behaviors analogous to frontal lobe dysfunction in children with attention-deficit hyperactive disorder. *Archives of Clinical Neuropsychology, 4,* 161–174.

Bower, T. G. R. (1989). *The rational infant: Learning in infancy.* New York: Freeman.

Bowers, S. D., Clement, P. W., Fantuzzo, J. W., & Sorensen, D. A. (1985). Effects of teacher-administered and self-administered reinforcers on learning disabled children. *Behavior Therapy, 16,* 357–369.

Bowlby, J. (1969). *Attachment and loss: Vol 1. Attachment.* New York: Basic Books.

Boyer, D., & Fine, D. (1992). Sexual abuse as a factor in adolescent pregnancy and child maltreatment. *Family Planning Perspectives, 24,* 4–11.

Bransford, J. D., Stein, B. S., Shelton, T. S., & Owings, R. A. (1981). Cognition and adaptation: The importance of learning to learn. In J. Harvey (Ed.), *Cognition, social behavior and the environment* (pp. 93–110). Hillsdale, NJ: Erlbaum.

Breen, M. J., & Barkley, R. A. (1988). Child psychopathology and parenting stress in girls and boys having attention deficit disorder with hyperactivity. *Journal of Pediatric Psychology, 13,* 265–280.

Bricker, D., & Veltman, M. (1990). Early intervention programs: Child focused approaches. In S. J. Meisels & J. P. Shonkoff (Eds.), *Handbook of early intervention* (pp. 373–399). New York: Cambridge University Press.

Briener, J. L., & Forehand, R. (1991). An assessment of the effects of parent training on clinic-referred children's school behavior. *Behavioral Assessment, 3,* 31–42.

Brody, G. H., & Forehand, R. (1985). The efficacy of parent training with maritally distressed and nondistressed mothers: A multimethod assessment. *Behaviour Research and Therapy, 23,* 291–296.

Bromwich, R. M. (1981). *Working with parents and infants: An interactional approach.* Baltimore: University Park Press.

Bronstein, P., Clauson, J., Stoll, M. F., & Abrams, C. L. (1993). Parenting behavior and children's social, psychological, and academic adjustment in diverse family structures. *Family Relations, 42,* 268–276.

Brooks-Gunn, J., & Furstenberg, F. F., Jr. (1989). Adolescent sexual behavior. *American Psychologist, 44,* 249–257.

Brophy, J. E. (1983). Research on self-fulfilling prophecy and teacher expectations. *Journal of Educational Psychology, 75,* 631–661.

Brophy, J. E., & Good, T. L. (1974). *Teacher–student relationships: Causes and consequences.* New York: Holt, Rinehart & Winston.

Broughton, J. (1978). Development of concepts of self, mind, reality, and knowledge. *New Directions for Child Development, 1,* 75–100.

Brown, R. T., & Borden, K. A. (1986). Hyperactivity at adolescence: Some misconceptions and new directions. *Journal of Clinical Child Psychology, 15,* 194–209.

Brown, B. B., Mounts, N., Lamborn, S., & Sternberg, L. (1993). Parenting practices and peer group affiliation in adolescence. *Child Development, 64,* 467–482.

Brown, R. T., Madan-Swain, A., & Baldwin, K. (1991). Gender differences in a clinic-referred sample of attention-deficit-disordered children. *Child Psychiatry and Human Development, 22,* 111–128.

Brown, R. T., & Pacini, J. N. (1989). Perceived family functioning, marital status, and depression in parents of boys with attention-deficit disorder. *Journal of Learning Disabilities, 22,* 581–587.

Buss, A. H., & Plomin, R. (1985). *Temperament: Early developing personality traits.* Hillsdale, NJ: Erlbaum.

Butter, C. M., Rapcsak, S. Z., Watson, R. T., & Heilman, K. M. (1988). Changes in sensory in attention, directional, hypokinesia and release of the fixation-reflex following a unilateral frontal lesion: A case report. *Neuropsychologia, 26,* 533–545.

Byrne, B. M., & Shavelson, R. J. (1987). Adolescent self-concept: Testing the assumption of equivalent structure across gender. *American Educational Research Journal, 24,* 365–385.

Calis, K., Grothe, D., & Elia, J. (1990). Therapy reviews: Attention-deficit hyperactivity disorder. *Clinical Pharmacy, 9,* 632–642.

Campbell, S. B. (1985). Hyperactivity in preschoolers: Correlates and prognostic implications. *Clinical Psychology Review, 5,* 502–524.

Campbell, S. B. (1990a). The socialization and social development of hyperactive children. In M. Lewis & S. Miller (Eds.), *Handbook of developmental psychopathology* (pp. 77–92). New York: Plenum Press.

Campbell, S. B. (1990b). *Behavior problems in preschool children: Clinical and developmental issues.* New York: Guilford Press.

Campbell, S. B., Breaux, A. M., Ewing, L. J., Szumowski, E. K., & Pierce, E. W. (1986). Parent-referred problem preschoolers: Mother–child interaction during play at intake and one-year follow-up. *Journal of Abnormal Child Psychology, 14,* 425–440.

Campbell, S. B., Endman, M., & Bernfield, G. A. (1977). A three-year follow-up of hyperactive preschoolers into elementary school. *Journal of Child Psychology and Psychiatry, 18,* 239–250.

Campbell, S. B., Ewing, L. J., Breaux, A. M., & Szumowski, E. K. (1986). Parent-identified behavior problem toddlers: Follow-up at school entry. *Journal of Child Psychology and Psychiatry, 27,* 473–488.

Campbell, S. B., Schleifer, M., & Weiss, G. (1978). Continuities in maternal reports and child behaviors over time in hyperactive and comparison groups. *Journal of Abnormal Child Psychology, 6,* 33–45.

Campbell, S. B., Szumowski, E. K., Ewing, L. J., Gluck, D. S., & Breaux, A. M. (1982). A multidimensional assessment of parent-identified behavior problem toddlers. *Journal of the American Academy of Child Psychiatry, 10,* 569–592.

Cantwell, D. P. (1972). Psychiatric illness in the families of hyperactive children. *Archives of General Psychiatry, 27,* 414–427.

Cantwell, D. P., & Baker, L. (1992). Association between attention-deficit hyperactivity disorder and learning disorders. In S. Shaywitz & B. Shaywitz (Eds.), *Attention-deficit disorder comes of age: Toward the twenty-first century* (pp. 145–164). Austin, TX: Pro-ed.

Cantwell, D. P., & Satterfield, J. H. (1978). The prevalence of academic underachievement in hyperactive children. *Journal of Pediatric Psychology, 3,* 168–171.

Carden-Smith, L. K., & Fowler, S. A. (1984). Positive peer pressure: The effects of peer monitoring on children's disruptive behavior. *Journal of Applied Behavior Analysis, 17,* 213–227.

Carey, W. B. (1989). Introduction: Basic issues. In W. B. Carey & S. C. McDevitt (Eds.), *Clinical and educational applications of temperament research.* Berwyn, PA: Swets North America.

Carlson, C. (1997, November). *Assessment and nonpharmacological treatment of ADHD.* Research abstract presented at the annual meeting of CH.A.D.D., San Antonio, TX.

Carlson, C., Lahey, B. B., Frame, C. L., Walker, J., & Hynd, G. W. (1987). Sociometric status of clinic-referred children with attention deficit disorders with and without hyperactivity. *Journal of Abnormal Psychology, 15,* 537–547.

Carlson, C., Lahey, B. B., & Neeper, R. (1986). Direct assessment of the cognitive correlates of attention-deficit disorders with and without hyperactivity. *Journal of Behavioral Assessment and Psychopathology, 8,* 69–86.

Carlson, C. L., Pelham, W. E., Milich, R., & Dixon, M. J. (1992). Single and combined effects of methylphenidate and behavior therapy on the classroom behavior, academic performance and self-evaluations of children with attention-deficit hyperactivity disorder. *Journal of Abnormal Child Psychology, 20,* 213–232.

Carlson, C. L., Pelham, W. E., Milich, R., & Hoza, B. (1993). ADHD boys' performance and attributions following success and failure: Drug effects and individual differences. *Cognitive Therapy and Research, 17,* 269–287.

Carlson, C. L., Tamm, L., & Gaub, M. (1997). Gender differences in children with ADHD, ODD, and co-occurring ADHD/ODD identified in a school population. *Journal of the American Academy of Child and Adolescent Psychiatry, 36,* 1706–1714.

Casey, B. J., Castellano, F. X., Giedd, J. N., Marsh, W. L., Hamburger, S. D., Schubert, A. B., Vauss, Y. C., Vaituzis, A. C., Dickstein, D. P., Sarfatti, S. E., & Rapoport, J. L. (1997). Implication of right frontostriatal circuitry in response inhibition and attention-deficit/hyperactivity disorder. *Journal of the American Academy of Child and Adolescent Psychiatry, 36,* 374–383.

Castellano, F. X., Giedd, J. N., Marsh, W. L., Hamburger, S. D., Vaituzis, A. C., Dickstein, D. P., Sarfatti, S. E., Vauss, Y. C., Snell, J. W., Lange, N., Kaysen, D., Krain, A. L., Richhie, G. F., Rajapakse, J. C., & Rapoport, J. L. (1996). Quantitative brain magnetic resonance imaging in attention-deficit hyperactivity disorder. *Archives of General Psychiatry, 53,* 607–616.

Cates, W., Jr., & Rauh, J. L. (1985). Adolescents and sexually transmitted diseases: An expanded problem. *Journal of Adolescent Health Care, 6,* 1–5.

Centers for Disease Control. (1993). *HIV/AIDS surveillance report* (Vol. 1, No. 22). Atlanta: Author.

Chance, P., & Fischman, J. (1987). The magic of childhood. *Psychology Today, 21,* 48–58.

Chandler, C. L. (1981). The effects of parenting techniques on the development of motivational orientations in children. *Dissertation Abstracts International, 42,* 4594B. (University Microfilms No. 82-09,943)

Chelune, G., Ferguson, W., Koon, R., & Dickey, T. (1986). Frontal lobe disinhibition in attention-deficit disorder. *Child Psychiatry and Human Development, 16,* 221–234.

Chesapeake Institute (1993). *Education of children with attention-deficit disorder.* Washington, DC: U.S. Department of Education.

Chess, S., & Thomas, A. (1984). *Origins and evolution of behavior disorders.* New York: Brunner/Mazel.

Chi, M. T. H. (1978). Knowledge structures and memory development. In R. S. Siegler (Ed.), *Children's thinking: What develops?* (pp. 73–96). Hillsdale, NJ: Erlbaum.

Chi, M. T. H. (1982). Knowledge development and memory performance. In M. Friedman, J. P. Das, & N. O'Connor (Eds.), *Intelligence and learning* (pp. 221–229). New York: Plenum Press.

Chi, M. T. H., & Koeske, R. D. (1983). Network representation of a child's dinosaur knowledge. *Developmental Psychology, 19,* 29–39.

Claes, M., & Simard, R. (1992). Friendship characteristics of delinquent adolescents. *International Journal of Adolescence and Youth, 3,* 287–301.

Coates, T. J., & Thoreson, C. E. (1981). Sleep disturbances in children and adolescents. In E. J. Mash & L. G. Terdal (Eds.), *Behavioral assessment of childhood disorders* (pp. 639–678). New York: Guilford Press.

Cohen, N. J., Davine, M., Horodezky, N., & Lipsett, L. (1993). Unsuspected language impairment in psychiatrically disturbed children: Prevalence and language and behavioral characteristics. *Journal of the American Academy of Child and Adolescent Psychiatry, 32,* 595–603.

Cohen, N. J., Bradley, S., & Kolers, N. (1987). Outcome evaluation of a therapeutic day treatment program for delayed and disturbed preschoolers. *Journal of the American Academy of Child and Adolescent Psychiatry, 26,* 687–693.

Cohen, N. J., Weiss, G., & Minde, K. (1972). Cognitive styles in adolescents previously diagnosed as hyperactive. *Journal of Child Psychology and Psychiatry, 13,* 203–209.

Colby, A., & Kohlberg, L. (1984). Invariant sequence and internal consistency in moral judgment stages. In W. M. Kertines & J. L. Gerwitz (Eds.), *Morality, moral behavior, and moral development.* New York: Wiley.

Colby, C. L. (1991). The neuroanatomy and neurophysiology of attention. *Journal of Clinical Neurology, 6,* S88–S118.

Comings, D. E. (1990). *Tourette syndrome and human behavior.* Duarte, CA: Hope Press.

Comings, D. E., Comings, B. G., Muhleman, D., Dietz, G., Shahbahrami, B., Tast, D., Knell, E., Kocsis, P., Baumgarten, R., Kovacs, B. W., Levy, D. L., Smith, M., Borison, R. L., Evans, D. D., Klein, D. N., MacMurray, J., Tosk, J. M., Sverd, J., Gysin, R., & Flanagan, S. D. (1991). The dopamine D2 receptor locus as a modifying gene in neuropsychiatric disorders. *Journal of the American Medical Association, 266,* 1793–1800.

Conners, C. K. (1975). Control trial of methylphenidate in preschool children with minimal brain dysfunction. *International Journal of Mental Health, 4,* 61–74.

Conners, C. K., & Wells, K. C. (1985). ADD-H Adolescent Self-Report Scales. *Psychopharmacology Bulletin, 21,* 921–922.

Cook, E., & Stein, M. (1996, November). *Genetics of ADHD: Current update and future directions.* Paper presented at the annual meeting of CH.A.D.D., Chicago, IL.

Cook, E. H., Stein, M. A., Krawowski, D. M., Cox, N. J., Olkon, D. M., Kieffer, J. E., & Leventhal, B. L. (1995). Association of attention deficit disorder and the dopamine transporter gene. *American Journal of Human Genetics, 56,* 993–998.

Copeland, E. D., & Copps, S. C. (1995). *Medications for attention disorders (ADHD/ADD) and related medical problems.* Plantation, FL: Speciality Press.

Crockenberg, S. B. (1986). Are temperamental differences in babies associated with predictable differences in care-giving? In J. V. Lerner & R. M. Lerner

(Eds.), *New directions for child development* (No. 31, pp. 53–74). San Francisco: Jossey-Bass.

Crockett, L. J., & Peterson, A. C. (1987). Pubertal status and psychosocial development: Findings from the Early Adolescent Study. In R. M. Lerner & T. T. Foch (Eds.), *Biological–psychosocial interactions in early adolescence: A life-span perspective.* Hillsdale, NJ: Erlbaum.

Cunningham, C. E. (1990). A family systems approach to parent training. In R. A. Barkley, *Attention-deficit hyperactivity disorder: A handbook for diagnosis and treatment* (pp. 432–461). New York: Guilford Press.

Cunningham, C. E., Benness, B. B., & Siegel, L. S. (1988). Family functioning, time allocation, and parental depression in families of normal and ADHD children. *Journal of Clinical Child Psychology, 17,* 169–177.

Cunningham, C. E., & Siegel, L. S. (1987). Peer interactions of normal and attention-deficit disordered boys during free-play, cooperative tasks, and simulated classroom situations. *Journal of Abnormal Child Psychology, 15,* 247–268.

Cunningham, C. E., Siegel, L. S., & Offord, D. R. (1985). A developmental dose response analysis of the effects of methylphenidate on the peer interactions of attention deficit disordered boys. *Journal of Child Psychology and Psychiatry, 26,* 955–971.

Cunningham, C. E., & Barkley, R. A. (1979). The interactions of hyperactive and normal children with their mothers during free play and structured tasks. *Child Development, 50,* 217–224.

Dadds, M. R., Schwartz, S., & Sanders, M. R. (1987). Marital discord and treatment outcome in behavioral treatment of child conduct disorders. *Journal of Consulting and Clinical Psychology, 55,* 192–203.

Darley, J. M., & Shultz, T. R. (1990). Moral rules: Their content and acquisition. *Annual Review of Psychology, 41,* 521–525.

Darling, C. A., Kallen, D. J., & Van Dusen, J. E. (1984). Sex in transition, 1900–1980. *Journal of Youth and Adolescence, 13,* 385–394.

Davidson, R. J. (1994). Affect, cognition, and hemispheric specialization. In C. E. Izard, J. Kagan, & R. Zajonc (Eds.), *Emotions, cognition and behavior* (pp. 320–365). New York: Cambridge University Press.

Davidson, R. J., & Fox, N. A. (1982). Asymmetrical brain activity discriminates between positive and negative affective stimuli in infants. *Science, 218,* 1235–1237.

Davidson, R. J., & Fox, N. A. (1989). Frontal lobe asymmetry predicts infants' response to maternal separation. *Journal of Abnormal Psychology, 98,* 127–131.

Dawson, G. (1994). Development of emotional expression and emotion regulation in infancy: Contributions of the frontal lobe. *Human behavior and the developing brain* (pp. 346–379). New York: Guilford Press.

DeMilio, L. (1989). Psychiatric syndromes in adolescent substance abusers. *American Journal of Psychiatry, 146,* 1212–1214.

Denckla, M. B. (1994). Measurement of executive function. In G. R. Lyon (Ed.), *Frames of reference for the assessment of learning disabilities: New views on measurement issues* (pp. 117–142). Baltimore: Brookes.

Denham, S. A., & Holt, R. W. (1993). Preschooler's likeability as cause or consequence of their social behavior. *Developmental Psychology, 29,* 271–275.

Dinges, M. M., & Oetting, E. R. (1993). Similarity in drug use patterns between adolescents and their friends. *Adolescence, 28,* 253–266.

Dishion, T. J., Patterson, G. R., Stoolmiller, M., & Skinner, M. L. (1991). Family, school, and behavioral antecedents to early adolescent involvement with antisocial peers. *Developmental Psychology, 27,* 172–180.

Dixon, E. B. (1995). Impact of adult ADHD on the family. In K. G. Nadeau (Ed.), *A comprehensive guide to attention deficit disorder in adults: Research, diagnosis, and treatment* (pp. 236–259). New York: Brunner/Mazel.

Dodge, K. A., Pettit, G. S., McClaskey, C. L., & Brown, M. M. (1986). Social competence in children. *Monographs of the Society for Research in Child Development, 51*(2, Serial No. 213).

Douglas, V., & Parry, P. A. (1994). Effects of reward and nonreward on frustration and attention-deficit disorder. *Journal of Abnormal Child Psychology, 22,* 281–302.

Douglas, V., & Peters, K. (1979). Toward a clearer definition of the attentional deficit of hyperactive children. In G. A. Hale & M. Lewis (Eds.), *Attention and the development of cognitive skills.* New York: Plenum Press.

Douglas, V. I. (1972). Stop, look, and listen: The problem of sustained attention and impulse control in children. *Canadian Journal of Behavioral Science, 4,* 259–282.

Douglas, V. I. (1983). Attention and cognitive problems. In M. Rutter (Ed.), *Developmental neuropsychiatry* (pp. 280–329). New York: Guilford Press.

Drabman, R. S., Spitalnik, R., & O'Leary, K. D. (1973). Teaching self-control to disruptive children. *Journal of Abnormal Psychology, 82,* 10–16.

Dunphy, D. C. (1963). The social structure of urban adolescent peer groups. *Sociometry, 26,* 230–246.

Dunst, C. J., & Trivette, C. M. (1990). Assessment of social support in early intervention programs. In S. J. Meisels & J. P. Shonkoff (Eds.), *Handbook of early childhood intervention* (pp. 326–349). Cambridge, UK: Cambridge University Press.

DuPaul, G. J., Barkley, R. A., & McMurray, M. B. (1991). Therapeutic effects of medication on ADHD: Implications for school psychologists. *School Psychology Review, 20,* 203–219.

DuPaul, G. J., Guevremont, D. C., & Barkley, R. A. (1991). Attention-deficit hyperactivity disorder. In T. R. Kratochwill & R. J. Morris (Eds.), *The practice of child therapy* (2nd ed., pp. 115–144). New York: Pergamon Press.

DuPaul, G. J., Guevremont, D. C., & Barkley, R. A. (1992). Behavioral treatment of attention-deficit hyperactivity disorder in the classroom: The use of the Attention Training System. *Behavior Modification, 16,* 204–225.

DuPaul, G. J., & Stoner, G. (1994). *ADHD in schools: Assessment and intervention strategies.* New York: Guilford Press.

Dykeman, R. A., & Ackerman, P. T. (1992). Attention-deficit disorder and specific reading disability: Separate but often overlapping disorders. In S.

Shaywitz & B. Shaywitz (Eds.), *Attention-deficit disorder comes of age: Toward the twenty-first century* (pp. 165–184). Austin, TX: Pro-ed.

Edelbrock, C. S., Rende, R., Plomin, R., & Thompson, L. (1995). A twin study of competence and problem behavior in childhood and early adolescence. *Journal of Child Psychology and Psychiatry, 36,* 775–786.

Egerton, H. A. (1987). Recapturing kindergarten for 5-year-olds. *Education Week, 19,* 28.

Elia, J., Borcherding, B. G., Potter, W. Z., Mefford, I. N., Rapoport, J. L., & Keysor, C. S. (1990). Stimulant drug treatment of hyperactivity: Biochemical correlates. *Clinical Pharmacology and Therapeutics, 48,* 57–66.

Elkind, D. (1967). Egocentrism in adolescence. *Child Development, 38,* 1025–1034.

Elkind, D. (1971). Two approaches to intelligence: Piagetian and psychometric. In D. R. Green, M. P. Ford, & G. B. Flamer (Eds.), *Measurement and Piaget* (pp. 12–28). New York: McGraw-Hill.

Elkind, D. (1984). *All grown up and no place to go.* Reading, MA: Addison-Wesley.

Elkind, D. (1987). *Miseducation: Preschoolers at risk.* New York: Knopf.

Elkind, D., & Bowen, R. (1979). Imaginary audience behavior in children and adolescents. *Developmental Psychology, 15,* 38–44.

Elliott, D. S., Huisinga, D., & Menard, S. (1989). *Multiple problem youth. Delinquency, substance use, and mental health problems.* New York: Springer-Verlag.

Epstein, M. A., Shaywitz, S. E., Shaywitz, B. A., & Woolston, J. L. (1992). The boundaries of attention-deficit disorder. In S. Shaywitz & B. Shaywitz (Eds.), *Attention deficit disorder comes of age: Toward the twenty-first century* (pp. 197–220). Austin, TX: Pro-ed.

Erickson, M., Egeland, B., & Sroufe, L. A. (1985). The relationship between quality of attachment and behavior problems in preschool in a high risk sample. In I. Bretherton & E. Waters (Eds.), Growing points in attachment theory and research. *Monographs of the Society for Research in Child Development, 50,* 147–186.

Erikson, E. H. (1950). *Childhood and society.* New York: Norton.

Erikson, E. H. (1959). *Identity and the life cycle: Selected papers.* (Psychological Issue Monograph Series I). New York: International Universities Press.

Erikson, E. H. (1961). The roots of virtue. In J. Huxley (Ed.), *The humanist frame.* New York: Harper & Row.

Erikson, E. H. (1968). *Identity: Youth and crisis.* New York: Norton.

Erikson, E. H. (1985). *The life cycle completed.* New York: Norton.

Ernst, M., Liebenauer, L. L., King, A. C., Fitzgerald, G. A., Cohen, R. M., & Zametkin, A. J. (1994). Reduced brain metabolism in hyperactive girls. *Journal of the American Academy of Child and Adolescent Psychiatry, 33,* 858–868.

Evans, S. W., & Pelham, W. E. (1991). Psychostimulant effects on academic and behavioral measures for ADHD junior high school students in a lecture format classroom. *Journal of Abnormal Child Psychology, 19,* 537–552.

Faraone, S. V., Biederman, J., Chen, W. J., Krifcher, B., Keenan, K., Moore, C.,

Sprich, S., & Tsuang, M. T. (1992). Segregation analysis of attention-deficit hyperactivity disorder. *Psychiatric Genetics, 2,* 257–275.

Faraone, S. V., Biederman, J., Chen, W. J., Milberger, R., & Tsuang, M. T. (1995). Genetic heterogeneity in attention-deficit hyperactivity disorder (ADHD): Gender, psychiatric comorbidity, and maternal ADHD. *Journal of Abnormal Psychology, 104,* 334–345.

Faraone, S. V., Biederman, J., Keenan, K., & Tsuang, M. T. (1991). A family-genetic study of girls with *DSM-III* attention deficit disorder. *American Journal of Psychiatry, 148,* 112–117.

Faraone, S. V., Biederman, J., Lehman, B., Spencer, T., Norman, D., Seidman, L. J., Kraus, I., Perrin, J., Chen, W. J., & Tsuang, M. T. (1993). Intellectual performance and school failure in children with attention deficit hyperactivity disorder and in their siblings. *Journal of Abnormal Psychology, 102,* 616–623.

Farran, D. C. (1990). Effects of intervention with disadvantaged and disabled children. In S. J. Meisels & J. P. Shonkoff (Eds.), *Handbook of early intervention* (pp. 501–539). New York: Cambridge University Press.

Farrell, A. D., Danish, S. J., & Howard, C. W. (1992). Relationship between drug use and other problem behaviors in urban adolescents. *Journal of Consulting and Clinical Psychology, 60,* 705–712.

Feldman, S., Denhoff, E., & Denhoff, E. (1979). The attention disorders and related syndromes outcome in adolescence and young adult life. In E. Denhoff & L. Stern (Eds.), *Minimal brain dysfunction: A developmental approach* (pp. 133–148). New York: Musson.

Filipek, P. A. (1996). Structural variations in measures in the developmental disorders. In R. W. Thatcher, G. Reid Lyon, J. Rumsey, & N. Krasnegor (Eds.), *Developmental neuroimaging: Mapping the development of brain and behavior* (pp. 169–186). San Diego, CA: Academic Press.

Filipek, P. A., Semrud-Clikeman, M., Steingard, R. J., Renshaw, P. F., Kennedy, D. N., & Biederman, J. (1997). Volumetric MRI analysis comparing subjects having attention-deficit hyperactivity disorder with normal controls. *Neurology, 48,* 589–601.

Fiore, T. A., Becker, E. A., & Nero, R. C. (1993). Educational interventions for students with ADD. *Exceptional Children, 60,* 771–773.

Fischer, M., Barkley, R. A., Edelbrock, C. S., & Smallish, L. (1990). The adolescent outcome of hyperactive children diagnosed by research criteria: II. Academic, attentional, and neuropsychological status. *Journal of Consulting and Clinical Psychology, 58,* 580–588.

Fischer, M., Barkley, R. A., Edelbrock, C. S., & Smallish, L. (1993). The stability of dimensions of behavior in ADHD and normal children over an 8-year follow-up. *Journal of Abnormal Child Psychology, 21,* 315–337.

Flavell, J. H. (1985). *Cognitive development* (2nd ed.). Englewood Cliffs, NJ: Prentice-Hall.

Fletcher, J., & Taylor, H. (1984). Neuropsychological approaches to children: Towards a developmental neuropsychology. *Journal of Clinical Neuropsychology, 6,* 39–56.

Flicek, M., & Landau, S. (1985). Social status problems of learning disabled and hyperactive/learning disabled boys. *Journal of Clinical Child Psychology, 14*, 340–344.

Forehand, R., & King, H. E. (1974). Pre-school children's compliance: Effects of short-term behavior therapy. *Journal of Community Psychology, 2,* 42–44.

Forehand, R., & King, H. E. (1977). Noncompliant children: Effects of parent training on behavior and attitude change. *Behavior Modification, 1,* 93–108.

Forehand, R., & McMahon, R. J. (1981). *Helping the noncompliant child: A clinician's guide to parent training.* New York: Guilford Press.

Forehand, R., Wierson, M., Frame, C., Kempton, T., & Armistead (1991). Juvenile delinquency entry and persistence: Do attention problems contribute to conduct problems? *Journal of Behavior Therapy and Experimental Psychiatry, 22,* 261–264.

Foster, S. L. (1978). Family conflict management: Skill training and generalization procedures. In A. Ciminero, K. S. Calhoun, & H. E. Adams (Eds.), *Handbook of behavioral assessment* (pp. 253–324). New York: Wiley.

Fowler, M. (1992). *CH.A.D.D. educator's manual: An in-depth look at attention-deficit disorders from an educational perspective.* Fairfax, VA: CASET.

Fox, N. A., & Davidson, R. J. (1986). Taste elicited changes in facial signs of emotion and the symmetry of brain electrical activity in human newborns. *Neuropsychologia, 24,* 417–422.

Foxx, R. M., & Shapiro, S. T. (1978). The timeout ribbon: A nonexclusionary timeout procedure. *Journal of Applied Behavior Analysis, 11,* 125–136.

Franklin, J. T. (1985). Alternative education as substance abuse prevention. *Journal of Alcohol and Drug Education, 30,* 12–23.

Freibergs, V., & Douglas, V. I. (1969). Concept learning in hyperactive and normal children. *Journal of Abnormal Psychology, 74,* 388–395.

Frick, P. J., & Lahey, B. B. (1991). Nature and characteristics of attention-deficit hyperactivity disorder. *School Psychology Review, 20,* 163–173.

Furstenberg, F. F., Jr., Brooks-Gunn, J., & Chase-Landale, L. (1989). Teenage pregnancy and childbearing. *American Psychologist, 44,* 313–320.

Gaensbauer, T., & Hiatt, S. (1984). *The psychobiology of affective development.* Hillsdale, NJ: Erlbaum.

Gibbs, J. C. (1987). Social processes in delinquency: The need to facilitate empathy as well as sociomoral reasoning. In W. M. Kurtines & J. L. Gerwitz (Eds.), *Morality, moral behavior, and moral development.* New York: Wiley.

Gilligan, C. (1982). *In a different voice: Psychological theory and women's development.* Cambridge, MA: Harvard University Press.

Gillis, J. J., Gilger, J. W., Pennington, B. F., & DeFries, J. C. (1992). Attention-deficit disorder in reading-disabled twins: Evidence for a genetic etiology. *Journal of Abnormal Child Psychology, 20,* 303–315.

Gittelman, R. (1983). *Stimulants: Neurochemical, behavioral and clinical perspectives.* New York: Raven Press.

Gittelman, R., Mannuzza, S., Shenker, R., & Bonagura, N. (1985). Hyperactive boys almost grown up. *Archives of General Psychiatry, 42,* 937–947.

Goldstein, A. P., Harootunian, B., Conoley, J. C. (1994). *Student aggression:*

Prevention, management, and replacement training. New York: Guilford Press.

Goldstein, A. P., & McGinnis, E. (1988). *The skillstreaming video.* Champaign, IL: Research Press.

Goldstein, A. P., Sprafkin, R. P., Gershaw, N. J., & Klein, P. (1980). *Skillstreaming the adolescent: A structured learning approach to teaching prosocial skills.* Champaign, IL: Research Press.

Goldstein, S., & Goldstein, M. (1990). *Managing attention disorders in children.* New York: Wiley-Interscience.

Goldstein, S., & Jones, C. (1998). Managing and educating children with ADHD. In S. Goldstein & M. Goldstein (Eds.), *Managing attention deficit hyperactivity disorder in children: A guide for practitioners* (2nd ed., pp. 545–591). New York: Wiley-Interscience.

Goodman, J. F., Cecil, H. S., & Barker, W. F. (1984). Early intervention with retarded children: Some encouraging results. *Developmental Medicine and Child Neurology, 26,* 47–55.

Goodman, R., & Stevenson, J. (1989). A twin study of hyperactivity: II. The aetiological role of genes, family relationships, and perinatal adversity. *Journal of Child Psychology and Psychiatry, 30,* 691–709.

Gordon, M. (1991). *ADHD/Hyperactivity: A consumer's guide.* DeWitt, NY: GSI.

Gordon, M., Thomason, D., Cooper, S., & Ivers, C. L. (1991). Nonmedical treatment of ADHD/hyperactivity: The Attention Training System. *Journal of School Psychology, 29,* 151–159.

Gorenstein, E. E., & Newman, J. P. (1980). Disinhibitory psychopathology: A new perspective and a model for research. *Psychological Review, 87,* 301–315.

Green, W. H. (1991). *Child and adolescent clinical psychopharmacology.* Baltimore: Williams & Wilkins.

Gronlund, N. E., & Holmlund, W. S. (1958). The value of elementary school sociometric status scores for predicting a pupil's adjustment in high school. *Educational Administration and Supervision, 44,* 255–260.

Gross, A. M., & Wojnilower, D. A. (1984). Self-directed behavior change in children: Is it self-directed? *Behavior Therapy, 15,* 501–514.

Guevremont, D. (1990). Social skills and peer relationship training. In R. A. Barkley, *Attention-deficit hyperactivity disorder: A handbook for diagnosis and treatment* (pp. 540–572). New York: Guilford Press.

Guidubaldi, J., & Perry, J. D. (1985). Divorce and mental health sequelae for children: A two-year follow-up of a nationwide sample. *Journal of the American Academy of Child Psychiatry, 24,* 531–537.

Hagen, J. W., & Stanovich, K. G. (1977). Memory: Strategies of acquisition. In R. V. Krail, Jr., & J. W. Hagen (Eds.), *Perspectives on the development of memory and cognition* (pp. 89–111). Hillsdale, NJ: Erlbaum.

Hallowell, E. M. (1993). Living and loving with attention-deficit disorder: Couples where one partner has ADD. *CH.A.D.D.E.R., 7,* 13–15.

Hallowell, E. M. (1995). Psychotherapy for adult attention-deficit disorder. In K. G. Nadeau (Ed.), *A comprehensive guide to attention-deficit disorder in adults: Research, diagnosis, and treatment* (pp. 144–167). New York: Brunner/Mazel.

Hallowell, E. M., & Ratey, J. J. (1994). *Driven to distraction.* New York: Pantheon Books.

Harlap, S., Kost, K., & Forrest, J. D. (1991). *Preventing pregnancy, protecting health: A new look at birth control choices in the United States.* New York: Guttmacher.

Harter, S. (1981). A new self-report scale of intrinsic versus extrinsic orientation in the classroom: Motivational and informational components. *Developmental Psychology, 17,* 300–312.

Harter, S. (1982). The perceived competence scale for children. *Child Development, 53,* 87–97.

Harter, S. (1990). Processes underlying adolescent self-concept formation. In R. Montemayor, C. R. Adams, & T. P. Gullotta (Eds.), *Advances in adolescent development: Vol. 2. From childhood to adolescence: A transitional period?* Newbury Park, CA: Sage.

Harter, S. (1987). The determinants and mediational role of global self-worth in children. In N. Eisenberg (Ed.), *Contemporary topics in developmental psychology.* New York: Wiley.

Hartup, W. W. (1978). Children and their friends. In H. McGurk (Ed.), *Issues in childhood social development.* London: Methuen.

Hartup, W. W. (1983). Peer relations. In P. Mussen & E. M. Hetherington (Eds.), *Manual of child psychology* (4th ed., pp. 103–196). New York: Wiley.

Hartup, W. W. (1989). Social relationships and their developmental significance. *American Psychologist, 44,* 120–126.

Hechtman, L. (1981). Families of hyperactives. *Research in Community and Mental Health, 2,* 275–292.

Hechtman, L., Weiss, G., & Metrakos, K. (1978). Hyperactive children as young adults: Current and longitudinal electroencephalographic evaluation and its relation to outcome. *Canadian Medical Association Journal, 118,* 919–923.

Heilman, K. M., & Van Den Abell, T. (1980). Right hemisphere dominance for attention: The mechanism underlying hemispheric asymmetries of inattention (neglect). *Neurology, 30,* 327–330.

Heilman, K. M., Voeller, K. K. S., & Nadeau, S. E. (1991). A possible pathophysiological substrate of attention-deficit hyperactivity disorder. *Journal of Child Neurology, 6S,* 576–581.

Heisel, B. E., & Retter, K. (1981). Young children's storage behavior in a memory for location task. *Journal of Experimental Child Psychology, 31,* 250–264.

Henker, B., & Whalen, C. K. (1980). The changing faces of hyperactivity: Retrospect and prospect. In C. Whalen & B. Henker (Eds.), *Hyperactive children: The social ecology of identification and treatment* (pp. 321–364). New York: Academic Press.

Hetherington, E. M., Cox, M., & Cox, R. (1982). Effects of divorce on parents and children. In M. E. Lamb (Ed.), *Nontraditional families: Parenting and child development* (pp. 233–288). Hillsdale, NJ: Erlbaum.

Higgins, A. T., & Turnure, J. E. (1984). Distractibility and concentration in children's development. *Child Development, 55,* 1799–1810.

Hill, C. R., & Stafford, F. P. (1980). Parental care of children: Time diary of quantity, predictability, and variety. *Journal of Human Resources, 15,* 219–239.

Hindelang, M. J. (1981). Variations in sex–race–age-specific incidence of offending. *American Sociological Review, 46,* 461–474.

Hinshaw, S. P. (1992). Externalizing behavior problems and academic underachievement in children and adolescents: Causal relationships and underlying mechanisms. *Psychological Bulletin, 111,* 127–155.

Hinshaw, S. P., & Anderson, C. A. (1996). Conduct and oppositional defiant disorders. In E. J. Mash & R. A. Barkley (Eds.), *Child psychopathology* (pp. 113–152). New York: Guilford Press.

Hinshaw, S. P., Henker, B., Whalen, C. K., Erhardt, D., & Dunnington, R. E. (1989). Aggressive, prosocial, and nonsocial behavior in hyperactive boys: Dose effects of methylphenidate in natural settings. *Journal of Consulting and Clinical Psychology, 57,* 636–643.

Hops, H., Walker, H. M., & Greenwood, C. R. (1987). *CLASS (Contingencies for learning academic and social skills) program* (rev. ed.). Delray Beach, FL: Educational Academic Systems.

Hoza, B., Pelham, W. E., Milich, R., Pillow, D., & McBride, K. (1993). The self perceptions and attributions of attention-deficit hyperactivity disordered and nonreferred boys. *Journal of Abnormal Child Psychology, 21,* 271–286.

Huesmann, L. R. (1986). Psychological processes promoting the relation between exposure to media violence and aggressive behavior by the viewer. *Journal of Social Issues, 42,* 125–139.

Hunt, R. D., Lau, S., & Ryu, J. (1991). Alternative therapies for ADHD. In L. Greenhill (Ed.), *Ritalin theory and practice* (pp. 75–95). New York: Liebert.

Hunt, R. D., Mandl, L., Lau, S., & Hughes, M. (1991). Neurobiological theories of ADHD and Ritalin. In L. Greenhill (Ed.), *Ritalin theory and practice* (pp. 267–287). New York: Liebert.

Hunt, R. D., Minderaa, R. B., & Cohen, D. J. (1985). Clonidine benefits children with attention deficit disorder with hyperactivity: Report of a double-blind placebo-crossover therapeutic trial. *Journal of the American Academy of Child Psychiatry, 24,* 617–629.

Hynd, G. W., Hern, K. L., Novey, E. S., Eliopulos, D., Marshall, R., Gonzalez, J., & Voeller, K. J. (1993). Attention-deficit hyperactivity disorder and asymmetry of the caudate nucleus. *Journal of Child Neurology, 8,* 339–347.

Hynd, G. W., Lorys, A., Semrud-Clikeman, M., Nieves, N., Huettner, M., & Lahey, B. (1991). Attention-deficit disorder without hyperactivity: A distinct behavioral and neurocognitive syndrome. *Journal of Child Neurology, 6,* S37–S43.

Hynd, G. W., Semrud-Clikeman, M., Lorys, A., Novey, E., & Eliopulos, D. (1990). Brain morphology in developmental dyslexia and attention-deficit disorder/hyperactivity. *Archives of Neurology, 47,* 919–926.

Hynd, G. W., & Willis, W. G. (1988). *Pediatric neuropsychology.* Orlando, FL: Grune & Stratton.

Irvine, J. J. (1986). Teacher–student interactions: Effects of student, race, sex, and grade level. *Journal of Educational Psychology, 78,* 14–21.

Isaac, G. (1992). Misdiagnosed bipolar disorder in adolescents in a special educational school and treatment program. *Journal of Clinical Psychiatry, 53,* 133–136.

Jacob, R. G., O'Leary, K. D., & Rosenblad, C. (1978). Formal and informal classroom settings: Effects on hyperactivity. *Journal of Abnormal Child Psychology, 6,* 47–59.

Jacobson, J. L., & Wille, D. E. (1986). Influence of attachment pattern on developmental changes in peer interaction from the toddler to the preschool period. *Child Development, 57,* 338–347.

Jacobvitz, D., Sroufe, A., Stewart, M., & Leffert, N. (1990). Treatment of attentional and hyperactivity problems in children with sympathomimetic drugs: A comprehensive review. *Journal of the American Academy of Child and Adolescent Psychiatry, 29,* 677–688.

Jaffe, S. L. (1991). Intranasal abuse of prescribed methylphenidate by an alcohol and drug abusing adolescent with ADHD. *Journal of the American Academy of Child and Adolescent Psychiatry, 30,* 773–775.

Johnston, C., & Pelham, W. E. (1986). Teacher ratings predict peer ratings of aggression at 3-year follow-up in boys with attention deficit disorder with hyperactivity. *Journal of Consulting and Clinical Psychology, 54,* 571–572.

Johnston, C., Pelham, W. E., & Murphy, H. A. (1985). Peer relationships in ADHD and normal children: A developmental analysis of peer and teacher ratings. *Journal of Abnormal Child Psychology, 13,* 89–100.

Jones, C. (1989, November/December). Managing the difficult child. *Family Day Caring,* pp. 6–7.

Jones, C. (1994). *Attention deficit disorder: Strategies for school age children.* San Antonio, TX: Communication Skill Builders: A Division of the Psychological Corporation.

Justice, E. (1985). Categorization as a preferred memory strategy: Developmental changes during elementary school. *Developmental Psychology, 21,* 1105–1110.

Kagan, J. (1965). *Matching Familiar Figures Test.* Cambridge, MA: Harvard University Press.

Kagan, J., & Snidman, N. (1991). Temperamental factors in human development. *American Psychologist, 46,* 856–862.

Kalat, J. W. (1975). Minimal brain dysfunction: Dopamine depletion? *Science, 194,* 450.

Kaplan, H. I., & Sadock, B. J. (1985). *Modern synopsis of psychiatry* (IV). Baltimore: Williams & Wilkins.

Kazdin, A. E. (1980). Acceptability of time out from reinforcement procedures for disruptive child behavior. *Behavior Therapy, 11,* 329–344.

Kelly, K., & Ramundo, P. (1993). *You mean I'm not lazy, stupid or crazy?!* Cincinnati: Tyrell & Jerem Press.

Kertesy, A., Nicholson, I., & Cancelliere, A. (1985). Motor impersistence: A right hemisphere syndrome. *Neurology, 35,* 662–666.

Khalli, A., & Shashaani, L. (1994). The effectiveness of computer applications: A meta-analysis. *Journal of Research on Computing in Education, 27,* 48–61.

Kinsbourne, M. (1996, October). *Quality of life in individuals with ADHD.* Paper presented at the spring conference of CH.A.D.D., Milwaukee, WI.

Klein, D. F., Gittelman, R., Quitkin, F., & Rifkin, A. (1980). *Diagnosis and drug treatment of psychiatric disorders: Adults and children.* Baltimore: Williams & Wilkins.

Klein, R. G. (1993). Clinical efficacy of methylphenidate in children and adolescents. *L'Encephale, 19,* 89–93.

Klein, R. G., & Abikoff, H. (1989). The role of psychostimulants and psychosocial treatments in hyperkinesis. In T. Sagvolden & T. Archer (Eds.), *Attention-deficit disorder: Clinical and basic research* (pp. 167–180). Hillsdale, NJ: Erlbaum.

Klein, R. G., & Mannuzza, S. (1988). Hyperactive boys almost grown-up: III. Methylphenidate effects on ultimate height. *Archives of General Psychiatry, 45,* 1131–1134.

Klein, R. G., & Mannuzza, S. (1989). The long-term outcome of the attention-deficit disorder/hyperkinetic syndrome. In T. Sagvolden & T. Archer (Eds.), *Attention-deficit disorder: Clinical and basic research* (pp. 71–91). Hillsdale, NJ: Erlbaum.

Klein, R. G., & Mannuzza, S. (1991). The long-term outcome of hyperactive children: A review [Special Section: Longitudinal research]. *Journal of the American Academy of Child and Adolescent Psychiatry, 30,* 383–387.

Klinderfuss, G. H., Lange, P. H., Weinberg, W. A., & O'Leary, J. (1965). Electroencephalographic abnormalities of children with hyperkinetic behavior. *Neurology, 15,* 883–891.

Klorman, R., Brumaghim, J. T., Fitzpatrick, P. A., & Borgstedt, A. D. (1990). Clinical effects of a controlled trial of methylphenidate on adolescents with attention deficit disorder. *Journal of the American Academy of Child and Adolescent Psychiatry, 29,* 702–709.

Knobel, M., Wolman, M. B., & Mason, E. (1959). Hyperkinesis and organicity in children. *Archives of General Psychiatry, 1,* 310–321.

Koella, W. P. (1982). A modern neurobiological concept of vigilance. *Experimentia, 38,* 1426–1437.

Kohlberg, L. (1969). Stage and sequence: The cognitive–developmental approach to socialization. In D. Gosslin (Ed.), *Handbook of socialization theory and research.* Chicago: Rand McNally.

Kohlberg, L., & Candee, D. (1984). The relationship of moral judgment to moral action. In W. M. Kurtines & J. L. Gerwitz (Eds.), *Morality, moral behavior, and moral development.* New York: Wiley.

Kohlberg, L., & Gilligan, C. (1971, Fall). The adolescent as philosopher: The discovery of the self in a postconventional world. *Daedalus,* 1051–1086.

Kolb, B., & Whishaw, I. (1990). *Fundamentals of human neuropsychology* (3rd ed.). San Francisco: Freeman.

Kolligan, J., & Sternberg, R. J. (1987). Intelligence, information processing, and specific learning disability. *Journal of Learning Disabilities, 20,* 8–17.

Kopp, C. (1982). Antecedents of self-regulation: A developmental perspective. *Developmental Psychology, 18,* 199–214.

Kopp, C. B., & Brownell, C. A. (1991). The development of self: The first 3 years. *Developmental Review, 11,* 195–196.

Koziol, L. F., & Stout, C. E. (1992). Use of a verbal fluency measure in understanding and evaluating ADHD as an executive function. *Perceptual and Motor Skills, 75,* 1187–1192.

Kreft, L., & Soriano, M. (1993). *Project mission possible: Final evaluation report.* Washington, DC: Unpublished manuscript.

Lachenmeyer, J. R., & Muni-Brander, P. (1988). Eating disorders in a nonclinical adolescent population: Implications for treatment. *Adolescence, 23,* 303–312.

Lahey, B. B., Pelham, W. E., Stein, M. A., Loney, J., Trapani, C., Nugent, K., Kipp, H., Schmidt, E., Lee, S., Cale, M., Gold, E., Hartung, C. M., Wilcutt, E., & Baumann, B. (1998). Validity of DSM-IV attention-deficit/hyperactivity disorder for younger children. *Journal of the American Academy of Child and Adolescent Psychiatry, 37,* 695–701.

Lahey, B., Piacentini, J. C., McBurnette, K., Stone, P., Hartdagen, S., & Hynd, G. W. (1988). Psychopathology in the parents of children with conduct disorder and hyperactivity. *Journal of American Academy of Child and Adolescent Psychiatry, 27,* 163–170.

Lahey, B., Schaughency, E., Hynd, G. W., Carlson, C., & Nieves, N. (1987). Attention-deficit disorder with and without hyperactivity: Comparison of behavioral characteristics of clinic-referred children. *American Academy of Child and Adolescent Psychiatry, 26,* 718–723.

Lahey, B., Schaughency, E., Strauss, C., & Frame, C. (1984). Are attention-deficit disorder with and without hyperactivity similar or dissimilar disorders? *Journal of the American Academy of Child Psychiatry, 23,* 302–309.

Lamb, M. E., Thompson, R. A., Gardner, W., Charnov, E. L., & Connell, J. P. (1985). *Infant–mother attachment: The origins and developmental significance of individual differences in Strange Situation behavior.* Hillsdale, NJ: Erlbaum.

Lambert, N. M., & Sandoval, J. (1980). The prevalence of learning disabilities in a sample of children considered hyperactive. *Journal of Abnormal Child Psychology, 8,* 33–50.

Landau, S., & Moore, L. (1991). Social skills deficits in children with attention-deficit hyperactivity disorder. *School Psychology Review, 20,* 235–251.

Latham, P. S., & Latham, P. H. (1995). Legal rights of the ADD adult. In K. G. Nadeau (Ed.), *A comprehensive guide to attention-deficit disorder in adults: Research, diagnosis, and treatment* (pp. 337–351). New York: Brunner/Mazel.

Laufer, M., Denhoff, E., & Solomons, G. (1957). Hyperkinetic impulse disorder in children's behavior problems. *Psychosomatic Medicine, 19,* 38–49.

LeFrancois, G. R. (1995). *An introduction to child development* (8th ed.). Belmont, CA: Wadsworth.

Lefkowitz, M. M., Eron, L. D., Walder, L. O., & Huesman, L. R. (1972). Television violence and child aggression: A follow-up study. In G. A.

Comstock & E. A. Rubinstein (Eds.), *Television and social behavior* (Vol. 3, pp. 35–135). Washington, DC: U.S. Government Printing Office.

Levine, M. (1993). *Developmental variation and learning disorders.* Cambridge, MA: Educator's Publishing Service.

Levine, M. (1994). *Educational care: A system for understanding and helping children with learning problems at home and at school.* Cambridge, MA: Educator's Publishing Service.

Levinson, D. (1986). A conception of adult development. *American Psychologist, 41,* 3–13.

Levy, F. (1980). The development of sustained attention (vigilance) and inhibition in children: Some normative data. *Journal of Child Psychology and Psychiatry, 21,* 77–84.

Levy, F. (1991). The dopamine theory of attention deficit hyperactivity disorder (ADHD). *Australian and New Zealand Journal of Psychiatry, 25,* 277–283.

Levy, F., Hay, D. A., McStephen, M., Wood, C., & Waldman, I. (1997). Attention-deficit hyperactivity disorder: A category or a continuum? Genetic analysis of a large-scale twin study. *Journal of the American Academy of Child and Adolescent Psychiatry, 36,* 737–744.

Lewis, M., Feiring, C., McGuffog, C., & Jaskir, J. (1984). Predicting psychopathology in six-year-olds from early social relations. *Child Development, 55,* 123–136.

Lewis, M., & Miller, S. M. (1990). *Handbook of developmental psychopathology.* New York: Plenum Press.

Loeber, R. (1990). Developmental risk factors of juvenile antisocial behavior and delinquency. *Clinical Psychology Review, 10,* 1–41.

Lombardino, L. J., & Mangan, N. (1983). Parents as language trainers: Language programming with developmentally delayed children. *Exceptional Children, 49,* 358–361.

Loney, J., Kramer, J., & Milich, R. (1981). The hyperkinetic child grows up: Predictors of symptoms, delinquency, and achievement at follow-up. In K. D. Gadow & J. Loney (Eds.), *Psychological aspects of drug treatment for hyperactivity.* Boulder, CO: Westview Press.

Loney, J., & Milich, R. (1982). Hyperactivity, inattention, and aggression in clinical practice. In D. Routh & M. Wolraich (Eds.), *Advances in developmental and behavioral pediatrics* (Vol. 3, pp. 113–147). Greenwich, CT: JAI Press.

Lou, H., Henriksen, L., & Bruhn, P. (1984). Focal cerebral hypo-perfusion in children with dysphasia and/or attention deficit disorder. *Archives of Neurology, 41,* 825–829.

Lou, H., Henriksen, L., Bruhn, P., Borner, H., & Nielsen, J. B. (1989). Striatal dysfunction in attention deficit and hyperkinetic disorder. *Archives of Neurology, 46,* 48–52.

Maccoby, E. E. (1980). *Social development.* New York: Harcourt Brace Jovanovich.

Maccoby, E. E. (1984). Middle childhood in the context of the family. In W. A. Collins (Ed.), *Development during middle childhood: The years from six to twelve.* Washington, DC: National Academy.

Maccoby, E. E., & Hagen, J. W. (1965). Effects of distraction upon central versus incidental recall. *Journal of Experimental Child Psychology, 2,* 280–289.

Maccoby, E. E., & Martin, J. A. (1983). Socialization in the context of the family. In E. M. Hetherington (Ed.), *Handbook of child psychology: Socialization, personality and social development.* New York: Wiley.

Mannuzza, S., Gittelman, R., Konig, P. H., & Giampino, T. L. (1989). Hyperactive boys almost grown up: IV. Criminality and its relationship to psychiatric status. *Archives of General Psychiatry, 46,* 1073–1079.

Mannuzza, S., Klein, R. G., Bessler, A., Malloy, P., & LaPadula, M. (1993). Adult outcome of hyperactive boys. *Archives of General Psychiatry, 50,* 565–576.

Marcia, J. E. (1980). Identity in adolescence. In J. Adelson (Ed.), *Handbook of adolescent psychology.* New York: Wiley.

Marholin, D., & Steinman, W. M. (1977). Stimulus control in the classroom as a function of the behavior reinforced. *Journal of Applied Behavior Analysis, 10,* 465–478.

Mariani, M., & Barkley, R. A. (1997). Neuropsychological and academic functioning in preschool children with attention-deficit hyperactivity disorder. *Developmental Neuropsychology, 13,* 111–129.

Markman, E. M. (1979). Realizing that you don't understand: Elementary school children's awareness of inconsistencies. *Child Development, 50,* 643–655.

Markus, H., & Nurius, P. S. (1984). Self-understanding and self-regulation in middle childhood. In W. A. Collins (Eds.), *Development during middle childhood: The years from six to twelve.* Washington, DC: National Academy.

Martin, J. A. (1981). A longitudinal study of the consequences of early mother–infant interaction: A microanalytic approach. *Monographs of the Society for Research in Child Development, 46*(3, Serial No. 190).

Martin, T. C., & Bumpass, L. L. (1989). Recent trends in marital disruption. *Demography, 26,* 27–51.

Mash, E. J., & Barkley, R. A. (Eds.). (1989). *Child psychopathology.* New York: Guilford Press.

Mash, E. J., & Barkley, R. A. (Eds.). (1996). *Child psychopathology* (2nd ed.). New York: Guilford Press.

Mash, E. J., & Dozois, D. A. (1996). Child psychopathology: A developmental systems perspective. In E. J. Mash & R. A. Barkely (Eds.), *Child psychopathology* (pp. 3–62). New York: Guilford Press.

Mash, E. J., & Johnston, C. (1982). Comparison of the mother–child interactions of younger and older hyperactive and normal children. *Child Development, 53,* 1371–1381.

Mash, E. J., & Johnston, C. (1983). Parental perceptions of child behavior problems, parenting self-esteem, and mothers' reported stress in younger and older hyperactives and normal children. *Journal of Consulting and Clinical Psychology, 51,* 86–99.

Masur, E. F., McIntyre, C. W., & Flavell, J. H. (1973). Developmental changes in apportionment of study time among items in a multi-trial free recall task. *Journal of Experimental Child Psychology, 15,* 237–246.

Matochik, J. A., Liebenauer, L. L., King, A. C., Szymanski, H. V., Cohen, R. M., & Zametkin, A. J. (1994). Cerebral glucose metabolism in adults with attention deficit hyperactivity disorder after chronic stimulant treatment. *American Journal of Psychiatry, 151,* 658–664.

Mattes, J., & Gittelman, R. (1983). Growth of hyperactive children on maintenance regimen of methylphenidate. *Archives of General Psychiatry, 40,* 317–321.

Matthews, K. A., & Rodin, J. (1989). Women's changing work roles: Impact on health, family, and public policy. *American Psychologist, 44,* 1389–1393.

McBurnett, K., Lahey, B. B., & Pfiffner, L. J. (1993). Diagnosis of attention deficit disorders in *DSM-IV*: Scientific basis and implications in education. *Exceptional Children, 60,* 108–117.

McCain, A. P., & Kelly, M. L. (1993). Managing the classroom behavior of an ADHD preschooler: The efficacy of a school–home note intervention. *Child and Family Behavior Therapy, 15,* 22–44.

McCullough, C. S. (1995). Using computer technology to monitor student progress and remediate reading problems. *School Psychology Review, 24,* 426–439.

McGee, R., Silva, P. A., & Williams, S. (1984). Perinatal, neurological, environmental, and developmental characteristics of seven-year-old children with stable behavior problems. *Journal of Child Psychology and Psychiatry, 25,* 573–586.

McGee, R., Williams, S., Moffitt, T., & Anderson, J. (1989). A comparison of 13-year-old boys with attention deficit and or reading disorder on neuropsychological measures. *Journal of Abnormal Child Psychology, 17,* 37–53.

McGuinness, D., & Pribram, K. (1980). The neuropsychology of attention and motivational controls. In M. C. Wittrock (Ed.), *The brain and psychology* (pp. 95–139). NY: Academic Press.

McLeer, S. V., Callaghan, M., Henry, D., & Wallen, J. (1994). Psychiatric disorders in sexually abused children. *Journal of the American Academy of Child and Adolescent Psychiatry, 33,* 313–319.

Meichenbaum, D. (1976). Cognitive functional approach to cognitive factors as determinants of learning disabilities. In R. Knights & D. Bakker (Eds.), *The neuropsychology of learning disorders.* Baltimore: University Park Press.

Mendelson, W. B., Johnson, N. E., & Stewart, M. A. (1971). Hyperactive children as adolescents: How they describe themselves. *Journal of Nervous and Mental Disease, 153,* 273–279.

Menkes, M. M., Rowe, J. S., & Menkes, J. H. (1967). A twenty-five-year follow-up study of hyperkinetic children with minimal brain dysfunction. *Pediatrics, 39,* 393–399.

Milich, R. (1994). The response of children with ADHD to failure: If at first you don't succeed, do try, try, again? *School Psychology Review, 23,* 11–28.

Milich, R., & Dodge, K. A. (1984). Social information processing in child psychiatric populations. *Journal of Abnormal Child Psychology, 12,* 471–490.

Milich, R., & Greenwell, L. (1991, December). An examination of learned helplessness among attention-deficit hyperactivity disordered boys. In B. Hoza & W. E. Pelham (Chairs), *Cognitive bases as mediators of childhood disorders: What do we know?* Symposium conducted at the annual meeting of the Association for Advancement of Behavior Therapy, New York.

Milich, R., & Kraemer, J. (1985). Reflections on impulsivity: An empirical investigation of impulsivity as a construct. In K. D. Gadow & I. Bialer (Eds.), *Advances in learning and behavioral disabilities* (Vol. 3, pp. 117–150). Greenwich, CT: JAI Press.

Milich, R., & Landau, S. (1989). The role of social status variables in differentiating subgroups of hyperactive children. In L. M. Bloomingdale & J. Swanson (Eds.), *Attention-deficit disorder: Current concepts and emerging trends in attentional and behavioral disorders of childhood* (Vol. 5, pp. 1–16). Elmsford, NY: Pergamon Press.

Milich, R., Landau, S., Kilby, G., & Whitten, P. (1982). Preschool peer perceptions of the behavior of hyperactive and aggressive children. *Journal of Abnormal Child Psychology, 10,* 497–510.

Milich, R., Licht, B. G., Murphy, D. A., & Pelham, W. E. (1989). ADHD boys' evaluation of and attributions for task performance on medication versus placebo. *Journal of Abnormal Psychology, 98,* 280–284.

Milich, R., Loney, J., & Landau, S. (1982). The independent dimensions of hyperactivity and aggression: A validation with playroom observation data. *Journal of Abnormal Psychology, 91,* 183–198.

Milich, R., & Okasaki, M. (1991). An examination of learned helplessness in attention-deficit hyperactivity disordered boys. *Journal of Abnormal Child Psychology, 19,* 607–623.

Miller, B., McCoy, J., Olsen, T., & Wallace, C. (1986). Parental discipline and control attempts in relation to adolescent sexual attitudes and behavior. *Journal of Marriage and the Family, 48,* 503–512.

Millstein, S. G. (1993). Perceptual, attributional, and affective processes in perceptions of vulnerability through the life span. In N. T. Bell & R. W. Bell (Eds.), *Adolescent risk taking* (pp. 55–65). Newbury Park, CA: Sage.

Minde, K., Weiss, G., & Mendelson, N. (1972). A five-year follow-up of 91 hyperactive children. *Journal of the American Academy of Child Psychiatry, 11,* 595–610.

Moffitt, T. E. (1993). Life-course-persistent and adolescent-limited antisocial behavior: A developmental taxonomy. *Psychological Review, 100,* 674–701.

Moffitt, T. E., & Henry, B. (1989). Neuropsychological assessment of executive functions in self-reported delinquents. *Development and Psychopathology, 1,* 105–118.

Moffitt, T. E., & Silva, P. A. (1988). Self-reported delinquency, neuropsychological deficit, and history of attention deficit disorder. *Journal of Abnormal Child Psychology, 16,* 553–569.

Montemayor, R., & Van Komen, R. (1980). Age segregation of adolescents in and out of school. *Journal of Youth and Adolescence, 9,* 371–381.

Morrison, G. M., Furlong, M. J., & Morrison, R. L. (1994). School violence to

References   351

school safety: Reframing the issue for school psychologists. *School Psychology Review, 23,* 236–256.

Morrison, J. (1980). Adult psychiatric disorders in parents of hyperactive children. *American Journal of Psychiatry, 137,* 825–827.

Morrison, J., & Stewart, M. (1971). A family study of the hyperactive child syndrome. *Biological Psychiatry, 3,* 189–195.

Muuss, R. E. (1988). Carol Gilligan's theory of sex differences in the development of moral reasoning during adolescence. *Adolescence, 23,* 229–243.

Nadeau, K. G. (1991). If your spouse has ADHD. . . . *Chesapeake Bulletin, 3,* 2–4.

Nadeau, K. G. (1993). Partners of ADD adults. *Chesapeake Bulletin, 5,* 1.

Nadeau, K. G. (1995). ADD in the workplace: Career consultation and counseling for the adult with ADD. In K. G. Nadeau (Ed.), *A comprehensive guide to attention-deficit disorder in adults: Research, diagnosis, and treatment* (pp. 308–336). New York: Brunner/Mazel.

National Center for Educational Statistics. (1987). *Who drops out of high school? From high school and beyond.* Washington, DC: U.S. Department of Education, Office of Educational Research and Improvement.

National Center for Health Statistics. (1990). *Health United States 1989 and prevention profile* (DHHS Publication No. 90-1232). Washington, DC: U.S. Government Printing Office.

Newby, R. F., Fischer, M., & Roman, M. A. (1991). Parent training for families of children with ADHD. *School Psychology Review, 20,* 252–265.

Newcome, M. D., & Bentler, P. M. (1988). *Consequences of adolescent drug use: Impact on the lives of young adults.* Newbury Park, CA: Sage.

Newcomer, S., & Udry, J. (1987). Parental marriage effects on adolescent sexual behavior. *Journal of Marriage and Family, 48,* 777–782.

Nezworski, T., Tolan, W., & Belsky, J. (1988). Intervention in insecure infant attachment. In J. Belsky & T. Nezworski (Eds.), *Clinical implications of attachment* (pp. 353–386). Hillsdale, NJ: Erlbaum.

Nunner-Winkler, G. (1984). Two moralities? A critical discussion of an ethic of care and responsibility versus an ethic of rights and justice. In W. M. Kurtines & J. L. Gerwitz (Eds.), *Morality, moral behavior, and moral development.* New York: Wiley.

Offer, D. O., & Offer, J. (1975). *From teenage to young manhood: A psychological study.* New York: Basic Books.

Offer, D. O., Ostrov, E., & Howard, K. (1984). *Patterns of adolescent self-image.* New York: Plenum Press.

Offer, D. O., Ostrov, E., Howard, K., & Atkinson, R. (1988). *The teenage world: Adolescents' self-image in ten countries.* New York: Plenum Press.

Offord, D. R., Sullivan, K., Allen, N., & Abrams, N. (1979). Delinquency and hyperactivity. *Journal of Nervous and Mental Disorders, 167,* 734–741.

Ohannessian, C., & Crockett, L. (1993). A longitudinal investigation of the relationship between educational investment and adolescent sexual activity. *Journal of Adolescent Research, 8,* 167–182.

Olson, R., Huszti, H., & Youll, L. K. (1995). Sexual behaviors and problems of adolescents. In M. C. Roberts (Ed.), *Handbook of pediatric psychology* (2nd ed., pp. 327–341). New York: Guilford Press.

Ornoy, A., Uriel, L., & Tennebaum, A. (1993). Inattention, hyperactivity, and speech delay at 2–4 years of age as a predictor for ADD–ADHD syndrome. *Israel Journal of Psychiatry and Related Sciences, 30,* 155–163.

Ornstein, P. A., Baker-Ward, L., & Naus, M. J. (1988). The development of mnemonic skill. In F. E. Weinert & M. J. Perlmutter (Eds.), *Memory development: Universal changes and individual differences.* Hillsdale, NJ: Erlbaum.

Paikoff, R. L., & Brooks-Gunn, J. (1991). Do parent–child relationships change during puberty? *Psychological Bulletin, 110,* 47–66.

Palfrey, J. S., Levine, M. D., Walker, D. K., & Sullivan, M. (1985). The emergence of attention deficits in early childhood: A prospective study. *Developmental and Behavioral Pediatrics, 6,* 339–348.

Palkes, H., Stewart, M., & Kahana, B. (1968). Porteus maze performance of hyperactive boys after training in self-directed verbal commands. *Child Development, 39,* 817–826.

Pangiagua, F. A. (1992). Verbal–nonverbal correspondence training with ADHD children. *Behavior Modification, 16,* 226–252.

Pangiagua, F. A., Morrison, P. B., & Black, S. A. (1990). Management of a hyperactive–conduct disordered child through correspondence training: A preliminary study. *Journal of Behavior Therapy and Experimental Psychiatry, 21,* 63–68.

Papalia, D. (1972). The status of several conservative abilities across the life-span. *Human Development, 15,* 229–243.

Papalia, D. E., & Olds, S. W. (1992). *Human development* (5th ed.). New York: McGraw-Hill.

Park, K. A., Lay, K. L., & Ramsey, L. (1993). Individual differences and developmental changes in preschoolers' friendship. *Developmental Psychology, 29,* 264–270.

Parker, J. G., & Asher, S. R. (1987). Peer relations and later personal adjustment: Are low-accepted children at risk? *Psychological Bulletin, 102,* 357–389.

Parmelee, A. H., Sigman, M., Garbanati, J., Cohen, S., Beckwith, L., & Asarnow, R. (1994). Neonatal electroencephalographic organization and attention in early adolescence. In G. Dawson & K. W. Fischer (Eds.), *Human behavior and the developing brain* (pp. 537–554). New York: Guilford Press.

Parry, P. (1973). *The effect of reward on the performance of hyperactive children.* Unpublished doctoral dissertation, McGill University, Montreal.

Parry, P. A., & Douglas, V. I. (1983). Effects of reinforcement on concept identification in hyperactive children. *Journal of Abnormal Child Psychology, 11,* 327–340.

Paternite, C. E., Loney, J., & Langhorne, J. E. (1976). Relationships between symptomology and SES related factors in hyperkinetic/MBD boys. *American Journal of Orthopsychiatry, 46,* 291–301.

Patterson, G. R. (1976). *Living with children: New methods for parents and teachers.* Champaign, IL: Research Press.

Patterson, G. R. (1982). *A social learning approach to family intervention: Vol. 3. Coercive family process.* Eugene, OR: Castalia.

Patterson, G. R., DeBaryshe, B. D., & Ramsey, E. (1989). A developmental perspective on antisocial behavior. *American Psychologist, 44,* 329–335.

Patterson, G. R., & Fleischman, M. J. (1979). Maintenance of treatment effects: Some considerations concerning family systems and follow-up data. *Behavior Therapy, 10,* 168–185.

Patterson, G. R., Reid, J. B., Jones, R. B., & Conger, R. E. (1975). *A social learning approach to family intervention: Vol. 1. Families with aggressive children.* Eugene, OR: Castalia.

Pederson, E., Faucher, T. A., & Eaton, W. W. (1978). A new perspective of the effects of first-grade teachers on children's subsequent adult status. *Harvard Educational Review, 48,* 1–31.

Patterson, G. R. (1986). *Living with children: New methods for parents and teachers.* Champaign, IL: Research Press.

Pelham, W. E. (1993a). Pharmacotherapy for children with attention-deficit hyperactivity disorder. *School Psychology Review, 22,* 199–227.

Pelham, W. E. (1993b, April). *Behavioral assessment and pharmacology in ADHD: An integrated approach.* Paper presented at the meeting of the National Association of School Psychologists, Washington, DC.

Pelham, W. E., & Bender, M. (1982). Peer interactions of hyperactive children: Assessment and treatment. In K. D. Gadow & I. Bialer (Eds.), *Advances in learning and behavior disabilities* (pp. 365–436). Greenwich, CT: JAI Press.

Pelham, W. E., Carlson, C., Sams, S. E., Vallano, G., Dixon, M. I., & Hoza, B. (1993). Separate and combined effects of methylphenidate and behavior modification of boys with attention-deficit hyperactivity disorder in the classroom. *Journal of Consulting and Clinical Psychology, 61,* 506–515.

Pelham, W. E., Carlson, C., Sams, S. E., Vallano, G., Dixon, M. J., & Hoza, B. (1993). Separate and combined effects of methylphenidate and behavior modification on the classroom performance of ADHD boys: Group effects and individual differences. *Journal of Consulting and Clinical Psychology, 61,* 506–515.

Pelham, W. E., & Hoza, J. (1987). Behavioral assessment of psychostimulant effects on ADD children in a summer day treatment program. In R. Prinz (Ed.), *Advances in behavioral assessment of children and families* (Vol. 3, pp. 3–33). Greenwich, CT: JAI Press.

Pelham, W. E., McBurnett, K., Harper, G. W., Milich, R., Murphy, D. A., Clinton, J., & Thiele, C. (1990). Methylphenidate and baseball playing in ADHD children: Who's on first? *Journal of Consulting and Clinical Psychology, 58,* 130–133.

Pelham, W. E., Murphy, D. A., Vannatta, K., Milich, R., Licht, B. G., Gnagy, E. M., Greenslade, K. E., Greiner, A. R., & Vodde-Hamilton, M. (1992). Methylphenidate and attributions in boys with attention-deficit hyperactivity disorder. *Journal of Consulting and Clinical Psychology, 60,* 282–292.

Pelham, W. E., & Murphy, H. A. (1986). Attention deficit and conduct disorders. In M. Hersen (Ed.), *Pharmacological and behavioral treatment: An integrative approach* (pp. 108–148). New York: Wiley.

Pelham, W. E., Schnedler, R. W., Bender, M. E., Miller, J., Nilsson, D., Budrow, M., Ronnei, M., Paluchowski, C., & Marks, D. (1988). The combination of behavior therapy and methylphenidate in the treatment of hyperactivity: A therapy outcome study. In L. Bloomingdale (Ed.), *Attention deficit disorder* (pp. 29–48). London: Pergamon.

Pennington, B. F., & Bennetto, L. (1993). Main effects or transactions in the neuropsychology of conduct disorder? Commentary on "The neuropsychology of conduct disorder." *Development and Psychopathology, 5,* 151–164.

Pennington, B. F., & Ozonoff, S. (1996). Executive functions and developmental psychopathology. *Journal of Child Psychology and Psychiatry, 37,* 51–87.

Petersen, A. C. (1988). Adolescent development. *Annual Review of Psychology, 39,* 583–607.

Pfiffner, L. J., & Barkley, R. A. (1990). Educational placement and classroom management. In R. A. Barkley, *Attention-deficit hyperactivity disorder: A handbook for diagnosis and treatment* (pp. 498–539). New York: Guilford Press.

Pfiffner, L. J. & O'Leary, S. G. (1987). The efficacy of all-positive management as a function of the prior use of negative consequences. *Journal of Applied Behavior Analysis, 20,* 265-271.

Pfiffner, L. J., Rosen, L. A., & O'Leary, S. G. (1985). The efficacy of an all-positive approach to classroom management. *Journal of Applied Behavior Analysis, 18,* 257–261.

Phelan, T. W. (1993). *Surviving your adolescents: How to manage and let go of your 13–18 year olds.* Glen Ellyn, IL: Child Managment.

Pianta, R. C., & Ball, R. M. (1993). Maternal social support as a predictor of child adjustment in kindergarten. *Journal of Applied Developmental Psychology, 14,* 107–120.

Pisterman, S., McGrath, P., Firestone, P., Goodman, J. T., Webster, I., & Mallory, R. (1989). Outcome of parent mediated treatment of preschoolers with attention-deficit disorder with hyperactivity. *Journal of Consulting and Clinical Psychology, 57,* 628–635.

Platzman, K. A., Stoy, M. R., Brown, R. T., Coles, C. D., Smith, I. E., & Falek, A. (1992). Review of observational methods in attention deficit hyperactivity disorder (ADHD): Implications for diagnosis. *School Psychology Quarterly, 7,* 155–177.

Pope, H. G., Hudson, J. I., Jurgelun-Todd, D., & Hudson, M. S. (1984). Prevalence of anorexia nervosa and bulimia in three student populations. *International Journal of Eating Disorders, 2,* 75–85.

Posner, M. I., & Petersen, S. E. (1990). The attention system of the human brain. *Annual Review of Neuroscience, 13,* 25–41.

Posner, M. I., & Raichle, M. E. (1994). Networks of attention. In M. I. Posner & M. E. Raichle (Eds.), *Images of mind* (pp. 153–179). New York: Scientific American Library.

Power, T. J., Atkins, M. S., Osbourne, M. L., & Blum, N. J. (1994). The school psychologist as manager for programming for ADHD. *School Psychology Review, 23,* 279–291.

Puig-Antich, J., & Chambers, W. J. (1978). *The Schedule for Affective Disorders and Schizophrenia for school-age children (Kiddie-SADS)*. New York: New York State Psychiatric Institute.

Quadrel, M., Fischhoff, B., & Davis, W. (1993) Adolescent invulnerability. [Special issue: Adolescence]. *American Psychologist, 48,* 102–116.

Quinn, P. O. (1995). Neurobiology of attention deficit disorder. In K. G. Nadeau (Ed.), *A comprehensive guide to attention deficit disorder in adults: Research, diagnosis, and treatment* (pp. 18–34). New York: Brunner/Mazel.

Rapoport, J. (1983). The use of drugs: Trends in research. In M. Rutter (Ed.), *Developmental neuropsychiatry* (pp. 385–403). New York: Guilford Press.

Rapoport, J. (1986). Antidepressants in childhood attention-deficit disorder and obsessive–compulsive disorder. *Psychosomatics, 27,* 30–36.

Rapoport, J. (1996, November). *Neurobiological research updates on attention-deficit disorders*. Paper presented at the annual meeting of CH.A.D.D., Chicago, IL.

Rapport, M. D., Murphy, H. A., & Bailey, J. S. (1982). Ritalin vs. response cost in the control of hyperactive children: A within-subject comparison. *Journal of Applied Behavior Analysis, 15,* 205–216.

Rapport, M. D., Stoner, G., DuPaul, G., Birmingham, B. K., & Tucker, S. (1985). Methylphenidate in hyperactive children: Differential effects of dose on academic, learning, and social behavior. *Journal of Abnormal Child Psychology, 13,* 227–244.

Rapport, M. D., Tucker, S. B., DuPaul, G. J., Merlo, M., & Stoner, G. (1986). Hyperactivity and frustration: The influence of control over and size of rewards in delaying gratification. *Journal of Abnormal Child Psychology, 14,* 191–204.

Ratey, J. J., Greenberg, S., Bemporad, J. R., & Lindem, K. (1992). Unrecognized attention-deficit hyperactivity disorder in adults presenting for outpatient psychotherapy. *Journal of Child and Adolescent Psychopharmacology, 4,* 267–275.

Ratey, J. J., Hallowell, E. M., & Miller, A. C. (1995). Relationship dilemmas for adults with ADD: The biology of intimacy. In K. G. Nadeau (Ed.), *A comprehensive guide to attention deficit disorder in adults: Research diagnosis and treatment* (pp. 218–235). New York: Brunner/Mazel.

Ratey, J. J., Miller, A. C., & Nadeau, K. G. (1995). Special diagnostic and treatment considerations for women with attention-deficit disorder. In K. G. Nadeau (Ed.), *A comprehensive guide to attention-deficit disorder in adults: Research, diagnosis, and treatment* (pp. 260–283). New York: Brunner/Mazel.

Rebok, G. W., & Balcerak, L. J. (1989). Memory self-efficacy and performance differences in young and old adults: The effect of mnemonic training. *Developmental Psychology, 25,* 714–721.

Reif, S. (1993). *How to reach and teach ADD/ADHD children*. West Nyack, NY: Center for Applied Research in Education.

Reynolds, W. M. (1989). *Reynolds Child Depression Scale*. Odessa, FL: Psychological Assessment Resources.

Rhode, G., Morgan, D. P., & Young, K. R. (1983). Generalization and maintenance of treatment gains of behaviorally handicapped students from resource rooms to regular classrooms using self-evaluation procedures. *Journal of Applied Behavior Analysis, 16,* 171–188.

Riccio, C. A., Hynd, G. W., Cohen, M. J., & Gonzalez, J. J. (1993). Neurobiological basis of attention-deficit hyperactivity disorder. *Exceptional Children, 60,* 118–124.

Richard, M. M. (1995). Students with attention deficit disorders in postsecondary education: Issues in identification and accommodation. In K. G. Nadeau (Ed.), *A comprehensive guide to attention deficit disorder in adults: Research, diagnosis, and treatment* (pp. 284–307). New York: Brunner/Mazel.

Richters, J. E., Arnold, L. E., Jensen, P. S., Abikoff, H., Conners, C. K., Greenhill, L. L., Hechtman, L., Hinshaw, S. P., Pelham, W. E., & Swanson, J. M. (1995). NIMH collaborative multisite multimodal treatment study of children with ADHD: I. Background and rationale. *Journal of the American Academy of Child and Adolescent Psychiatry, 34,* 987–1000.

Riddle, M., Hardin, M., Cho, S., Woolston, J., & Leckman, J. (1988). Desipramine treatment of boys with attention-deficit hyperactivity disorder and tics: Preliminary clinical experience. *Journal of the American Academy of Child and Adolescent Psychiatry, 27,* 811–814.

Riddle, M., Nelson, J. C., Kleinman, C. S., & Cohen, D. J. (1991). Sudden death in children receiving noripramine: A review of three reported cases and commentary. *Journal of the American Academy of Child and Adolescent Psychiatry, 30,* 104–108.

Robin, A. L. (1975). *Communication training: A problem-solving approach to parent–adolescent conflict.* Unpublished doctoral dissertation. State University of New York, Stony Brook.

Robin, A. L. (1981). A controlled evaluation of problem-solving communication training with parent–adolescent conflict. *Behavior Therapy, 12,* 593–609.

Robin, A. L. (1990). Training families with ADHD adolescents. In R. A. Barkley (Ed.), *Attention-deficit hyperactivity disorder: A handbook for diagnosis and treatment* (pp. 462–497). New York: Guilford Press.

Robin, A. L., & Foster, S. L. (1989). *Negotiating parent–adolescent conflict: A behavioral–family systems approach.* New York: Guilford Press.

Robin, A. L., Kraus, D., Koepke, T., & Robin, K. A. (1987, August). *Growing up hyperactive in single versus two-parent families.* Paper presented at the 95th annual convention of the American Psychological Association, New York.

Robins, L. N. (1978). Sturdy childhood predictors of adult outcomes: Replications from longitudinal studies. *Psychological Medicine, 8,* 611–622.

Robinson, P. W., Newby, T. J., & Ganzell, S. L. (1981). A token system for a class of underachieving hyperactive children. *Journal of Applied Behavior Analysis, 14,* 307-315.

Roche, J. P., & Ramsbay, T. W. (1993). Premarital sexuality: A five-year follow-up study of attitudes and behavior by dating stage. *Adolescence, 28,* 67–80.

Roosa, M. W. (1991). Adolescent pregnancy programs collection: An introduction. *Family Relations, 40,* 370–372.

Rosen, L. A., Gabardi, L., Miller, C. D., & Miller, L. (1990). Home-based treatment of disruptive junior high school students: An analysis of positive and negative consequences. *Behavioral Disorders, 15,* 227–232.

Rosen, L. A., O'Leary, S. G., Joyce, S. A., Conway, G., & Pfiffner, L. J. (1984). The importance of prudent negative consequences for maintaining the appropriate behavior of hyperactive students. *Journal of Abnormal Child Psychology, 12,* 581–604.

Rosenberg, M. (1979). *Conceiving the self.* New York: Basic Books.

Rosenfield, P., Lambert, N. M., & Black, A. (1985). Desk arrangement effects on pupil classroom behavior. *Journal of Educational Psychology, 77,* 101–108.

Rosenthal, R., & Jacobson, L. (1968). *Pygmalion in the classroom: Teacher expectations and pupils' intellectual development.* New York: Holt, Rinehart & Winston.

Ross, D. M., & Ross, S. A. (1982). *Hyperactivity: Current issues, research, and theory* (2nd ed.). New York: Wiley.

Rubin, Z. (1980). *Children's friendships.* Cambridge, MA: Harvard University Press.

Rutter, M. (1979). Maternal deprivation 1972–1977: New findings, new concepts, new approaches. *Child Development, 50,* 283–305.

Rutter, M. (1983). Behavioral studies: Questions and findings on the concept of a distinctive syndrome. In M. Rutter (Ed.), *Developmental neuropsychiatry* (pp. 259–279). New York: Guilford Press.

Rutter, M. (1984). Resilient children. *Psychology Today, 18,* 57–65.

Rutter, M. (1985). Resilience in the face of adversity: Protective factors and resistance to psychiatric disorder. *British Journal of Psychiatry, 147,* 598–611.

Rutter, M. (1987). Psychosocial resilience and protective mechanisms. *American Journal of Orthopsychiatry, 57,* 316–331.

Rutter, M. (1989). Attention deficit disorder/hyperkinetic syndrome: Conceptual and research issues regarding diagnosis and classification. In T. Sagvolden & T. Archer (Eds.), *Attention deficit disorder: Clinical and basic research* (pp. 1–24). Hillsdale, NJ: Erlbaum.

Rutter, M., Korn, S., & Birch, H. G. (1963). Genetic and environmental factors in the development of "primary reaction patterns." *British Journal of Social and Clinical Psychology, 2,* 162–173.

Saarni, C. (1982). Social and affective functions of nonverbal behavior: Developmental concerns. In R. Feldman (Ed.), *Development of nonverbal behavior in children* (pp. 123–147). New York: Springer-Verlag.

Safer, D. J., & Allen, R. P. (1976). *Hyperactive children.* Baltimore: University Park Press.

Sagvolden, T., Wultz, B., Moser, E. I., Moser, M. B., & Morkrid, L. (1989). Results from a comparative neuropsychological research program indicate altered reinforcement mechanisms in children with ADD. In T. Sagvolden & T. Archer (Eds.), *Attention-deficit disorder: Clinical and basic research* (pp. 261–286). Hillsdale, NJ: Erlbaum.

Sameroff, A. (1975). Transactional models in early social relations. *Human Development, 18,* 56–79.

Sameroff, A., & Chandler, M. (1975). Reproductive risk and the continuum of caretaker casualty. In F. D. Horowitz (Ed.), *Child development research* (Vol. 4). Chicago: University of Chicago Press.

Sander, L. W. (1975). Infant and caretaking environment. In E. J. Anthony (Ed.), *Exploration in psychiatry.* New York: Plenum Press.

Sandler, A. D. (1995). Attention deficits and neurodevelopmental variation in older adolescents and adults. In K. G. Nadeau (Ed.), *A comprehensive guide to attention-deficit disorder in adults: Research, diagnosis, and treatment* (pp. 58–73). New York: Brunner/Mazel.

Satterfield, J. H., Hoppe, C. M., & Schell, A. M. (1982). A prospective study of delinquency in 110 adolescent boys with attention deficit disorder and 88 normal adolescent boys. *American Journal of Psychiatry, 139,* 795–798.

Satterfield, J. H., Satterfield, B. T., & Cantwell, D. P. (1980). Multimodal treatment. *Archives of General Psychiatry, 37,* 915–919.

Satterfield, J. H., Satterfield, B. T., Cantwell, D. P. (1981). Three-year multimodality treatment study of 100 hyperactive boys. *Journal of Pediatrics, 98,* 650–655.

Satterfield, J., Swanson, J., Schell, A., & Lee, F. (1994). Prediction of antisocial behavior in attention-deficit hyperactivity disorder boys from aggression/defiance scores. *Journal of the American Academy of Child and Adolescent Psychiatry, 33,* 185–190.

Savin-Williams, R. C., & Small, S. A. (1986). The timing of puberty and its relationship to adolescent and parent perceptions of family interactions. *Developmental Psychology, 22,* 342–347.

Schachar, R., Tannock, R., & Logan, G. (1993). Inhibitory control, impulsiveness, and attention-deficit hyperactivity disorder. *Clinical Psychology Review, 13,* 721–740.

Schachar, R. J., Rutter, M., & Smith, A. (1981). The characteristics of situationally and pervasively hyperactive children: Implications for syndrome definition. *Journal of Child Psychology and Psychiatry, 22,* 375–392.

Schaughency, E., & Hynd, G. W. (1989). Attentional control systems and the attention-deficit disorder. *Learning and Individual Differences, 1,* 423–449.

Schaughency, E. A., Vannatta, A., & Mauro, J. (1993). Parent training. In J. L. Matson (Ed.), *Handbook of hyperactivity in children* (pp. 256–281). Needham Heights, MA: Allyn & Bacon.

Schleifer, M., Weiss, G., Cohen, N. J., Elman, M., Cvejic, H., & Kruger, E. (1975). Hyperactivity in preschoolers and the effect of methylphenidate. *American Journal of Orthopsychiatry, 45,* 38–50.

Schumaker, J. B., Hovell, M. F. & Sherman, J. A. (1977). An analysis of daily report cards and parent managed privileges in the improvement of adolescent's classroom performance. *Journal of Applied Behavior Analysis, 10,* 449-464.

Scruggs, T. E., & Wong, B. Y. L. (1990). *Intervention research in learning disabilities.* New York: Springer-Verlag.

Sebald, H. (1984). *Adolescence: A social psychological analysis* (3rd ed.). Englewood Cliffs, NJ: Prentice-Hall.

Secord, P., & Peevers, B. (1974). The development and attribution of person concepts. In T. Mishel (Ed.), *Understanding other persons*. Totowa, NJ: Rowman & Littlefield.

Seiden, L. S., Miller, F. E., & Heffner, T. G. (1989). Neurotransmitters in attention-deficit disorder. In T. Sagvolden & T. Archer (Eds.), *Attention-deficit disorder: Clinical and basic research* (pp. 223–234). Hillsdale, NJ: Erlbaum.

Seidman, L. J., Biederman, J., Faraone, S. V., Weber, W., Mennin, B. A., & Jones, J. (1997). A pilot study of neuropsychological function in girls with ADHD. *Journal of the American Academy of Child and Adolescent Psychiatry, 36*, 366–373.

Seitz, V., & Provence, S. (1990). Caregiver focused models of early intervention. In S. J. Meisels & J. P. Shonkoff (Eds.), *Handbook of early intervention* (pp. 400–427). New York: Cambridge University Press.

Selman, R. L. (1980). *The growth of interpersonal understanding*. New York: Academic Press.

Selman, R. L., & Selman, A. P. (1979). Children's ideas about friendship: A new theory. *Psychology Today, 13*, 71–80.

Semrud-Clikeman, M., Biederman, J., Sprich-Buckminster, S., Krifcher, B., Lehman, B., Faraone, S. V., & Norman, D. (1992). The incidence of ADHD and concurrent learning disabilities. *Journal of the American Academy of Child and Adolescent Psychiatry, 31*, 439–448.

Semrud-Clikeman, M., Filipek, P. A., Biederman, J., Steingard, R., Kennedy, D., Renshaw, P., & Bekken, K. (1994). Attention-deficit hyperactivity disorder: Magnetic resonance imaging morphometric analysis of the corpus callosum. *Journal of the American Academy of Child and Adolescent Psychiatry, 33*, 875–881.

Shapiro, E. S., & Cole, C. L. (1994). *Behavior change in the classroom: Self-management interventions*. New York: Guilford Press.

Shapiro, E. S., DuPaul, G. J., & Bradley, K. L. (in press). Self-management as a strategy to improve the classroom behavior of adolescents with ADHD. *Journal of Learning Disabilities*.

Shapiro, E. S., DuPaul, G. J., Bradley, K. L., & Bailey, L. T. (1996). A school-based consultation program for service delivery to middle school students with attention-deficit/hyperactivity disorder. *Journal of Emotional and Behavioral Disorders, 4*, 73–81.

Shaw, G. A., & Brown, G. (1991). Laterality, implicit memory and attention disorder. *Educational Studies, 17*, 15–23.

Shaywitz, S. E., Holahan, J. M., Marchione, K. E., Sadler, A., & Shaywitz, B. A. (1992). The Yale Children's Inventory: Normative data and their implications for the diagnosis of attention-deficit disorder in children. In S. E. Shaywitz & B. A. Shaywitz (Eds.), *Attention-deficit disorder comes of age* (pp. 29–68). Austin, TX: Pro-ed.

Shaywitz, S. E., & Shaywitz, B. A. (1989). Critical issues in attention-deficit disorder. In T. Sagvolden & T. Archer (Eds.), *Attention-deficit disorder: Clinical and basic research* (pp. 53–70). Hillsdale, NJ: Erlbaum.

Shaywitz, S. E., & Shaywitz, B. A. (1992). *Attention-deficit disorder comes of age*. Austin, TX: Pro-ed.

Shaywitz, B., Shaywitz, S., Anderson, G., Jatlow, P., Gillespie, S., Sullivan, R., Riddle, M., Leckman, J., & Cohen, D. (1988, September). D-*Amphetamine effects on central nonadrenergic mechanisms in children with attention-deficit hyperactivity disorder.* Paper presented at the 17th national meeting of the Child Neurology Society, Halifax, Canada.

Shaywitz, S. E., Shaywitz, B.A., Cohen, D.J., & Young, J. G. (1983). Monaminergic mechanisms in hyperactivity. In M. Rutter (Ed.), *Developmental neuropsychiatry* (pp. 330–347). New York: Guilford Press.

Shedler, J., & Block, J. (1990). Adolescent drug use and psychological health: A longitudinal inquiry. *American Psychologist, 45,* 612–630.

Shekim, W. O., Asarnow, R. F., Hess, E., Zaucha, K., & Wheeler, N. (1990). A clinical and demographic profile of a sample of adults with attention-deficit hyperactivity disorder, residual state. *Comprehensive Psychiatry, 31,* 416–425.

Shekim, W. O., Javid, J., Dans, J. M., & Bylund, D. B. (1983). Effects of D-amphetamine on urinary metabolites of dopamine and norepinephrine in hyperactive children. *Biological Psychiatry, 18,* 707–714.

Shelton, T. (1992). *UMASS kindergarten behavior management program.* Unpublished manuscript.

Shennum, W. A., & Bugenthal, D. B. (1982). The development of control over affective expression of nonverbal behavior. In R. Feldman (Ed.), *Development of nonverbal behavior in children* (pp. 101–121). New York: Springer-Verlag.

Sheridan, S. (1995). *The tough kid social skills book.* Longmont, CO: Sopris West.

Sherman, M., & Hertzig, M. (1991). Prescribing practices of Ritalin: Suffolk County, New York study. In L. Greenhill & B. Osman (Eds.), *Ritalin: Theory and patient management.* New York: Liebert.

Sieg, K. G., Gaffney, G. R., Preston, D. F., & Hellings, J. A. (1995). SPECT brain imaging abnormalities in attention-deficit hyperactivity disorder. *Clinical Nuclear Medicine, 20,* 55–60.

Singh, N. N., Landrum, T. J., Donatelli, L. S., Hampton, C. (1994). Characterisitics of children and adolescents with serious emotional disturbance in systems of care: I. Partial hospitalization and inpatient psychiatric services. *Journal of Emotional and Behavioral Disorders, 2,* 13–20.

Singer, R. S. (1982). Childhood, aggression and television. *Television and Children, 5,* 57–63.

Solden, S. (1995). *Women with attention deficit disorder: Embracing disorganization at home and in the workplace.* Grass Valley, CA: Underwood Books.

Soriano, M., Soriano, F. I., & Jimenez, E. (1994). School violence among culturally diverse populations: Sociocultural and institutional considerations. *School Psychology Review, 23,* 216–235.

Speltz, M. L., Varley, C. K., Peterson, K., & Beilke, R. L. (1988). Effects of dextroamphetamine and contingency management of a preschooler with ADHD and oppositional defiant disorder. *Journal of the American Academy of Child and Adolescent Psychiatry, 27,* 175–178.

Spencer, T., Biederman, J., Kerman, K., Steingard, R., & Wilens, T. (1993).

Desipramine treatment of children with attention-deficit hyperactivity disorder and tic disorder or Tourette's syndrome. *Journal of the American Academy of Child and Adolescent Psychiatry, 32,* 354–360.

Spitzer, R. L., Williams, J. B. W., Gibbon, M., & First, M. B. (1990). *Structured Clinical Interview for DSM-III-R—Patient Edition, Version I.O.* Washington, DC: American Psychiatric Press.

Sroufe, L. A. (1979). The coherence of individual development. *American Psychologist, 34,* 834–841.

Sroufe, L. A. (1983). Infant–caregiver attachment and patterns of adaptation and competence. In M. Perlmutter (Ed.), *Minnesota Symposia in Child Psychology* (Vol. 16). Hillsdale, NJ: Erlbaum.

Sroufe, L. A. (1985). Attachment classification from the perspective of infant–caregiver relationships and infant temperament. *Child Development, 56,* 1–14.

Sroufe, L. A., & Cooper, R. G. (1985). *Child development: Its nature and course.* New York: Knopf.

Sroufe, L. A., Jacobvitz, D., Mangelsdorf, S., DeAngelo, E., & Ward, M. J. (1987). Generational boundary dissolution between mothers and their preschool children: A relationship systems approach. *Child Development, 56,* 317–325.

Sroufe, L. A., & Waters, E. (1982). Issues of temperament and attachment. *American Journal of Orthopsychiatry, 52,* 743–746.

Stander, V., & Jensen, L. (1993). The relationship of value orientation to moral cognition: Gender and cultural differences in the United States and China explored. *Journal of Cross-Cultural Psychology, 24,* 42–52.

Stattin, H., & Magnusson, D. (1990). *Pubertal maturation in female development.* Hillsdale, NJ: Erlbaum.

Steinberg, L. (1988). Latch-key children and susceptibility to peer pressure: An ecological analysis. *Developmental Psychology, 22,* 295–296.

Steingard, R., Biederman, J., Spencer, T., Wilens, T., & Gonzalez, A. (1993). Comparison of clonidine response in the treatment of attention-deficit hyperactivity disorder with and without comorbid tic disorder. *Journal of the American Academy of Child and Adolescent Psychiatry, 32,* 350–353.

Stern, S. (1984). *A group cognitive-behavioral approach in the management and resolution of parent–adolescent conflict.* Unpublished doctoral dissertation, University of Chicago.

Sternberg, R. J. (1980). A sketch of a componential subtheory of human intelligence. *Behavioral and Brain Sciences, 3,* 573–614.

Sternberg, R. J. (1985). *Beyond IQ: A triarchic theory of human intelligence.* New York: Cambridge University Press.

Sternberg, R. J. (1987). A unified theory of intellectual exceptuality. In J. G. Borkowski & J. Day (Eds.), *Cognition and intelligence in special children: Comparative approaches to retardation, learning disabilities, and giftedness* (pp. 135–172). Norwood, NJ: Ablex.

Stevenson, J. (1992). Evidence for a genetic etiology in hyperactivity in children. *Behavior Genetics, 22,* 337–343.

Stewart, M. A., deBlois, C. S., & Singer, S. (1979). Alcoholism and hyperactivity revisited. In M. Gallanter (Ed.), *Biomedical issues and clinical effects of alcoholism* (Vol. 5). New York: Grune & Stratton.

Stokes, T. F., & Osnes, P. G. (1989). An operant pursuit of generalization. *Behavior Therapy, 20,* 337–355.

Stoutjesdyk, D., & Jevne, R. (1993). Eating disorders among high performance athletes. *Journal of Youth and Adolescence, 22,* 271–279.

Streater, A., & Chertkoo, J. (1976). Distribution of rewards in a triad: A developmental test of equity theory. *Child Development, 47,* 800–805.

Streitmatter, J. (1993). Gender differences in identity development: An examination of longitudinal data. *Adolescence, 28,* 55–66.

Sullivan, M. A., & O'Leary, S. G. (1990). Differential maintenance following reward and cost token programs with children. *Behavior Therapy, 21,* 139–149.

Swaim, R. C., Oetting, E. R., Thurman, P. J., Beauvais, F., & Edwards, R. W. (1993). American Indian adolescent drug use and socialization characteristics: A cross-cultural comparison. *Journal of Cross-Cultural Psychology, 24,* 53–70.

Swanson, J. (1988). Discussion. In J. Kavanaugh & T. Truss, Jr. (Eds.), *Learning disabilities: Proceedings of the national conference* (pp. 542–546). Parkton, MD: York Press.

Swanson, J. (1992). *School-based assessments and interventions for ADD students.* Irvine, CA: K. C.

Swanson, J. (1993). Medical intervention for children with attention-deficit disorder. *Education of children with attention-deficit disorder.* Washington, DC: U.S. Department of Education, Chesapeake Institute.

Swanson, J., Cantwell, D., Lerner, M., McBurnett, K., & Hanna, G. (1993). Effects of stimulant medication on learning in children with ADHD. *Journal of Learning Disabilities, 24,* 219–230.

Swanson, J., McBurnett, K., Wigal, T., Pfiffner, L. J., Lerner, M. A., Williams, L., Christian, D. L., Tamm, L., Willcutt, E., Crowley, K., Clevenger, W., Khouzam, N., Woo, C., Crinella, F. M., & Fisher, T. D. (1993). Effect of stimulant medication on children with attention deficit disorder: A "review of reviews." *Exceptional Children, 60,* 154–162.

Szatmari, P. (1992). The epidemiology of attention-deficit hyperactivity disorders. In G. Weiss (Ed.), *Child and adolescent psychiatry clinics of North America: Attention deficit hyperactivity disorder* (pp. 361–372). Philadelphia: Saunders.

Szatmari, P., Offord, D. R., & Boyle, M. H. (1989). Correlates, associated impairments, and patterns of service utilization of children with attention-deficit disorders: Findings from the Ontario child health study. *Journal of Child Psychology and Psychiatry, 30,* 205–217.

Tallmadge, J., & Barkley, R. A. (1983). The interactions of hyperactive and normal boys with their mothers and fathers. *Journal of Abnormal Psychology, 11,* 565–579.

Tant, J. L., & Douglas, V. I. (1982). Problem solving in hyperactive, normal, and reading-disabled boys. *Journal of Abnormal Child Psychology, 10,* 285–306.

Taylor, E. A. (1986). Childhood hyperactivity. *British Journal of Psychiatry, 149, 562–573.*

Taylor, J. (1994). *Helping your hyperactive/attention deficit child.* Rocklin, CA: Prima.

Teeter, P. A. (1991). Attention-deficit hyperactivity disorder: A psychoeducational paradigm. *School Psychology Review, 20, 266–280.*

Teeter, P. A. (1993, April). *A developmental model for interventions for children with ADHD.* Paper presented at the meeting of the National Association of School Psychologists, Washington, DC.

Teeter, P. A., & Semrud-Clikeman, M. (1995). Integrating neurobiological, psychosocial, and behavioral paradigms: A transactional model for ADHD. *Archives of Clinical Neuropsychology, 10, 433–461.*

Teeter, P. A., & Semrud-Clikeman, M. (1997). *Child neuropsychology: Assessment and interventions for neurodevelopmental disorders.* Boston, MA: Allyn & Bacon.

Teeter, P. A., & Smith, P. L. (1993). WISC-III and WJR: Predictive and discriminant validity for students with severe emotional disturbance. *Journal of Psychoeducational Assessment, WISC-III Monograph, 113–124.*

Teeter, P. A., & Stewart, P. (1996, November). *Getting research on educational best practices off the book shelves and into the classroom.* Paper presented at the annual meeting of CH.A.D.D., Chicago, IL.

Teeter, P. A., & Stewart, P. (1997). *ADD and problem-solving communication: A model for home–school–physician partnerships.* Wisconsin Department of Public Instruction Report.

Thomas, A., & Chess, S. (1977). *Temperament and development.* New York: Brunner/Mazel.

Thomas, A., & Chess, S. (1981). The role of temperament in the contribution of individuals to their development. In R. M. Lerner & N. A. Busch-Rossnagel (Eds.), *Individual as producers of their development.* New York: Academic Press.

Thomas, A., & Chess, S. (1984). Genesis and evolution of behavioral disorders: From infancy to early adult life. *American Journal of Orthopsychiatry, 141,* 1–9.

Thomas, A., Chess, S., & Birch, H. G. (1968). *Temperament and behavior disorders in children.* New York: New York University Press.

Thomas, A., Chess, S., & Birch, H. G. (1970). The origin of personality. *Scientific American, 223, 102–109.*

Thorne, B. (1986). Girls and boys together . . . but mostly apart: Gender arrangements in elementary schools. In W. Hartup & Z. Rubin (Eds.), *Relationships and development.* Hillsdale, NJ: Erlbaum.

Tisak, M. S. (1993). Preschool children's judgments of moral and personal events involving physical harm and property damage. *Merrill–Palmer Quarterly, 39, 375–390.*

Torgensen, A. M., & Kringlen, E. (1978). Genetic aspects of temperamental differences in infants. *Journal of the American Child Psychiatry, 17,* 433–444.

Traskman, L., Asberg, M., Bertilisson, L., & Sjostrand, L. (1981). Monamine metabolites in CSF and suicidal behavior. *Archives of General Psychiatry, 38,* 631–636.

Tremblay, R. E., Pagani-Kurtz, L., Masse, L. C., Vitara, F., & Pihl, R. O. (1995). A bimodal prevention for disruptive kindergarten boys: Its impact through mid-adolescence. *Journal of Consulting and Clinical Psychology, 63,* 560–568.

Trommer, B. L., Hoeppner, J. B., Lorber, R., & Armstrong, K. (1988). Pitfalls in the use of a continuous performance test as a diagnostic tool in attention-deficit disorder. *Developmental and Behavioral Pediatrics, 9,* 339–346.

Tucker, D. M., & Williamson, P. A. (1984). Asymmetric neural control systems in human self-regulation. *Psychological Review, 91,* 185–215.

Tzelepis, A., Schubiner, H., & Warbasse, L. H., III. (1995). Differential diagnosis and psychiatric comorbidity patterns in adult attention-deficit disorder. In K. G. Nadeau (Ed.), *A comprehensive guide to attention-deficit disorder in adults: Research, diagnosis, and treatment* (pp. 35–57). New York: Brunner/Mazel.

U.S. Bureau of the Census. (1989). *Marital status and living arrangements.* Washington, DC: U.S. Government Printing Office.

U.S. Bureau of the Census. (1992). *Statistical Abstracts of the United States: 1992* (112th ed.). Washington, DC: U.S. Government Printing Office.

U.S. Department of Education. (1993). *Education of children with attention-deficit disorder.* Washington, DC: Chesapeake Institute.

U.S. Department of Education. (1986). *What works: Research about reading and learning.* Washington, DC: Office of Educational Research and Improvement.

Vaillant, G. E. (1977). *Adaptation to life.* Boston: Little, Brown.

Vaillant, G. E., & Vaillant, C. O. (1990). Natural history of male psychological health, XII: A 45-year study of predictors of successful aging. *American Journal of Psychiatry, 147,* 31–37.

Varley, C. K. (1983). Effects of methylphenidate in adolescents with attention deficit disorder. *Journal of the American Academy of Child and Adolescent Psychiatry, 22,* 351–354.

Vygotsky, L. S. (1962). *Thought and language.* Cambridge, MA: MIT Press.

Vygotsky, L. S. (1978). *Mind in society: The development of higher psychological processes.* Cambridge, MA: MIT Press.

Vygotsky, L. S. (1986). *Thought and language* (Translated and revised by A. Kozulin). Cambridge, MA: MIT Press.

Vyse, S. A., & Rapport, M. D. (1989). The effects of methylphenidate in children with ADDH: The stimulus equivalence paradigm. *Journal of Consulting and Clinical Psychology, 57,* 425–435.

Waldrop, M. F., Bell, R. Q., McLaughlin, B., & Halverson, C. (1978). Newborn minor physical anomalies predict short attention span, peer aggression, and impulsivity at age 3. *Science, 199,* 563–565.

Walker, H. M., & Hops, H. (1979). The CLASS program for acting out children: R and D procedures, program outcomes and implementation issues. *School Psychology Digest, 8,* 370–381.

Walker, H. M., Todis, B., Holmes, D., & Hortin, G. (1988). *The Walker Social Skills Curriculum: The ACCESS Program: Adolescent curriculum for communication and effective social skills.* Austin, TX: Pro-ed.

Walker, J. L., Lahey, B. L., Hynd, G. W., & Frame, C. L. (1987). Comparison of specific patterns of antisocial behavior in children with conduct disorder with or without coexisting hyperactivity. *Journal of Consulting and Clinical Psychology, 55,* 910–913.

Walker, L. J. (1988). The development of moral reasoning. In R. Vasta (Ed.), *Annals of child development* (Vol. 5). Greenwich, CT: JAI Press.

Walker, L. J., & De Vries, B. (1985, August). *Moral stages/moral orientations: Do the sexes really differ?* Paper presented at the annual meeting of the American Psychological Association, Los Angeles.

Walker, L. J., De Vries, B., & Trevethan, S. D. (1987). Moral stages and moral orientations in real-life and hypothetical dilemmas. *Child Development, 58,* 842–858.

Wallander, J. L., Schroeder, S. R., Michelli, J. A., & Gualtiere, C. T. (1987). Classroom social interactions of attention deficit disorder with hyperactivity children as a function of stimulant medication. *Journal of Pediatric Psychology, 12,* 61–76.

Wallerstein, J. S. (1985). Children of divorce: Preliminary ten-year follow-up of older children and adolescents. *Journal of American Academy of Child Psychology, 24,* 545–553.

Wallerstein, J. S., & Kelly, J. B. (1980). *Surviving the break-up: How children actually cope with divorce.* New York: Basic Books.

Warren, B., & Rosebery, A. S. (1988). Theory and practice: Uses of the computer in reading. *Remedial and Special Education, 9,* 29–38.

Weiss, G. & Hechtman, L. (1986). *Hyperactive children grown up.* New York: Guilford Press.

Weiss, G. & Hechtman, L. (1993). *Hyperactive children grown up* (2nd ed.): *ADHD in children, adolescents, and adults.* New York: Guilford Press.

Weiss, G., Hechtman, L. T., Milroy, T. & Perlman, T. (1985). Psychiatric status of hyperactives as adults: A controlled perspective 15-year follow-up of 63 hyperactive children. *Journal of the American Academy of Child and Adolescent Psychiatry, 24,* 211–220.

Weiss, G., Kruger, E., Danielson, R., & Elman, M. (1975). Effect of long term treatment of hyperactive children with methylphenidate. *Canadian Medical Association Journal, 112,* 159–165.

Weiss, G., Minde, K., Werry, J. S., Douglas, V. I., & Nemeth, E. (1971). Studies of hyperactive children VIII: Five-year follow-up. *Archives of General Psychiatry, 24,* 409–414.

Weiss, L. (1992). *Attention deficit disorder in adults.* Dallas, TX: Taylor.

Wellman, H. M. (1988). The early development of memory strategies. In F. E. Weinert & M. Perlmutter (Eds.), *Memory development: Universal changes and individual differences.* Hillsdale, NJ: Erlbaum.

Wellman, H. M., Sommerville, S. C., & Haake, R. J. (1979). Development of search procedures in real-life spatial environments. *Developmental Psychology, 15,* 530–542.

Wenar, C. (1994). *Developmental psychopathology: From infancy through adolescence.* New York: McGraw Hill.

Wenar, E. E., & Smith, R. S. (1992). *Overcoming the odds: High risk children from birth to adulthood.* Ithaca, NY: Cornell University Press.

Wender, P. H. (1971). *Minimal brain dysfunction in children.* New York: Wiley.

Wender, P. H. (1987). *The hyperactive child, adolescent, and adult.* New York: Oxford University Press.

Wender, P. H. (1995). *Attention-deficit hyperactivity disorder in adults.* New York: Oxford University Press.

Wender, P. H., & Reimherr, F. W. (1990). Bupropion treatment of attention deficit hyperactivity disorder in adults. *American Journal of Psychiatry, 147,* 1018–1020.

Werner, E. E., & Smith, R. S. (1977). *Kauai's children come of age.* Honolulu: University of Hawaii Press.

Werry, J. S., Weiss, G., & Douglas, V. (1964). Studies on the hyperactive child: I. Some preliminary findings. *Canadian Psychiatric Journal, 9,* 120–130.

Whalen, C. K., Collins, B. E., Henker, B., Alkus, S. R., Adams, D., & Sapp, J. (1978). Behavior observations of hyperactive children and methylphenidate (Ritalin) effects in systematically structured classroom environments: Now you see them, now you don't. *Journal of Pediatric Psychology, 3,* 177–187.

Whalen, C. K., & Henker, B. (1985). The social worlds of hyperactive children. *Clinical Psychology Review, 5,* 1–32.

Whalen, C. K., & Henker, B. (1991). Therapies for hyperactive children: Comparisons, combinations, and compromises. *Journal of Consulting and Clinical Psychology, 59,* 126–137.

Whalen, C. K., Henker, B., Buhrmester, D., Hinshaw, S. P., Huber, A., & Laski, K. (1989). Does stimulant medication improve peer status of hyperactive children? *Journal of Consulting and Clinical Psychology, 57,* 5435–5449.

Whalen, C. K., Henker, B., Collins, B. E., Finck, D., & Dotemoto, S. (1979). A social ecology of hyperactive boys: Medication effects in systematically structured classroom environments. *Journal of Applied Behavior Analysis, 12,* 65–81.

Whalen, C. K., Henker, B., & Dotemoto, S. (1980). Teacher response to the methylphenidate (Ritalin) versus placebo status of hyperactive boys in the classroom. *Child Development, 52,* 1005–1014.

White, S., & DeBlassie, R. R. (1992). Adolescent sexual behavior. *Adolescence, 27,* 183–191.

Whitney, E. N., & Hamilton, E. M. N. (1984). *Understanding nutrition* (3rd ed.). St. Paul, MN: West.

Wilens, T. E., Biederman, J., Geist, D. E., Steingard, R., & Spencer, T. (1993). Nortriptyline in the treatment of ADHD: A chart review of 58 cases. *Journal of the American Academy of Child and Adolescent Psychiatry, 32,* 343–349.

Wilens, T. E., Biederman, J., Mick, E., & Spencer, T. (1995). A systematic assessment of tricyclic antidepressants in the treatment of adults with attention-deficit disorders. *Journal of Nervous and Mental Disease, 183,* 48–50.

Wilens, T. E., Spencer, T., & Biederman, J. (1995). Pharmacotherapy of adult ADHD. In K. G. Nadeau (Ed.), *A comprehensive guide to attention deficit disorder in adults: Research, diagnosis, and treatment* (pp. 168–190). New York: Brunner/Mazel.

Williams, L. B., & Pratt, W. F. (1990). Wanted and unwanted childbearing in the United States, 1973–88: Data from a National Survey of Family Growth. *Advance Data from Vital and Health Statistics of the National Center for Health Statistics, 189*, 1–5.

Winnicott, D. W. (1953). Transitional object and transitional phenomena. *International Journal of Psycho-Analysis, 34*, 89–97.

Wolfson, A., Lacks, P., & Futterman, A. (1992). Effects of parent training in infant sleeping patterns, parents' stress, and perceived parental competence. *Journal of Consulting and Clinical Psychology, 60*, 41–48.

Wong, B. Y. L. (1991). *Learning about learning disabilities*. San Diego, CA: Academic Press.

Worland, J. (1976). Effects of positive and negative feedback on behavior control in hyperactive and normal boys. *Journal of Abnormal Child Psychology, 4*, 315–325.

Zabin, L. S., Hirsch, M. B., Smith, E. A., & Hardy, J. B. (1984). Adolescent sexual attitudes and behavior: Are they consistent? *Family Planning Perspectives, 16*, 185.

Zametkin, A., Gross, M., King, A., Semple, W., Rumsey, J., Hamburger, S., & Cohen, R. (1990). Cerebral glucose metabolism in adults with hyperactivity of childhood onset. *New England Journal of Medicine, 323*, 1361–1366.

Zametkin, A., & Rapoport, J. (1987). Neurobiology of attention deficit disorder with hyperactivity. *Journal of American Academy of Child and Adolescent Psychiatry, 26*, 676–686.

Zani, B. (1991). Male and female patterns in the discovery of sexuality in adolescence. *Journal of Adolescence, 14*, 163–178.

Zentall, S. S. (1985). Stimulus-control factors in search of performance of hyperactive children. *Journal of Learning Disabilities, 18*, 480–485.

Zentall, S. S. (1988). Production deficiencies in elicited language but not in the spontaneous verbalizations of hyperactive children. *Journal of Abnormal Child Psychology, 16*, 657–673.

Zentall, S. S. (1995). Modifying classroom tasks and environments. In S. Goldstein (Ed.), *Understanding and managing children's classroom behavior*. New York: Wiley.

Zentall, S. S., & Dywer, A. M. (1988). Color effects on the impulsivity and activity of hyperactive children. *Journal of School Psychology, 23*, 83–93.

Zentall, S. S., Falkenberg, S. D., & Smith, L. B. (1985). Effects of color stimulation and information on the copying performance of attention-problem adolescents. *Journal of Abnormal Child Psychology, 13*, 501–511.

Zentall, S. S., Harper, G., & Stormont-Spurgin, M. (1993). Children with hyperactivity and their organizational abilities. *Journal of Educational Research, 87*, 112–117.

Zentall, S. S., & Meyer, M. J. (1987). Self-regulation of stimulation for ADD-H children during reading and vigilance task performance. *Journal of Abnormal Child Psychology, 15,* 519–536.

Zentall, S. S., & Shaw, J. H. (1980). Effects of classroom noise on performance and activity of second-grade hyperactive and control children. *Journal of Educational Psychology, 72,* 830–840.

Zentall, S. S., & Zentall, T. R. (1983). Optimal stimulation: A model for disordered activity and performance in normal and deviant children. *Psychological Bulletin, 94,* 446–471.

Zuckerman, B. S., & Beardslee, W. R. (1987). Maternal depression: A concern for pediatricians. *Pediatrics, 79,* 110–117.

Index